Money, Politics, and Campaign Finance Reform Law in the States

MONEY, POLITICS, AND CAMPAIGN FINANCE REFORM LAW IN THE STATES

David Schultz

CAROLINA ACADEMIC PRESS

Durham, North Carolina

340.73
M742

ISBN 0-89089-072-2
LCCN 2002107845

CAROLINA ACADEMIC PRESS
700 Kent Street
Durham, NC 27701
Telephone (919) 489-7486
Fax (919) 493-5668
www.cap-press.com

Printed in the United States of America

CONTENTS

Money, Politics, and Campaign Finance Reform Law in the States

Money, Politics, and Campaign Financing in the States

David Schultz

Introduction

Americans are deeply concerned about the role and impact of money upon politics and government. Since the Watergate scandals in the 1970s, public opinion polls suggest that the American public overwhelmingly believes that money corrupts politics and that reforms are needed in the way that campaigns and elections are financed in the United States. Continued support for such reform, no doubt, is due in part to the media coverage of national political campaigns, including stories of $100,000 sleep-overs in the White House, large stealth contributors or organizations financing attack ads on television, and unprecedented millions of dollars raised and spent to run for the presidency and Congress.

But recent revelations that Enron corporation gave millions of dollars in political contributions to President Bush and most members of Congress also renewed concern that money purchased political favors at the expense of employee retirement accounts. Enron's tale seemed to confirm often told stories of lobbyists and special interest organizations spending huge sums of money to influence legislation or otherwise being granted special access or opportunity to meet with elected officials or their staff (Drew 1999; Birnbaum 2000).

In the 2000 elections, the Democratic and Republican parties together raised over $457 million in soft money to finance a host of activities that were outside the regulated activity of the 1971 Federal Election Campaign Act and its subsequent amendments (FECA)— the main federal law governing the financing of federal election activities (Common Cause 2000). Additionally in

2002, as the House of Representatives moved towards passage of Shays-Meehan and a ban on soft money contributions seemed likely, the two major parties went on fund-raising sprees and collected record-setting soft money donations for fear they would no longer be able to solicit this money in the future.

One result of the public's distrust with the current practices of financing elections was the emergence of Arizona Senator John McCain as a major presidential candidate for the Republican Party nomination in 2000. His support, along with that of Wisconsin Senator Russ Feingold, who both fought for the McCain-Feingold bill and its effort to eliminate soft money (along with the parallel House bill authored by Representatives Christopher Shays and Marty Meehan), made campaign finance reform a major political issue. Almost singularly, campaign finance reform transformed Senator McCain into a hero among the American public who supported this issue.

While numerous efforts have been underway for the last twenty years or more in Congress to enact campaign finance reform, a somewhat quiet revolution has been underway in the states. With reform stalled at the national level, groups have increasingly turned their efforts towards individual states, seeking to pass a diversity of laws regarding political contribution limits, disclosure, campaign financing, and lobbyist regulation, just to mention a few reforms. While American impressions of money and politics are almost singularly influenced by what is happening regarding events at the national level (Thompson and Moncrief 1998), little serious scholarly work has explored what impact money has upon state politics, elections, and governance. In many ways, state activity and experiences are a great scholarly void.

While the literature seeking to examine the impact of money on national politics is extensive and includes studies of FECA and federal regulation (see, for example, Corrrado 2000; Green 1999; Sorauf 1988; Sorauf 1992; Rosenbranz 1998; Alexander 1995), there has also been little effort to examine what reforms have been undertaken at the state level to address the impact of money on politics. The goal of this book is to address part of this void.

In their *Campaign Finance in State Legislative Elections*, Joel Thompson and Gary Moncrief (1998) undertake a cross-aggregate study of eighteen states and their legislative races over three election cycles from 1986 to 1992. This study yielded important information about the role of PACs, parties, financing, and legislative races in those states. They found clear evidence of rising campaign spending where between 1986 and 1994 the median spending for candidates in contested races increased from 13 % to 159 %, with a median increase of 67 % (212). The impact was an increased difficulty for challengers to raise the resources necessary to mount a serious race, resulting in incumbent reelection rates of over 90 % (213) and, in the latter, winning by greater and greater percentages since the 1960s. In addition, PACs were more likely at the state level to give to parties than to individual candidates (218), and they were more prone to giving in support of incumbents than challengers. Similarly, political parties remain a major source of funding for state candidates, leading critics to argue that limits on party contributions and legislative caucuses are required to promote more competitive elections and weaken the influence of lobbyists and PACS at the state level (221). However, at the conclusion of the book, the authors indicate that "[n]ow that we finally have a large-scale study covering more than one-third of the states, it may seem strange to call for more in-depth studies of individual states" (230). Yet their book does call for more focused case studies that examine the individual experiences of different states, covering not simply legislative races but perhaps the history of money and politics in that state on several fronts, including an analysis of reform efforts and an overall assessment of what seems to be working or not working in the arena of campaign finance reform.

The only other recent book examining money and politics on the state level is Michael Malbin's and Thomas L. Geis' *The Day After Reform: Sobering Campaign Finance Lessons From the American States* (1998). It examined four states in some depth, concentrating on a limited range of issues, including enforcement of then-existing laws, regulation of contributions to state political parties, and adaption of interest groups to campaign finance regulation. While the book is good in what it does, it is only a partial attempt at exploring the diversity of experiences and reform efforts underway at the state level. Moreover, it lacks real in-depth analysis of states across a range of issues, and it was written prior to the recent wave of state action in regulating money in politics.

Several other scholarly studies examine specific states or various aspects of money and campaign finance reform at the state level. Frank Sorauf's *Inside Campaign Finance* (1992) examines the Minnesota voluntary partial public financing system as one reform option. Yet the author dismisses the efficacy of such a system because state fiscal austerity would produce insufficient money to fund a public system, and because significant financial incentives or punishments ("carrots and sticks," in Sorauf's words) to induce participation(152-156). Jeffrey M. Brindle (2000) details the law and enforcement powers of the New Jersey Election Law Enforcement Commission, yet his discussion does not address the role of money in that state or how the regulations impact spending and contribution patterns, little alone the conduct of the state's elections or policy making.

Ronald D. Michaelson's "Campaign Finance Activity in the States" (2001) provides an important overview of what states have done from 1995 to 2000 to enact and regulate campaign financing. His discussion is significantly case-law-driven, looking to whether the courts have upheld laws limiting or prohibiting contributions, what enforcement powers state agencies possess, how technology drives disclosure, the role of ballot initiatives in pushing campaign finance reform, and what types of public financing systems have been adopted. Again, while informative, the study lacks in-depth analysis of the specific impact that money has on state elections and policy making. Finally, the National Institute on Money in State Politics at http://www.followthemoney.org/ and the Center for Responsive Politics at http://www.opensecrets.org/ maintain Web pages that track money at the state level through the construction of rich databases. But little comparative scholarly analysis is undertaken that permits drawing of generalizations from state experiences.

Overall, the definite focus of most studies on money and politics has been directed towards the presidential and congressional elections and federal legislation on this topic. Yet states also must confront the role of money in their political systems, and they have responded legislatively in various ways.

The Constitutional Framework for Campaign Finance Reform

The constitutional ability of states to regulate the role of money in campaigns and elections is significantly framed by four United States Supreme Court decisions: *Buckley v. Valeo*, 424 U.S. 1 (1976); *Nixon v. Shrink*, 528 U.S. 377 (2000); *Colorado Republican Party v. Federal Election Commission*, 518 U.S. 604 (1996); and *Colorado Republican Party v. Federal Election Commission*, 533 U.S. 431 (2001).[1]

In *Buckley*, at issue were several challenges to the 1974 amendments to the Federal Election Campaign Act (FECA), which mandated disclosure of political contributions and expenditures, limited to $1,000 political contributions by individuals or groups and to $5,000 by political action committees and party organizations to candidates for federal elective office per election cycle, with a cap of $25,000 by an individual per election cycle. In addition, individuals and groups were limited to $1,000 as the amount they could expend per election to a clearly identified candidate. Finally, other restrictions on how

---

1. State constitutional mandates, along with lower federal court decisions, may also place certain limits upon the ability of specific states to enact or regulate money and political activity. Yet the main part of the regulatory framework defining the case law in this area comes from these four Supreme Court decisions.

much of one's personal wealth could be spent on a campaign were also imposed, as well as overall expenditure limits. In upholding and in striking down several parts of the law as unconstitutional, the Supreme Court defined the basic legal terrain of campaign finance reform law that remains to this day.

In examining limits on contributions and expenditures, in a *per curiam* opinion the Court applied very different lines of constitutional analysis. First, the Court noted that Congress had broad power to regulate federal elections, yet the question in this case was whether the contribution and expenditure limitations violated the First Amendment free speech clause. The Court of Appeals, in upholding the FECA contribution and expenditure limitations, held that the restrictions were directed towards conduct and not speech and that, accordingly, the frame of analysis as dictated by *United States v. O'Brien*, 391 U.S. 367 (1968) should apply. The Court rejected the assertion that contribution and expenditure limits were conduct and not speech, stating that

> We cannot share the view that the present Act's contribution and expenditure limitations are comparable to the restrictions on conduct upheld in *O'Brien*. The expenditure of money simply cannot be equated with such conduct as destruction of a draft card. Some forms of communication made possible by the giving and spending of money involve speech alone, some involve conduct primarily, and some involve a combination of the two. Yet this Court has never suggested that the dependence of a communication on the expenditure of money operates itself to introduce a nonspeech element or to reduce the exacting scrutiny required by the First Amendment. (16)

Hence, the Court seemed to equate the giving of money for political purposes as a form of protected speech, which the FECA sought to regulate. Specifically, in terms of the limits on independent expenditures, the Court saw the restrictions as a "substantial rather than merely theoretical restraints on the quantity and diversity of political speech" (19). In addition, the Court described contributions as a means of expressing support for a candidate or otherwise indicating one's preference for political candidates such that restricting political contributions also imposed First Amendment associational limitations upon political dialogue. In short, both contributions and expenditures were protected speech, subject to First Amendment analysis.

In terms of contributions, the Court indicated that restrictions upon them were allegedly justified by three claims:

> [T]he primary interest served by the limitations and, indeed, by the Act as a whole, is the prevention of corruption and the appearance of

corruption spawned by the real or imagined coercive influence of large financial contributions on candidates' positions and on their actions if elected to office. Two "ancillary" interests underlying the Act are also allegedly furthered by the $1,000 limits on contributions. First, the limits serve to mute the voices of affluent persons and groups in the election process and thereby to equalize the relative ability of all citizens to affect the outcome of elections. Second, it is argued, the ceilings may to some extent act as a brake on the skyrocketing cost of political campaigns and thereby serve to open the political system more widely to candidates without access to sources of large amounts of money. (25-6)

The Court rejected the muting of wealthy voices and the controlling of the skyrocketing costs of elections as compelling enough to justify restrictions on contributions, yet preventing corruption was sufficiently compelling enough to justify restrictions upon contributions:

It is unnecessary to look beyond the Act's primary purpose to limit the actuality and appearance of corruption resulting from large individual financial contributions in order to find a constitutionally sufficient justification for the $1,000 contribution limitation. Under a system of private financing of elections, a candidate lacking immense personal or family wealth must depend on financial contributions from others to provide the resources necessary to conduct a successful campaign. The increasing importance of the communications media and sophisticated mass-mailing and polling operations to effective campaigning make the raising of large sums of money an ever more essential ingredient of an effective candidacy. To the extent that large contributions are given to secure a political quid pro quo from current and potential office holders, the integrity of our system of representative democracy is undermined. Although the scope of such pernicious practices can never be reliably ascertained, the deeply disturbing examples surfacing after the 1972 election demonstrate that the problem is not an illusory one. (27-8)

Similarly, in addition to recognizing the prevention of corruption as a compelling governmental interest to limit contributions, preventing the appearance of corruption was also accepted by the Court as a legitimate reason to limit contributions:

Of almost equal concern as the danger of actual quid pro quo arrangements is the impact of the appearance of corruption stemming from public awareness of the opportunities for abuse inherent in a regime of large individual financial contributions. In *CSC v. Letter Carriers, supra*, the Court found that the danger to "fair and effective government" posed by partisan political conduct on the part of federal employees charged with administering the law was a sufficiently important concern to justify broad restrictions on the employees' right of partisan political association. Here, as there, Congress could legitimately conclude that the avoidance of the appearance of improper influence "is also critical...if confidence in the system of representative Government is not to be eroded to a disastrous extent." (28-9)

Thus, the interest of preventing corruption was enough to uphold the $1,000 limit on individual contributions and, by the same logic, the Court upheld the $5,000 contribution limit on political committees (35-6) and the overall $25,000 contribution limit during any calendar year (38).

Despite Congress finding no reason to treat contributions and expenditures differently, the Court failed to treat the two the same, contending that restrictions on expenditures are a violation of the First Amendment. First, the Court indicates that the expenditure restrictions, while neutral, still restrict the "quantity" of the speech individuals, groups, and candidates may express (39). However, while preventing corruption or its appearance was compelling enough to restrict contributions to candidates, these two justifications did not obtain in terms of independent expenditures that were not made in coordination with a candidate:

> We find that the governmental interest in preventing corruption and the appearance of corruption is inadequate to justify §608(e)(1)'s ceiling on independent expenditures. First, assuming, arguendo, that large independent expenditures pose the same dangers of actual or apparent quid pro quo arrangements as do large contributions, §608(e)(1) does not provide an answer that sufficiently relates to the elimination of those dangers. Unlike the contribution limitations' total ban on the giving of large amounts of money to candidates, §608(e)(1) prevents only some large expenditures. So long as persons and groups eschew expenditures that in express terms advocate the election or defeat of a clearly identified candidate, they are free to spend as much as they want to promote the candidate and his views. The exacting interpretation of the statutory language necessary to avoid unconstitutional vagueness thus undermines the limitation's effectiveness as a loophole-closing provision by facilitating circumvention by those seeking to exert improper influence upon a candidate

or office-holder. It would naively underestimate the ingenuity and re-
sourcefulness of persons and groups desiring to buy influence to believe that they would have much difficulty devising expenditures that
skirted the restriction on express advocacy of election or defeat but
nevertheless benefited the candidate's campaign. Yet no substantial
societal interest would be served by a loophole-closing provision designed to check corruption that permitted unscrupulous persons and
organizations to expend unlimited sums of money in order to obtain
improper influence over candidates for elective office. (45-6)

Because independent expenditures are not tied into candidates or otherwise
not coordinated with candidates, the Court felt that there was no danger of *quid
pro quo* corruption or its appearance. The independent expenditure ceiling thus
failed to serve any substantial governmental interest and was therefore unconstitutional in terms of its application to individual expenditures, expenditures by
candidates from personal or family resources, and total campaign expenditures.

The Court also rejected as a valid compelling interest the restriction on expenditures to equalize the influence of individuals and groups upon the political process. Such restrictions, for the Court, were invalid because "the concept
that government may restrict the speech of some elements of our society in
order to enhance the relative voice of others is wholly foreign to the First
Amendment," since the basic goal of the First Amendment was to enhance political dialogue and the widest amount of dialogue, including views from an-
tagonistic groups (48). Hence, while preventing corruption and its appearance
were considered compelling enough to justify restrictions on contributions, it
appeared that no such compelling justifications could be found to justify restrictions on expenditures. In essence, the Court categorically stated that restrictions on contributions were permissible in some cases, while categorically
stating that no restrictions on expenditures could be justified in 1976. However, the Court articulated two caveats to its discussion of independent expenditures. First, the Court noted that independent expenditures do "not presently
appear to pose dangers of real or apparent corruption comparable to those
identified with large campaign contributions"(46). Second, the *per curiam*
opinion also asserted that "independent expenditures may well provide little
assistance to the candidate's campaign and indeed may prove to be counter-
productive" (47) In making these two claims, the Court held out the possibil-
ity that at some point independent expenditures may be restricted if evidence
could be provided that they posed dangers of corruption or its appearance.
Also, if it could be shown that such expenditures had some impact or assistance to a candidate's campaign, then some restrictions might be permissible.

In addition to defining the distinctions between expenditures and contributions, the Court also articulated three other important points in regards to disclosure, express advocacy versus issue advocacy, and the public financing of campaigns and elections.

In terms of disclosure, the Court upheld the FECA requirements and stated that there must be a correlation between the disclosure requirements and the state interest being advocated. According to the Court:

> The governmental interests sought to be vindicated by the disclosure requirements are of this magnitude. They fall into three categories. First, disclosure provides the electorate with information "as to where political campaign money comes from and how it is spent by the candidate" 77 in order to aid the voters in evaluating those who seek federal office. It allows voters to place each candidate in the political spectrum more precisely than is often possible solely on the basis of party labels and campaign speeches. The sources of a candidate's financial support also alert the voter to the interests to which a candidate is most likely to be responsive and thus facilitate predictions of future performance in office....
>
> Second, disclosure requirements deter actual corruption and avoid the appearance of corruption by exposing large contributions and expenditures to the light of publicity.78 This exposure may discourage those who would use money for improper purposes either before or after the election. A public armed with information about a candidate's most generous supporters is better able to detect any post-election special favors that may be given in return. 79 And, as we recognized in Burroughs v. United States, 290 U.S., at 548, 54 S.Ct., at 291, Congress could reasonably conclude that full disclosure during an election campaign tends "to prevent the corrupt use of money to affect elections."...
>
> Third, and not least significant, recordkeeping, reporting, and disclosure requirements are an essential means of gathering the data necessary to detect violations of the contribution limitations described above.

According to the Court, disclosure would be permitted so long as one of these three criteria were met.

Second, the Court made a crucial distinction between what has come to be referred to as express advocacy versus issue advocacy. If a political message specifically referred to a candidate for office and urged her election or defeat, this would be considered express advocacy, while communications that did not expressly advocate a candidate's election or defeat would be a form of issue advocacy. The test to distinguish between the two forms of communication was articulated in footnote 52 of the *Buckley* opinion, where the Court defined *express advocacy* as "[C]ommunications contain[ing]...express words of advocacy of election or defeat, such as 'vote for,' 'elect,' 'support,' 'cast your ballot for,' 'Smith for Congress,' 'vote against,' 'defeat,' 'reject.'" Often referred to as the "magic words" test, the importance of this distinction is multi-fold. First, issue advocacy was clearly a form of protected First Amendment speech that could not be limited or regulated (at least according to the *Buckley* Court, whereas in some circumstances express advocacy could be subject to contribution limits. In addition, in some cases, specific agents can be denied the ability to engage in express advocacy. For example, labor unions and corporations are prohibited from expending funds to directly influence a federal election (many states have similar laws that apply to their own elections) through expressly advocating for or against the election of a candidate. However, they may engage in issue advocacy and participate in discussion of issues that are important to them. Thus, depending on how the political communication is classified—as express advocacy or issue advocacy—the speech of a union or a corporation may or may not be subject to regulation.

Many groups have used this important distinction to escape federal campaign finance regulation and thereby solicit or expend virtually unregulated sums of money. Often, issue- advocacy communications are, effectively, forms of express advocacy, yet the absence of the magic words has placed this form of speech almost beyond the domains of regulation.

Finally, the express/issue distinction is important because it leads to another form of money that has come to dominate campaigns and elections, namely soft money. Subsequent to *Buckley*, a Federal Election Commission (FEC) ruling in 1978 permitted contributions to political parties for the purposes of internal communication, get-out-the-vote (GOTV) efforts, voter registration, and party-building to fall outside of the FECA hard money limits. As a result, labor unions and corporations could now make contributions, and in unlimited amounts. While in1978 the soft money loophole was minor, it has grown over time to the point where in the 2000 elections the Democratic and Republican parties each raised over $457 million in soft money. Soft money, for many, is now one of the biggest problems in campaign finance in that it permits virtually unlimited and unregulated money to flow into elections, thereby rending any hard money limits meaningless.

One final legal legacy of *Buckley* is that while the Court struck down mandatory expenditure limits, it did rule that voluntary limits were permissible. In footnote 65 the Court stated: " Congress may engage in public financing of election campaigns and may condition acceptance of public funds on an agreement by the candidate to abide by specified expenditure limitations. Just as a candidate may voluntarily limit the size of the contributions he chooses to accept, he may decide to forgo private fund raising and accept public funding." Under a voluntary public financing schema, Congress and states can impose a variety of conditions upon candidates running for office. These conditions could include overall spending caps and limits on how much a candidate may contribute to one's own campaign, among other stipulations.

Overall, the constitutional legacy of *Buckley* was to place the expenditure of money for political purposes under protection of the First Amendment. The *Buckley* Court stated that it would uphold contribution limits if one could show that certain contributions corrupt or lead to the appearance of corruption. The Court also declared that limits on expenditures were effectively unconstitutional. It held that disclosure was permitted in some circumstances, that there was a difference between express and issue advocacy, and that independent expenditures effectively could not be banned. Yet a voluntary public financing system could permit Congress and the states to legislate additional limits or regulations upon candidates as a condition of their receiving public financing.

In addition to *Buckley*, several other Supreme Court cases also have been significant in defining the constitutional landscape for the regulation of money in politics. For our purposes, three cases are worth noting. First, in *Colorado Republican Party v. Federal Election Commission*, 518 U.S. 604 (1996) ("*Colorado Republican I*"), the Court ruled that the FECA ban on party-independent expenditures was unconstitutional. This decision, building upon earlier Court jurisprudence that protected independent expenditures (Schultz 1998), thereby freed parties to solicit money from donors and then spend that money specifically on behalf of one of their candidates. The implication here would be that, despite any voluntary public financing system that would place limits on candidate expenditures, additional spending by parties to support that candidate would render spending limits for the latter immaterial. Moreover, a lifting of the prohibition of party-independent expenditures, along with the soft-money loopholes, gave parties tremendous incentive to raise and expend money. However, despite the Court permitting party-independent expenditures, in *Colorado Republican Party v. Federal Election Commission*, (2001) ("*Colorado Republican II*"), the Court upheld a ban on party expenditures coordinated with the candidate.

The last major case to consider is *Nixon v. Shrink Missouri Government PAC*, 528 U.S. 377 (2000). At issue here were whether state contribution limits set lower than those upheld in *Buckley* were constitutional (in this case, some limits were as low as $250). In upholding the limits, the Court appeared to rethink some of its *Buckley* assumptions, specifically what standard of proof was necessary to demonstrate corruption or its appearance. According to the Court:

> The quantum of empirical evidence needed to satisfy heightened judicial scrutiny of legislative judgments will vary up or down with the novelty and plausibility of the justification raised. *Buckley* demonstrates that the dangers of large, corrupt contributions and the suspicion that large contributions are corrupt are neither novel nor implausible....
>
> While *Buckley's* evidentiary showing exemplifies a sufficient justification for contribution limits, it does not speak to what may be necessary as a minimum. As to that, respondents are wrong in arguing that in the years since *Buckley* came down we have "supplemented" its holding with a new requirement that governments enacting contribution limits must "'demonstrate that the recited harms are real, not merely conjectural,'" a contention for which respondents rely principally on. We have never accepted mere conjecture as adequate to carry a First Amendment burden, and *Colorado Republican* did not deal with a government's burden to justify limits on contributions. Although the principal opinion in that case charged the Government with failure to show a real risk of corruption, the issue in question was limits on independent expenditures by political parties, which the principal opinion expressly distinguished from contribution limits: "limitations on independent expenditures are less directly related to preventing corruption" than contributions are. In that case, the "constitutionally significant fact" that there was no "coordination between the candidate and the source of the expenditure" kept the principal opinion "from assuming, absent convincing evidence to the contrary, that [a limitation on expenditures] is necessary to combat a substantial danger of corruption of the electoral system." *Colorado Republican* thus goes hand in hand with *Buckley*, not toe to toe. (391-2)

The Court thus appeared to make it easier to enact some forms of contribution limits, opening up the use of public opinion polls and other sources of data that could constitute evidence of corruption or its appearance. Yet the Court did appear to impose some outer limit on how low contribution limits could be:

> In *Buckley*, we specifically rejected the contention that $1,000, or any other amount, was a constitutional minimum below which legislatures could not regulate. As indicated above, we referred instead to the outer limits of contribution regulation by asking whether there

was any showing that the limits were so low as to impede the ability of candidates to "amas[s] the resources necessary for effective advocacy." We asked, in other words, whether the contribution limitation was so radical in effect as to render political association ineffective, drive the sound of a candidate's voice below the level of notice, and render contributions pointless. Such being the test, the issue in later cases cannot be truncated to a narrow question about the power of the dollar, but must go to the power to mount a campaign with all the dollars likely to be forthcoming. (393)

Thus, so long as candidates were not impeded in their ability to acquire the resources they needed to mount an effective campaign, it appeared that the Court was willing to let states set contribution limits lower than the $1,000 *Buckley* amount.

Overall, *Nixon* appeared to breathe new life into the campaign finance reform debate. That decision, along with *Buckley*, and the two *Colorado Republican* decisions, thus not only have shaped the constitutional parameters within which regulation of money in politics is currently permitted, but these decisions have also defined the political debate on campaign finance reform, with some arguing that money is speech and that, short of disclosure, no other limits are constitutionally permitted or desirable (Smith 2001; Redish 2001),while others argue that money is not speech and that more extensive contribution and expenditure limits, among other regulations, are needed (Rosenkranz 1998).

States as Laboratories in Campaign Finance Regulation

Justice Louis Brandeis, in *New State Ice Company v. Liebman*, 285 U.S. 262 (1932), described states as laboratories of democracy where "a single courageous state may, if its citizens choose, serve as a laboratory; and try novel social and economic experiments without risk to the rest of the country" (311). Justice Brandeis argued that, in the context of the Depression, the courts should not halt state efforts to experiment with different means of addressing the social welfare needs their people face. Thus, as advocates of federalism argue, there are potentially fifty different experiments in policy or regulation regarding an issue. Letting states first experiment and then reviewing the results permits scholars and policy advocates to draw from these experiments to see what works and thereby to produce either better national or state policy.

Along with each of the states serving as regulatory laboratories, each state also faces a host of different conditions regarding the role money plays within its political system. Some states have opted to let the money play free; others have chosen some disclosure, while still others have opted for a variety of other mechanisms, including contribution limits, voluntary public funding, lobbyist registration, bans on corporate or union political activity, or other regulations. This volume provides a broad examination of a diversity of states in terms of how they deal with money, politics, campaigns, and elections within their borders. It examines how each of these states has decided to regulate money and politics to ascertain the impact of these policies upon governance and elections. While the book does not cover all fifty states, it provides a diverse spectrum of state experiences. Effort has been made to make the inclusion of case studies as diverse as possible in terms of geographic location (the South, Midwest, West and East), population, political cultures (traditional, individualistic, and moralistic) (Elazar 1966), and regulatory schemes (i.e., minimal regulation of campaign contributions, partial or full public financing, disclosure, and lobbyist regulations). As a result, the book offers the first major attempt at providing a realistic picture about what we know regarding how money influences state politics and what different governments are doing to address this issue.

Hence, when it comes to campaign finance reform and the regulation of money in politics, the states selected for this book provide one effort to see what the different laboratory experiments have produced, perhaps laying the groundwork for legal regulatory models that could be adopted by the federal government or other states.

The states selected for inclusion in this book represent a diversity of regulatory practices across a range of geographic and demographic criteria. Among states that minimally regulate campaign contributions are Iowa, Texas, Wyoming, Illinois, and South Carolina. States with partial public financing of campaigns include Florida, for the governor's office, and all legislative and statewide offices in Minnesota. In fact, Minnesota, with its strong moralistic culture, is often pointed out as a model in its efforts to police the political process. Its partial public financing system is unique in its funding—state rebates to citizens who make up to $50 in donations and overall limits on how much money candidates may take from PACs, lobbyists, and big donors. It is also only one of two states to have instituted a total ban on lobbyist gifts to public officials.

Massachusetts is an example of the new "clean money" system that calls for total public financing of state races, yet, for reasons to be noted in the chapter on that state, the "clean money" option had yet to be implemented or funded at the time of the this book's publication. Arizona is also awaiting implementation of this financing option. This leaves Maine, in the 2000 election, as the only state so far with any experience in terms of a total public financing schema. Hence, there is little data thus far regarding how well total public financing systems work.

California's importance stems from the fact the it is the most populous and costly of all states in terms of running campaigns. In addition, because of California's use of ballot measures, the state is also a significant case study, both in terms of how money is spent for these initiatives and how the initiatives have been used to enact campaign finance reform measures. Iowa's importance generally stems from its being the starting point in the presidential election, but this state, along with Minnesota, bans corporate but not labor contributions, thus creating an interesting test on how these two groups battle it out for influence. States such as South Carolina, Florida, and Oklahoma are included not only because they are representatives of Southern states, but also because, in the election of 2000, they were battleground states for the presidency, or because, as in the case of Florida and Oklahoma, they are examples of reform in areas not traditionally noted for reformist efforts. Wyoming provides an interesting contrast of a western state that has opted not to enact many regulations, yet, nonetheless, it has produced results far different from other states like Texas and Illinois, which also lack contribution limits. Finally, Michigan is examined to see what impact term limits have had upon money and politics. Supporters of term limits hoped that they would diminish the power of incumbency and weaken the connection between elected officials and special interest money, yet so far this claim has not been tested adequately.

Finally, besides states, many local governments throughout the country have adopted mandatory and voluntary reforms, ranging from contribution limits to disclosure, public financing, and conflict-of-interest laws. Their experiences are also instructive in telling scholars and reformers what impact both money and the regulations have had on campaigns and policy making.

Overall, this book will look at money and reform in state politics through the 2000 elections, and in so doing, will offer the most comprehensive and up-to-date analysis of money and campaign finance reform at the state level on the market. The book will be useful to scholars in American politics, including those in state and local politics, campaigns and elections, and money and politics. But, outside of political science, lawyers who litigate in the area of election law will also find the book to be of interest. A comprehensive treatment of money, politics, and state campaign finance reform efforts is sadly needed and perhaps will serve as one part of the effort to document evidence regarding what impact money has on political contributions and expenditures and how regulations succeed or fail to address their corrupting influence. As the Supreme Court indicated in *Buckley v. Valeo*, 424 U.S. 1 (1976), states can regulate contributions and expenditures if they can show that contributions and expenditures either corrupt or lead to corruption of the political process. Evidence of corruption (Schultz 1998), thus, is critical to legislation being upheld, and the material gathered in this book will thus be useful to those seeking to document the money paper-trail.

The Lessons of State Experiments and Experiences

The cases studies presented in this book demonstrate that state campaigns, and, to a lesser extent, local campaigns, are increasingly facing the same problems with money and politics as federal races confront. This means that there is a general pattern of increased costs associated with running for election, including growth in average and aggregate contributions and expenditures, as well as a rise in the use of issue advocacy, soft money and independent expenditures by both party and non-party organizations and individuals.

Several forces contribute to state races' and local races' mimicking characteristics found in federal elections. First, recent moves to limit the size of the federal government or to redefine governmental authority under some type of rejuvenated federalist vision mean states and local governments are increasingly being asked to assume important new policy functions. This means that state and local policy decisions carry with them more significance than in the recent past and, therefore, elections at these levels are more important because the stakes are greater than in the past (Nathan 1996). With additional responsibility to resolve policy disputes, it is now worth the effort of many groups and individuals to get involved and try to influence elections and policy deliberations.

Second, there has been a general trend towards the "nationalizing" of state elections. State and local elections are increasingly more media-driven, run by professionals, or are otherwise adopting techniques traditionally employed only in presidential or congressional elections (Salmore and Salmore 1996). As a result, more money is required to run these campaigns.

Third, political party realignments over the last two decades have broken down many of the traditional single-party-dominated states, thereby producing either more competitive races, or splitting party control at the state level or between the state and federal offices, or shifting domination to another party (Maisel 1999). As a result of these realignments, or as fuel to help them, more money has flowed into states' races.

Fourth, both term-limits and reapportionment as a result of population and demographic shifts within and across states have resulted in the creation of more open or contested seats, thereby making them attractive for new candidates, especially in states where party control of the government is divided or close.

Finally, as a result of the soft money loopholes, state parties are often used by the national political parties as conduits for money and campaign activity that cannot be undertaken at the federal level. For example, as noted earlier, federal law prohibits corporations and unions from contributing to federal campaigns. However, many states do not have this prohibition, resulting in these entities contributing to state parties (Corrado 2000). State parties, thus, have not only become surrogate banks for the national parties, but their use of this new found money for GOTV, voter registration, issue advocacy, and other activities have also impacted the cost and tenor of local races. Overall, for the above reasons, and perhaps others, state and local political environments have been more affected or dominated by money than in the past.

It would be impossible to summarize the campaign finance trends of all fifty states, let alone the twelve examined in detail here. However, several patterns are definitely clear.

First, states and local governments demonstrate a variety of patterns of regulatory behavior to address the impact money has upon their campaigns and governance. These techniques range from doing practically nothing, (as in Texas), to simple disclosure (as in Illinois), to other patterns, including forms of contribution limits (as in Wyoming, Oklahoma, and California), bans on corporations or union contributions and restrictions on lobbyist activity (as in South Carolina and Minnesota), and forms of public financing for elections (as in Minnesota, Massachusetts, and Florida). At the local level, cities such as Austin, Texas, New York City, Seattle, San Francisco, and Fort Collins, Colorado, have enacted similar types of regulations, but cities, such as Boulder, Colorado, have also experimented with voluntary spending limits. Finally, cities such as Westminister, Colorado, and Belmont, California, have sought to sever the link between political contributions and the awarding of city contracts or political favors by redefining local conflict-of-interest statutes. Subject to limits placed upon them by home rule authority, local governments have demonstrated enormous creativity in seeking to police their elections and policy processes.

Yet, despite this creativity on the part of state and local governments in varying ways, the states examined here are increasingly affected by soft money, independent expenditures, rising campaign costs, and issue advocacy. With the notable exception of Wyoming, all of the states examined have experienced significant increases in contributions and expenditures over the last decade, and perhaps over the last quarter of a century. For example, in 1976, the total aggregate spending for races in California was $20 million, while in 2000 it was $130 million. Similarly, in 1976, the aggregate cost of running for governor was $5.7 million; in 1998, it was $52.5 million. In Massachusetts, the average House member in 1998 spent nearly $40,000, a 38 % increase over the previous election cycle, while Paul Cellucci spent $6.7 million in 1998 to be elected Governor, eclipsing the spending of the previous winning candidate, Republican Bill Weld, who spent $3.6 million to get elected in 1994. In Iowa, total contributions to state legislative campaigns increased from $3,606,739 in 1994 to $9,800,515 in 2000. The average successful State Senate candidate spent $111,363 (not counting primary spending), while the average State House candidate spent $42,866. Candidates running in 1998 in contested races for the Florida House raised $79,976 on average.

Contested Florida Senate races found candidates raising an average of $194,110. Total expenditures in the 120-member House, where all seats are up for election every two years, were $18,505,767. Ninety-six incumbents raised $10 million, compared to $2.8 million for sixty-five challengers and $5.7 million for eighty-four candidates in open-seat races. On the Senate side, where only one-half of the forty seats are contested every two years, total expenditures amounted to $6,774,943. Sixteen Senate incumbents raised $4 million. Finally, in the 2000 Oklahoma elections, Senate legislative candidates raised $53,572 and spent $47,349 on average, while House candidates raised $27,647 and spent $26,495 on average; both expenditures represented significant increases from previous election cycles.

In short, it is far more expensive to run for office today than it was in the past, and the different case studies demonstrate that the increased costs are not simply related to inflation. Often the increases far outstrip any cost-of-living changes. Because of those increased costs, there is now increased pressure for candidates to raise money. California Governor Davis is referred to as the "$100,000 man" because he refuses to make an appearance for less than that amount. The impact of all this is that there is pressure on contributors to give more to campaigns, that candidates must spend more time raising money, and, presumably, that there is more expected by donors from candidates who win election.

A second theme to emerge in the states is that soft money has clearly become a problem at the state level. Minnesota, Florida, South Carolina, Indiana, and California particularly note the influence of soft money. In Minnesota, for example, the total aggregate amount of soft money is far greater than that of hard money. In 1994, soft money totaled $5.9 million, while in 2000 it was $20 million. In contrast, total hard money in those years amounted to $3.1 and $7.8 million, respectively. Moreover, Minnesota, Iowa, South Carolina, and Florida, especially after the 2000 ballot disputes, noted large influxes of national-party or out-of-state money into state parties. In Minnesota, both the Democrats and the Republicans received well over $1.5 million dollars from national parties to fuel local GOTV, issue ads, and other activities.

Third, many states, including Texas, Minnesota, Oklahoma, and California, have also noted a rise in the use of independent expenditures and issue ads, both by parties and PACs. However, no such corresponding rise in soft money or independent expenditures has occurred in Indiana and Illinois, in part because, lacking limits on individual contributions, these states provide no need or incentive to work around the hard money contributions that exist at the federal level or in other states. Along with this growth in independent expenditures, there has also been an increase in party-independent expenditures since the 1996 *Colorado Republican I* decision declared bans on them to be unconstitutional. Thus, in Minnesota, for example, since the time the state ban on these expenditures has become invalidated, party-independent expenditures–and with them, soft money contributions and party fund raising to fuel them–have exploded.

A fourth lesson learned from examining these states is that the patterns by which groups give money and how they give it vary not only according to the resources and goals of the local group (Wilson 1973), but the patterns also depend on the regulatory framework of the state in question, as well as the local issues that are most salient. For example, in Illinois, gambling and liquor interests contribute heavily, while, in South Carolina, textile and gambling interests are heavy contributors. In Wyoming, mining contributes heavily, in Oklahoma, oil and gas, and, in Texas, just about anyone is a heavy contributor to political campaigns. However, in some states, either corporate or union contributions may be prohibited, forcing groups to spend more money on lobbyist activity. This is clearly the case in Florida, Minnesota, Oklahoma, and South Carolina (the last of which recently restricted the ability of lobbyists to contribute to candidates or give gifts to elected officials). Yet, as the Indiana and Illinois examples reveal, if the regulatory environment allows for unlimited individual contributions, then money will come from individuals and not groups. In part, the evidence appears to show that soft money and independent expenditures are an outgrowth of hard money restrictions: Place limits on the ability to give in one arena, and the money will resurface elsewhere. Even in South Carolina, where new efforts were undertaken to limit special interest influence, the decrease in the ability of lobbyists to give resulted in other forms of contributions, which raised a record amount of $11.5 million for lobbyists in the 2000 election campaigns. In fact, several case studies here point to the increasingly powerful role of lobbyists and PACs at the state level, thereby questioning the uniqueness of their activities and their financial impact on the national scene.

The moral from state experiences can be used to confirm an old political adage that regulating money in politics is like a water balloon: if one squeezes one end of the balloon, the water will shift elsewhere. Regulations that seek to limit money in politics do not seem to prevent contributors from giving; they simply shift their donations to another venue. The range of options appear to be hard money contributions to candidates, soft money contributions to parties and political groups, independent expenditures, and lobbyist activity. Interests shift their resources among at least these four venues, dependent upon state law and the organizational tactics and resources the interests seek to pursue.

State experiences also pose questions about or throw empirical light on some debates taking place in the legal and academic community regarding campaign finance reform. For one, there is little evidence that disclosure alone is enough to address problems associated with money and politics. This is true for two reasons. First, the pattern of state disclosure is very uneven and often inadequate at the state level. Some states require disclosure of all money down to a certain threshold, the threshold varying from $50 to $500 or more. Some states do not require some parties to disclose, or some do not make disclosure mandatory, or some set dates for filing so late that no citizen could ever review the information in time to make an electoral choice. In other cases, states such as Texas, have no real enforcement power to mandate disclosure, and in many states that have electronic disclosure–a recent innovation that only disclosure advocates trumpet–the disclosure is often not mandatory, or it is spotty at best .

Another problem with disclosure directly affected the writing of this book. In many states, specific information on candidate-behavior, PAC-behavior, or contributor-behavior does not have to be reported. In other states, such as South Carolina, Florida, and Wyoming, the lack of reporting and disclosure has made it difficult to ascertain the exact scope of soft- money or party-independent expenditures in the state. Lacking facts or evidence, it is impossible to generate conclusions about phenomena. Finally, some states, such as Michigan, either destroy the data or change the format in which it is available after several years, making multi-year analysis difficult, while, in other states, the various authors in this book indicate that underfunded or uncooperative state ethical or campaign finance boards have mis-coded data, changed coding from year to year, or have otherwise organized data in ways that have made any multi-state or multi-year analysis difficult. The point here is that if experts in politics, data analysis, and political funding have had difficulty working with or interpreting any state data, the prospects that average citizens or reporters could do better are doubtful, thereby questioning the claim that disclosure laws are currently adequate and able to police the potential abuses in the politics. If anything, the case studies in this volume reveal a need for some standards regarding disclosure that are consistent across states and time.

But state experience in campaign financing also demonstrates that disclosure alone does not produce more competitive races or equalize the spending inequities between challengers and incumbents. Several state studies note the overwhelming power of incumbents to raise money compared to that of challengers. The experiences of Texas, Illinois, California and Massachusetts illustrate this. There is some evidence that the competitiveness of races in Iowa and Indiana may be due in part to the lack of limits on contributions, but the only state where the gap between the money raised by challengers and incumbents has narrowed such that it has produced more competitive races is Minnesota, where there exists a partial public financing system. It has resulted in the election of a third- party candidate, Jesse Ventura, and it has made state legislative races more competitive.

After surveying the various state regulatory mechanisms among the twelve states, ranging from disclosure through some combination of disclosure and contribution limits, this volume finds that only Minnesota, with its system of public funding, demonstrates any evidence of being able to remedy incumbent advantage. Not even term limits, as the Michigan study reveals, can address that issue. As Michigan reveals, term limits have produced more competitive races, more reliance on a candidate's own money, and an increased role for party and PAC giving. However, there is no evidence that term limits have severed the connection between legislators and special interests or have produced a legislature more diversified; instead, term limits seem to be generating wealthier candidates. Thus, for those seeking to mitigate the power of incumbency and produce more competitive elections, neither disclosure alone nor term limits seem to be the solution. Instead, some move towards public funding is needed. But, even then, the water balloon analogy suggests that money will shift elsewhere, perhaps to soft money, issue advocacy, independent expenditures, or to lobbyist activity. Thus, efforts to address the impact of money on state politics need to be more comprehensive than at present.

All of the above clearly begs the question: Does money corrupt the political process, or is all this worry much ado about nothing? The current constitutional justification to permit the regulation of money in politics is a need to demonstrate that money corrupts or leads to the appearance of corruption. Exactly what is corruption? For some, it is merely the *quid pro quo* exchange of money for votes or influence. If that is the case, the experiences of California, Oklahoma, Illinois, and Florida, for example, reveal clear patterns of bribery-like behavior where individuals are convicted in sting operations or money is found in a shoe box. Other states in this study also report individual patterns of abuse. Perhaps these individual abuses are enough to justify some action, but perhaps they also justify tougher criminal enforcement against specific offenders.

Dennis Thompson (1995) suggests an important distinction between individual and institutional corruption. The latter refers to the abuse of office for political and not personal reasons, while the former refers to the abuse of office for personal benefit. Building upon this distinction, corruption may also be considered institutionally in terms of how money affects a state political system as a whole. Indeed, the state experiences detailed in this book demonstrate a wide pattern of how money affects the political process. For instance, many of the case studies here report public opinion polls that question how much influence citizens of that state have over their elected representatives as opposed to those who give money to their representatives' campaigns. If nothing else, citizens sense money corrupts, and perhaps that is enough evidence–per the *Nixon v. Shrink*-test–to enact reforms or be concerned about the impact of money on political campaigns.

But, moving beyond appearance, the various case studies reveal the plethora of ways that money institutionally impacts both state campaigns and governance. In Iowa, legislation is unable to reach the floor. In Minnesota, there is evidence that tobacco money is killing legislation or that money has decreased voter turnout. In Illinois, gambling and liquor money has achieved significant policy goals, and the same is true in Florida, in Texas, and in other states. In Massachusetts, money appears even to be precluding efforts to fund the voter initiative to clean up the role of money in politics. Elsewhere, the case studies document uncompetitive or noncompetitive races, incumbency advantages, the powerful ability of caucus or party leaders to raise and transfer money to those who support them, a turn towards the use of personal wealth to run for office, and dramatic increases in the costs of running for office, among a host of other activities that result in candidates spending more time fund-raising or in decreased opportunities for new people to enter the political system, mount credible challenges, or influence public policy. All of this should be considered when one assesses the evidence regarding the impact of money on politics and whether money leads to corruption or the *appearance* of corruption.

The experiences of these states perhaps demonstrate that current efforts to regulate money in politics are insufficient, or that perhaps the First Amendment limits imposed by *Buckley* need to be rethought. But, at the very least, they demonstrate that there is much for us to learn about money and its impact on politics by turning away from federal experiences and instead examining what the state laboratories can tell us.

References

Alexander, Herbert E. 1995. *Financing the 1992 election*, Armonk, NY: M.E. Sharpe.

Birnbaum, Jeffrey H. 2000. *The money men: The real story of fund-raising's influence on political power in America*. New York: Crown.

Brindle, Jeffrey M. 2000. Mission and method: Regulating campaign financing in New Jersey. *Public Integrity* 4: 2 (Fall 2000): 289-302.

Corrado, Anthony. 2000. *Campaign finance reform*. New York: The Century Foundation Press.

Common Cause. 2000. National parties raise record $457 million in soft money this election cycle through November 27, 2000. Retrieved October 1, 2001: http://commoncause.org/publications/dec00/121500st.htm

Drew, Elizabeth. 1999. *The corruption of American politics: What went wrong and why*. Secaucus, NJ: Birch Lane Press.

Elazar, Daniel J. 1966. *American federalism: A view from the states*. New York: Thomas Crowell Company.

Graham, Cole Blease Jr., and William V. Moore. 1994. *South Carolina politics and government*. Lincoln: University of Nebraska Press.

Green, John C., ed. 1999. *Financing the 1996 election*. Armonk, NY: M.E. Sharpe.

Kuzenski, John C. 1998. South Carolina: The heart of GOP realignment in the South. In *The new politics of the Old South*, edited by Charles S. Bullock and Mark Rozell. New York: Rowman and Littlefield.

Maisel, L. Sandy. 1999. *Parties and elections in America: The electoral process*. 3d ed. Lanham, MD: Rowman & Littlefield.

Malbin, Michael J., and Thomas L. Geis. 1998. *The day after reform: Sobering campaign finance lessons from the American states*. Albany, NY: The Rockefeller Institute.

Michaelson, Ronald D. 2001. Campaign finance activity in the states: Where the action is. *Public Integrity*, 3:1 (Winter 2001): 33-51.

Nathan, Richard P. 1996. The role of the states in American federalism. In *The state of the states*, edited by Carl E. Van Horn. Washington, D.C.: Congressional Quarterly Press.

Redish, Martin H. 2001. *Money talks: Speech, economic power, and the values of democracy*. New York: NYU Press.

Rosenkranz, Joshua. 1998. *Buckley stops here: Loosening the judicial stranglehold on campaign finance*. New York: The Century Foundation Press.

Salmore, Stephen A., and Barbara G. Salmore. 1996. The transformation of state electoral politics. In *The state of the states*, edited by Carl E.Van Horn. Washington, D.C.: Congressional Quarterly Press.

Schultz, David. 1998. Proving political corruption: Documenting the evidence required to sustain campaign finance reform laws. *Texas Review of Litigation* 18: 86.

————. 1998. Revisiting *Buckley v. Valeo*: Eviscerating the line between candidate contributions and independent expenditures. *Journal of Law and Politics* 14: 33.

Smith, Bradley A. 2001. *Unfree speech: The folly of campaign finance reform*. Princeton: Princeton University Press.

Sorauf, Frank J. 1988. *Money in American politics*. Scott, Foresman and Company.

———. 1992. *Inside campaign finance: Myth and realities*. New Haven, CT: Yale University Press.

Thomas, Clive S., and Ronald J. Hrebner. 1990. Nationalization of interest groups and lobbying in the States. In *Interest group politics*, edited by Allen J. Cigler and Burdett A. Loomis. Washington DC: Congressional Quarterly.

Thompson, Dennis F. 1995. *Ethics in congress: From individual to institutional corruption*. Washington, D.C.: The Brookings Institution.

Thompson, Joel A., and Gary F. Moncrief. 1998. *Campaign finance in state legislative elections*. Washington, D.C.: Congressional Quarterly.

Wilson, James Q. 1973. *Political organizations*. New York: Basic Books.

CHAPTER 1

BIG MONEY IN THE LONE STAR STATE: THE ABSENCE OF CAMPAIGN FINANCE REGULATION AND POLITICS IN TEXAS

John David Rausch, Jr.

The Texas system is just so wide open. The federal situation is terrible,
and the Texas system makes the federal system look like the Golden Rule.
    —John Hirschi, former Democratic House
        member from Wichita Falls (Hirschi 2001)

On November 7, 2000, Republican Todd Staples, a three-term state representative, rancher and businessman from Palestine, defeated Silsbee attorney David Fisher, the Democratic candidate, to claim Texas Senate District Three. This race was important for a number of reasons. Senate District Three was the only open seat in the Senate, because the incumbent declined to seek re-election after having been convicted of a crime. Because of Staples' victory, the Republican Party maintained its one-seat advantage in the thirty-one-member Senate. Staples was only the second Republican since Reconstruction to be elected to represent the heavily Democratic district in east Texas. Finally, Staples and Fisher combined to raise more than $5 million to campaign for an office with a salary of $7,200 a year (Robison 2000).

Texans for Public Justice, a policy and research organization that tracks the influence of money in elections, examined the financial disclosure reports filed by both campaigns through the end of October 2000. The organization found that both candidates benefitted from a small number of contributors with deep pockets. Staples raised $2.4 million, with approximately 50% coming from thirty contributors. The Democrat Fisher raised $1.7 million. Texans for Public Justice noted "the $982,113 supplied by Fisher's top 30 donors came from contributors that have an interest in blocking the business agenda promoted by Staples' top donors." This race was the most expensive campaign for a state senate seat in Texas history (2000a).

Campaign financing in Texas is largely unregulated. This chapter examines the effect of this lack of regulation on politics in the state. Was the 2000 Senate District Three race an aberration or simply one point on a trend? What is the role of money in a new political arena with a very competitive Republican Party? Why is it difficult to enact incremental campaign finance changes much less more significant reforms? What is the role of public opinion in driving a campaign finance reform "movement" in the Lone Star State?

To answer these questions, I first briefly examine the context of politics in Texas. Second, I examine the current state of campaign finance regulation. Third, I analyze the effects of unregulated money flowing into campaigns for state-level offices and discuss recent attempts to enact regulation. I conclude by looking into the future of campaign financing regulation in the Lone Star State.

The Context of Texas Politics

Any Texan will tell a questioner that Texas is a unique state. Geographically, the state is considered part of the South, but culturally it is an amalgam of a number of different regions. Bass and DeVries note:

> The cultural blend of the South and the West, the presence of two substantial minority population groups, the prolonged frontier period, the massive deposits of oil and natural gas, the dramatic rate of urbanization in recent decades and the massive size of the state (801 miles from north to south and 773 miles east to west) all combine to make Texas unique. (1976)

Lamis argues that the political arena in Texas is a "world unto itself" (1984). This chapter examines how campaign financing affects, and is affected by, that political arena.

Population growth has been significant in Texas during the last three decades. The state's population in 1960 was 9.5 million. By 1992 it was estimated to be 17.6 million. In 1994, Texas exceeded the 18 million mark, becoming the second most populous state in the nation. According to the 2000 Census, 20.9 million people reside in Texas.

The rural and agrarian nature of Texas remains largely as a memory. Most of the newcomers and natives of Texas reside in four major metropolitan regions: Dallas-Fort Worth, Houston-Galveston, Austin-San Antonio, and El Paso. Altogether, 83.4% of the population lives in the twenty-nine metropolitan areas of the state. The ethnic/racial composition is approximately 55% Anglo, 31% Hispanic, 11% African-American, and 4% other. The Hispanic population has grown rapidly in the last few decades. Demographers project that by 2030 no ethnic group will have a majority (Maxwell and Crain 2002).

The state's image, portrayed on television shows like *Dallas,* is that of a very wealthy state. Empirical data present a different picture. The income gap between the wealthiest and poorest families is greater in Texas than in other states. According to Texans for Public Justice, "the wealthiest fifth of Texas' population (averaging $130,302 a year) makes almost 12 times the annual earning of the poorest fifth (averaging $11,200 a year)" (2000b). This income disparity is reflected in voter participation in elections at the ballot box and with the checkbook.

Texas was once a one-party Democratic state, with most competition occurring between liberal and conservative Democrats. Conservative Democrats were much more successful than their liberal counterparts because the semi-open primary laws allowed Republican voters to cross over into the Democratic primary. In the general election, the conservative Democratic candidate usually defeated the Republican because the Democrats were the traditional party (Maxwell and Crain 2002). The Republican Party's growth was stymied while the conservative Democrats remained dominant (Lamis 1984).

During the late 1980s and early 1990s, the Republican Party began to show significant signs of life, in part because campaign contributors began to fund Republican candidates. In 1978, the GOP held ninety-two elected offices in the state. Maxwell and Crain report that "before the presidential election of 1988, only three contemporary Republicans won statewide races in Texas: former U.S. Senator John Tower, Governor Bill Clements, and U.S. Senator Phil Gramm"(2002). The Republican Party had a difficult time shaking its image as "the party of Reconstruction."

By the end of the twentieth century the state became a two-party competitive state (Bibby and Holbrook 1999). In 1992, Kay Bailey Hutchison, a Republican, was elected to the U.S. Senate in a special election to replace the new Secretary of the Treasury Lloyd Bentsen, a conservative Democratic Senator. For the first time since Reconstruction, the Republican Party held both U.S. Senate seats. The watershed year for the Republican Party was 1998, when Republicans won all statewide races. Incumbent Governor George W. Bush was reelected and joined by Rick Perry, the Republican candidate for Lieutenant

Governor. Republicans were elected to the Railroad Commission, the Texas Supreme Court, and the Court of Criminal Appeals. The GOP maintained its hold on statewide offices in the 2000 elections. In fact, newspapers reported, "Texas Democrats...have fielded the fewest number of candidates for statewide office of the four parties on the ballot" (Gott 2000). After the 2000 elections, Republicans held 1,500 offices. The rise of the Republican Party has been attributed to the defection of conservative Democrats to the Republican Party. These defections occurred primarily because many conservative Democrats believed that the Democratic party had left them (Cannon 1998; Attlesey 1995).

Voters may benefit from increased two-party competition, and this may be reflected in increased participation in elections. Moderate and conservative Republicans will challenge liberal and conservative Democrats. It is possible that this increased competition also will result in more expensive campaigns, as both parties fight to mobilize their key constituencies. These constituencies can be difficult to mobilize.

Political culture plays a significant role in defining the political activity of a state's citizens. According to Elazar, Texas is a hybrid of traditionalistic and individualistic subcultures (1972). The key feature of the traditionalistic subculture is the view that the government's job is to maintain the existing social order. An established social elite runs the government, and ordinary citizens are not expected to play a significant role in the political process. The traditionalistic subculture, derived from the plantation society of the Old South, and was carried to east Texas by immigrants from that region. On the other hand, the individualistic subculture emphasizes limited government, with a strong reliance on private initiative. The government should protect individual rights and maintain a social order based on merit. This subculture emerged in the Middle Atlantic states and was carried across the lower Midwest and into west Texas (Tannahill 2000). Political culture can explain low Texas-voter turnout, the few restrictions on campaign financing, as well as the large contributions seen in recent Texas campaigns.

A Texas voter faces a long ballot when he or she enters the polling place on Election Day. Almost every office, at all levels of government, is filled by election. With the exception of some local governments and school boards, most of the elections are partisan. At the state-level, the focus of this chapter, Texans elect the governor and lieutenant governor separately, not as a ticket. The lieutenant governor holds the most powerful position in the state, because the he or she also serves as state senate president. Senate rules have allowed the presiding officer significant powers to appoint committee chairs and refer legislation. Texans also elect all executive-branch officials, creating the so-called plural executive. These officials are the attorney general, comptroller of public accounts, commissioner of the General Land Office, and commissioner of agriculture. Texans elect the three members of the Railroad Commission in a statewide vote, while the fifteen members of the State Board of Education are elected in districts. Despite its name, the Railroad Commission currently regulates the oil and gas industry in Texas. The nine justices of the state supreme court and the nine judges of the court of criminal appeals are elected statewide in partisan elections; other judges are elected in smaller districts.

The Texas Legislature is comprised of a House of Representatives, with 150 members and a thirty-one-member Senate. The Legislature meets biennially in a 140-day regular session. All 150 representatives are elected every two years, while senators serve four-year terms. After the decennial redistricting, all senators must stand for election. Given the frequency of elections and the number of people running for office, a person or a group with an interest in influencing government has ample opportunity to contribute to campaigns. Observers argue that the long ballot also works to decrease turnout by diffusing interest in the election and confusing voters.

The Current State of Campaign Finance Regulation

Campaign financing in Texas is largely unregulated. This lack of regulation can be attributed to the state's individualistic political culture. Texas is one of the few states that do not limit individual contributions to legislative and executive campaigns. The Texas Ethics Commission summarizes and explains campaign finance regulations in its *Campaign Finance Guide for Candidates and Officeholders Who File with the Texas Ethics Commission* (1997a). Before a candidate may raise or spend money, he or she must file a report naming an official campaign treasurer. Candidates and political action committees may not accept aggregate contributions of more than $100 in cash. Corporations and labor unions have been prohibited from directly contributing to campaigns since 1903, but they may form political action committees (Graves 1997). Candidates and treasurers of campaign committees are required to file disclosure reports for a designated reporting period. These disclosure reports must include amounts of all contributions and expenditures, but the reports do not include an indication of the cash balance on hand at the time of filing. In 1999, the Legislature enacted a statute requiring most candidates to file their reports electronically to make the information more accessible (Texans for Public Justice 2001a). "The Texas Ethics Commission may impose fines for filing late or failing to file. Also, any citizen may file a criminal complaint with the district attorney, a civil complaint with the Ethics Commission, or a civil action against a candidate or officeholder for violations." The penalties are assessed against the candidate or officeholder, not the campaign treasurer (Texas Ethics Commission 1997a). Candidates may not spend campaign contributions on personal expenses and the law requires them to itemize the expenses on their disclosure reports. Legislators may not accept campaign contributions during a regular session of the legislature and thirty days before it.

Legislators are prohibited from accepting contributions, and potential contributors are prohibited from making them in the Capitol in Austin. A person who violates this regulation commits a Class A misdemeanor and is subject to a year in jail and a $4,000 fine. The Legislature enacted this regulation in 1991 in the wake of an incident involving Lonnie "Bo" Pilgrim, majority stockholder and CEO of Pilgrim's Pride. The company is a large poultry-processor in East Texas. In 1989, Governor Bill Clements called a special session of the Legislature to rewrite worker's compensation law. As noted above, legislators are prohibited from accepting campaign contributions during regular sessions, but the prohibition does not extend to special sessions. Pilgrim had a special interest in worker's compensation, since workers in poultry-processing facilities frequently suffer on-the-job injuries. To insure that the legislation would not impede his business, Pilgrim went on the floor of the Texas Senate immediately after it recessed one afternoon and handed checks, each for $10,000, to eight senators (Elliott, Hofer, and Biles 1998). The recipients returned the checks; several waited a few days. The Travis County district attorney could not prosecute Pilgrim because the law did not prohibit contributions during special sessions. In 1991, the Legislature passed a package of campaign finance regulations that included a prohibition on contributions being made in the Capitol (Robison 2001a). Pilgrim continues to be one of the state's largest contributors, usually mailing the checks to campaign committees.

There are significant loopholes in campaign finance regulation. The first loophole is the inability of the Texas Ethics Commission to enforce current law. According to Fred Lewis of Campaigns for People, the commission "was structured to fail" (Berger 2001). The Texas Ethics Commission was created in 1991 when Texas voters approved a constitutional amendment. While it had been established in statutory law during the 1991 legislative session, the constitutional amendment was required in order to provide the commission with the power to recommend legislative pay raises for voter approval and to increase government officials' per diem payments without voter input. In addition to these constitutional powers, the Ethics Commission also "requires financial disclosure from public officials, and publishes recommendations and rules for public officials. It assumed the secretary of state's duties on advisory opinions, lobbyist registration and expenditures, and review of campaign spending and contributions." The commission is made up of eight members, four selected by the governor and two members, one selected by the lieutenant governor and the other by speaker of the House (Johnson 1999). It also is bipartisan, with an equal number of Democrats and Republicans (Graves 1997).

While the commission has the power to enforce campaign finance rules and maintain disclosure data, it does not appear to review the disclosure reports and only investigates irregularities when there is a complaint. Since 1992, the commission has held "one informal and one formal hearing," and it has never issued a subpoena (Berger 2001). The affirmative vote of six of the eight commissioners is required to issue a subpoena, and the commission's investigators are limited by very strict confidentiality rules. If an investigator interviews a potential witness, he or she risks severe civil and criminal penalties for revealing information about the complaint. Releasing information on a pending investigation is a Class A misdemeanor, punishable by a $4,000 fine and up to one year in jail. The violator could also receive a $10,000 fine or be responsible for the damages, whichever sum is higher, including court costs and attorneys' fees (Berger 2001). Attempts to change this law have been unsuccessful.

The inability of the Ethics Commission to independently investigate campaign finance irregularities means that most elected officials are able to spend money on expenses not directly related to a campaign. The *Houston Chronicle* reviewed the 1998, 1999, and 2000 campaign finance records of Houston area legislators and found that "at least four of seven senators and 10 of 25 representatives...broke the itemizing laws" (Berger 2001). The senators and representatives used campaign contributions to pay for "various small expenses on credit cards" and "for political expenditures made from personal funds during prior campaigns for state representative" (Berger 2001). Members of the Texas Legislature receive a salary of $600 per month, and some probably see campaign contributions as a way to supplement that salary. The Ethics Commission receives its appropriation from the Legislature and, thus, commissioners are unwilling to provoke that body's ire by closely examining expenditures from the legislators' campaign funds.

The campaign finance disclosure forms filed by campaigns do not have to identify contributors' occupations or employers. This loophole makes it difficult for researchers to uncover possible connections among individual contributors and interest groups or corporations. Unless a citizen or candidate complains, it appears that a corporation can provide "bonuses" to employees with the "hope" that the employees will contribute to the corporation's favored candidate. Makinson describes a similar process uncovered in Alaska (1994).

While legislation was passed in 1999, requiring electronic filing of disclosure reports, the Legislature created two exemptions. If candidates promise not to accept more than $20,000 or spend more than $20,000 in the calendar year, they do not have to file electronically. Those who do not use computer equipment to keep contribution and expenditure records also are not required to file electronically (Texans for Public Justice 2001a).

Out-of-state political action committees do not have to register with the Texas Ethics Commission or file disclosure reports. The definition of an out-of-state committee is not completely clear:

Whether a committee is an out-of-state committee depends on the proportion of expenditures made by the political committee on elections voted on in Texas (including elections for federal offices) in the last 12 months to all political expenditures made by the political committee in the last 12 months. If the expenditures in connection with elections voted on in Texas (not including the anticipated expenditure) do not exceed 20% of the committee's total political expenditures, the committee may make the anticipated expenditure without filing a campaign treasurer appointment in Texas. If the expenditures in connection with elections voted on in Texas (not including the anticipated expenditure) exceed 20% of the committee's total political expenditures, the committee may not make the anticipated expenditure without filing a campaign treasurer appointment in Texas. (Texas Ethics Commission 1997b)

Soft money and independent expenditures are also not regulated in Texas, but these types of campaign financing are less important in a state with few regulations on "hard money" contributions. The Texas Supreme Court protected the confidentiality of soft money contributors with its ruling in *In Re Bay Area Citizens Against Lawsuit Abuse* (982 S.W.2d 371 [Tex. 1998]). The Court, in a unanimous decision, found that the open records provision of the Texas Nonprofit Corporations Act violates the U.S. Constitution's First Amendment rights of contributors to nonprofit organizations. A nonprofit corporation must identify its board of directors, but the sources of its funding do not have to be reported to the Texas Ethics Commission (Ratcliffe 1997a).

Candidates for judicial offices must follow different campaign finance regulations, primarily as a result of the Judicial Campaign Fairness Act of 1995 (Texans for Public Justice 2001b; Texas Ethics Commission 2001; Farrar-Myers and Frier 2000). There are two courts of last resort in Texas. The Court of Criminal Appeals primarily reviews death penalty appeals and other challenges to criminal punishment in the state. The Texas Supreme Court hears civil appeals and reviews cases involving juveniles. While members of both courts are selected in partisan elections, campaign contributions may have more influence on the Supreme Court because the litigants (especially the defendants) in these cases have more financially at stake. Most discussion of campaign finance regulations involves candidates for the Supreme Court (Cheek and Champagne 2000).

Judicial candidates are limited to spending $2 million for each statewide election; candidates for non-statewide judicial positions (court of appeals, district court, county court at law, etc.) have lower limits, based on the size of the judicial district. Individuals may contribute no more than $5,000 to each statewide campaign per election. Law firms and legal political action committees can give no more than $30,000 in each statewide election. The $30,000 limit includes contributions from individuals employed by that firm. Once a candidate receives $30,000 from a law firm, employees of that firm are limited to contributing no more than $50 apiece for that candidate's election campaign. General-purpose political action committees may contribute no more than 15% of a candidate's total contributions. A candidate can take a total of $300,000 from PACs. Contributors must be identified by name, address, occupation and job title, and the full name and business address of the contributor's employer or law firm. Judicial candidates may begin soliciting contributions approximately seven months (210 days) before the deadline for applying to have their names put on the ballot. They can continue to solicit money until approximately four months (120 days) after the last election (primary, runoff, or general election) in which the candidate has an opponent. Judges who were appointed by the governor to fill a vacancy may accept contributions for sixty days once their official duties commence, whether or not the appointed judge is appointed during an election cycle.

The significant loophole in judicial campaign finance regulation is that the contribution limits are voluntary. A candidate does not have to abide by the limits if his or her opponent does not. Contribution limits are calculated separately for each election, not for each election cycle. For example, a contributor may give a Texas Supreme Court candidate $5,000 for the primary election, $5,000 more for any runoff election, and an additional $5,000 for the general election. Such a candidate would be able to raise three times as much money as the candidate who faces only a contested general election (Kinch 2001). In addition, judges do not have to recuse themselves from cases involving lawyers, law firms, or individuals who contributed to their campaigns.

The Judicial Campaign Fairness Act was a result of the expensive 1994 Democratic primary for the Texas Supreme Court. The incumbent Raul Gonzalez, favorite of the Texas defense bar, raised $2 million. The trial lawyers' candidate, Rene Haas, raised more than $2.4 million in her unsuccessful attempt to win the nomination (Borges and Ballard 1994). The campaign was also marked by a degree of nastiness not previously seen in judicial campaigns (Borges 1994). Kinch notes that the race forced the two legal factions to agree on some restraint (2001). Former Chief Justice John L. Hill, heading a judicial reform lobby organization, was able to persuade the Legislature to enact the Judicial Campaign Finance Act. He also lobbied unsuccessfully to change the judicial selection process in the state. Judicial selection continues to be a hotly debated issue in Texas politics.

The Effects of Limited Regulation

The lack of campaign finance regulation affects Texas politics. The impact of no regulation must be viewed through the lens of political culture; thus, it may be difficult to attribute many of the findings to the lack of campaign finance regulation. This section examines the amount of money raised and spent by candidates and political committees. It also analyzes the level of competition in political campaigns in Texas. Voter turnout percentages are also presented. Competition and voter turnout may be two areas where political culture plays a significant role as the antecedent variable. Finally, this section will survey the opinions of Texans on the issues of campaign financing, corruption, and trust in government.

Trends in Political Money

The focal point of politics in Texas is often the campaign for governor, and campaigns for governor are getting much more expensive. Graves reports that the seven candidates running for governor in both parties in 1990 spent a total of $46 million (1997). The total hides some interesting facts about the nature of contributions to campaigns. The Democrat's nominee, Ann Richards, received 21,161 contributions of less than $100 and only 152 contributions of more than $10,000. Tolleson-Rinehart and Stanley argue that traditional large donors did not think a woman was an electable candidate for governor (1994). In his February 1990 disclosure report, Clayton Williams, the Republican nominee, reported raising $1.3 million from 151 separate contributors and $2 million from 271 contributors. These contributors provided an average individual contribution of $7,000. By the end of the campaign, Williams' average individual contribution had dropped to $214; thus, Williams was able to appeal to more contributors in the general election campaign (Tolleson-Rinehart and Stanley 1994). Williams spent more than Richards in his losing effort.

Governor Ann Richards raised $15 million for her reelection campaign in 1994, while her Republican opponent, George W. Bush, raised $16.1 million. Interestingly, Bush received a number of sizable contributions after his election victory. Bush raised $3.3 million from October 30 through December 31, 1994, with fifteen contributors each giving more than $20,000 (Ratcliffe 1995).

Both candidates in the 1998 gubernatorial race combined to raise $29.9 million. Incumbent Governor George W. Bush raised $25.1 million, while his Democratic opponent, Garry Mauro, raised $4.6 million. Texans for Public Justice examined the Bush campaign's disclosure reports for 1994 and 1998 and found that the contributions totaled $41 million. Nearly one-quarter of this money came from "207 donors who gave Bush at least $25,000 apiece." About 67% of the contributors in the 1994 and 1998 campaigns gave $100 or less (2000c).

The National Institute on Money in State Politics examined the disclosure reports to find who contributed to Republican Bush and Democrat Mauro in 1998. More than 24% of Bush's funds came from contributors in the Finance, Insurance, and Real Estate sectors, as defined by the Institute. The Energy and Natural Resources sector came in second with 17% of the contributions. Lawyers and lobbyists gave the most to Mauro, contributing 36%. Interestingly, Energy and Natural Resources concerns contributed 11% of Mauro's total (Dixon 2000).

While gubernatorial campaigns have become more expensive throughout the 1990s, some observers are predicting that the 2002 gubernatorial race may be even more expensive. It is possible that the incumbent, Republican Rick Perry, will be able to raise more than $25 million, while the leading Democrats also have strong fund-raising capabilities and sizable personal fortunes (Burka 2001).

The contributions for the 1998 campaigns for the remainder of the plural executive illustrate an important concept: the candidate who raises the most money wins. In the race for lieutenant governor, Republican Rick Perry raised $12 million, compared to Democrat John Sharp's $7.8 million. The Republican candidate for attorney general, John Cornyn, raised $6 million while his Democratic opponent, former Attorney General Jim Mattox, collected $3 million. David Dewhurst, the Republican candidate for commissioner of the General Land Office, collected $4.7 million, but almost $3 million of that came out of his own pocket. The Democratic candidate, Richard Raymond, raised $682,000. In the race for one of the Railroad Commission seats, Republican Tony Garza raised $2.5 million; his Democratic opponent, Joe Henderson, raised $68,000. Republican Susan Combs, candidate for Agriculture Commissioner, collected $1.4 million, while her opponent, Democrat Pete Patterson, raised $187,000 (Dixon 2000).

The race for comptroller was the only exception to the rule that the candidate with the most money wins. Democrat Paul Hobby raised more money ($5.8 million) than his Republican opponent, Carole Keeton Rylander, who collected $4.1 million. Hobby received more than $100,000 from a political action committee created by his father, former Lieutenant Governor Bill Hobby.

It is becoming more expensive to run for the Texas Legislature. In 1996, candidates for the House of Representatives received a total of $14.6 million (Tran and Wheat 1998). By 1998, the total had risen to $23.6 million (Dixon 2000). The total amount contributed to House candidates in 2000 was $27.8 million (Texans for Public Justice 2001c).

Trends in contributions to Senate candidates are more difficult to uncover because only half of the Senate seats are up for election every two years. Candidates in the sixteen Senate races in 1998 raised a total of $9.2 million. There was one open seat, District 11, which was won by a Republican, who raised $416,000. One incumbent, Republican Michael Galloway, lost to a Democrat. Galloway raised $362,000, but he faced a challenger in the Republican primary. The challenger, Bill Leigh, raised $175,000. David Bernsen, the successful Democratic candidate, raised $1.4 million (Dixon 2000). In 2000, Senate candidates in fifteen races raised $15.4 million. The total includes the more than $5 million raised by both candidates in the only open seat race, Senate District Three (Texans for Public Justice 2001c).

Redistricting is the primary explanation for the increase in contributions from 1998 to 2000. The parties worked hard to have control of both chambers for redistricting. The Texas Democratic Party contributed $2.28 million to legislative candidates, while the Republican Party of Texas gave $1.47 million (Texans for Public Justice 2001c). The parties also were positioning to decide who would replace Lieutenant Governor Rick Perry if George W. Bush were elected President.

A question emerges to challenge our notion of representative democracy. In an interview, Fred Lewis of the pro-campaign finance reform group Campaigns for People, inquired: "Who are the constituents: the voters or the contributors?" (2001). On average, 80% of all contributions to legislative candidates come from sources outside of the legislative district. In their report *Mortgaged House*, Tran and Wheat found that in the period from July 1, 1995 through the end of 1996, only eleven members of the House of Representatives raised more than half of the $100-or-larger contributions from within the district. In fact, the researchers found that nine zip codes in Austin, Houston, and the Dallas Metroplex accounted for 48% of all House contributions of $100 or more. Businesses and political action committees contributed more than 62% of the money to House members with three zip codes in Austin, the state capital, accounting for 35% of all contributions over $100 (1998).

The funding of judicial campaigns in the state of Texas has received national attention. The news shows *Frontline* and *60 Minutes* have examined the role of money in campaigns, especially in races for the Texas Supreme Court.[1] Despite the fact that judicial candidates are subject to contribution and expenditure limitations, Supreme Court candidates remain able to build large war chests. In 1994, Raul Gonzalez, a Democrat, raised $2 million in contributions over $100. His opponent, Republican John Hawley, raised $11,628. Gonzalez was the incumbent and much of his money was used in a contentious primary, one of the factors that led to campaign finance reform for judicial candidates. Republican Nathan Hecht also raised $2 million in his 1994 campaign. His opponent, Alice Oliver-Parrott, collected $738,748. Republican Priscilla Owen was successful, even though she raised 10% less money than her opponent ($1.1 million to $1.2 million) (Texans for Public Justice 1998a).

The Judicial Campaign Fairness Act, limiting Supreme Court candidates to a voluntary $2 million expenditure limit, took effect in 1995. Contribution levels are going down, although it would be difficult to attribute the decrease to the 1995 law. In the later part of the decade, Republican candidates for Supreme Court Justice often faced third-party challengers or no opposition at all. Chief Justice Tom Phillips, a Republican, raised $1.3 million for his reelection campaign in 1996. His opponent, Andrew Kupper, was able to collect $20,057. Republican John Cornyn outspent Democrat Patrice Barron $1.2 million to $86,000. James Baker, a Republican, raised $1 million while his opponent Gene Kelly raised $3,200. Republican Greg Abbott outspent his Libertarian opponent John Hawley $712,000 to $500.

Republicans were elected to all three Supreme Court seats up for election in 1998. Harriet O'Neill raised $1.2 million to defeat Democratic incumbent Justice Rose Spector who collected $563,000. O'Neill had to campaign in a primary contest. Incumbent Justices Deborah Hankinson, Greg Abbot, and Craig Enoch, all Republicans, spent over $1 million each to easily defeat their Democratic opponents (Elliott, Council, and Borreson 1998). None of the Republican Supreme Court candidates faced a Democratic opponent in 2000.

---

1. Farrar-Myers and Frier (2000) examine campaign financing trends at the other levels of Texas court system.

Contributions have played a significant role in Texas judicial campaigns for a number of decades. Cheek and Champagne find that the amount of campaign contributions best explains electoral outcomes in Texas Supreme Court races. The researchers suggest, however, that incumbency is becoming a more important factor in explaining success in Supreme Court races. In short, winning a seat on the Texas Supreme Court is just like winning a seat in the Texas Legislature: the incumbent candidate with the most money usually wins (2000).

Political action committees play a significant role in campaigns in Texas, as in many states. The only difference is that, in Texas, PAC contributions to legislative and executive branch candidates are not limited. Texans for Public Justice identified a number of trends by examining PAC contributions from the 1996 election cycle. During the period from 1995 through 1997, 974 general-purpose PACs[2] reported expenditures of $56 million. The thirty-six largest PACs spent more than $300,000 apiece. The largest PAC was the Texas Democratic Party, with $4.1 million. Texans for Public Justice identified fifty PACs as "Democratic/Liberal." These PACs spent $6.8 million. The 157 "Republican/Conservative" PACs spent a total of $6.3 million. Business PACs spent the most, $37.2 million. The research group found that "more than half of Texas' active PACs (517) were affiliated with businesses that promote the interests of a particular private-sector industry. In fact, thirty-seven of the state's fifty largest general-purpose PACs are directly affiliated with a particular business interest" (1998b). Besides the Texas Democratic Party, the largest PACs in terms of spending were: the Texas Republican Campaign Committee, $2.2 million; Texas Association of Realtors, $1.4 million; Vinson & Elkins, a defense law firm, $1.4 million; Texans for Lawsuit Reform, $1.3 million; and Texas Trial Lawyers Association, $867,000.

The number of active PACs declined in the 1998 election cycle, while the amount spent by PACs increased. "In the 1998 election cycle, 891 general purpose PACs spent $52 million" (Texans for Public Justice 1999). The fifty largest PACs spent a total of $32.3 million, 63% of PAC expenditures. Business PACs spent $31.5 million, while single-issue PACs spent $17.7 million. The Texas Democratic Party was the largest PAC, spending $6.1 million. The Texas Republican Campaign Committee spent $3.3 million. The other large committees were Associated Republicans of Texas, spending $1.4 million; Vinson &

---

2. A general-purpose political committee supports general issues and multiple candidates. Specific-purpose PACs are created to support or oppose specific candidates or ballot measures.

Elkins, spending $1.2 million; Texans for Lawsuit Reform, spending $1.2 million; Texas Association of Realtors, spending $1 million; and Texas Trial Lawyers Association, spending $957,000.

Competition

Large sums of money change hands during campaigns in the state of Texas. Does this flow of money affect the level of competition? The data presented above on fund raising by plural executive and Supreme Court candidates suggest that the amount of money does have an effect on the level of competition: the candidate with the most money usually wins.

This pattern also can be seen in legislative campaigns. In 2000, 155 of the 165 winning candidates were incumbents. Of the candidates winning their seat, 162 of the 165 raised more money than the losing candidate. Only one candidate was elected who was neither the incumbent nor the leading fundraiser in his race (Texans for Public Justice 2001c). The trend in competitiveness has not changed much in the late 1990s. In 1996, "out of 66 contested general elections, the least-funded candidate prevailed in just seven races" (Tran and Wheat 1998). Reviewing the 1998 election cycle, Kinch reports that in "the 16 Senate races and the 150 House races, 97% of the winners were incumbents or raised the most money or both. Only five legislative candidates in all of those legislative campaigns won without the advantage of incumbency or the advantage of having the most money" (2001).

The Arkansas Policy Foundation (APF) examined the number of legislative primary candidates in contested races during the 1990s in Texas, Arkansas, and Oklahoma, in order to better understand the impact of term limits in Arkansas. The foundation's data are presented in Figure 1 (on next page). The foundation report suggested that fewer Texans are running in contested primary elections. In 1992, there were sixty-eight contested primaries with a total of 192 candidates. The study did not note that 1992 was an unusual year because all senators had to run due to redistricting. All senators ran again in 1994 because of a further redistricting under court order.

By 1998, nine-four candidates ran in forty-two contested primaries. I extended the APF's study to the 2000 elections, using the same simple methodology of counting the number of candidates, and I found ninety-six candidates in contested primaries. Only forty-three of the 330 individual races (150 House seats plus fifteen Senate seats, times two parties) were contested.

The number of candidates filing for legislative seats declined in the 1990s, a result of the fund-raising abilities of incumbents. The list of candidates avail-

Figure 1
Primary Competition in Texas Legislative Races, 1992–2000

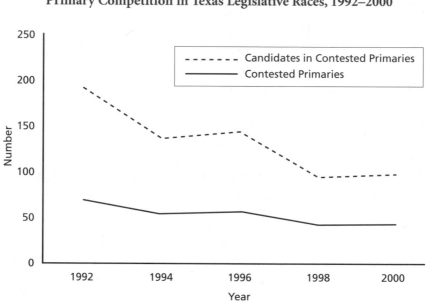

Source: 1992–1998, Patel (2001); 2000, Texas Secretary of State Historical Data
<http://www.sos.state.tx.us/elections/historical/index.shtml>

able from the Texas Secretary of State reveals that 376 candidates filed in the 1992 primaries; however, in the election immediately following redistricting, all 181 legislative seats (150 in the House and thirty-one in the Senate) were up for election. By 2000, only 264 candidates filed for 165 seats in the House and the Senate.

Figure 2 presents another measure of competition. The figure illustrates the growing percentage of single-candidate races in House seats and Senate seats in Texas. Percentages must be used because of the unequal number of seats available across elections. In 1992, candidates who did not face an opponent in the general election filled 48.6% of the 181 available seats. By 2000, this number grew to over 60% (165 available seats). Apparently, in a majority of legislative seats, the winner of a contested primary becomes a legislator because he or she does not face a competitor from the other party in November.

It is hard to attribute the lack of competitiveness in Texas legislative elections solely to campaign financing. Clearly, some potential candidates do not run because their opponent is well-financed. Acting Lieutenant Governor Bill Ratliff, a Republican, is an example of a candidate who decided to forgo a

Figure 2
Single-Candidate Races in Legislative General Elections, 1992–2000

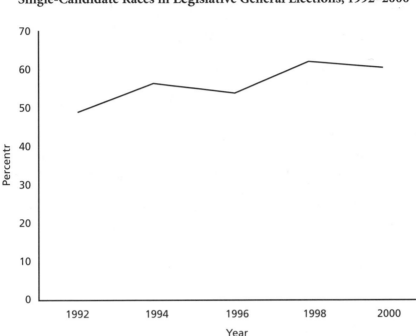

Source: Texas Secretary of State Historical Data <http://www.sos.state.tx.us/elections/his-
torical/index.shtml>

campaign because of money. His fellow senators appointed Ratliff to the position after Rick Perry became governor in December 2000. Another Republican candidate for lieutenant governor, Land Commissioner David Dewhurst,
was reported to be able to spend $10 million of his own money in the race to
become lieutenant governor. Ratliff bowed out of the campaign "rather than
alter his independent message to attract financial contributors" (Robison
2001b). Ratliff decided to run for reelection to the Senate. A second Republican senator, David Sibley of Waco, also decided not to continue his campaign
for lieutenant governor, although it was not clear if fund raising was the problem (McNeely 2001). It is hard to determine exactly how much one needs to
raise, because incumbents are not required to disclose the amount of money
they have on hand.

The 2002 elections probably will be more competitive because of redistricting. The campaigns will also be more expensive, since candidates will need
to bring their messages to areas new to the district. In the wake of redistrict-

ing, some incumbents will choose not to run, opening a seat to a potentially large number of new faces.

Campaign Finance and Voter Turnout

Voter participation in Texas elections seems to be more a result of political culture, socioeconomic status, and legal requirements, than a result of the increase in the size of campaign contributions. Since the 1970s, Texas, in campaign finance regulation and voter turnout, has ranked very low when compared to those of other states. The high point was in the 1992 presidential election, when 49% of the voting age population went to the polls. The peak in non-presidential election years came in 1994, when 31.3% of voting-age Texans voted (Maxwell and Crain 2002). The low turnout rate could also explain why there is little campaign finance regulation. Legislators have decided that the voting public does not care about the political arena in Texas and, thus, legislators are free to do as they wish.

Campaign Financing and Public Policy

Finding a connection between a campaign contribution and a public policy outcome is challenging. Several watchdog groups and the media in Texas uncover and present evidence to show how large contributions have affected public policy in the state. The connection between spending in Supreme Court races and court rulings has been hypothesized by national television shows like *Frontline* and *60 Minutes*. Texans for Public Justice, a nonpartisan group, has worked to uncover the links between contributions and policy. While its research reports are interesting, the group has been criticized for exaggerating the possible connections (Robison 1998).

Texans for Public Justice argue that the contributions made by Texans for Lawsuit Reform (TLR) eased passage of significant tort reform legislation in 1995. Three Houston businessmen founded TLR in 1994. Two of the men, Richard Weekley and Leo Linbeck, Jr., are in the construction industry, while the third, Richard Trabulsi, Jr., owns a chain of liquor stores. During the legislative session in 1995, the Legislature enacted significant limits on the liability of corporations. According to Texans for Public Justice, the tort reform legislation passed because of contributions made by TLR (2001d). An analysis of campaign contributions conducted by the *Dallas Morning News* found that Governor Bush, who lobbied for the reform measures, received at least $550,000 from members of TLR's board after he signed the legislation. The analysis further revealed that TLR board members "contributed at least $1.8

million to [Bush's] campaign since he began running for governor in 1994" (Slater 1996). Interestingly, tort reform has not found fertile ground in the Legislature since 1995 (Robbins 2001).

Contributions made by trial lawyers have also played a role in limiting the success of tort reform groups. As a candidate for governor in 1994, George W. Bush cited a study by the American Tort Reform Association that found that trial lawyers contributed almost $9 million to legislative candidates in the early 1990s. Bush used the data to attack Governor Ann Richards for being against lawsuit reform (Ratcliffe 1994). Lawsuit reform is one area in which campaign contributions make a difference. Despite the importance of this issue to the average Texan, it is difficult to find a role for him or her in the debate.

Campaign Financing and Public Opinion

Texans think the amount of money flowing into political campaign presents a problem, especially in judicial elections. Caution must be exercised while interpreting public opinion because the wording of a question can influence responses (Traugott and Lavrakas 1996). A 1997 Harte-Hanks Texas poll found that 72% of respondents believed judges were influenced in some cases by pressure from campaign contributors. The poll also found that 62% believed judicial elections should be non-partisan (Texans for Public Justice 1998c). A study conducted by the Texas Supreme Court's Office of Court Administration and the State Bar of Texas found that an "overwhelming majority of Texans (83%) felt that campaign contributions made to judges have a 'very significant' (43%) or 'somewhat significant' (40%) influence on the decisions judges make in the courtroom." Despite their conviction that campaign contributions influence judicial decision-making, 70% of the respondents believed that the people should continue to elect judges. Unfortunately, the survey did not ask about partisan or non-partisan elections. About 48% of judges felt that campaign contributions have a "fairly" or "very" significant influence on judicial decisions. Large majorities of other court personnel (69%) and attorneys (79%) agreed that campaign contributions affect judicial decision-making (1998).

Less is known about the public attitude towards the role of money in Texas legislative and executive races. A 1999 poll commissioned by Public Citizen and conducted by Austin Trends revealed the opinions of 400 respondents from across the state. A very large majority (92%) indicated that they favored spending limits for legislative candidates, and 86% believed campaign contributions have too much influence on public policy. This poll also asked about judicial campaigns and found that 71% opposed allowing lawyers and law firms to contribute to judicial campaigns. A majority (68%) favored collecting a fee from attorneys to fund judicial campaigns (Associated Press 1999).

Despite the strong public support of reform in theory, the Texas Legislature has not been able to enact any changes in campaign finance regulation. The next section considers the reasons for the lack of action.

Obstacles to Campaign Finance Reform

Alas, there is no subject—with the possible exception of sexual morality—that stretches the Machiavellian gap between what politicians say and do quite like campaign finance reform (Wheat 2001).

At the end of the 2001 legislative session, the *Corpus Christi Caller-Times* reported that "for the third consecutive legislative session, Texas lawmakers failed to pass meaningful campaign finance reform" (Meighan 2001). Observers watching from outside the state would find that "meaningful campaign finance reform" in Texas would be considered incremental change in most other states. Even small changes experience difficulty navigating the legislative process in Texas.

Campaign finance reform was blocked by a technicality during the waning days of the 1997 legislative session. The legislation, as introduced, would have set limits on spending and contributions for statewide candidates. It also would have prohibited "push polling." These provisions were removed from the bill in committee and replaced by a proposal requiring political consultants to register with the Texas Ethics Commission. The bill was killed on the House floor when Representative Kent Grusendorf (R-Arlington) made a point of order arguing that the "the Elections Committee had failed to report in its minutes what action the committee had taken on the bill." The House would have violated its rules had it allowed further consideration of the bill (Hughes and Gonzalez 1997).

Since the Texas Legislature meets in regular session only once every two years, members of both chambers regularly meet in study committees during the interim period. Two House committees studied campaign financing during the interim between the 75th Legislature (1997) and the 76th Legislature (1999). The *Houston Chronicle* reported that Speaker Pete Laney (D-Hale Center) asked the committees to study tactics like those used against him by term-limits groups. In 1996, Texans for Term Limits ran radio commercials throughout Laney's district, accusing the Speaker of not allowing term limits legislation to be brought the floor. As a nonprofit organization, Texans for Term Limits was not required to disclosure its funding sources. While Laney's aides disputed the claim that the interim committees were "payback" for running the ads (Ratcliffe 1997b), Speaker Laney has been a strong supporter of disclosure in "soft money" and issue-advocacy campaigns.

Campaign finance regulation was not enacted during the 1999 session, despite Speaker Laney's support. The only measure to reach the governor's desk for approval was a bill requiring electronic disclosure of campaign financial reports. A bill requiring campaigns to disclose the occupations and employers of contributors was allowed to die in the Senate. The bill (House Bill 4) was being debated when the deadline passed for approving legislation. The Senate never voted on the bill. A bill that would have established limits on contributions died in committee (Greenberger 1999). As Texas governor, George W. Bush expended little political capital to see that campaign finance reform was enacted, only signing the electronic disclosure bill that came to his desk.

The House Committee on Elections met during the interim between the 1999 and 2001 session to consider a number of issues relating to campaigns and elections in Texas. A "Subcommittee on Campaign Finance" was charged to "review and assess all issues related to the financing of campaigns, including so-called 'soft money' and other funds whose source is unclear, the influence of out-of-state political action committees, and so-called 'late train' contributions" (Texas House of Representatives 2001).[3] The subcommittee found that Texas election law has loopholes "which deny the public the capability to determine the source of campaign funds." In order to close these loopholes, the subcommittee recommended nineteen actions:

1. Require contributors' occupation on reports with the filer of the reports making his or her best effort to comply with the requirement if information is not provided by contributor.
2. Require the name of employer and occupation of contributors of $500 or more.
3. Require out-of-state PACS to report as in-state PACs.
4. Require 527s (issue-advocacy groups) to disclose contributors and expenditures.
5. Require cash-on-hand balances for each report.
6. Define promises and offers of contributions and require inclusion of same in contributor reports.
7. Define coordinated contributions and include them in reports.
8. Increase the penalty for intentional failure to file a Class A misdemeanor.

---

3. Late train contributions are donations to candidates after they have won the election.

9. Allow only one principal campaign committee for candidates for statewide, legislative, State Board of Education and appellate courts.
10. Allow only one principal campaign committee for all candidates for public office, including local offices.
11. Require description of in-kind contributions in reports.
12. Require itemization of contributions and expenditures more than $100 rather than more than $50 (current law).
13. Require the listing of loans outstanding, if the loans total more than $100 at the end of reporting period.
14. Expand the loan reimbursement restriction in current law to include not just personal loans from the candidate but also loans by financial institutions or others guaranteed or backed by the candidate or their family.
15. Expand late reporting (occurring between the ninth and the second day before the election) requirements to include opposed statewide candidates who receive contributions from a person for more than $1,000, general purpose committees that receive contributions for more than $5,000 from a person, and other committees required to file with the Ethics Commission that receive contributions from a person for more than $5,000.
16. Require late reporting (between the ninth and the second day before the election) within twenty-four hours of direct expenditures for more than $5,000. Reports must include the amount and the purpose of the expenditure and the occupation of the recipient. Expenditures made by political parties for more than $5,000 within this time frame are not included.
17. Require reporting of the contributors, or their business entity in which they have a substantial interest (10% or more), who have executory contracts with the agency of the official receiving the contribution.
18. Require PACs to report administrative expenses if they exceed $ 100.
19. Require political parties to compile and report aggregate totals of contributions and expenditures made on behalf of candidates and officeholders. (Texas House of Representatives 2001).

Many of these recommendations were written into three pieces of legislation introduced by Representative Pete Gallego (D-Alpine) when the 77th Legislature convened in January 2001. Each bill had the support of Speaker Laney; its low bill number indicated the importance of each measure. House Bill 3 required a limit on contributions. Individuals and political action committees would be able to give $5,000 per calendar year to House candidates, $10,000 to Senate candidates, and $25,000 for statewide candidates. House Bill 2 called for candidates to consolidate their fund-raising activities into one committee in order to make it easier for the public to track contributions. This measure also included a provision requiring that candidates would have to report the occupations and employers of contributors. House Bill 2 received a mention in Republican Governor Rick Perry's State of the State address. The bill was similar to the legislation that died in the Senate in 1999. House Bill 4, the third piece of legislation, called for public financing of judicial campaigns. At its introduction, many observers did not think it had a chance of emerging from the Legislature (Davidson 2001). Acting Lieutenant Governor (and Senate President) Bill Ratliff (R-Mount Pleasant) added his support to broader campaign finance disclosure in several speeches (Fikac 2001).

Despite the support of Governor Perry, Acting Lieutenant Governor Ratliff, and Speaker Laney, no campaign finance bill made its way through the legislative maze during the regular session of the 77th Legislature. House Bill 3, on contribution limits, never made it to the House floor. It was reported out of the Elections Committee, but it never gained a place on the House calendar. In the Texas House of Representatives, the Speaker appoints all members of the House Calendars Committee. This committee schedules all bills for floor debate.

The bill on public financing of judicial campaigns, House Bill 4, died in House committees. The House Judicial Affairs Committee reported out Senate Bill 129, creating retention elections for non-partisan judicial candidates and prohibiting straight-ticket voting for judges. The Senate approved the bill and the accompanying Senate Joint Resolution 3, a constitutional amendment providing for gubernatorial appointment of all appellate judges. However, Senate Bill 129 never reached the House floor for a vote.

Campaign finance reform proponents had high hopes for Representative Gallego's House Bill 2. In what observers from outside Texas might view as a marginal change, this bill focused largely on improving disclosure (Texans for Public Justice 2001e). The bill enjoyed bipartisan support. Besides Representative Gallego, Representatives Debra Danburg (D-Houston), Rob Junell (D-San Angelo), Jerry Madden (R-Richardson), and David Swinford (R-Dumas), cosponsored the bill. House Bill 2 passed the House by 21 votes, even though a similar bill passed the House in 1999 by a vote of 138–3. Interestingly, Representative Swinford voted against the bill, even though he was a cosponsor. Wheat argues that the close vote in 2001 occurred because the Senate had already approved a companion bill; in 1999, House members knew the Senate would kill any campaign finance bill emerging from the House (2001).

Any hopes for campaign finance reform emerging from the 77th Legislature were crushed when a House-Senate conference committee could not agree on provisions that differed in the House and Senate versions. The major stumbling block was a provision requiring disclosure of "candidate-specific advertising," a form of issue advocacy according to conservative interest groups who wanted to have the provision removed. These groups feared that the provision would render voters guides illegal (Texas Eagle Forum 2001). A second controversial provision was the requirement that campaigns identify the occupations and employers of contributors. Opponents claimed that this provision "would be too burdensome for poorly paid, overworked legislators" (Wheat 2001). Texas remains the largest state with no significant campaign finance regulations on legislative and executive candidates.

Prospects for the Future

The prospects for significant campaign finance regulation are dim. The challenge for reformers is succinctly identified in Fred Lewis' inquiry, "Who are the constituents: the contributors or the voters?" As long as legislators continue to view contributors as their constituents, money in campaigns will remain unregulated. Pro-reform groups have to work to mobilize average Texas voters to let their legislators know that the voters are the constituents. These groups have only begun their work. Texans for Public Justice has been in operation for about four years while Campaigns for People was founded in 1999.

Judicial campaign reform has been more successful. The success can be attributed to the fact that Texans, like most Americans, feel that the judicial system should be free from bias. There is an almost visceral reaction to the notion that the courts can be bought. In contrast, most people believe that legislature and the executive branch have always been under the control of moneyed interests, and campaign finance reform will not change much. A second factor is the relationship of the court system, especially the Texas Supreme Court, with its constituents. The Legislature enacted the Judicial Campaign Fairness Act in 1995 after the defense bar and trial lawyers, with the support of a number of former justices, asked for the changes. While the Judicial Campaign Fairness Act is a useful example, it seems improbable that legislators' constituents, either contributors or voters, will ask for campaign finance reform.

If the Texas Ethics Commission were able to thoroughly investigate all campaign disclosure reports, the public probably would learn that some campaign contributions are being used for personal expenses. In this case, enacting more regulations will not solve the problem. Observers of the campaign finance system have suggested that the Ethics Commission should be allowed to do the job for which it was created.

The best hope for campaign finance reform in the state of Texas is local government. In November 1997, voters in Austin approved a change in the city charter limiting campaign contributions and providing for voluntary expenditure limits. Candidates for city offices may not accept contributions over $100 per election from individuals (Smith 2001). PACs may not contribute more than $15,000 per election. While these limits appear to be a workable solution to the problem of big money, there are no limits on candidates spending large sums of their own money on their campaigns. The contribution limits have failed to reduce the amount of money raised and spent in campaigns. During the summer of 2001, Clean Campaigns for Austin circulated petitions for a new campaign finance proposal that includes public financing of campaigns (2001). The Austin experience suggests that campaign finance reform will not have the effect of increasing grassroots candidates until mandatory campaign expenditure limits can be enacted.

It is expensive to run for statewide office in Texas because of the state's physical size and residential patterns. Campaigns need money to reach voters often separated by distance or disengaged from politics. Even legislative candidates need significant financial resources; Texas senate districts encompass populations of over 670,000. While the amount of money needed to run a campaign is the problem, the solutions, particularly public financing, are politically impossible in the current environment. More marginal measures like additional disclosure of contributor information are possible, but only if Texans demand them.

References

Associated Press. 1999. Poll shows Texans favor campaign spending limits. 18 April.

Attlesey, Sam. 1995. Democrats welcomed into GOP. *Dallas Morning News*, 21 February.

Bass, Jack, and Walter DeVries. 1976. *The transformation of Southern politics*. New York: Basic Books.

Berger, Eric. 2001. Campaign funds are a regularly milked cash cow. *Houston Chronicle*, 2 April.

Bibby, John F., and Thomas M. Holbrook. 1999. Parties and elections. In *Politics in the American states: A comparative analysis*, 7th ed., edited by Virginia Gray, Russell L. Hanson, and Herbert Jacob. Washington, DC: CQ Press.

Borges, Walt. 1994. Secret to Gonzalez's success is no secret; incumbency meant more than money, nastiness in runoff. *Texas Lawyer*, 18 April.

Borges, Walt, and Mark Ballard. 1994. Vested interests and firms bankroll court campaigns. *Texas Lawyer*, 3 October.

Burka, Paul. 2001. 2002: A race odyssey. *Texas Monthly*, March.

Cannon, Thure Barnett. 1998. The Texas political system: Shifting dynamics in political party power. M.P. Aff. Report. University of Texas at Austin.

Cheek, Kyle, and Anthony Champagne. 2000. Money in Texas Supreme Court elections, 1980–1998. *Judicature* 84:20–25.

Clean Campaigns for Austin. 2001. Support clean elections for Austin! Retrieved August 13, 2001: <http://www.cleancampaigns.org/>

Davidson, Bruce. 2001. Campaign reform has a chance. *San Antonio Express-News*, 8 February.

Dixon, Mark. 2000. *Summary of Texas 1998 statewide & legislative races*. Retrieved August 5, 2001: <http://www.followthemoney.org/reports/texas/texas98.html>

Elazar, Daniel. 1972. *American federalism: A view from the states*, 2nd ed. New York: Crowell.

Elliott, Charles P., Kay Hofer, and Robert E. Biles. 1998. *The world of Texas politics*. New York: St. Martin's Press.

Elliott, Janet, John Council, and Susan Borreson. 1998. Judicial sweep shocking, yet expected: *60 Minutes* report, key endorsements don't save Dems. *Texas Lawyer*, 9 November.

Farrar-Myers, Victoria, and Amber Frier. 2000. Electing judges: Accountability or corruptibility? Presented at the annual meeting of the Southern Political Science Association, Atlanta.

Fikac, Peggy. 2001. Ratliff favors broad disclosure, *San Antonio Express-News*, 27 February.

Gott, Natalie. 2000. Democrats post fewer statewide candidates. Retrieved September 28, 2000: <http://www.amarillonet.com/stories/092800/tex_democrats.shtml>

Graves, Patrick Kelly. 1997. What they get—How moneyed interests influence the Texas legislature. M.P. Aff. Report. University of Texas at Austin.

Greenberger, Scott S. 1999. Blame swirls in death of campaign bill. *Austin American-Statesman*, 28 May.

Hirschi, John. 2001. John Hirschi interview with Anne Marie Kilday. In *Too much money is not enough*. Austin, TX: Campaigns for People.

Hughes, Polly Ross, and John W. Gonzalez. 1997. Campaign finance reform dies in the House. *Houston Chronicle*, 16 May.

Johnson, John G. 1999. Texas ethics commission. In *The handbook of Texas online*. Retrieved August 3, 2001: <http://www.tsha.utexas.edu/handbook/online/articles/view/TT/mdtkr.html>

Kinch, Sam. 2000. *Too much money is not enough: Big money and political power in Texas*. Austin, TX: Campaigns for People.

Lamis, Alexander P. 1984. *The two-party South*. New York: Oxford University Press.

Lewis, Fred. 2001. Phone interview by author, 1 August.

McNeely, Dave. 2001. Sibley still looking for change, but not as lieutenant governor. *Austin American-Statesman*, 27 July.

Makinson, Larry. 1994. *Follow the money handbook*. Washington, DC: Center for Responsive Politics.

Maxwell, William Earl, and Earnest Crain. 2002. *Texas politics today*, 10th ed. Belmont, CA: Wadsworth/Thomson Learning.

Meighan, Ty. 2001. Campaign finance reform fails once again. *Corpus Christi Caller-Times*, 2 June.

Patel, Ushma. 2001. Study says fewer candidates running election primaries. *Austin American-Statesman*, 18 July.

Ratcliffe, R.G. 1994. Richards criticized on tort reform. *Houston Chronicle*, 14 September.

———. 1995. Bush coffers swell by $3 million. *Houston Chronicle*, 18 January.

———. 1997a. Suit attempts to reveal list of nonprofit group donors. *Houston Chronicle*, 13 October.

———. 1997b. Speaker authorizes studies of campaign finance tactics. *Houston Chronicle*, 23 September.

Robbins, Mary Alice. 2001. Trial lawyers, tort reformers agree mistake was made in '95. *Texas Lawyer*, 2 April.

Robison, Clay. 1998. Ex-high court judges dispute payola claims. *Houston Chronicle*, 15 August.

———. 2000. GOP guaranteed to keep majority in Texas Senate; Democrats likely will keep their six-seat edge in House. *Houston Chronicle*, 8 November.

———. 2001a. Lesson in influence-peddling lost on lawmakers. *Houston Chronicle*, 25 March.

———. 2001b. Statewide races about money, lots of it. *Houston Chronicle*, 10 June.

Slater, Wayne. 1996. Donations to governor tied to issue. *Dallas Morning News*, 2 February.

Smith, Susan. 2001. New plan for city campaign finance reform. *Austin American-Statesman*, 1 August.

Supreme Court of Texas, Office of Court Administration and State Bar of Texas. 1998. *Public trust and confidence in the courts and the legal profession in Texas: Summary report*. Retrieved August 6, 2001: <http://www.courts.state.tx.us/publicinfo/publictrust/index.htm>

Tannahill, Neal. 2000. *Texas government: Policy & politics*, 6th ed. New York: Addison Wesley Longman.

Texans for Public Justice. 1998a. *Payola justice: how Texas Supreme Court justices raise money from court litigants*. Retrieved August 6, 2001: <http://www.tpj.org/reports/payola/toc.html>

———. 1998b. *Texas pacs: a roundup of the special interests driving Texas' political action committees*. Retrieved August 9, 2001: <http://www.tpj.org/report/pacs/toc.html>

———. 1998c. *Factsheet 2. Time to reform judicial selection*. Retrieved August 6, 2001: <http://www.tpj.org/campfin/factsheet2.html>

———. 1999. *Texas PACs: 1998 election cycle spending*. Retrieved August 9, 2001: <http://www.tpj.org/reports/pacs98/cover.html>

———. 2000a. Funding reveals class struggle for priciest State Senate seat. Retrieved July 30, 2001: <http://www.tpj.org/Lobby_Watch/staplesfisher.html>

———. 2000b. *The state of the Lone Star State: How life in Texas measures up*. Austin, TX: Texans for Public Justice.

———. 2000c. *The governor's gusher: the sources of George W. Bush's $41 million Texas war chest*. Retrieved August 5, 2001: <http://www.tpj.org/reports/gusher/cover.html>

———. 2000d. *Checks & imbalances: How Texas Supreme Court justices raised $11 million*. Retrieved August 6, 2001: <http://www.tpj.org/reports/checks/toc.html>

———. 2001a. *Luddite lawmakers & other officials: Politicians who dodged electronic donor disclosure by claiming they don't track donors with computers*. Austin, TX: Texans for Public Justice.

———. 2001b. *Pay to play: How big money buys access to the Texas Supreme Court*. Austin, TX: Texans for Public Justice.

———. 2001c. Texas legislative candidates raise $43.2 million in 2000. *Press release*. Received via email, 12 June.

———. 2001d. *Texans for lawsuit reform: How the Texas tort tycoons spent millions in the 2000 elections*. Austin, TX: Texans for Public Justice.

————. 2001e. *Campaign reform heroes & zeros: How members of the Texas house voted on campaign reform.* Austin, TX: Texans for Public Justice.

Texas Eagle Forum. 2001. *Alert: House campaign reform bill would ban voter guides.* Retrieved August 12, 2001: <http://www.texaseagle.org/alert/2001/0326.html>

Texas Ethics Commission. 1997a. *Campaign finance guide for candidates and officeholders who file with the Texas Ethics Commission.* Retrieved July 31, 2001: <http://www.ethics.state.tx.us/guides/state.htm>

————. 1997b. *Campaign finance guide for political committees.* Retrieved August 4, 2001: <http://www.ethics.state.tx.us/guides/pac97.htm>

————. 2001. *Campaign finance guide for judicial candidates and officeholders.* Retrieved July 31, 2001: <http://www.ethics.state.tx.us/guides/judicial.htm>

Texas House of Representatives. 2001. House Committee on Elections. *Interim report 2000.* Austin: Texas House of Representatives: House Committee on Elections.

Tolleson-Rinehart, Sue, and Jeanie R. Stanley. 1994. *Claytie and the lady: Ann Richards, gender, and politics in Texas.* Austin: University of Texas Press.

Tran, Lynn, and Andrew Wheat. 1998. *Mortgaged house: Campaign contributions to Texas representatives, 1995–1996.* Retrieved July 27, 2001: <http://www.onr.com/tpj/reports/house/index.htm>

Traugott, Michael W., and Paul J. Lavrakas. 1996. *The voter's guide to election polls.* Chatham, NJ: Chatham House Publishers.

Wheat, Andrew. 2001. Memorial Day massacre. *Texas Observer,* 8 June.

CHAPTER 2

Sunshine and the Shoe Box: Money and Politics in the Unregulated State of Illinois

Kent Redfield

Illinois is the Land of Lincoln. If Illinois politics has a face, then for many people, it is the tired face of Abraham Lincoln as he struggled to keep a civil war-torn nation together. For those with a more contemporary view of history, the face of Illinois politics may be the television pictures of Chicago Major Richard J. Daley screaming insults at Senator Abraham Ribicoff during the 1968 Democratic Convention, while the police battled anti-war protestors in the streets. However, when it comes to the role of money in Illinois politics, the perfect image is not a face. It is a shoe box. It has been more than thirty years since the death of Illinois Secretary of State Paul Powell and the subsequent discovery of more than $800,000 in cash in his hotel room, some of it stored in shoe boxes. Yet the image still endures.

Powell was the "gray fox of Vienna", three-time Speaker of the Illinois House, the deal-maker extraordinaire. Since Powell never made more than $30,000 a year from elected office, those outside Illinois politics may have been shocked to discover that Powell died with $800,000 in cash in his hotel room and an estate valued at more than $2.6 million (Hartley 1999). Those on the inside knew all too well that, in the Land of Lincoln, money can drive politics and that politics can drive money. When Powell died in 1970, the playing field was remarkably wide open. In keeping with the political culture of the time, laws regulating campaign finance, lobbying and political ethics were either nonexistent or weak and un-enforced. In practice, there were no restrictions on giving money or gifts to elected officials and no restrictions on what elected officials did with them. Bribery, extortion, theft, and fraud were crimes, as they are now. But the subtle and not-so-subtle ways that private money and public power intertwine to distort and corrupt the political process were unabated by laws or public scrutiny. But a lot has happened over the past thirty years. A comforting thought would be that Powell represents a different kind of politics and a different era. The truth is that, when it comes to money and politics, Powell's politics, and perhaps his ethics, would fit quite nicely in contemporary Illinois.

From 1970 to 1997, only two substantive changes were made in the official rules of the game of money and politics in Illinois. In 1976 a reporting and disclosure law covering the contribution and expenditure of campaign funds passed in the wake of the Watergate scandal. The law did not regulate the sources, amounts, or the use of campaign contributions. In 1993 the legislature strengthened the existing lobbyist registration and reporting law by expanding the definition of who had to register under the act and by requiring lobbyists to report direct expenditures on their lobbying activities, but not the fees they charged their clients. At best, these were weak laws with grossly under-funded agencies providing minimal oversight and enforcement.

What about recent changes? In 1997, a bill became law, requiring the State Board of Elections to post candidate campaign finance reports on a web site (PA 90-495). That law also eliminated the requirement that anyone examining campaign contribution and expenditure reports fill out a detailed form, giving his or her address, occupation and employer. A copy of the form was sent to the committee that filed the report being examined. In 1998, a bill became law (PA 90-737) that required electronic disclosure of campaign contributions and expenditures and increased disclosure of details on contributors. It added a ban on using campaign funds for personal use, added other ethics reforms, provided much stronger lobbying registration and reporting, and required a limited ban on gifts to public officials. By Illinois standards, these are remarkable reforms. The successes in passing these reforms have greatly energized and empowered public interest groups who are pushing for more sweeping changes. The ethical climate in Illinois has also changed since Powell's day. Public corruption is not as easily dismissed with a wink and a nod. The press is also much more attentive, much more knowledgeable, and much more aggressive in reporting the role that money plays in Illinois politics.

Surely the day is near when we can confidently say that Powell's politics, as well as his ethics, are hopelessly out of place in the Illinois political scene. Or are they? In the fall of 2000, the gift ban provisions of the 1998 law were challenged in a state court. An Illinois circuit court judge declared the entire law unconstitutional and issued an injunction against its enforcement (*Flynn v. Ryan*, 12th Judicial Circuit Court, No. 99 CH 340). In the fall of 2001 that law still faced an uncertain future before the Illinois Supreme Court. With or without the reforms of 1998 law, the records from the 1998 and 2000 state elections do not suggest a new day for the role of money in Illinois politics. Elections in general were more expensive. Legislative elections were less competitive than ever before and were still dominated by the legislative leaders. Neither is the record from the 1999–2000 legislative sessions encouraging. As in previous sessions, the legislative leaders dominated the process, and large campaign contributions and high paid lobbyists drove issues that had little public support, but huge financial implications for their supporters. From the perspective of a quarter of a century of inaction, the 1997 and 1998 successes in changing Illinois campaign finance law are certainly encouraging. But reports of the death of Illinois's wide-open system of campaign finance are very premature.

Why Study Illinois?

The usual menu of campaign finance reforms includes campaign disclosure, strict contribution limits, and public financing tied to spending limits. One alternative to a system of regulation is a pure "sunshine" system. Such a system would combine a complete deregulation of money in politics with a real-time electronic reporting and disclosure system. The idea is that public scrutiny will cause candidates and contributors to modify their behavior in regard to campaign contributions and expenditures. It is assumed that they will refrain from actions that they would not like their opponents to find out about or their mothers to read about in the newspapers or see on the TV news. Many academic researchers and policy analysts have advocated disclosure as the only truly sound policy option for regulating the relationship between private money and politics. (Gurwitt 1992; Sabato 1989) No one has to wonder what the elections and the legislative process would look like in a completely unregulated campaign finance system. They need only come to Illinois.

Illinois had been operating with a completely unregulated campaign finance system, except for reporting and disclosure, for more than a quarter of a century. Given the diversity of the politics and demographics of the state, it is often argued that Illinois is a microcosm of the nation. (Gove and Nowlan 1996) To suggest that the same patterns of election competition, interest group activity, legislative leadership power and executive power that we find in Illinois would develop at the federal level under a completely deregulated campaign finance system is not an unreasonable hypothesis. As the federal campaign system continues to deteriorate under the crush of soft money and issue ads, the time of such a natural experiment may not be far off.

Where Illinois falls short of being a pure sunshine system is in its system of reporting and disclosure. Illinois does have a system of electronic filing and Internet posting of campaign reports. It was fully implemented in the spring of 2000, following the filing of reports for the last six months of 1999. This system is arguably the best of any state in the nation. However, the most complete data is only available after elections take place and after the legislature goes home, not before. And because this system is so new, it is impossible to know what effect, if any, increased public access to campaign finance information will have on the patterns of competition and influence that have developed since 1974 under a completely deregulated system.

Researching Campaign Finance in Illinois

The data presented in this chapter come from a database developed and maintained by the Sunshine Project, one of the activities of the Illinois Legislative Studies Center, which is located within the Institute for Public Affairs at the University of Illinois at Springfield. The Joyce Foundation has provided the primary funding for the Sunshine Project. The database covers the period from January 1, 1993 to June 30, 2001. Those eight plus years contain four separate election cycles. For the period of 1993 through 1998, the database contains reports from incumbent office holders and candidates for statewide and legislative office, all legislative-leader-controlled chamber committees, and the two state political parties. For 1999–2000, reports from candidates for the state supreme court are also included in the database. Beginning in 2001, reports from candidates for appellate court positions are also included.

All of the contribution and spending data presented below come either directly from reports filed with the State Board of Elections or the Sunshine data base, which is built from the electronic and paper reports filed with the State Board of Elections. The Illinois State Board of Elections has been constructing limited contribution databases since 1994. With the advent of electronic filing, the amount of data entry required to construct the database has been significantly reduced, although there are committees for legislative candidates that still file paper reports.

The Sunshine database consists of three sub-databases, an aggregate receipt-and-expenditure portion, a contribution-record portion and an expenditure-record portion. The expenditure-record portion is only partially complete.

Approximately 60% of the paper records from 1993 through 1999 have been entered and coded. Electronic records filed after July 1, 1999 are only partially coded. The contribution-record portion of the database is complete and currently contains 399,725 contribution records from 708 political committees formed by candidates for statewide and legislative office, from legislative chamber committees, and from state political parties. The aggregate receipt-and-expenditure portion of the database is also complete for the 708 political committees included in the contribution portion of the database.

Each contribution record is coded according to the nature of its source, using a modified version of the coding scheme developed by the Center for Responsive Politics for their Open Secrets database (Makinson 1994). The data are organized in a three-table relational database. The contribution table contains fields for name, dollar amount, address, date, source's code, and recipient. The candidate table contains party and demographic data fields. The election-cycle table contains election and office/district data. The three tables are linked by a common field, containing the unique ID number assigned by the State Board of Elections to each political committee set up by a candidate, party organization, association, union, or corporation.

All of the tables presented in this chapter are based on original data from the campaign finance database maintained by the author or the official records of the Illinois State Board of Elections. Most of the data presented or analyzed in this chapter can be found on-line at the Web sites either of the Illinois Campaign for Political Reform (www.ilcampaign.org) or of the Illinois State Board of Elections (www.elections.state.il.us).

The Illinois Campaign Finance Law

When it comes to campaign finance, Illinois has a well-deserved reputation as a no-holds-barred and take-no-prisoners free-for-all: an ethical swamp. References to Illinois as the "wild, wild west of campaign finance" strike home with citizens and political players alike. With the modest disclosure and ethics changes enacted in1998 in legal limbo, it was almost impossible to violate Illinois campaign finance law, short of refusing to file disclosure reports. The Microsoft Corporation could form an organization called Friends of the Earth and transfer $1 billion in corporate funds to it. A representative of Friends of the Earth could meet a candidate for county coroner on the steps of the state capitol and given him a $1 billion campaign contribution. The county coroner candidate could give $200 million each to the Governor, the Speaker of the House, and the State Senate President; spend $200 million on his campaign; and use the remaining $200 million to build a house, buy a car, play the stock market and throw a hell of a Christmas party. It is not even clear under Illinois law if Friends of the Earth would have to form an official political committee and file campaign finance reports. If the Illinois State Supreme Court reinstates the 1998 law, the $1 billion contribution would still be OK, but it could no longer take place on state property, and none of it could be converted to personal use. So the car, the house, and the on-line trading would be out, but the Christmas party is probably still on, if it involves campaign workers or constituent relations. And unlimited transfers of money from one political campaign to another are still allowed.

The Illinois campaign finance system is a sunshine system that relies on reporting and disclosure to regulate the flow of money into and through the political system. Except for two long-since-repealed laws that prohibited contributions from certain types of insurance companies and horse-racing interests, Illinois has never tried to limit the individuals or groups who can give money or how much they can give. No public financing bill has ever been signed into law in Illinois. The state law regulating campaign finance in Illinois was passed in 1974 (10 ILCS 5/9-1 et al.). It applies to candidates for public office and groups who support or oppose candidates for public office or support or oppose questions of public policy whose receipts and expenditures exceed certain dollar thresholds ($1,000 or $3,000, depending on circumstances) during a twelve month period. Individuals and groups who are covered by the law are required to form a political committee and file reports. The application of the law to interest groups, labor unions and corporations is somewhat ambiguous. In practice, all candidates for office and political parties and most interest-group associations form political committees and file reports. Some corporations and labor unions file repots; some do not. Individuals are not required to file reports, regardless of how much they contribute.

Candidates and groups who form political committees are required by law to keep records of their receipts and expenditures and to file reports at regularly specified intervals. Candidates for statewide or legislative office and groups who contribute to them have to file reports with the State Board of Elections. Disclosure reports relating to campaigns for local public offices or local referendum questions within a single county are filed with the county clerk. Under the suspended 1998 law, political committees with receipts or contributions above $25,000 in a six-month period have to file all reports electronically. The changes, passed in 1997, require the State Board to make all disclosure reports filed with it available on the Internet in a searchable database. The State Board of Elections also has the power to investigate complaints and to assess civil penalties for willful violations of the disclosure law. Those who willfully violate it may also be subject to the criminal penalties provided by the law.

There are no restrictions in Illinois on who can contribute. Individuals, political parties, interest groups, and associations can contribute to candidates, parties or other political groups. In contrast to federal and many state laws, unions and corporations can also contribute directly to candidates in Illinois. There are no limits on how much a contributor can give. There are no restrictions on the number of political committees a candidate, a party, or contributor can form. Most importantly, there are no limits on transfers among political committees. Legislative leaders can—and do—raise millions of dollars from private interests and then spend that money directly on legislative elections.

Except for a ban on the personal use of campaign funds by a candidate in the now-suspended 1998 law, there have never been any restrictions in Illinois on how money in a political committee can be spent. Even after leaving office, public officials can continue to spend any money they have left in their political funds, as long as they keep their committees open. In a 1980 case involving an Illinois State Attorney General's using his campaign fund to pay his lawyers to fight a criminal indictment, the Illinois Supreme Court ruled that the State Board of Elections has no authority to question how a political committee spends its money (*Troy v. State Board*, IL. App. 406 N.E. 2nd 562 (1980)). The old joke in Illinois is that, if a politician takes money from an organized crime group and hires a hit man to kill his opponent, the only concerns of the State Board of Elections would be that the politician's receipts and expenditures are reported on the proper forms and in a timely manner.

Expenditure records from the 1999–2000 election cycle show that a state senator who had resigned prior to the end of his term paid himself more than $125,000 out of his campaign fund after leaving office. They also show that the Chicago ward committee controlled by the Speaker of the Illinois House spent more than $50,000 on tickets for the Chicago Cubs and the Chicago White Sox. Reinstating the ban on personal use would eventually eliminate public officials' converting campaign funds to income, but not until all of those politicians grandfathered in 1998 close out their political funds. And the personal-use ban does not apply to non-electoral expenditures like the baseball tickets or the gifts for constituents and supporters.

All political committees who are participating in an election must file pre-election reports of campaign contributions no later than fifteen days preceding each election (primary and general). These pre-election reports have to be complete as of the thirtieth day preceding the election. Any contribution of $500 or more received by the committee between the last date covered in their pre-election campaign report and the date of the election has to be reported to the State Board within two business days after its receipt. The intention of requiring pre-election reports and the reporting of large contributions received during the last month of the campaign is to provide information to the voters when it is most useful: prior to the election.

All political committees must file comprehensive reports every six months. Reports covering the period of January 1 to June 30 have to be filed no later than July 31, and reports covering the period of July 1 to December 31 have to be filed no later than January 31 of the following year.

The comprehensive six-month campaign finance reports filed by political committees must contain aggregate information for the reporting period on the beginning balance of the committee, the total amount of funds received by the committee from contributions, transfers, loans and other receipts, and the total amount of in-kind contributions of goods and services received by the committee. The same aggregate information is also required for all expenditures, transfers out of the committee, loans made, long term investments, and ending balances. All receipts and expenditures that exceed $150 for the reporting period from a single source must be reported individually. Each itemized report of a receipt or expenditure over $150 must list the name and mailing address of the source of the receipt or the recipient of the expenditure, the amount of the receipt or expenditure, the date either was made, and the aggregate total from the source or to the recipient for the reporting period. Under the suspended 1998 law, reports of contributions from individuals of over $500 are required to include occupation and employer information. Pre-election reports must also contain itemized reports for contributions, but not for expenditures.

Most of the issues that dominate the national debate on the role of money in politics are not relevant to Illinois. Illinois does not have hard money or soft money. It does not have independent expenditures or issue ads. In Illinois money is just money, and expenditures are just expenditures. A group or individual who provides goods or services on behalf of a candidate is required to notify the candidate, and the candidate is required to report those goods or services as an in-kind contribution. But these requirements constitute a disclosure issue, not an issue of complying with limits on contributions. The same is true of national-political-party money that comes to the state political parties and the legislative leaders. State-party expenditures involving federal candidates may raise federal issues concerning hard and soft money and issue ads. State-party expenditure of national-party money involving state candidates cannot violate state limits on how much money can be spent or on what the money can be spent, because Illinois has no limits.

The Illinois Supreme Court and Illinois' Campaign Finance Law

The major Illinois State Supreme Court cases dealing with the state campaign finance law are two in number. The *Troy* case was discussed earlier. The Court's ruling prohibited the State Board of Elections from considering the propriety of an expenditure of campaign funds by a candidate. In an earlier ruling, the Court addressed the question of the general intent and applicability of the Illinois Campaign Disclosure Act in a case brought by former Governor Daniel Walker (*Walker v State Bd of Elections*, 391 N.E.2nd 507 (1979)). He challenged the State Board of Elections' finding that a committee formed to pay off campaign debts from his 1972 gubernatorial campaign was required to report its receipts and expenditures to the Board. In ruling for the State Board of Elections, the Court held that:

> The Act is designed to preserve the integrity of the electoral process by requiring full public disclosure of the sources and amounts of campaign contributions and expenditures and the regulation of practices incident to political campaigns. The legislature wished the public to be informed of the total contributions received and expended by a political committee, the names of significant contributors and of individuals to whom a political committee is indebted.

Within the narrow scope of the law, as set down by *Troy,* the *Walker* decision provides the Illinois State Board of Elections with a very broad grant of power.

The 1998 amendments to the Illinois campaign finance law, contained in PA 90-737, were held unconstitutional by an Illinois circuit court in the case of *Flynn v. Ryan* in September 2000. The case was appealed to the Illinois State Supreme Court. The Court heard oral arguments in November 2001, but it has yet to rule. The major issue in the case was the constitutionality of the gift-ban portions of the Act that covered gifts to public officials from persons with interests before state government. While most of the changes to the Illinois campaign finance law were not challenged (electronic filing, disclosure of occupation and employer, ban on personal use of contributions, etc) the Circuit Court judge questioned the clarity of some provisions, such as the ban on receiving or soliciting contributions on state property. The Circuit Court judge held that the campaign finance provisions of the Act could not be severed and ruled the entire Act unconstitutional.

Table 1
Total Two Year Election Cycle Receipts*
(in millions of dollars)

Election Cycle	1993–94	1995–96	1997–1998	1999–2000
Offices Contested	House ⅓ Senate State Wide	House ⅔ Senate	House ⅔ Senate State Wide	House ⅓ Senate
Corporate, Union, PAC, & Individual Contributions	64.3	60.6	89.4	64.9
Candidate & Party Committee Contributions	13.3	23.9	26.0	29.4
Internal Transfers/Loans	5.6	6.0	11.4	9.4
Total Receipts ($ millions)	$83.2	$90.5	$126.8	$103.7

*Money Contributed to: Legislative leaders and legislative chamber committees
Legislators and candidates for legislative office
Constitutional officers and candidates for constitutional office
State political parties

Money in Illinois Politics: The Big Picture

By any measure, a great deal of money flows into and through the political system in Illinois. Aggregate data from the last four election cycles are presented in Table 1. The total receipts for statewide and legislative office holders and candidates and for the two major state political parties have ranged from $83.5 million to $126.8 million. Part of the variation in the amounts can be attributed to the kind of elections being held. In 1994 and 1998, a governor and five other statewide officers were elected for four-year terms. The Illinois legislature has 118 House members and fifty-nine Senate members. All 118 House seats are up for election every two years. Because state senators serve differing combinations of one two-year term and two four-year terms between each redistricting, one third of the Senate seats were up for reelection in 1994 and 2000, while two thirds of the Senate seats were up for reelection in 1996 and 1998. A comparison of the 1993–1994 cycle—holding elections for Governor, for all seats in the House, and for one third of the seats in the Senate—with the 1998 cycle—holding elections for Governor, for all seats in the House and for two thirds of the seats in the Senate—shows an increase of $43.6 million in campaign receipts. A comparison of the 1995–1996 cycle—holding elections for all seats in the House and for two thirds of the seats in the Senate—with the 1999–2000 cycle—holding elections for all seats in the House and one third of the seats in the Senate—shows an increase of $13.2million. Clearly, the trend in overall receipts is upward.

The money received from corporations, unions, association PACs and individuals amounts, fairly consistently, to $60 million–$65 million over three of the four election cycles. In 1997–98 the data show an increase of almost 50%—to $89.4 million—from the previous election cycle. An increase in the 1997–1998 election cycle over the 1995–1996 election cycle, when no statewide elections were being held, is expected. An increase over the last cycle, 1993–94, when statewide offices were contested, is also expected. But the size of the increase in 1997–98 is surprising. It is partially explained by the fact that the campaigns for the two top statewide offices, Governor and Secretary of State, were open races with no incumbent. While the sources of money for campaigns for the legislature do overlap with those for governor and other statewide offices, there is a separate pool of money for gubernatorial and other statewide campaigns that is not part of the legislative pool.

Another factor in the large increase in private contributions in 1997–98 was a number of high-profile legislative issues that the legislature brought to the floor in 1997, 1998, and 1999. A large portion of the contributions from interest groups, unions, and corporations to incumbent office holders has little to do with elections and everything to do with gaining or maintaining access to power. The role of campaign contributions in legislative policy decisions will be examined in a later section. The relatively small increase of private contributions in 1999–2000 over those of 1995–1996 also makes the increase in 1997–1998 look even larger. The decline in private-sector money contributed in 1999–2000 reflects both a smaller number of legislative elections and the continuing decline of competition in legislative elections. This topic will also be addressed in a later section.

Candidates and parties in Illinois can raise money from any source and then transfer that money to another political committee without limit. As shown in Table 1, the amount of money that is raised by one political committee and then transferred to another political committee accounts for between a quarter and a third of all receipts. The high was $29.4 million for the 1999–2000 election cycle. In one sense, this is recycled money. The ultimate source of a contribution from one political committee to another is a contribution from an individual or private entity. But it is not double-counting to include these transfers as part of the total receipts. If the Illinois State Medical Society gives the Republican leader of the State Senate $200,000 and the leader spends $200,000 on the campaign of a state senator, a total of $400,000 worth of obligations have been created, not $200,000. One is a $200,000 relationship between the interest group and the leader, and one is a $200,000 relationship between the leader and the legislative candidate. The growth in political transfers reflects the growth in the power of the legislative leaders and their direct role in legislative elections.

Table 2
Spending in Primary and General Elections* for Statewide Office**

Year	1994	1998
Primary	15.7 (Governor $9.8m)	18.5 (Governor $12.2m)
General	<u>22.8</u> (Governor $12.5m)	<u>22.2</u> (Governor $13.4m)
Total	$38.5 million	$40.7 million

*Primary Period = January 1 to June 30, General Election Period = July 1 to December 31
** Governor, Lieutenant Governor, Secretary of State, Attorney General, Treasurer, Comptroller

The internal transfers and loans listed in Table 1 represent transfers between the personal committees of legislative leaders and the legislative chamber committees they control, or between the political committees and the state political parties. For example, a legislative leader uses his personal committee to raise money and then transfers the funds to a chamber committee or a state party committee that spends the money directly on legislative elections. These transactions are paper transfers that do not affect the amount of money operating in the state political system or the relationships created by the flow of that money. These transfers could be subtracted to provide a "working total" of money which was part of a political transaction that affected an election or a policy decision.

Spending on Elections

Like the total amount of money that flows into the Illinois political system, the total amount spent on campaigns during an election cycle varies with the offices that are being contested. Candidates for statewide office in Illinois spent $38.5 million in 1994 and $40.7 million in 1998. (See Table 2.) Spending by candidates for governor accounted for 58% of the total spending on campaigns for statewide office in 1994 and 66% of the total in 1998. The $25.6 million spent by candidates for Governor in the 1998 primary and general elections does not exhaust the potential for spending in a gubernatorial campaign in Illinois. In 1998 the governor's race was for an open seat, but the Democratic candidate who won the primary voluntary placed a limit on contributions from PACs and individuals to his campaign. As a result he was outspent by the Republican by a margin of 3 to 1. Incumbent statewide officials also raise and spend money during the election cycles when no statewide races are contested, but only a small portion of this activity shows up in direct election spending on legislative races. In 1999–2000 incumbent statewide officials raised $10.5 million.

Table 3
Spending on Primary and General Elections* for Legislative Office

Seats Contested	House ⅓ Senate	House ⅔ Senate	House ⅔ Senate	House ⅓ Senate
Year	1994	1996	1998	2000
Primary	6.4	7.8	5.9	10.6
General Election	18.5	26.3	25.0	28.6
Total ($ millions)	$24.9	$34.1	$30.9	$39.2

*Primary Period = January 1 to June 30, General Election Period = July 1 to December 31

Spending on legislative elections, as seen in Table 3, increased dramatically over the four election cycles. From1994 to1998 the increase is almost 50%—more than $12 million. However, most of that increase occurred between 1994 and 1996. The aggregate figures mask a lot of variation. When we look at individual elections, we will see that the trend over the four cycles was for candidates to spend more and more on fewer and fewer contested seats.

At the same time, the number of seats being contested and the political climate of a particular election cycle has a strong impact on spending. In 1994 the Republicans won control of the Illinois house. That gave them control of both chambers of the legislature for the first time in more than twenty-five years. In 1996 there was a major battle over control of the legislature. At that time, two thirds of the Senate seats and all of the House seats were up for election. Total spending in 1996 increased by more than $9 million over total spending in 1994. The Democrats regained control of the House in 1996, setting up the same election dynamics for 1998. The result was a status quo election, with control of the legislature split between the two parties. Spending was up in 2000, but primarily because of primary fights in House elections between rival ward organizations in the city of Chicago. A total of five incumbent Democratic legislators from Chicago were defeated in the primary in 2000.

Competition in Legislative Elections

One of the articles of faith among critics of contribution limits is that strict contribution limits and limits on what entities can contribute make elections less competitive because they make it too difficult for challengers to raise enough money to be competitive (Smith 2001). Illinois provides a test of the converse of that proposition: does the complete absence of campaign finance

Table 4
General Election Competition in Legislative Elections

House				
Election Cycle	1993–1994	1995–1996	1997–1998	1999–2000
Seats up	118	118	118	118
Unopposed	35	31	58	75
Weak	52	56	31	24
Competitive	7	11	13	7
Targeted by Leaders	24	20	16	12
Senate				
Election Cycle	1993–1994	1995–1996	1997–1998	1999–2000
Seats up	21	40	41	22
Unopposed	7	16	21	13
Weak	9	13	7	3
Competitive	0	4	5	1
Targeted by Leaders	5	7	8	5

Unopposed = Winner had no opponent or token opponent who spent less than $1,000.
Weak = Winner had an opponent who spent more than $1,000, but less than $50,000.
Competitive = Winner had an opponent who spent more than $50,000.
Targeted = One or both of those running received more than $100,000 in support from a legislative leader.

regulations create more competition? The data in Table 4 clearly suggest that the answer is no. Legislative elections in Illinois are very uncompetitive and they have become less competitive over the last four elections. What competition exists is largely a function of the actions of the legislative leaders.

The number of House seats where the winner had no general election opponent or a weak opponent who spent less than $50,000 increased from eighty-seven seats in 1994 (74%) to ninety-nine seats (84%) in 2000. In the Senate the number of uncompetitive seats was between 71% and 74% of all seats for the four election cycles. The number of races that were competitive without major funding from the legislative leaders ranged between 0% and 11% of all seats for both the House and the Senate for the four election cycles. The standard of competition in the general election being used as an example is fairly low, since the losing candidate spent more than $50,000. Candidates in races targeted by the legislative leaders spent four times that amount for house races in 1994 and eight times that amount in 2000. The disparity was even greater for Senate races.

The real competition in legislative elections came from races where one or both of the legislative leaders provided $100,000 or more to a candidate. These targeted races accounted for 17% to 24% of the Senate races and 10% to 24% of the House races between 1994 and 2000. The decline in targeted races in

Table 5
Reelection Rates and Partisan Shifts —House

Election Cycle	1993–1994	1995–1996	1997–1998	1999–2000
Incumbents running	105/118	106/118	103/118	113/118
Incumbents reelected	91/105 (87%)	101/106 (95%)	102/103 (99%)	107/113 (95%)
Incumbent Primary Losses	2	1	1	6
Incumbent General Election Losses	12	4	0	0
Incumbent Losses in Non-targeted races	0	0	0	0
Partisan Shift Open Seat	0	2	2	0
Partisan Shifts	Rep +12	Dem +6	Dem +2	0
Partisan Balance	D54/R64	D60/R58	D62/R56	D62/R54

the House reflects a focusing on targets of opportunity by the legislative leaders and their unwillingness to spend good money after failing to defeat incumbents who had won twice or three times in a potentially competitive district. For example, the Republican incumbent in the 99th House district faced a Democratic opponent in 1992 and 1994 who received the majority of her funding from a legislative leader and spent more than $300,000 in each election. In 1996 the Democrats offered only a token opponent. In 2000, there was no Democratic challenger in the 99th house district. What made the district competitive or uncompetitive were the strategic choices made by the legislative leaders. In the Senate, the number of targeted seats was more constant across the four election cycles because the number of seats being contested limited the number of strategic choices for the leaders.

Overall, Illinois legislative elections are largely uncompetitive. The absence of campaign contribution limits has not generated large numbers of candidates or a high level of competition. At the same time, the legislative leaders control competition in legislative elections through their unfettered ability to raise money and move it into legislative races.

Another way of looking at competition is to examine reelection rates for incumbent legislators. Looking at results from House elections over four election cycles in Table 5, one sees that the reelection rates for incumbents who run for reelection are very high (87% to 99%), even with the heavy losses suffered by the Democrats in the national Republican landslide of 1994. The picture in the Senate presented in Table 6 is the same, with reelection rates of 95% for all four of the election cycles. A total of sixteen House incumbents

Table 6
Reelection Rates and Partisan Shifts —Senate*

Election Cycle	1993–1994	1995–1996	1997–1998	1999–2000
Incumbents running	19/21	37/40	39/41	22/22
Incumbents reelected	18/19 (95%)	35/37 (95%)	37/39 (95%)	21/22 (95%)
Incumbent Primary Losses	0	1	2	1
Incumbent General Election Losses	1	1	0	0
Incumbent Losses in Non-targeted races	0	0	0	0
Partisan Shift Open Seat	0	1	1	0
Partisan Shifts	Rep +1	Dem +2	Rep +1	0
Partisan Balance	D26/R33	D28/R31	D27/R32	D27/R32

* Senate districts are divided in three groups with terms of 2-4-4, 4-2-4 or 4-4-2 after redistricting. In 1994 and 2000 one-third of the seats were up for election, while in 1996 and 1998 two-thirds of the seats were up for election.

lost in the general election in 1994 and 1996, and none have lost since. During the same four election cycles, ten House incumbents lost in the primary. In the Senate one incumbent senator lost in 1994 and one in 1996, and none have lost since. Twice as many incumbent senators lost in the primary in the four election cycles. Incumbent legislators were almost always reelected, but if they lost, they were just as likely to lose in the primary as in the general election.

For political parties, elections are about control. In 1992, under a new legislative map drawn by a Republican majority on a redistricting commission, the Republicans took control of the state Senate by a margin of 32 to 27, while the Democrats maintained control of the house by a margin of 66 to 52. Tables 5 and 6 show the shifts in partisan control between 1994 and 2000. In the national Republican landslide of 1994, the Republicans took control of the House by defeating twelve Democratic incumbents. In 1996 the Democrats regained control of the House by defeating four Republican incumbents and winning two open seats in districts that had previously elected Republicans. In 1998 the Democrats picked up two more seats by winning two open seats in districts that had previously elected Republicans. In 2000 no seats changed hands.

In the Senate, control was maintained by the Republicans through the four election cycles. The Republicans picked up a seat in 1994 by defeating an incumbent. The Democrats picked up two seats in 1996 by defeating an in-

Table 7
Average General Election Spending per Candidate—Targeted Races*

	House	Senate
1994	$200,000 (24/118 races)	$297,000 (5/21 races)
1996	$291,000 (20/118 races)	$417,000 (7/40 races)
1998	$286,000 (16/118 races)	$364,000 (8/41 races)
2000	$415,000 (12/118 races)	$504,000 (5/22 races)

*Targeted Race = One or both of those running received more than $100,000 in support from a legislative leader.

cumbent and winning an open seat, while the Republicans picked up a seat in 1998 by winning an open seat. No seats changed hands in the 2000 election.

For all the money spent on legislative elections in races targeted by the legislative leaders, a grand total of one seat changed hands in the1998 election, and no seats changed hands in 2000. Both parties spent more and more money in fewer and fewer targeted races. As a result, the status quo was maintained.

Each of the eighteen incumbent legislators defeated in the four general elections between 1994 and 2000 were in races targeted by the legislative leaders. Of the six open seats that shifted from one party to the other, only one was not a targeted race. In other words, in the four general elections between 1994 and 2000, 242 candidates ran without the support of the legislative leader of their party against an incumbent legislator, or ran for open seats that had been controlled by the opposite party. Of those 242 candidates, only one of them won. At the same time, 276 legislative candidates ran in the general election without opposition.

Spending in Legislative Elections

The fight for control of the legislature takes place in a relatively small number of races. These races are called targeted races because the legislative leaders focus on them as races where a shift of seats between parties is possible. A threshold of $100,000 from a legislative leader in support of a candidate for the general election has been used to designate races as "targeted." In most cases, the amount has been much greater. The role of the legislative leaders in Illinois in legislative elections is much broader than just providing money. They recruit candidates, raise the money to fund the campaigns, and provide the staff who run the campaigns. The leaders function as political parties for their political caucuses, and the legislative campaigns in targeted races have the characteristics of party-centered rather than candidate-centered elections. The average spending by candidates in targeted races is presented in Table 7.

Table 8
Average General Election Spending in Non-Targeted Races*

Year	1994	1996	9998	2000
House				
Winner	$81,000	$91,000	$78,000	$94,000
Loser**	$31,000	$24,000	$36,000	$28,000
Senate				
Winner	$80,000	$70,000	$91,000	$121,000
Loser**	$11,000	$23,000	$27,000	$ 32,000

* Includes both weak and competitive races from Table 1.
** Excludes token candidates who spent less than $1,000.

In 1994 the average candidate in a targeted House race spent $200,000, while the average candidate in a targeted Senate race spent $297,000. In 2000 those averages had increased to $415,000 for a House candidate and $504,000 for a Senate candidate. In the 2000 general election, four Senate races exceeded $1 million in combined spending. The most expensive Senate race cost more than $1.40 million, which broke the old record of $1.37 million. In the House, five races exceeded $1 million in total spending. The most expensive race cost $1.36 million, which was also a new record. Prior to 2000, no House race had exceeded $850,000 in spending for the general election.

The contrast between spending in targeted and non-targeted races is dramatic. Table 8 shows the average spending of the winning and losing candidates in non-targeted races. The amount spent by losing candidates in non-targeted races is less than 10% of the amount spent by candidates in targeted races. The average amounts spent by these losing candidates have been virtually flat over the past four election cycles. The disparity between winning and losing candidates in non-targeted races is just as dramatic. In 2000 winners outspent losers by a margin of almost four to one. These figures understate the advantage of the winners. Losing candidates in non-targeted races generally spend all that they raise. In 2000, the total of the fund balances reported by winners in non-targeted races at the end of the general election period exceeded the total amount they spent during the period.

The Financial Role of the Legislative Leaders

Legislative leaders in Illinois raise money through their own personal political committees and through legislative chamber committees which they control. For example, the Republican Senate President has his own committee. He raises money in his committee and then transfers money to the Sen-

Table 9
Money Raised by Legislative Leaders* per 2-Year Election Cycle

1993–1994	$16.0 Million
1995–1996	$21.0 Million
1997–1998	$18.5 Million
1999–2000	$21.5 Million

*Includes both personal committees and chamber committees controlled by the legislative leaders.

ate Republican Campaign Committee. The Senate Republican Campaign Committee both raises money and provides money and services to legislative candidates. The House Republican leader and the Senate Democratic leader follow the same arrangement. The relationship is even more complicated for the Democratic Speaker of the House. Unlike the other three legislative caucuses, the House Democrats do not have a chamber committee. But their leader, the House Speaker, is also the Chairman of the Democratic Party of Illinois. The Democratic Speaker raises money through his personal committee and then transfers money to the State Democratic Party. The Democratic leader of the Senate also transferred money to the Democratic Party of Illinois in 1998 and 2000. The Democratic Party of Illinois then provides money and services to House and Senate candidates running as Democrats.

As a result of these funding arrangements, legislative leaders in Illinois control the spending of millions of dollars in legislative elections. In 2000, they raised more than $21.5 million. The total amounts raised by legislative leaders and their chamber committees for the last four election cycles are presented in Table 9.

The extent of the financial support that legislative leaders provide to candidates in targeted races can be seen in Table 10. On average the legislative

Table 10
General Election Support* Provided by Leader in Targeted Races**

Election Year	1994	1996	1998	2000
House				
Democrats	68%	55%	68%	70%
Republicans	56%	58%	67%	76%
Senate				
Democrats	74%	64%	54%	72%
Republicans	70%	69%	68%	73%

 * General election receipts from a legislative leader as a % of general election spending.
** Targeted Race = One or both of those running received more than $100,000 in support from a legislative leader.

leaders provided money and services to candidates in targeted races that equaled between 55% and 76% of the total amounts spent by those candidates in the general election. Only a small part of this support was in the form of transfer of money. Most of it came in the forms of in-kind contributions such as direct-mail advertising, media buys on TV and radio, polling, and full-time campaign staff.

In the 2000 general election, the losing Republican challenger in the 116th House district spent $521,000. During the general election period, he received $401,000 of in-kind support from the House Republican leader and an additional $37,500 cash contribution, for a total of $438,500 in leadership support. In essence, the legislative leader funded and ran the campaign, providing more than 84% of the candidate's resources used in the general election. While extreme, this example is in no way atypical for a targeted legislative race in Illinois. The winning Democratic incumbent in the 116th house district spent $807,000 in the general election. During that period, he received almost $438,000 from the Democratic Party of Illinois. These figures represent support directly linked to the leaders. The 116th district is a rural district located in deep southern Illinois. When a campaign contribution from a Chicago labor union or a Rockford manufacturing firm finds it way to a candidate in the 116th district, it is reasonable to assume that the legislative leader helped direct that money to that candidate—who needed it.

Can Private Money Buy Happiness in Elections?

The top twenty contributors to Illinois elections in the 1999–2000 election cycle are shown in Table 11. Because Illinois' law allows unlimited contributions from corporations and unions, for a corporation or a union to make the top twenty list requires $270,000 in contributions over a two-year election cycle.

All of the groups and companies listed in Table 11 contribute to candidates who are running for office and to the legislative leaders. But they vary widely in their direct interest in elections, particularly contested, partisan elections. Most interest groups, unions, corporations, and individuals are interested primarily in access to power. These groups give to legislative leaders, incumbent legislators, and statewide officials who can help them in achieving their policy goals. They are not primarily concerned with partisan goals and are very comfortable shifting contribution strategies from one party to another with a change in legislative power. Among the top twenty contributors, the Illinois Hospital and Health Systems Association, the Associated Beer Distributor of Illinois, Ameritech, the Cable TV Association, The Banker Association, the

Table 11
Top 20 Private Sector Contributors*
1999–2000 Election Cycle (1/1/1999–12/31/2000)

1.	IL Education Assn	$1,394,000
2.	IL State Medical Society	$1,026,000
3.	IL Fed of Teachers	$ 975,000
4.	IL Hospital Assn	$ 881,000
5.	Assoc Beer Distributors (ABDI)	$ 775,000
6.	IL Manufacturers Assn	$ 712,000
7.	Ameritech	$ 600,000
8.	IL Trial Lawyers Assn	$ 564,000
9.	Public Employee Union AFSCME	$ 486,000
10.	Cable TV Assoc of IL	$ 473,000
11.	IL Realtors Assn	$ 466,000
12.	IL Power/Illinova	$ 444,000
13.	Commonwealth Edison	$ 434,000
14.	IL Bankers Assn	$ 426,000
15.	Philip Morris Corp.	$ 349,000
16.	Personal PAC (Pro-choice Assn)	$ 327,000
17.	United Dist & Vintners UDV	$ 325,000
18.	Mayer Brown & Platt	$ 292,000
19.	IL State Chamber of Commerce	$ 284,000
20.	Empress Casino	$ 270,000

* Money Contributed to:
   Legislative leaders and legislative chamber committees
   Legislators and candidates for legislative office
   Constitutional officers and candidates for constitutional office
   State political parties

Realtors Association., Illinois Power, Commonwealth Edison, Philip Morris, United Distillers and Vintners, the law firm of Mayer Brown and Platt, and the Empress Casino all fall into this general pattern. One of the axioms shared by political science and practical politics is that money flows to power. In Illinois it flows more freely than almost anywhere else. As a result, incumbent legislators from safe districts are able to raise much more money than they need to continue winning elections, and the legislative leaders are able to raise the huge sums of money they need to contest targeted races.

Some interest groups care about who wins elections. They want to elect legislators and statewide officials who favor their policy goals. Such groups may be intensely partisan, but not always. They focus a large portion of their contributions on contested races and are usually big contributors to the legislative leaders. The Illinois Federation of Teachers, the Illinois Trial Lawyers Association, and AFSCME (a public employee union) are very Democratic and election-oriented in their contribution strategies. The Illinois State Medical

Society, the Illinois Manufactures Association, and the Illinois State Chamber of Commerce are also very election-oriented in their contribution strategies, but they favor Republican candidates.

In contrast, the Illinois Education Association (IEA) gives to candidates primarily in terms of the candidates' support for the education goals of the IEA. It is heavily involved in contested elections, but it gives very little to the legislative leaders. While it contributes more to Democratic than to Republican candidates, it actively supports Republican candidates in contested races. The IEA has both the resources and the issues that give it confidence it can make a difference without going through the legislative leaders. Personal PAC, a pro-choice group, uses the same general strategy. It gets involved in legislative contests to provide contributions and in-kind services to candidates in contested races where abortion is an issue between candidates. Personal PAC is even more bi-partisan that the IEA.

Overall, most interest group-, union-, and corporation-money that goes directly to candidates goes to incumbents. Interests groups do get involved in contested races, and they do make a difference in the margins in some races (Redfield 2001). But contested legislative races in Illinois are very expensive because of the involvement of the legislative leaders. The Illinois Education Association has contributed as much as $40,000 in one State Senate race (Redfield 2000). In an uncontested Senate race, that would be a huge amount of money. In a targeted Senate race, where a legislative leader contributes $300,000 and the candidate spends more than $500,000, a $40,000 contribution is valued, but not decisive.

Can Money Buy Happiness in the Legislature?

In Illinois elections, money is a critical factor. But it is not the only factor. And money alone will not guarantee victory. So it is with a group's trying to influence policy in the Illinois General Assembly. Money is important. But it is not the only factor, and money alone will not insure that a group will succeed. The most effective groups in Springfield have large memberships that are widely distributed throughout the state, and they actively participate in grass-roots lobbying activities. They also have effective organizations with a strong policy analysis and public information staffs. They are active and effective in legislative elections with both campaign contributions and manpower. Finally, they have strong, full-time Springfield lobbying operations supplemented by access-oriented contribution strategies (Redfield 2001).

Only a few organizations that lobby in Springfield come close to meeting every one of these criteria. Certainly, the Illinois State Medical Society, the two major teacher unions (the Illinois Education Association and the Illinois Federation of Teachers), the Illinois Manufacturers Association, the Illinois Trial Lawyers Association and the Illinois State AFL-CIO have strong elements of each of these criteria. Money and membership allow them to build strong organizations, to employ full-time lobbyists and policy research staff, to create and sustain ongoing, district-based, grass-roots activities, and to be directly involved in political campaigns. Campaign contributions are a key component of their successes in Springfield. These groups could mount a strong presence in Springfield without making large campaign contributions, but they are much more effective when they make them. In general, campaign contributions are more effective as a partner with the other resources than as a substitute for them.

While it takes a board range of resources to engage in all of the aspects of lobbying, not every group with the necessary resources will pursue every strategy available. Some groups in the top twenty in total campaign contributions (listed in Table 11) take a more narrow approach to lobbying, based on the nature of their issues. For example, the Beer Distributors, the Realtors, and the Bankers may have the money necessary to take the same aggressive approach to legislative elections as the teacher unions, the Medical Society, the Manufacturers or the Trial Lawyers. But they choose not to do so, largely because of the nature of their issues, which tend to be less partisan than traditional labor/management conflicts. In contrast, Personal PAC, a pro-choice group, focuses almost exclusively on election activities to achieve its policy goals. Because of the nature of its major issue, the group believes it is much more effective to elect pro-choice candidates to office than to come to Springfield to lobby legislators to take a pro-choice position. As a result, Personal PAC is different from all most every other group that ranks high in campaign contributions, because it does not have the full-time lobbying presence in Springfield.

Some interests are more limited in the resources they can bring to bear on their behalf. Corporations, such as Commonwealth Edison and Illinois Power, while Illinois-based, are limited by the regional impact of their business activities and by their lack of manpower in undertaking board-based grass-roots campaigns on a statewide basis. As a result, they are more dependent on campaign contributions to provide access to the policy process than groups with large, well-organized, well-distributed memberships. In a few cases, campaign contributions provide the primary basis for a lobbying effort because there are no other options.

Taxing and regulating the use of tobacco products has been a very controversial issue in Illinois for more than two decades. The major supporter of the interests of the tobacco companies has been the Philip Morris Corporation. Philip Morris has very little business activity in Illinois, even with its acquisition of Kraft Foods and Miller Beer. The corporation doesn't have a key contact grass-roots lobbying organization or an army of volunteers to work in campaigns. Its ability to generate and direct a constituent-based lobbying campaign is very limited. Out of necessity, it relies on campaign contributions to provide the access for their lobbying efforts in Springfield. Because direct corporate contributions are legal in Illinois, the opportunity exists for a corporation to use money as a substitute for constituent linkages or grass-roots activities. With more than $2 million in contributions to legislative leaders, legislators, and Governors between the beginning of 1993 and the end of 2000, Philip Morris has made the most of that opportunity.

The organized opponents of the tobacco industry are primarily not-for-profit groups, such as the American Cancer Society and the American Heart Association. The tax-exempt status of such groups does allow them to engage in some lobbying activities, but they are prohibited from making campaign contributions or engaging in election activities. The record of tax increases on tobacco and limitations on smoking in public places suggests that being a top-twenty contributor does not insure success in Springfield. But those taxes and limitations have come more slowly and have been less severe than in other states because of the strong lobbying effort Philip Morris has led on behalf of tobacco interests throughout the 1990s. While there are public-policy arguments based on economic- and personal-freedom rationales to support the positions of the tobacco companies, the primary reason for the successes of the tobacco interests in Illinois has been money. Legislative leaders, in particular, need money to fund election campaigns that keep them in power. Tobacco companies have been more than willing to provide campaign contributions ($2.02 million since 1993) in exchange for access in Springfield and a seat at the table.

Many lobbying battles in Springfield are contests between two well-financed interests, complete with dueling grass-roots campaigns, campaign contributions, press releases, position papers, and lobbyists. A public debate will usually take place with a full airing of the issues. Even in a lobbying battle between two interests, one much more heavily financed than the other—in a debate, for example, between the tobacco industry and public health interests—the issues at stake will be publicly engaged, in part because public health interests are organized and have a full-time presence in Springfield, and in part because their issue wears a white hat.

Table 12
Contributions by Categories of Private Sector Groups
(millions of dollars)

Election Cycle	1993–1994	1995–1996	1997–1998	1999–2000
Manufacturing	$4.2	$4.2	$4.9	$4.2
Finance	$3.0	$2.9	$3.9	$4.3
Construction	$2.3	$2.7	$3.3	$3.7
Health Facilities	$1.6	$1.8	$2.5	$2.1
Trade Unions	$3.2	$3.6	$5.2	$4.7
Teacher Unions	$1.5	$1.8	$3.0	$2.6
Public Employee Unions	$0.6	$0.8	$1.0	$1.1
Lawyers	$5.6	$4.3	$5.6	$5.8
Physicians/Health Prof.	$2.5	$2.6	$2.6	$2.0
Gambling	$1.4	$1.6	$1.9	$1.8
Lobbyists	$0.4	$0.7	$1.1	$0.9

The real danger for distortion and bias in public policy occurs when un-represented or under-represented interests face off against well-organized, well-funded interests. When one side is organized and well-funded and the other side is unorganized and unfunded, the policy result is usually one-sided. A look at the sources of Illinois campaign contributions broken down into a set of broad categories can make the same point. Table 12 presents those sources for the past four election cycles. Lawyers, unions, manufacturing, finance, physicians, financial institutions, and construction firms dominate the list. Absent are issue-groups, consumer-groups, patient-rights-groups, anti-gambling groups, children advocates and environmental groups.

The record of the 1999 General Assembly in dealing with gambling expansion and liquor distributor contracts suggest that the current system gives narrow interests with money a huge advantage over unorganized, unrepresented interests. Part of that dynamic is the result of the role that campaign contributions play in maintaining the power of the legislative leaders (Redfield 2001).

Money, Legislative Leaders, and Policy

Political parties are alive and well in the Illinois General Assembly. But these are not the traditional Republican and Democratic parties. Rather, the parties that controlled the Illinois General Assembly in the 2001–2002 legislative session were the House-Speaker Michael-Madigan Party, the Senate-President-James-"Pate"-Philip Party, the House-Minority Leader-Lee-Daniels-Party, and the Senate-Minority-Leader-Emil-Jones-Party. These legislative leaders perform all of the traditional functions of political parties. The leaders recruit the candidates, raise the funds and run the campaigns. They also set the legislative agenda and consistently deliver the votes of their members on important roll calls. And they do all of this in a manner about which legislative leaders at the national level can only dream.

Longevity and experience are certainly two of the sources of legislative leadership power in Springfield. All four of the legislative leaders serving in 2001 came to Springfield before Jimmy Cater was elected President. All four have been the leaders of their political caucuses for more than a decade. The leaders are all very talented, politically savvy men who have survived by making the right decision at the right time. Yet the long tenure or the political skills of the leaders do not explain why they are so powerful or why their power has increased steadily over the past two decades.

What lies at the heart of legislative leader-power in Illinois is the near monopolies the leaders hold over campaign fund-raising in key legislative elections, over legislative staff, and over the formal procedures of the legislative process (Redfield 1998). These monopolies allow the leaders to control the course of legislative elections and to control the legislative process when the legislature comes into session. Individual legislators are simply not able, on their own, to raise the funds necessary to be competitive in a race targeted by the legislative leaders. Individual legislators also lack the personal- and policy-staff necessary to establish political and substantive autonomy from their leaders. Strong leaders and relatively weak members of the legislature in Springfield mean that interest groups concentrate their campaign contributions on the leaders, which gives the leaders more control over the financing of elections, which makes them stronger in Springfield, which makes them more dominate in raising money which....and so on.

Trying to beat an incumbent legislator in the general election in Illinois without the help of a legislative leader is almost always a suicide mission. Beating an incumbent with the help of a legislative leader is still very difficult, but clearly possible, based on the results of the past four elections. In addition to financial support, leadership staffs usually run the campaigns of challengers in targeted races, and the legislative leaders informally recruit most of the challengers. The result of the system of legislative elections, which has evolved since the early 1980s, is a legislature where the incumbents in districts that have been targeted are there primarily because of the financial and campaign support of the legislative leaders.

Each Illinois legislator has a district office allowance. This allowance is sufficient to open one or two offices in the district. One full-time person, along with some part-time help and student volunteers, usually staffs these offices. Rank and file House members have individual offices in the capitol, but they usually share a secretary with one or two other members. Each senator has a capitol office and a secretary. Members have no personal-policy staff. When the General Assembly is in session, a committee staff provides information on bills and amendments and provides support in drafting and shaping legislation. But the legislative members, or even the committee chairmen, do not hire those staff people. All the partisan staff who do the substantive and appropriation committee work are part of four centralized staffs, each controlled by one of the legislative leaders. The committee chairmen and minority spokesmen are appointed by the leaders and work with staff people assigned from the leaders' staffs. The executive directors of the bi-partisan legislative service agencies are hired by the four leaders and serve at their pleasure. Ultimate control over staff rests not with individual members or even committee chairmen, but with the legislative leaders.

Beginning in 1993, when the Republicans took control of the Senate, the rules of the legislative process in both the Senate and the House have been significantly changed to increase the formal power of the legislative leaders over the movement, content, and passage of legislation. Leaders have always exercised these powers informally, but the rule changes of 1993 created formal steps that reduced the power of individual members and increased the control of the leaders. Long-time observers note that the process has come full circle. The 1970s was a period when a very closed, leader- and committee-chairman-dominated process was opened up for individual members. Large increases in partisan committee staff and nonpartisan policy staff during that era also gave the individual members and the legislature as a whole more policy independence from the governor, interest groups, and the legislative leaders than had been the case before. The 1990s have seen a wholesale retrenchment of the power and autonomy of individual members in the legislative process and a failure to extend the policy and bi-partisan staffing resources of the legislature.

In addition to leadership staff doing committee work, there is a wide range of staff members who provide support for the members that is more political in nature. They do the press releases, write the newsletters, organize district activities, and provide information on legislation directly to members. These are many of the same tasks performed by a United States congressman's Capitol and district staff. The key difference is that the Illinois staff works not for the individual member, but for the legislative leader.

The general support provided by the political staff to members is important, but staff's real value lies in what it allows the legislative leaders to do during elections. It constitutes an experienced, professional campaign organization that exists from election to election. Each election cycle, the leaders deploy the political staff in the races that will determine whether their party will gain or retain control of their chamber of the legislature. The legislative leader's political staff goes out into the targeted districts in the spring and then leaves the state payroll in the summer and fall to work full-time on campaigns in the targeted districts. They are the ones who organize and run the campaigns. Because the leaders, not the candidates, control the money and the campaign staff, the leaders can shift resources during the course of the campaign, pulling the plug on a candidate whose campaign has failed to take off and pouring money and staff into a district where a contest is unexpectedly close.

The combination of the campaign organizations and the campaign money that the legislative leaders control gives them enormous power to shape the outcome of legislative elections in the districts they target. Which party controls each chamber of the legislature is a result of a small number of campaigns that are fought with the legislative leaders' money and that are directed by the legislative leaders' staffs.

When the legislature convenes in Springfield, the leaders have a monopoly over staff and the political clout and formal power necessary to control the legislative agenda and determine most of the outcomes. The most significant impact of leadership power on the legislative process over the past two decades has been the appropriation process.

In the 1970s the state budget was acted on by the legislature through a set of separate agency budget bills. The result was often an uncoordinated, chaotic process. During the 1980s the number of appropriation bills was steadily reduced, making it easier to comprehend and manage the entire budget during the appropriation process. Through this process, individual agencies' budgets and specific spending programs were considered in committee, and budgets were shaped by amendments in committee and on the House and Senate floors. But, after the 1992 elections, fewer and fewer of the budget decisions were made in committee or on the floor. Instead, more and more of the budget was negotiated among the four leaders and the Governor and then presented to the legislators for ratification in a single vote at the end of the session. By the end of the decade, the appropriation process in the legislature had ceased to function. Agency budgets were discussed in House and Senate committees, but the decisions were made by the leaders and the Governor and then presented to the members at the end of the session.

The ultimate symbol of leadership control over the appropriation process is the current practice of handling what used to be called pork-barrel spending, but which is now referred to as "member initiatives." The budget for the fiscal year 2001 contained more than $380 million in spending authority divided among the four legislative caucuses. No specific projects were listed. Instead, the money would be designated for projects at the discretion of each leader, with an eye toward maximizing the election prospects of their members. All of this leadership power led one long-time observer of the process to refer to the role of rank-and-file legislators as supernumeraries, the non-speaking spear-carriers and support characters in an opera production (Wheeler 2000). When one considers the limit imposed by House Speaker Madigan during the 2001 spring session of the legislature that no House member could call more than three bills for a final passage roll call, "supernumeraries" seems almost too kind.

The power of the legislative leaders over the process means that almost every group who makes campaign contributions gives a significant portion of their contributions to the leaders, regardless of the nature of their issues or whether their concerns are partisan or regional. Because the leaders can never be sure about how much money is enough for the next set of political campaigns, they exert great pressure on interest groups and corporations to contribute. Because these groups and corporations want to be important players in the process, or, at a minimum, to have access to the legislature, they continue to contribute more each election cycle. Control in the capitol enhances control in elections and control in elections enhances control in the capitol. No incentives exist for the leaders to share their power with individual members or to alter the campaign finance system they have created. The individual legislative members become less independent, less influential, while power becomes more and more concentrated in the hands of the legislative leaders. Limiting the role of money in the process, particularly as it relates to the power of the legislative leaders, would go along way toward opening up the process and empowering individual members of the legislature.

Gambling with Public Policy

The public's perception of the legislative process in Springfield is often that of a backroom game of "let's make a deal politics" dominated by powerful legislative leaders, by the Governor, by powerful special interests, by huge campaign contributions, and by high-priced lobbyists. There are occasions when that perception is a very accurate one—for example, the process that produced the gambling subsidy and the expansion bill that the legislature passed and the Governor signed in the spring of 1999.

No one ran for the legislature or for Governor in 1998 on a platform of dramatically expanding casino gambling in the state. No one made subsidizing the horse-racing industry the cornerstone of his or her TV ads or direct mail pieces. There was no army of concerned citizens pressing for more horse-racing, more casino gambling. More gambling was not at the top of any public opinion polls measuring the concerns of Illinois citizens as they moved into the twenty-first century. The gambling industry is sharply divided between casino interests and horse-racing interests that are, in turn, fragmented into individual gambling facilities that compete with every other facility for the gambling dollar. Anyone politician seeking to expand gambling faced opposition from the existing gambling interests. Opponents of gambling expansion, while small in number and poorly funded, had intensity and organization and a "good guy/white hat" issue. All of this hardly seems like a recipe for passing a gambling subsidy and expansion bill.

Except for the money. There was a huge amount of money to be made from expanding and subsidizing gambling. Just as important, there was a huge amount of money at the disposal of those who would benefit from the subsidies and expansion and from a campaign finance system that allowed those with money to make maximum use of it. With the openness of the Illinois campaign finance system, those individuals, groups, and corporations seeking to use money to influence the passage of the gambling bill were able to contribute as much as they wanted to the political committees of elected public officials and candidates for public office. As a result, by the end of the 1999 spring legislative session, a bill was signed into law providing for subsidies and tax breaks for horse-racing tracks, for dockside gambling in river-boat casinos, and for the shifting of a casino license to the city of Rosemont in Cook County.

Publicly sanctioned gambling has become a very big deal in Illinois. In 1999 wagers in legal gambling in Illinois topped $23.6 billion. While the Illinois State Lottery is a public operation (run by the Illinois Department of Lottery), horse racing and river-boat casinos are not. They are private operations that are licensed, regulated, and taxed by the state. State-sanctioned gambling is also an important source of state and local revenue. River-boat casinos, horse racing, and the state lottery generated more than $957 million in revenue for the state and local governments in 1999.

Given all of this, it is not surprising that gambling policy has become an increasingly visible and contentious issue before the Illinois General Assembly. The stakes have been very high. And with those high stakes has come an explosion of campaign contributions from gambling interests. Since 1993 the various interests contending over state gambling policy have battled in the legislature and sought to influence the Governor or candidates for governor. The amounts contributed by gambling interests during the past four election cycles are presented in Table 13. In 1991–92 the first river-boat casinos in Illi-

Table 13
Gambling Contributions

1991–1992	$ 100,000 (est.) River-boat casinos established in 1992
1993–1994	$1,371,000
1995–1996	$1,634,000
1997–1998	$1,944,000
1999–2000	$1,792,000

nois were just becoming operational. Gambling activity from horse racing had reached a plateau. During those two years, contributions from gambling interests to incumbents and candidates for legislative and state office totaled less than $100,000. In 1993–1994 contributions from horse-racing interests, river-boat casino license holders, and those seeking to expand river-boat casino gambling exploded to $1.346 million. In 1995–96 the total grew to $1.634 million. The gambling subsidy and expansion bill was passed and signed in the spring of 1999. During 1997–98, gambling interests contributed $1.949 million to incumbents and candidates for legislative and statewide office. During 1999–2000 they gave an additional $1,792,000. Between the beginning of 1993 and the end of 2000, gambling interests made more than $6.84 million in campaign contributions.

Given both the wide-open nature of Illinois' campaign finance system and the extreme centralization of legislative power in the hands of the four legislative leaders and the Governor, it is not surprising that campaign contributions from gambling interests flow to the centers of power within the system. Over the past seven years, those receiving the largest share of campaign contributions from gambling interests have been the legislative leaders and the legislative chamber political committees which they control. This also includes Governor Edgar and then candidate, and now Governor George Ryan.

A comparison of contributions from gambling interests to Governor Jim Edgar with contributions to Secretary of State (now Governor) George Ryan illustrates the point that, in Illinois, money flows to power. In 1993–94, when Governor Jim Edgar was winning re-election, he received $184,969 in contributions from gambling interests. In 1995–96 the total dropped to $82,561. In 1997 Governor Edgar announced he would not run for re-election. His 1997–98 contributions from gambling interests plummeted to $34,100. In 1993–94 George Ryan won re-election as Secretary of State. He received $57,250 in contributions from gambling interests. In 1995–96 the amount declined to $51,811. After becoming an announced candidate for Governor in 1997 and then the presumptive favorite to win in 1998, contributions from gambling interests to candidate and then Governor-elect Ryan skyrocketed.

His 1997–98 total was $428,209, with a majority of those contributions received during the last six months of 1998. Governor Ryan's 1997–98 total was more than eight times his total from the previous two years and more than twice the total Governor Edgar received in 1993–94 from the same sources. Part of the dramatic increase can be attributed to Governor Ryan's reputation as a deal maker and to his somewhat ambiguous position during the campaign on the expansion of river-boat gambling.

The pattern with respect to the four legislative leaders is just as clear. Between 1993 and 1999, the four legislative leaders took more than $2.80 million in contributions from gambling interests. Of that total, the leaders received $914,000 in 1997–98 and an additional $323,000 in 1998. Senate President James "Pate" Philip and the Senate Republican campaign committee received a total of $267,000 from gambling interests in 1997–98 and an additional $89,000 in 1999. Senate Democratic leader Emil Jones and the Senate Democratic campaign committee received $62,000 in 1997–98 and $37,000 in 1999. House Speaker Michael Madigan received a total of $123,000 from gambling interests in 1997–98 and an additional $33,000 in 1999. House Republican leader Lee Daniels and the House campaign committee received $452,000 in 1997–98 and $164,000 in 1999. In addition, the State Republican Party received $111,000 in 1997–98 and $17,000 in 1999, while the State Democratic Party received $64,000 in 1997–98 and $22,000 in 1999.

Overall, only 25% of gambling contributions went to rank-and-file legislators or legislative candidates. The other 75% went to the legislative leaders, the Governor and the other constitutional officers, and the two state political parties. The primary lessons learned from these election years are that money flows to power and that interests with significant financial resources can bring them quickly to bear on the centers of power in Illinois politics.

An examination of the contributions from the horse-racing interests illustrates what can happen in Illinois when a single group of interests with huge financial resources seeks access to power through a wide-open campaign finance system. Campaign contributions from horse racing interests are dominated by the companies and family members associated with the Duchossois name. Richard Duchossios is both the owner of Arlington International Race Track and Hill N' Dale Farms. His son is president of Duchossois Industries. Chamberlain Manufacturing and Thrall Car Manufacturing are both subsidiaries of Duchossois Industries. In addition, three Duchossois family members who made campaign contributions all list their address as that of Duchossois Industries. Interests associated with the Duchossois name contributed more than $672,000 in 1997–98 to the statewide elected officials, legislators, and legislative leaders.

Assuming that the contributions from these individuals and companies share a common interest, the Duchossois companies and family members are the largest non-association or non-group contributor to Illinois state level political campaigns. In 1997–98, only the Illinois Medical Society, the Illinois Education Association, the Illinois Federation of Teachers, the Illinois Manufacturer's Association and the Illinois Hospital and Health Systems Association gave more than the Duchossois total of $672,000.

Prior to 1999, the interests of the horse-racing, river-boat casino, and casino expansion groups were generally in conflict. As a result, campaign contributions from gambling interests were not all pushing in the same direction in terms of trying to influence public policy. Horse-racing interests wanted assistance from the state in the form of reduced taxes and direct subsidies to support what had become a stagnate industry. Pressure from river-boat casinos and off-track betting has hurt the horse-racing industry in Illinois. The state's major racetrack, Arlington International Race Track, suspended operation for the 1998 and 1999 seasons due to concerns over its economic viability. In addition to state assistance, horse-racing interests were opposed to the expansion of casino gambling, although there was some sentiment for expansion if it included casino gambling operations at horse-racing tracks. The river-boat casino interests were primarily concerned with resisting efforts to expand the number of casino gambling licensees and with resisting efforts to raise state or local taxes on their operations. The one positive legislative goal the casinos all shared was a change in law that would allow their continuous access to gamblers, through the elimination of the requirement that a river-boat casino actually leave the dock and sail. They were also opposed to any legislation that would strengthen the horse-racing industry. Those who wanted to increase the number of river-boat casino licensees faced strong opposition from the existing river-boat casinos and the horse-racing interests.

At the beginning of 1999, gambling interests had tremendous access to the Governor and the legislative leaders, based on a decade of ever-increasing campaign contributions. But their influence was severely limited by the seemingly conflicting goals of casinos, horse-racing, and those seeking an increase in the number of casino licenses. Those opposed to legalized gambling, in general, and the expansion of gambling in Illinois, in particular, found allies among horse-racing and river-boat casino interests when proposals were made to bring a casino to Chicago or Cook County. The anti-gambling forces could count on the river-boat casinos to oppose legislation aimed at helping horse-racing tracks and could count on horse-racing tracks to oppose legislation aimed at helping the river-boat casino industry. The prospect was that the long-term stalemate over changes in Illinois gambling policy would continue.

All of this changed in the spring of 1999. The potential for a grand coalition between the warring factions of the gambling interests had always been present in Illinois. Each of the groups had significant needs that could be addressed by changes in state law. The troubled economics of horse racing continued to be a concern for the industry, particularly for the owners of racetracks. The record for river-boat casinos was more positive, but still mixed. While three of the casino operations had financial problems, the overall health of the industry was excellent. The amount of casino gambling activity exceeded even the most optimistic of the early projections for the industry. However, like horse racing and the lottery, participation in casino gambling has been flat since 1996.

Those in Cook and Lake Counties seeking to expand casino gambling had been completely unsuccessful in their efforts to expand casino gambling through an increase in the number of licensees and a removal of the prohibition on river-boat casino gambling in Cook and Lake counties prior to 1998. But the potential economic bonanza kept the casino interests active in the legislature and contributing to political leaders.

When river-boat casino gambling was sold to the legislature in 1992, the principal argument was that it would provide tourism and economic development for depressed areas in the state. The reality is that the casinos with the largest base of potential customers (in Joliet, Peoria, Aurora, Elgin, East St. Louis, and Alton) have been the most successful. Casinos in smaller markets have not been the anchors for economic revival that early supporters suggested. The owners of the Silver Eagle in East Dubuque (H.P. Inc.) were denied a license renewal in July 1997 largely because the casino failed as a business. The boat halted operations at the end of the year. The availability of a casino gaming license became the lynch pin for the 1999 gambling agreement. It is ironic that the impetus for the 1999 law, which dramatically expanded gambling, came from the failure of casino gambling to achieve its stated public policy goal of promoting the redeveloping of smaller, economically depressed communities.

A gambling deal depended on four critical factors: satisfying horse-racing interests (particularly Duchossois), satisfying the owners of existing casino licenses, finding a way to bring a licensed casino to Chicago or Cook County in a way that would satisfy the mayor of Chicago, Richard Daley, and crafting a bill that the legislature would pass and the Governor would sign. In politics, a tried and true strategy for passing a bill is to make sure that everyone gets a piece of the pie. With the potential economic benefit for gambling interests, the potentially huge profits from a Cook-County-based casino, and a booming state budget as a source of money to sweeten the deal, the pie was more than adequate to do the job.

The basics of the agreement were (1) to provide tax breaks and subsidies to the horse-racing industry, particularly the owner of horse-racing tracks, (2) to provide dockside gambling for river-boat casinos, with continuous access to customers, and (3) to allow the owners of the casino in East Dubuque to regain their license and to move to the Village of Rosemont, which is in Cook County, next to O'Hare Airport. The side payments included (1) taking revenue from the relocated boat and using it to fund criminal justice facilities in Cook County and to fund renovations for the University of Illinois football stadium, (2) requiring that a portion of the ownership of the relocated casino be a female or a member of a minority ethnic group, (3) providing $30 million in general revenue-funding for economic development in depressed communities over five years, and (4) an agreement that the Village of Rosemont would share the local government portion of gambling tax revenue from the new casino with more than seventy villages in Cook County.

Unless one was a gambling opponent or a downstate legislator without a casino in his or her district, this truly was a bill with something for everyone. Richard Duchossois got tax breaks worth at least $6 million dollars a year, with the prospect of another $6–9 million in subsidies from the Rosemont casino. Owners of Illinois' other horse-racing tracks and the thoroughbred- and harness-racing industries also benefitted, but to a smaller extent. Existing casinos were able to expand the amount of time when gambling could take place in their facilities. Mayor Don Stephens of Rosemont got a huge engine to drive economic development and activity in his community. The owners of the re-licensed and re-located East Dubuque casino were able to dramatically increase its value. Mayor Daley got a gambling facility in Cook County with all the attendant economic benefits, plus a subsidy for county government operations. Minority legislators who initially blocked the bill in the Senate got money for economic development and diversity in the ownership of the new license. Legislative leaders, in general, and the Republican leaders, in particular, as well as the Governor, were able to assist some of their most important campaign contributors.

In the end, this agreement is a classic example of powerful interests and big money dominating the law-making process, with little regard for the overall public-policy merits of the legislation. These were not a set of good, stand-alone ideas that happened to be in the same bill. Most complex legislation contains a severability clause: if some portion of the bill is found unconstitutional, the rest of the bill will continue in force. The gambling bill had a non-severability clause. If the courts were to invalidate the transfer of the casino license, then dockside gambling and tax breaks for horse-racing track owners would also fall. The gambling interests did not trust each other or share their diverse goals, but the combination of access and influence and the potentially huge financial pay-off drove the deal and ultimately made it happen.

The danger of money and influence dominating policy-making is that important changes can be made without any serious public debate over the public-policy issues involved. Expanding gambling in Illinois raises a series of important public-policy questions. Is horse-racing a viable industry, even with massive public subsidies? Should Illinois facilitate a major expansion in the amount of casino gambling taking place? What are the implications of having (for all practical purposes) land-based casino gambling instead of river-boat excursion gambling? Having established casino gambling and expanded it to Cook County, can further expansion be resisted? Should it be? What are the social costs of increasing gambling in Illinois and how do they compare with the economic benefits of gambling? These are important questions, but the process that produced the 1999 gambling expansion bill largely ignored them.

Events since the gambling bill was signed into law suggest that the gambling debate is far from over. Revenue from the newly docked casino rose dramatically as soon as the new law was implemented. Proponents of gambling expansion will take that rise as a clear indication that the gambling market has not been saturated. A lawsuit was filed in a State court by supporters of a casino for Lake County to block the transfer of the East Dubuque casino to Rosemont. That litigation has halted construction activity by the Rosemont group and has led to an impasse before the Illinois State Gaming Board. If the Courts throw out the 1999 gambling bill, the pressure to construct an even more extensive gambling bill would be overwhelming.

The success of the 1999 gambling bill is a tribute to the power of money in Illinois politics. Money alone did not pass the bill, but the advantage in access and influence to those who have money over those who do not is painfully evident. Campaign contributions did not guarantee that the 1999 gambling bill would become law. But it would not have become law without them.

Liquor Distributors Distribute Money and Clout

On May 21, 1999, Governor George Ryan signed the Wine and Spirits Fair Dealing Act into law. The new law prohibited liquor manufactures with existing contracts with Illinois liquor distributors from canceling or changing those contracts unless they made a showing of "good cause" before the Illinois State Liquor Control Commission. The law was designed primarily to protect the financial interests of one company: Judge & Dolph, which is a subsidiary of the Wirtz Corporation. The legislation was intended as protection in Illinois against problems that Wirtz-owned liquor distributorships had been having with liquor manufacturers in Nevada.

William Wirtz heads the Wirtz Corporation. He is also owner of the Chicago Black Hawks and a major figure in Chicago sports and business. The story of the Fair Dealing Act is a classic example of the ease with which big money flows in the political process in Illinois and of the direct and indirect ways big money shapes the outcomes of public policy.

Campaign contributions buy access. Individuals, corporations, and groups with money will often make contributions, even though there are no pressing issues that affect the givers. Contributions are an investment in the future, actions of good will for a time when the interests of the giver are at stake. In early November 1994, a Nevada liquor distributor owned by the Wirtz Corporation gave House Democratic Leader Michael Madigan a $15,000 contribution. The House Republicans won a majority in the November election, and, a month later, a Minnesota liquor distributor owned by the Wirtz Corporation gave House Republican leader Lee Daniels a $6,250 contribution. The Wirtz Corporation also gave Governor Jim Edgar a total of $5,000 in 1993 and 1994. The Democrats regained control of the House in 1996. On November 5, 1996, a Texas-based liquor distributor owned by the Wirtz Corporation gave the House Democratic chamber committee $20,000. The same day a Wisconsin-based liquor distributor, also owned by the Wirtz Corporation, gave the House Republican chamber committee a $20,000 contribution. Judge & Dolph also made a $1,000 contribution to Governor Edgar in 1996. In most states and in federal elections, direct corporate contributions to candidates are illegal, but not in Illinois. When William Wirtz decided to seek help from the State of Illinois for his liquor distributor business in 1998, he was not a stranger in Springfield, particularly with legislative leaders in the house.

Legislation creating the Fair Dealing Act was formally introduced in the legislature in November 1998, but the campaign began almost a year earlier and proceeded on three fronts. In December 1997, the IWAPAC was formed as a political committee with the State Board of Elections. The IWAPAC is a political action committee for the Wine and Spirits Distributors of Illinois (WSDI). The IWAPAC was initially funded by contributions from individual liquor distributors, including Judge & Dolph. In the second half of 1998, the funding for IWAPAC was changed to lump-sum transfers from the WSDI. It is currently impossible to tell who is funding the WSDI and with what dollar amount, because the WSDI are not registered as a political committee and do not file disclosure reports with the Illinois State Board of Elections. Hence, the failure to file disclosure reports makes it impossible to tell who is funding the IWAPAC and in what amounts.

The IWAPAC did not exist until the last month of 1997. In 1998 it gave more than $123,000 to legislators and to the candidate who would be elected Governor in the fall election. A total of $15,000 went to House Speaker Madigan, $21,650 to House Republican Leader Daniels, $19,700 to Senate President Philip, and $7,500 to Senate Democratic Leader Jones. In addition to the $68,850 contributed to the four legislative leaders, the IWAPAC gave $4,300 to gubernatorial candidate George Ryan and most the remaining $55,000 to individual legislators.

In addition to working through the IWAPAC in 1998, the Wirtz Corporation was giving money directly to Illinois political leaders. On May 11, 1998 five out-of-state liquor distributors owned by the Wirtz Corporation each contributed $10,000 to the Republican candidate for Governor, Illinois Secretary of State George Ryan. In all, Ryan received $50,250 directly from corporate interests controlled by the Wirtz Corporation, plus an individual contribution of $1,000 from William Wirtz. Between September 15 and October 13, 1998, liquor distributors controlled by the Wirtz Corporation gave $70,000 to the four legislative leaders, with all but $10,000 coming from out-of-state companies. House Speaker Madigan received $25,000, as did House Republican Leader Daniels, while Senate President Philip and Senate Democratic Leader Jones each received $10,000. The combined 1998 total of contributions to the four legislative leaders and to the Governor-elect from companies owned by the Wirtz Corporation and the IWAPAC was more than $193,000. Individual legislators also received more than $55,000 in contributions from the IWAPAC. All of this money was contributed before the Fair Dealing bill was introduced in November.

In addition to making direct contributions, groups, corporations, and individuals with money can hire lobbyists to represent their interests before the legislature and the governor. In 1998, the Wirtz Corporation had a number of people employed directly by the corporation who were registered lobbyists in Springfield. It had also retained a small number of contract lobbying firms and individual lobbyists. By the time the Fair Dealing Act passed the legislature in 1999, the number of contract lobbying firms and individual lobbyists employed by the Wirtz Corporation had grown to twenty-two. Most notable among the lobbyists were former Governor James Thompson of the Winston and Strawn law firm, former Senate President Phil Rock, and a number of prominent Chicago law firms. Contract lobbyists are hired because they know the process, know the people, and have access and credibility with the governor, the legislative leaders or the members. They build relationships and gain expertise over time. This type of representation gives a corporation a huge home-court advantage over individuals or other groups who either can't afford Springfield-based people to represent them or don't realize they need such people.

The top contract lobbyists or lobbying firms in Springfield do not come cheap. Unlike some states, fee arrangements do not have be disclosed in Illinois, but a fee for a single project at this level will run from five to six figures. Part of what one is paying for is the access and good will that the lobbyists and lobbying firms have built up over time. And part of that access and good will is built by the campaign contributions the lobbyists make. Money going to a lobbyist with the understanding that it will be passed on to a specific politician is not considered money laundering. Such contributions are general ones made in the name of the lobbyist or lobbying firm. But their fees are set to include the cost of making general campaign contributions in the name of the firm or lobbyist.

The lobbying firms and lobbyists employed by the Wirtz Corporation gave more than $360,000 to legislative leaders, legislators, and constitutional officers in 1997–98. Those contributions buy general visibility, access, and good will that are employed on behalf of a client, such as the Wirtz Corporation. Part of the fees charged by these lobbying firms and lobbyists go toward campaign contributions, but the linkage to the client is almost always indirect. The Wirtz Corporation was buying the lobbyist's access and influence. That access and influence was built partially on campaign contributions financed by fees charged to previous clients. Future clients of these lobbying firms will be buying access and influence that have been sustained by campaign contributions funded in part by fees paid by the Wirtz Corporation in 1998 and 1999.

In 1999, both before and after the Fair Dealing Act became law, the IWAPAC contributed an additional $103,000, with $11,000 going to Governor Ryan, $31,000 to the four legislative leaders, and $61,000 to individual legislators. The Wirtz Corporation contributed less than $5,000 in 1999. During 1998 and 1999, total contributions from corporations controlled by the Wirtz Corporation and from the IWAPAC were more than $357,000. Governor Ryan received more than $77,000, House Republican leader Daniels $55,000, House Speaker Madigan $52,000, and Senate President Philip and Senate Democratic Leader Jones $30,000 each. Individual legislators received more than $123,000 altogether.

The Wirtz interests were successful from the beginning in characterizing the conflict as one between an Illinois business and big international companies. In contrast to the campaign contributions from the Wirtz side, the principal corporations involved in the dispute with Wirtz contributed almost nothing during 1998 or 1999. They did hire a prominent contract-lobbying firm to represent them. The liquor manufacturers' strategy was largely one of framing the issue as a protectionist, anti-competitive measure that was bad public policy.

The Fair Dealing Act passed the House in the fall of 1998 during the veto session, but it stalled in the Senate. The Wirtz group re-started its lobbying in the spring of 1999. In spite of strong editorial opinion against the bill and at least verbal support from general business groups, the bill passed both the House and the Senate by large margins and was signed into law at the end of the spring session. While the liquor manufacturers probably won the policy debate, they lost the lobbying battle.

Did the Wirtz Corporation buy a law? In terms of a straight quid pro quo, the answer is no. But it did sell the new law to the legislature and the governor with the help of campaign contributions and high-priced contract lobbyists. As a prominent Illinois businessman, would Wirtz have been able to get the attention of the legislative leaders and the governor without making more than $300,000 in contributions and hiring twenty-two contract lobbyists? Probably. Would the legislation have been considered in the veto session at the end of the two-year legislative session? Probably not. Did Wirtz's advantage in campaign contributions and in lobbying activity make it much more difficult for the opponents to make their case with the legislative leaders and the Governor? Certainly. Would limits on the role of money in Illinois politics produce a different outcome? Probably, if the result was a less leadership-dominated, more open process, with more independent members. But, as with all political reforms, that is a big if.

Interest groups, corporations, and individuals with narrow issues and legislative access and skill, or the money to purchase access and skill, will flourish in a system where power is concentrated in the hands of a few leaders and the campaign finance process is wide-open. The Fair Dealing Act is not the kind of issue that a legislator is likely to feature in a constituent newsletter or a campaign ad. Very few legislators and even fewer citizens understood or cared about the Fair Dealing Act as it moved through the legislature But the legislative leaders and the governor did.

Once the Fair Dealing Act became law, the liquor manufactures brought suit in Federal court to overturn it. They were successful, and the case is now on appeal. The expectation is that this issue will come before the Illinois legislature again. The contribution activity by the liquor distributors and the liquor manufactures since the litigation began also speaks volumes about the role of money in lobbying strategies in Illinois. Table 14 shows these contributions since 1995. Contributions for liquor manufactures were less than $9,000 in the two years before the bill was signed. In the fall of 1999, contributions from liquor manufacturers under the UDV name (United Distillers and Vintners of North America) started appearing in the campaign finance reports of legislators and constitutional officers. The total from UDV for 1999–2000 was $368,000. UDV's dramatic entry was followed by over

Table 14
Liquor Distributor and Liquor Manufacturer Contributions

	Liquor Distributors*	Liquor Manufacturers**
1995–1996	$48,000	$6,000
1997–1998	$283,000	$9,000
1999–2000	$280,000	$369,000
2001 (six months)	$200,000	$64,000

* Wine & Spirits Distributors (IWA) & Wirtz-owned distributors
** Distilled Spirits Council prior to 1999, United Distillers & Vintners (UDV) after 1999

$200,000 in campaign contributions from the liquor distributors in the first six months of 2001. One lesson the liquor manufacturers seem to have learned from their fight over the Fair Dealing Act is that major campaign contributions are an important part of a lobbying strategy in Illinois, particularly if one is facing an opponent who is a big contributor.

Money and Policy in Illinois Politics

Money does not always win. Every bill that the legislature passes and the governor signs has a public-policy content. The boilerplate language in the 1999 gambling bill stressed the need for economic development and the importance of horse-racing as an agri-business. But money is critically important to lobbying, both in terms of campaign contributions and in terms of hiring lobbyists to push legislation. One of the gambling bill supporters talked about having a hundred lobbyists working on the bill. Even if one discounts that figure by 50%, the impact of such an effort is critical. And the cost is tremendous. Public-policy questions can get lost when big money and organizations fight big organizations and money. When unrepresented or under-represented interests face off against well-organized, well-funded interests, the potential for distortion and bias in public-policy jumps dramatically. The result is often one-sided, with outcomes ranging from the dramatic (the 1999 gambling bill and the 1999 Wirtz liquor distributor bill) to the quiet (the bills that are not introduced or amended because no one is willing to take on powerful interests).

Campaign Finance Reform in Illinois

What are the prospects for campaign finance reform in the unregulated state of Illinois? The Illinois State Constitution contains no general initiative process through which a new campaign finance law could be placed before the state's voters for consideration. If one combines this lack with a political culture that is primarily about winning, power, control, jobs and financial gain, and legislative leaders and governors who have learned to be successful under the existing system, one does not have a recipe for change. The history of campaign finance reform in Illinois is both limited and recent. The basic state law was unchanged from 1976 to 1997. The reforms of 1997 and 1998, while monumental by Illinois standards, would strike most observers as very modest. After the legislature has passed "reform," its natural tendency is to say "our job is done here" and then move on. So the short-term prospects for change are not good.

Long-term prospects are another story. Illinois has the best electronic filing and disclosure system in the country. Having completed a thirty-year natural experiment in how a political system would evolve with a completely unregulated campaign finance system, the mechanisms are in place for another natural experiment. Will transparent access by the press, the public, and political actors to knowledge of where money comes from and how it is spent really make a difference in how the actors in the political system behave? Will the result be a silent yawn? Or will an aroused and enraged public demand contribution limits and public financing? If the response is a silent yawn, then Illinois will continue to be Illinois. As one long-time incumbent legislator summed it up, "I like to be the people's representative. The problem is that the people don't have any money."

References

Gove, Samuel K., and James D. Nowlan. 1996. *Illinois politics and government: The expanding metropolitan frontier*. Lincoln NB and London: University of Nebraska Press.

Gurwitt, Rob. 1992. The mirage of campaign reform. *Governing* (August): 48–55.

Hartley, Robert E. 1999. *Paul Powell of Illinois: A lifelong Democrat*. Carbondale and Edwardsville, IL: Southern Illinois University Press.

Makinson, Larry. 1994. *Follow the money handbook*. Washington, D.C.: Center for Responsive Politics.

Redfield, Kent D. 1995. *Cash clout: Political money in Illinois legislative elections*. Springfield, Illinois: Institute for Public Affairs, University of Illinois at Springfield.

———. 1998. What keeps the Four Tops on top? Leadership power in the Illinois General Assembly. In *Almanac of Illinois politics—1998*, edited by Jack R. Van Der Slik. Springfield, Illinois: University of Illinois at Springfield.

———. 2000. Political education: The role of teacher unions in funding Illinois politics. In *Almanac of Illinois politics—2000*, edited by David A. Joens. Springfield, Illinois: University of Illinois at Springfield.

————. 2001. *Money counts: How dollars dominate Illinois politics and what we can do about it*. Springfield, Illinois: Institute for Public Affairs, University of Illinois at Springfield.

Sabato, Larry J. 1989. *Paying for elections: The campaign political thicket*. New York: Priority Press Publications.

Smith, Bradley A. 2001. *Unfree speech: The folly of campaign finance reform*. Princeton, NJ: Princeton University Press.

Wheeler, Charles N., III. 2000. The days of pork and pander: Politicians begin the fall campaign. *Illinois Issues* (May): 42–43.

CHAPTER 3

THE "BAYH"-ING OF INDIANA POLITICS: THE CHANGING FACE OF CAMPAIGN FINANCE IN THE HOOSIER STATE

James L. McDowell
Robert K. Goidel

The 1990s were a time of considerable change in laws governing the flow of money into state campaigns. Indiana, with its individualistic political culture and part-time legislature, has not been at the forefront of this reform movement. In fact, laws governing campaign finance in Indiana state elections have remained virtually unchanged since the last great wave of reform spurred by Watergate in the mid-1970s. Yet, if the laws have remained relatively constant, electoral politics in Indiana have undergone a sea change, and not necessarily in ways that one would expect. Understanding the nature of this change helps to illustrate the malleability of campaign finance systems, even in the absence of legal reform.

The results of presidential campaigns since 1968 suggest that Indiana is a Republican state, but state politics tells a much different story. Since the election of Evan Bayh in 1988, Democrats have occupied the governor's mansion, while either controlling or sharing control of the state House of Representatives (except for the 1995–1996 session). Democrats also captured the Indianapolis mayor's office in 1999 in the most expensive municipal campaign in state history. While explanations for the resurgence of the Democratic Party are complex and varied, at least part of the story involves successful Democratic fund-raising within a context that, by all accounts, should have favored the Republican Party.

Several themes emerge in this chapter. First, once considered a state dominated by strong party organizations, Indiana moved into the era of candidate-centered campaigns with the election of Evan Bayh as governor. Bayh's campaigns stressed fiscal responsibility and conservative "Hoosier" values, with little mention of partisan affiliation. Frank O'Bannon, Bayh's less charismatic successor, has run similar, successful campaigns. Second, the most notable change in state legislative campaigns has been the growth in leadership fund-raising efforts and the distribution of those funds to other candidates. Using leadership positions as a fund-raising tool has allowed the Democrats to surpass the Republicans in terms of total money raised, thus assuring that Democratic candidates in competitive districts will not be outspent by their Republican opposition. Like Republicans at the national level, minority-party status encouraged the Democrats to be innovative in their fund-raising efforts. Increased competition—as partisan control of the House hangs continually in the balance—has encouraged a more aggressive and more innovative pursuit of campaign contributions.

Overall, the case study of Indiana campaign finance laws demonstrates the remarkable fluidity of campaign finance systems. Even with relatively modest legal change, campaign finance systems are in a constant state of flux, as candidates and parties attempt to manipulate the system to their advantage.

Party Competition and Change in Indiana

To outside observers, Indiana is considered a "safe" and conservative Republican state. The state is usually the first one awarded to the Republican presidential candidate by the television networks on Election Night broadcasts, and with good reason. Republican candidates carried the Hoosier State in 21 of 25 presidential elections in the 20th century, with Democrats gaining the state's electoral votes only in years when Republicans were politically divided (1912 and 1964) or during the Depression Era (1932 and 1936). Although Indiana produced two liberal Democratic U.S. Senators, Vance Hartke (1958–76) and Birch Bayh (1962–80), the state, more often than not, has been represented nationally by conservative Republican Senators and Representatives, notably William Jenner, whom Republican state leaders shunted off to the nation's capital from 1947 to 1959, where "he could do less harm as one of ninety-six senators in Washington than as governor of the state of Indiana" (Fenton 1966, 173).

Indiana's external political reputation also came about because Indianapolis, the capital and largest city, elected Republican mayors from 1967 to 1999. Often, Indianapolis was the nation's only large city with Republican political leadership during this time. The partisan success was enhanced by a unique governmental setting, engineered by party leadership. The combination of the election of a Republican mayor, Richard G. Lugar, in 1967, and the election of both a Republican governor and a Republican majority in both houses of the General Assembly in 1968, produced a governmental reorganization of Indianapolis and a political move of untold value. The legislature, in its 1969 session, merged most Indianapolis and Marion County functions (without submitting the measure to a public referendum) into the consolidated government of Indianapolis-Marion County, or "Unigov." This unification not only streamlined local government to some degree but also permitted the heavily Republican townships in the county to vote for mayor and a county-wide legislative body. The then-Marion County Republican chairperson later called the creation of Unigov "my greatest coup ever…, taking in 65,000 more Republican voters" (Roberts 1987, 6).

Republican mayoral candidates won seven consecutive elections through 1995 and so dominated the twenty-nine-member City-County Council that their numbers alone usually constituted a quorum (twenty members). However, Republican success in Indianapolis was attributable not only to this political masterstroke but also to the superior financial resources and campaign skills of the party's central committee. The general ineffectiveness of Marion County Democrats also contributed to Republican fortunes. In 1987, for example, Democrats could not find a viable mayoral candidate and drafted a political unknown on the final day of the primary filing period. In 1995, the party was unable to afford television advertising for yet another political unknown. This situation, however, abruptly changed in 1999, when Democrats captured the Indianapolis mayor's office in the most expensive municipal campaign in state history and also held Republicans to a 15–14 majority on the City-County Council.

In terms of *state* politics, however, Indiana emerged in the late twentieth century as a competitive two-party state. Republicans dominated the General Assembly from 1921 to 1969, a situation attributed to the legislature's refusal to redistrict after 1921. (The legislature was later forced to do so after the U.S. Supreme Court's "one person, one vote" ruling.) But both Democrats and Republicans elected six governors during this period. While indices of party control, using gubernatorial- and legislative-election results, classified Indiana as a "modified one-party Republican" state from 1964 to 1973, these same measures placed Indiana among the ranks of "two-party states"—albeit just barely—for the 1974–88 time frame. Employing the same "party control index" used in previous calculations, researchers placed Indiana at the midpoint of "two-party competition" for the period 1989–94 (Bibby and Holbrook 1996). Democratic victories in the governor's races of 1996 and 2000, and Democratic control of the Indiana House in 1998 and 2000, following a 50–50 split in 1996, have sustained this ranking.

In many ways, Indiana politics have been the inverse of national politics over the last several decades, with minority Democrats wresting control from an entrenched Republican establishment. While the increased competitiveness of Indiana Democrats reflects a myriad of complex and overlapping factors, at least part of the change is rooted in the success of Democratic fund-raising efforts. Since the election of Evan Bayh in 1988, Democratic candidates have achieved rough parity with Republicans in terms of campaign spending in most competitive races. Indeed, while Democratic candidates might be outspent, they are less likely to lack sufficient resources to mount a credible and competitive campaign. Notably, these changes in electoral competition and fund-raising are not associated with major or drastic revisions in Indiana campaign finance laws but reflect the skillful manipulation of loopholes in, and a lackadaisical enforcement of, existing laws.

A Brief History of Indiana Campaign Finance Laws

Campaign finance laws can generally be divided into four distinct categories: disclosure requirements, contribution limits, spending ceilings, and public financing. Indiana, along with other states and the national government, wrestled periodically and largely inadequately with the problems associated with money in politics throughout the twentieth century. In its legislative attempts to deal with these issues, Indiana initially focused on disclosure and spending limits, and prohibited corporations and unions from making political contributions. The state never embraced public financing up front but created a backdoor approach in the 1930s by which political party committees received funding through the sale of automobile license plates.

For most of this period, the state functioned under the Indiana Corrupt Practices Act of 1911. Virtually unchanged over the next sixty-five years, the law required that candidates file reports of campaign receipts and expenditures within forty-five days after a primary or general election. This law also imposed spending limits of $25,000 for statewide offices, $10,000 for congressional races, $5,000 for city or county offices, and $2,000 for any other offices. The law, however, provided exceptions to these spending limits for a candidate's *personal* expenditures, which specifically included postage, telegrams, telephone calls, printing, advertising, travel, and room and board. Further, the law classified a candidate's failure to file a report as only a misdemeanor, subject to a $500 fine, and a corporation's and a union's failure to report also as a misdemeanor, with the same penalty.

Under this statute, a candidate found guilty of engaging in "corrupt practices" simply had his election voided and was rendered ineligible to hold appointive or elective office for four years. Few individuals were ever found to have violated this law, however, because the statute created no statewide enforcement agency. Implementation of the law was the responsibility of local prosecuting attorneys.

The loopholes in the Indiana law were painfully obvious and invited exploitation. Since the only required reports of campaign contributions and disbursements came more than six weeks after an election, there could be virtually no adverse reaction from the voters. The list of exceptions for a candidate's personal spending was so broad that evasion of the stated limits seemed unnecessary and enforcement virtually impossible. The section voiding a candidate's election was so broadly interpreted that it was all but inapplicable. For example, courts held that candidates were not responsible for any action taken by an "agent." Corporations and unions easily sidestepped and flagrantly ignored prohibitions on political donations. Recognizing these practices, the legislature in the 1950s authorized these groups to advertise in a "bipartisan political almanac" that was created as a fund-raising device. But this action did not deter business and labor from continuing to circumvent the law.

In the aftermath of the Watergate scandal, the Indiana General Assembly substantially reformed the state's campaign finance law. Essentially, Hoosier legislators joined a national trend by abolishing spending limitations and adopting more stringent disclosure requirements, including lower contribution thresholds and more timely filings of reports.

In 1974, the legislature required candidates for statewide and legislative offices to file statements of economic interest and reports of campaign contributions in excess of $50 with their declarations of candidacy. In 1975, conceding that corporations and unions provided political money in one form or another, the legislature legitimized the practice by limiting contributions from these sources to a total of $8,000 each year: to $3,000 to either a statewide candidate or a state central committee, and to $1,000 to either a local candidate or a local political committee.

In 1976, the General Assembly passed its most extensive campaign practices regulations. Applicable to all state and local candidates, except those whose annual salaries were less than $2,000, the law provided for extensive record-keeping requirements, filing of pre-election and post-election reports, state and local campaign supervision, and substantially increased penalties.

Under the new legislation, each candidate had to establish a political committee with a chairman and treasurer, although the candidate could fill these positions. The law required treasurers to maintain records of all contributions and expenditures of more than $25, report the names and addresses of persons making aggregate contributions of $100 or more, and the names, addresses, occupations and principal places of business to whom payments of $100 or more are made. The law also required political committees to complete reports of contributions and expenditures fifteen days before and twenty days after either a primary or general election and to deliver these reports to the appropriate agency no later than eight days before or forty-seven days after an election. Political committees also had to file an annual report by January 31, covering all activity in the preceding calendar year.

This new law also mandated the state election board and county election boards to report apparent violations of the statute to the Attorney General or the local prosecuting attorney, respectively. Each election board could also report alleged violations to the appropriate grand jury for its investigations. The new statute made the filing of a fraudulent report or willfully failing to file a report a felony, punishable by a fine of up to $10,000 or by a term of up to two years in prison, or both. The law also made failing to file a report within thirty days, after being notified of the failure to file, a misdemeanor, punishable by a fine of up to $5,000 or by a term of up to one year in prison, or both.

For all this rather bold approach and break with tradition, this attempt at campaign finance reform in Indiana neither met its announced intentions nor was strictly enforced. Indeed, the General Assembly took a significant step back in 1986 with little, if any, public concern. The legislature that year revised the law to permit *increased* contributions by corporations and unions. The new limits allowed corporate and union donations of up to $5,000 apportioned among all statewide candidates; a total of $5,000 apportioned among all state central committees; an aggregate of $2,000 in *each* of the following cases—among all candidates for the state Senate, among all candidates for the state House of Representatives, and among all candidates for school boards and other local offices; and, meaningfully, an aggregate of $2,000 in *each* of these cases—among campaign committees organized by the Senate and House legislative caucuses. Not coincidentally, Indiana's legislative caucus campaign committees became major financial factors in assembly races in the next election cycle.

The General Assembly in recent years also significantly watered down the importance of campaign reports. While a committee must complete a report twenty-five days prior to an election, it has seven days to deliver this report by hand or by mail, or to file it by electronic mail to the appropriate election board. The law also abolished the post-election report, requiring only that a candidate's committee, legislative caucus committee, or political action committee file an annual report by the third Wednesday in January of the following year. Regular state party committees must file annual reports by March 1 of the following year. Initially, the legislature set a penalty for failure to file reports to a fine not exceeding $100, but it increased this penalty to a maximum of $1,000 in 1993.

Essentially, Indiana's approach to campaign finance issues may be summed up by the legislature's response to a joint investigation of interest-group influence in the 1995 General Assembly by the Center for Public Integrity, a Washington, D.C.-based public interest research group, and by the *Indianapolis Star*, the state's major newspaper. Published in the *Indianapolis Star*, February 11, to February 15, 1996, during the assembly's short session under the provocative title "Statehouse $ellout," a week-long series of articles detailed, in the newspaper's terms, "how special interests highjacked the legislature." The exposé made campaign finance and lobbyist reform become major discussion items in the fall gubernatorial campaign. But neither newly-elected Democratic Governor Frank O'Bannon nor the General Assembly strongly pursued the topics in the 1997 session.

Lawmakers that year responded to public- and press-criticism of their relationships with lobbyists by prohibiting fund-raising efforts during the session, but they did not seriously disturb their connections with interest group representatives. In Indiana, social interaction between lawmakers and lobbyists has been a way of life that neither side has wished to end. Luncheons and dinner affairs have developed to the point that interest groups schedule receptions through the official legislative offices to reduce conflicting events. While banning individual and small-group meetings, the legislature exempted social occasions to which all members of the General Assembly were invited.

Finally, Indiana never endorsed public financing of statewide or legislative campaigns, but the legislature for years permitted the indirect support of state central committees and county political organizations through the sale of automobile license plates. Initiated under the administration of Democratic Governor Paul V. McNutt (1933–37), Indiana did not provide these services through a state agency but franchised this operation to the chairperson of the governor's political party in each county. Under state law, each county chair employed all personnel from the party faithful, collected a portion of the service charge to support local party activities, and forwarded another share to help fund state central committee activities. Thus, all Indiana drivers contributed to the governor's political party, not necessarily by choice.

Both parties benefitted from and supported the system since its inception. Democrats held the governor's office twenty-four of the thirty-six years from 1933 to 1969, but Republicans won five consecutive gubernatorial elections and controlled the license branches from 1969 through 1989, which aided their domination of state government during this period. However, a series of scandals in the early 1980s, involving mismanagement of license branch accounts and the conviction of several branch managers for embezzlement, brought an end to the system in 1989. Coupled with other administrative scandals during this decade, the license branch mishaps convinced the General Assembly to restructure the system, turning the licensing procedure over to the Bureau of Motor Vehicles. Newly-elected Democratic Governor Bayh did not object, although the change provoked complaints from party officials, since it cost Democrats their first chance at this source of both patronage and funding in two decades.

In summary, Indiana's approach to campaign finance regulation has evolved from modest efforts at disclosing receipts and expenditures that were easily evaded and rarely enforced; through a period of more restrictive disclosure requirements, also seldom implemented; to the current relaxed policies that emphasize disclosure but permit corporate and union contributions, and allow unlimited individual and political action committee contributions. Public access to campaign finance information has been enhanced in recent years, although this information is available on-line only from 1994. That the state has progressed this far is largely the product of external forces. Only after a Washington, D.C.-based public interest research group and the state's largest newspaper combined to produce a comprehensive examination of the state's campaign finance sources and practices did the legislature in 1997 fund conversion of the paper-based campaign report filing system to an electronic database.

The Money and Politics Mix

Indiana's largely deregulated campaign finance environment might lead one to believe that election costs are skyrocketing. But, while spending in election campaigns has increased significantly, Indiana campaigns are, relatively speaking, not terribly expensive. During the 2000 elections, total spending for gubernatorial elections remained under $20 million, a slight decrease under 1996 levels, once inflation is taken into account. In a competitive statewide campaign for Attorney General, campaign spending topped $1.6 million, certainly not an insignificant amount, but unusually large by Indiana standards. Aside from the race for governor, this was the most expensive statewide race in Indiana during the 2000 election cycle. Total campaign spending for a seat in the narrowly divided Indiana House was roughly $7.3 million, or approximately $73,000 per election. As in most states, however, totals and averages

Table 1
Contributions and Expenditures by Party and Office Sought

	Contributions	Expenditures
Governor		
Democratic	$9,831,379	$9,657,955
Republican	$8,746,057	$8,349,167
Total	$18,577,436	$18,007,123
Attorney General		
Democratic	$973,876	$885,722
Republican	$698,037	$649,752
Total	$1,671,913	$1,535,475
State Representative		
Democratic	$5,973,820	$4,400,354
Republican	$5,567,278	$2,969,851
Total	$11,541,101	$7,370,205
State Senate		
Democratic	$762,247	$471,361
Republican	$1,660,970	$1,144,478
Total	$2,423,222	$1,245,842

Source: Indiana Elections Commission, based on annual reports filed by the respective committees. (Spending prior to January 1, 2000 would not be included). Data may include spending by candidates not in the general election.

are somewhat misleading, given that much of the spending occurs in a handful of races both parties deem competitive.

With the Indiana Senate firmly in Republican hands and with generally fewer competitive elections, spending in Indiana State Senate campaigns is considerably less than spending in state House campaigns. During the 2000 elections, total spending in twenty-five Indiana Senate races was estimated at $1.2 million, or roughly $48,000 per election. The Indiana Senate is an anomaly as well, in terms of the partisan breakdown in candidate campaign spending. In each of the other races included in Table 1, Democratic spending exceeds or is in rough parity with Republican spending. In Indiana Senate elections, Democrats were outspent two to one during the 2000 election cycle, and, not coincidentally, control only nineteen of fifty seats.

Gubernatorial Elections

Indiana's Constitution of 1851 limited the governor to one four-year term. As one of several elements of constitutional reform in the late 1960s and early 1970s, the state's voters amended their charter in 1972 to permit their chief executive to seek re-election to a second term. Since adoption of this provi-

Figure 1.
Campaign Spending in Indiana Gubernatorial Elections, 1980–2000
(in millions of real 1992 dollars)

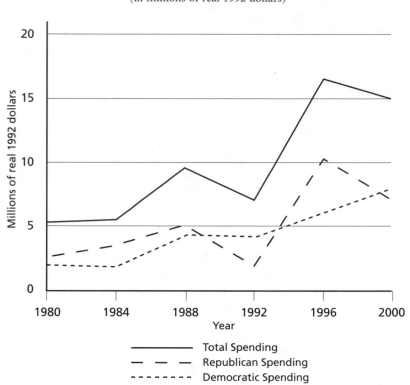

sion, each governor won two terms: Republicans Otis Bowen (1973–81) and Robert Orr (1981–89), and Democrats Bayh (1989–97) and O'Bannon (1997–date).

While Indiana elections have been relatively inexpensive, there has been a discernable trend toward increasingly expensive gubernatorial campaigns, with a dramatic increase in 1996, when Bayh was term-limited from office. As a general rule, open-seat elections are more expensive than elections in which an incumbent seeks reelection. On this particular point, Indiana is no exception. As can be seen in Figure 1, the more expensive open-seat election in 1988, the year Bayh first won election, was followed by a less expensive campaign in 1992, when Bayh ran as the incumbent. In 1996, without Bayh's presence, campaign spending skyrocketed. In 2000, total spending (in current dollars) increased yet again, surpassing the record spending in 1996, though once inflation is accounted for, spending was actually less in the 2000 gubernatorial campaign than in 1996. Notably, from 1980–2000, the only races in which Democratic spending exceeded Republican spending involved Democratic incumbents seeking reelection.

Competitive primaries tend to bode poorly for Indiana gubernatorial candidates. In 1980 and 1984, the eventual Democratic nominee won the primary with 52% and 57% of the vote, respectively, but then went on to lose the general election with 42% and 47% of the vote, respectively. In both elections Orr, the Republican candidate, faced either no primary opposition (in 1980) or minimal opposition (in 1984). In 1988, Bayh faced minimal opposition on his way to the first Democratic gubernatorial victory in Indiana since 1964, and then, in 1992, faced no opposition as the Democratic incumbent. In 1988, his Republican opponent, John Mutz, won the primary without opposition, while in 1992, eventual Republican nominee, Linley Pearson, failed to carry a majority of the Republican electorate. In 1996, the cast of Republican gubernatorial candidates ran deep enough to mount a three-way primary fight. Collectively, losing Republican primary candidates spent nearly $3 million, not enough to win the nomination, but enough to create real problems for eventual Republican nominee, Steven Goldsmith, the Indianapolis mayor who won the primary with 55% of the vote. Goldsmith, however, then narrowly lost to Lieutenant Governor O'Bannon in the general election, a major factor being his loss of Indianapolis-Marion County. O'Bannon secured the Democratic nomination in 1996 without a primary fight, enabling him to reap the benefits of an expensive and negative Republican primary. In the 2000 campaign, Republican challenger David McIntosh faced only modest opposition in the primary but couldn't overcome a popular incumbent, running with the benefits of both a then-strong economy and a $1.9 billion state surplus.

While Bayh was term-limited in 1996, his political persona has provided the basic contour of Indiana politics since his emergence as a gubernatorial candidate in 1988. Since that time, Democrats have controlled the governor's office and elected a majority or managed an even division of the Indiana House in all but the 1995–1996 sessions. In some ways, Bayh's election in 1988 resembles a critical election with an apparent partisan realignment following, but the realignment is more apparent than real. If anything, Bayh moved the state toward a more candidate-centered form of politics, in which partisan affiliation takes a backseat to candidate image and generic appeals to "Hoosier values." In 1996, four years before George W. Bush popularized the term at the national level, Bayh's successor, O'Bannon, ran as a "compassionate conservative." By downplaying partisan affiliation, Democrats have been more successful in state elections, but there has been little, if any, liberalizing of either the electorate or public policy.

State Legislative Elections

The Indiana General Assembly consists of a House of Representatives, whose 100 members serve two-year terms, and a fifty-member Senate, whose members serve four-year terms, with half of the membership elected every two years. Hoosier lawmakers are not subject to term limits, and, while legislative service is not the primary occupation of most members, Indiana ranks among states with the lowest turnover percentages. One study, covering the 1987–1997 period, indicates that Indiana turnover rate of 58% for the state Senate and 64% for the state House was not only well below the national averages of 72% (senates) and 84% (houses) but lower than figures for all but five other state senates and three state houses of representatives (Rosenthal 1998).

For all practical purposes, Indiana provided a prototypical state legislature prior to the reform movement of the late 1960s. Each odd-numbered year, members suspended their work as farmers and lawyers and in small businesses to convene for sixty-one calendar days to conduct the state's affairs. This period was viewed as sufficient time to provide representative government at low cost but to prevent members from gathering long or often enough to enact drastic or foolish changes in state law. Members serving in 1969 received an annual salary of $1,800, with no expense allowances.

Since adoption of a constitutional amendment in 1970 that permits the legislature to determine the length and frequency of its sessions, the Indiana General Assembly has met annually. While not a "professional" legislature by any definition, the Indiana assembly has become considerably more "professionalized," now meeting for sixty days (through April 29) in odd-numbered years and twenty-nine days (through March 14) in even-numbered years. Although a "part-time" legislature, Hoosier lawmakers serve in what Alan Rosenthal (1998) describes as a highly work-intensive environment and consider themselves to have year-round commitment. Their monetary rewards also reflect their enhanced responsibilities. Although their annual salary is $11,600, daily expense allowances tied to federal levels, between-sessions allocations for legislative duties, and mileage allotments combine to boost the total annual compensation of members into the low- to mid-$30,000 range.

With the increased responsibilities has developed a greater emphasis on legislative campaigns and, necessarily, increased campaign spending. At least some portion of these changes can be traced to the court-ordered switch to population-based legislative districts. Prior to the 1964 U.S. Supreme Court decision in *Reynolds v. Sims*, Indiana's constitution barred the crossing of county lines in drawing district lines. Moreover, Indiana did not revise its assembly boundaries from 1921 to 1965. As a result, legislators were either the product of individual efforts or the result of county organizational politics, being all but ignored by the party's state central committees. Indiana's House Republican leader, who resigned his seat in 2001 to accept a lobbyist position, recalled the time when his party's candidates conducted only a single golf outing to finance their campaigns. One thirty-six-year veteran, now the Senate's most influential member on taxing and spending policies, won his first campaign for a House seat in 1966 for less than $600.

The creation of districts, including all or parts of several counties, not only negated the influence of county committees and chairs but necessitated creation of individual campaign committees and, more importantly, establishment of legislative caucus campaign committees. Relaxed campaign finance laws enhanced legitimate interest group contributions. Further, from a relatively inauspicious beginning in 1984, the lawmakers' election organizations, particularly in the House of Representatives, have become a significant factor in assembly campaigns.

For all of members' insistence that they serve in a "citizen legislature," it is not Indiana citizens who are principal contributors to legislative campaigns, especially successful efforts. In 1994 legislative races, 75.3% of campaign funds came from interest groups and legislative party committees; in the 1996 assembly campaigns, interest groups provided 53.3% and legislative committees 22.4% of all candidate backing. One recent study concludes that from 1994 to 1998, all candidates who received more than three-fourths of their funding from individual giving or contributions under $100 lost their races (McDowell 2001).

Indiana's campaign spending increased from $3.8 million in 1988 to $9 million in 1998, relatively modest figures compared to spending in other states, but sufficiently larger that the state's major newspaper lamented that legislative election costs were at "alarming levels." The rise in campaign costs is not distributed equally between the legislative chambers. As the Indiana Senate has been dominated by Republicans since the 1979 session, most campaign spending is directed toward control of the Indiana House of Representatives. Since 1988, not coincidentally the year of the first election of Governor Bayh, House races have been competitive: the lower chamber was deadlocked at 50–50 following both the 1988 and 1996 elections, while Democrats won narrow control in all other years through 2000, with the exception of 1994.

As Figure 2 indicates, the major increase in spending (73.7%) occurred in1990, the election that would determine control of redistricting for the coming decade. Slightly higher, but considerably more modest increases, occurred

Figure 2
Campaign Spending in Indiana State Legislative Elections
(in millions of dollars)

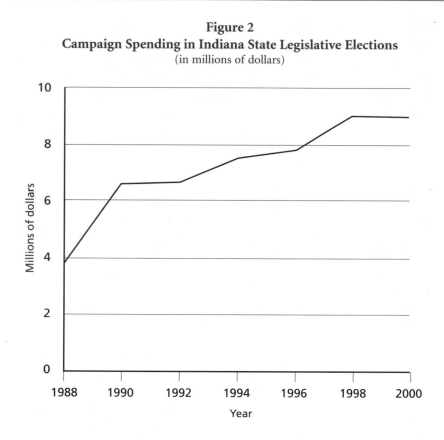

in the off-year elections of 1994 (11.9%) and 1998 (15.4%), with minuscule increases in presidential/gubernatorial election years. The ensuing redistricting produced by Democratic House wins in 1990 resulted in forty "safe" seats for each party, with control of the chamber depending on the outcome of the remaining twenty races. In reality, by the end of the decade, political observers suggested that while twenty House seats were "contested," only ten districts were truly "competitive." Each of these races in 1998 produced combined spending in excess of $234,000. The lack of competition is further indicated by House primary elections in 2000: only ten districts generated nominating contests in both political parties.

With control of redistricting again a major motivation in the elections of 2000, Indiana's legislative campaign committees focused attention and money on a dozen House districts. Although the combined spending for the two chambers has been approximately the same as in 1998, candidates for House seats spent nearly $8 million, or $1.3 million more than they spent two years

THE "BAYH"-ING OF INDIANA POLITICS · 113

earlier. Despite the millions expended, the partisan division remained the same after the 2000 elections, with Democrats retaining a 53–47 margin in the lower chamber. However, despite Governor O'Bannon's easy re-election, Indiana Republican House candidates fell only 1,900 votes short among the four closest races that would have given them control of the House.

By retaining their House margin, Democrats fashioned a redistricting plan in 2001 that many expect will permit the party to retain control—at least in the 2002 elections. Indiana's overall population increased 9.7%—to just over six million in the 2000 census (but not enough to prevent the state from losing a seat in the U.S. House of Representatives). The major population gains occurred in the heretofore generally Republican collar counties surrounding Indianapolis, but demographic shifts indicate these areas—like Marion County—are becoming more competitive.

Increased campaign funding in targeted districts by legislative committees is not the only source of election assistance provided by Indiana's lawmaking organizations. Both party caucuses in each chamber have authorized members to send constituent mailing not just to voters who elected them in 2000 but also to residents of new districts in which they will run in 2002. Clearly, the orientation of state legislative campaigns has changed in Indiana in recent years.

The Role of Political Parties

Since at least the 1980s, scholars have noted the resurgence of state and local political parties (Cotter, Gibson, Bibby, and Huckshorn 1984). As electoral politics was transformed from party-centered to candidate-centered campaigns, parties adapted to these changes by raising money and providing services to candidates. This transformation of the political parties assured that they would play an important, though perhaps not primary role, in the electoral process. As the minority party in national politics, Republicans were more innovative and effective in their party-building efforts. At the state, and at the local level as well, Republican party organizations were generally better funded and more professional than their Democratic counterparts. Much of these efforts were born out of Republican frustrations with their "permanent minority" status in national politics.

In the early 1980s, Indiana politics was similar to national politics in that a "permanent minority" struggled to find ways to compete with an entrenched majority. In Indiana, however, the players were on the opposite sides of the field. As such, it has been the Democrats who have been more innovative and aggressive in their fund-raising efforts. While the literature is ripe with warnings about attributing causality between money and votes (Jacobson 1980,

Table 2
Political Party Contributions and Expenditures
During the 2000 Election Cycle

	Contributions	Expenditures
State Central Committees		
Democrats	$6,028,999	$5,973,915
Republicans	$2,997,954	$2,879,916
State House Campaign Committees		
Indiana House Democratic Caucus	$2,257,755	$2,220,041
Indiana Republican Campaign Comm.	$1,964,817	$1,834,793
State Senate Campaign Committees		
Indiana Senate Democratic Comm.	$339,524	$284,310
Senate Majority Campaign Comm.		
(Republican Senate Comm)	$285,436	$276,770
Total Democratic State Party Spending	$8,626,278	$8,478,266
Total Republican State Party Spending	$5,248,207	$4,991,479
Total Spending State Parties	$13,874,485	$13,469,745

Source: Indiana Elections Commission, based on annual reports filed by the respective committees. (Spending prior to January 1, 2000 would not be included).

1990; Green and Krasno 1988; Goidel and Gross 1994), Democratic electoral success and Democratic fund-raising have clearly coincided, with Democratic electoral success following Democratic success in attracting campaign contributions.

As a general rule of politics, money follows political power. It is not surprising then that Democrats enjoyed a financial advantage over Republicans during the 2000 election cycle (See Table 2). With an incumbent and popular Democratic governor, the Democratic State Central Committee outpaced the Republican Committee roughly two to one in campaign contributions and expenditures. Democrats also have enjoyed a slim majority in the Indiana House, a fact reflected in the campaign fund-raising activities of the House campaign committees. The Indiana House Democratic Caucus raised and spent roughly $2.2 million, while the Indiana Republican Campaign Committee raised and spent just under $2 million. Among the state party committees, the least active have been the state Senate Campaign Committees, which spent just over $1.8 million. As noted earlier, the Senate is securely in Republican control, reducing the incentive for party-based fund raising. While the differences are small (as are the totals), the minority Indiana Senate Democratic Committee raised more money than the Republican Senate Majority Campaign Committee.

Table 3
National Party Transfers to Indiana Parties, Federal and Non-Federal

	Federal (Hard Money)	Nonfederal (Soft Money)	Total
National Party Committees			
DNC	$74,334	$329,815	$404,149
RNC	$37,113	$1,119,469	$1,156,582
Senate Campaign Committees			
Democratic	$25,000	$216,000	$241,000
Republican	—	$16,000	$16,000
House Campaign Committees			
Democratic	$284,879	$674,712	$959,591
Republican	$476,880	$586,615	$1,063,495
Total Democratic National Party	$384,213	$1,220,527	$1,604,740
Total Republican National Party	$513,993	$1,722,084	$2,236,077
Total National Party	$898,206	$2,942,611	$3,840,817

Source: Federal Election Commission Data.

The national parties also played a role in Indiana during the 2000 election cycle, with most of the assistance coming in the form of soft money and with national Republican Party organizations outpacing their Democratic counterparts. Aside from the figures displayed in Table 3, the Republican House Campaign Committee filtered $687,500 in hard dollars directly to state and local candidates, while the Democratic House Campaign Committee contributed $29,000. In addition, the Republican and Democratic House Campaign Committees filtered approximately $1 million to state and local parties in hard- and soft-money contributions. In contrast, the national Senate committees, but particularly the Republican Committee, had a much less visible presence in Indiana state politics. The Republican Senate committee filtered just $16,000 in soft money through Indiana state and local Republican parties. The Democratic Senate committee transferred a more substantial $241,000 but still lagged behind their counterparts in the House. This difference between chambers should hardly be surprising, given the importance of the 2000 election cycle for redistricting purposes and the narrow divisions between the parties both in the Indiana State House and the U.S. House of Representatives.

In total, the national parties filtered roughly $4.4 million to Indiana parties or candidates.[1]Consistent with recent trends, the overwhelming bulk of

---

1. This total includes direct contributions to state and local candidates, which are not included in the table.

national party money (nearly two-thirds of the total from national parties) has come in the form of soft money dollars. Approximately 60% of these funds come from Republican party organizations, with the Republican advantage apparent in both hard dollars and soft dollars. Of the national party sources, only the Republican Senate Committees were outpaced by their Democratic counterparts, but this is also the source from which we see the least financial activity.

Other Sources of Campaign Money

One of the myths of American campaign finance is that it is dominated by "fat cat" contributors and special interests. In fact, the U.S. system of campaign finance is remarkably broad-based. As Frank Sorauf has noted "no other system of campaign funding anywhere in the world enjoys so broad a base of support. None even approaches it" (1992). As in national politics, individual contributions dominate Indiana campaign finance. In the 2000 election cycle, individuals contributed roughly $42.1 million to Indiana candidates and parties, dwarfing all other sources of campaign contributions. Though corporations and labor unions are allowed to make direct contributions to candidates under Indiana law, their impact is fairly marginal. In the 2000 elections, corporations contributed just $141,000, while labor unions contributed a paltry $4,900. Even political action committees, which are allowed unlimited contributions by state law, contributed only $1.2 million during the 2000 election cycle.

Why the limited role of PACs, corporations, and labor unions despite lenient state laws? Money in politics has been likened to water flowing downhill: Any attempt to divert the water will simply send it in another direction (Sorauf 1992). With unlimited individual contributions and lax enforcement of existing laws, there is little need to filter money into these other avenues. Lest this sound like an endorsement of deregulated campaign finance systems, the relative importance of individual contributions and the disclosure of these records on the Internet hardly makes for a more informed public on the influence of interested money in state and local campaigns.

At the national level, individual "hard dollar" contributions are limited to $1000 per candidate per election, assuring at least some role for the small contributor (though that role has been greatly reduced by the increasing predominance of soft money and the issue-advocacy loophole that allows these non-federal dollars to spent on federal campaigns). Indiana places no such restrictions on individual contributions. Even without legal limits, however, most contributions remain under $1000. According to the data made available by the Indiana Elections Commission, only 843 contributions of $1000 or more were reported during the 2000 election cycle. More than half of these were for $1500 or less, and more than three-quarters were for $5000 or less. On the other end of the spectrum, less than twenty of these contributions were for $20,000 or more, while the single largest reported contribution was for $50,000.

Yet, if this alleviates some concern about the dominance of individual "fat cat" contributors, problems with disclosure remain. For contributions under $1000, there are no disclosure requirements for the contributor's occupation, making it virtually impossible to tie individual contributions to specific interests. Moreover, many contributions are made in $99 increments, allowing the contributor (as well as his or her occupation) to remain anonymous. As is the case in national politics, bundling is a common practice in Indiana, allowing special interests to magnify their influence by aggregating and disseminating individual contributions to preferred candidates and parties. Fundamentally, if one raises the question: How much money have specific corporate or labor interests contributed to Indiana legislative candidates? The only valid answer is that we simply do not know.

Conclusions

Unlike many other states, Indiana has not been swept up by the reformist urges of "Clean Money" campaigns, nor is it likely to move toward comprehensive reform at any point in the near future. Despite only modest changes in the law, the party system has been transformed by a resurgent Democratic Party. What is perhaps most remarkable about this transformation is that it occurred in direct opposition to national partisan tides and in a deregulated campaign finance system that should, by all accounts, have protected the status quo.

Several lessons emerge from this case study. First, the absence of reform does not equate with an absence of change. Campaign finance systems are in a constant state of flux, as candidates and parties seek advantages by exploiting loopholes in existing laws. The contours of partisan change are not easily predicted by the presence or absence of campaign reform. Likewise, because campaign finance systems are not static, reform may be necessary simply to preserve the status quo. Second, as long as the playing field is uneven, "minority" party candidates have the greatest incentive to pursue new avenues of campaign financing and to aggressively exploit loopholes in existing laws. As competition increases, both parties will have incentives to discover and exploit loopholes in campaign finance laws. These incentives, when combined with lax enforcement, help to explain the elasticity of state campaign finance regulations. Third, in an era of candidate-centered campaigns, entrepreneurial candidates (such as Evan Bayh) may spark broader-based partisan realignments, as electoral success translates into increased party fund-raising, which in turn translates into greater electoral success. Therefore, candidate-centered campaigns, often seen as a sign of the "decline-of-parties" thesis, may help resuscitate parties struggling against entrenched partisan majorities. This may be particularly true in deregulated campaign finance systems where entrepreneurial candidates may have their greatest impact. In these states, electoral politics breaks down to a very simple formula: Find the right candidates and make sure they have enough money to mount competitive campaigns.

References

Bibby, John F., and Thomas Holbrook. 1996. Parties and elections. In *Politics in the American States: A comparative analysis*, edited by Virginia Gray and Hebert Jacob. Washington D.C., Congressional Quarterly Press.

Cotter, Cornelius P., James L. Gibson, John F. Bibby, and Robert J. Huckshorn. 1984. *Party organization in American politics*. New York: Praeger.

Fenton, John H. 1966. *Midwest Politics*. New York: Holt, Rinehart and Winston.

Goidel, Robert K., and Donald A. Gross. 1994. A systems approach to campaign finance in United States House elections. *American Politics Quarterly* 22: 125–53.

Green, Donald P., and Jonathan S. Krasno. 1988. Salvation for the spendthrift incumbent. *American Journal of Political Science* 32: 844–907.

Jacobson, Gary C. 1980. *Money and congressional elections*. New Haven: Yale University Press.

———. 1990. The effects of spending in House elections: New evidence for old arguments. *American Journal of Political Science* 34: 334–62.

McDowell, James L. 2001. The citizen legislators as an endangered species: The influence of "carpetbagger cash" on legislative elections. *Political Chronicle* 13: 16–27.

Roberts, Bill. 1987. "Schreiber's chemistry prone to politics," Indianapolis News, March 23: 6.

Sorauf, Frank J. 1992. *Inside campaign finance reform: Myths and realities*. New Haven: Yale University Press.

CHAPTER 4

WYOMING: MONEY, POLITICS, AND A CITIZEN LEGISLATURE

Richard N. Engstrom

The amount of money in play in Wyoming electoral politics is remarkably small. Figure 1 shows the total amount contributed to Wyoming electoral campaigns between 1990 and 2000. Within those years, the average amount raised for campaigns for a seat in the State Legislature was $9,258. At its lowest in 1996 (average money raised per seat: $5,660), the amount compares favorably to the price of a used automobile, and certainly does not compare to the vast sums raised by state legislative candidates in many other states. Also, campaign contributions in Wyoming have declined during the 1990s, which is not the case nationally. Why is so little money raised campaigning for office in Wyoming? And why have campaign contributions decreased?

Some may argue that low-cost campaigns (as well as decreasing amounts of campaign dollars) are quite desirable, implying that something right is going on when legislative campaigns can be waged with amounts of money that are accessible to a large proportion of citizens. Also, low campaign costs suggest that legislators are not devoting themselves entirely to fund-raising—leaving them ample time to work on their legislative duties. Finally, many may feel comforted by the idea of a legislature in which policy change (or lack of change) undertaken by the legislature may have less to do with the movement of vast sums of money and more to do with the merits of the issue at hand.

These are heady implications, so the causes and effects of a reduced role of money in Wyoming politics bear investigation. Wyoming itself, as well as its legislature, has characteristics that encourage low campaign costs. Recent trends in the amounts of money raised for campaigns in the state also point to institutional causes for the lowering of campaign money inflows even further in recent years.

Figure 1
Contributions

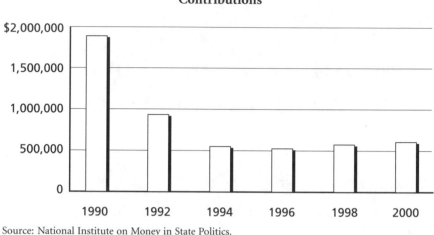

Source: National Institute on Money in State Politics.

The ultimate question in any study of money and politics is whether or not moneyed interests have undue influence over policy-makers. Moneyed interests are indeed donors to political campaigns for government office in Wyoming. And low campaign costs allow such interests to spread money around in ways that might not be possible in states where campaign contributions would have to be much higher to make a meaningful impact. However, the institutional bias toward the status quo stands in the way of all change, and it is difficult to conclude that the small campaign donations typical in Wyoming are buying much in terms of policy outcomes.

But before we celebrate the success of the "citizen legislature" in holding down campaign spending and money's influence in policymaking, it makes sense to consider the costs. In fact, the policy-making process in Wyoming may not be overly responsive to moneyed interests because, given its institutional makeup, it has trouble responding to any interests. Nonetheless, that same institutional makeup does minimize the role of money in Wyoming politics.

Explaining Low Campaign Costs

Characteristics of the State

Low campaign costs in Wyoming may have to do with some of the state's general characteristics. Wyoming's economy has not kept up with the nation's, and there may well be little money to go around. As an energy-producing state, Wyoming's economy did not fare well in the 1990s era of cheap energy prices. Wyoming, in fact, has been noted for its failure to ride the nation's recent wave of economic prosperity (Broder 1999). This failure is mostly due to the fact that the state has not diversified its economic base and relies overwhelmingly on coal and oil for jobs and economic growth (Engstrom and Schuhmann 2001). When energy prices are down (as they were during most of the 90s), the pool of money available for electoral campaigns may simply not be there.

Another characteristic that may keep Wyoming's campaign costs down is the fact that it is a rural state. The economies of scale that justify costly media campaigns do not apply to the nation's least populous state. Wyoming's House districts contain about 8,000 people apiece, and its Senate districts contain about 15,000. Given that the state has only four commercial television stations with limited reach and that most regions in Wyoming exist in media markets that extend beyond the state, spending on modern media campaigns is impractical, to say the least.

Though the characteristics of the state are certainly not the only reasons for Wyoming's inexpensive campaigns, economic conditions, the state's rural landscape and the lack of media outlets may explain at least part of why it has low campaign costs. However, a look at how its government is structured, specifically its legislature, further explains why such small amounts of money are involved in electoral politics in Wyoming.

Institutional Structure of the Legislature

Many of the features of Wyoming's legislature can be seen to contribute to the low costs of campaigning in the state. The state's legislature is made up of sixty Representatives, serving two-year terms, and thirty Senators, serving four-year terms (with half of the Senate seats up for reelection every two years). Wyoming is noted for having a "citizen legislature"—one exhibiting low levels of professionalization. Representatives meet for only a brief time during the year, and receive little in the way of institutional support. Legislators typically keep their regular jobs while serving in office. They must also do a great deal of their own legwork in researching and crafting legislation, owing to the fact that the support staff for all Wyoming legislators consists of the thirty-two-person Legislative Service Office.

Public office is not particularly attractive from a professional standpoint, and one would expect individuals to devote relatively few resources to winning such an office. Not only are salaries low and support staff minimal, but the lawmaking process in Wyoming is designed to limit the power of legisla-

tors. As Cawley et al. note: "The Wyoming Constitution does not specify legislative power as much as it limits legislative power" (2000).

One way in which power is limited is in the very short amount of time that
legislators have to propose and pass bills. The state Constitution requires that
legislative sessions last no longer than sixty days within two calendar years. Of
those sixty days, only twenty are allocated to dealing with budgetary matters.

Passing a bill through the Wyoming state legislature requires that one have
almost no opposition, given that such a small window exists in which bills can
be considered. Any parliamentary delay on a bill by a party or a committee
leader can easily mean that the legislature will not return to the bill before the
end of the legislative session. In addition, the Governor has line-item veto
power on all budgetary matters. The fact that most important legislation is
passed toward the end of the legislative session often means that a governor's
pocket veto is final—legislators cannot conduct an override vote.

Even on bills that enjoy a fair amount of consensus, the legislative process
is designed to slow the passage of bills, potentially frustrating legislators and
limiting the number of possible legislative accomplishments. Each bill must
be assigned to a committee and must go through the committee process. Bills
are limited to only one subject, preventing representatives from attaching rid-
ers onto bills or bundling policies together to pass many at once. After bills
emerge from the committee process and are scheduled for a floor vote, legislative rules require that bills be read three times on three separate days before they can be passed. On the bill's final vote, having majority approval for
a bill on the floor does not necessarily mean that the bill has passed, because
absent representatives are considered to have voted "no" on the bill.

Accomplishing one's legislative goals is difficult in Wyoming, given these
institutional rules that govern policymaking. Such limitations might cause potential candidates to think twice about running for office, and they could very
well cause people to choose not to invest much money in winning the office
or supporting people who seek it. But there are other benefits to holding public office that can make elected public service attractive. Public office-holding
can provide members with a career and, eventually, positions of power and
leadership. But here, too, Wyoming's institutional rules explain why one might
choose not to invest a great deal of money standing for legislative office. State
Representatives and Senators are term-limited to twelve years, limiting the legislature's appeal as a career option. However, it seems that the term limits that
are in place are not forcing people out of office. So far, no sitting legislator has
been ineligible for reelection—legislators tend to step down (or up to a higher
office) before twelve years of service. This pattern existed in Wyoming even
before term limits were in place (King 1993).

Additionally, Wyoming's State House has a tradition that requires the Speaker of the House to serve for only one term. After one term, the Speaker is not only required to leave the leadership position, he or she is also expected to step down from his or her legislative seat. Rising to a position of leadership in the majority party in the House, then, often means stepping onto an escalator of party leadership that accelerates one's exit from office. The potential benefits of a career of office-holding and the power associated with rising to leadership positions have been reduced in the Wyoming legislature by both law and institutional tradition. Wyoming's legislators are citizen legislators, and they are expected to return to citizen status after a brief time in the legislature.

In sum, the Wyoming legislature does not encourage potential members to invest a great deal of resources into winning office. Given little time or resources with which to accomplish policy goals, and few lasting leadership benefits, it is not surprising that those who do choose to run spend very little in pursuit of that goal. However, institutional reasons, though compelling, are not the only explanations for low levels of campaign spending in Wyoming. The state also has a set of laws on the books designed to limit the role of money in politics in the state.

Campaign Finance Laws

The role of money in campaigns is regulated by the set of campaign finance laws that are in place. The state of Wyoming limits both who can contribute to political campaigns and how much can be contributed. These limits are similar to Federal campaign contribution limits in many ways. And, as is the case under federal rules, loopholes do exist that allow some forms of political contributions and activities to escape legal limits.

Wyoming law stipulates that only individuals or political committees (registered PACs, party committees, or campaign committees) are permitted to contribute to campaigns for state office. All other organizations, profit and non-profit, are prohibited from making campaign contributions. These include organizations such as corporations, unions, and civic and religious groups.

Contributions from individuals to a campaign are restricted to $1,000 per contest. This means that individuals may contribute $1,000 to a candidate's primary election campaign and $1,000 to a candidate's general election campaign. This limit covers the two-year period that includes the year before and the year of the general election. State-sponsored PACs are limited by their ability to raise funds. Contributors are restricted to a total of $25,000 in donations to all candidates and to Political Action Committees in a two-year election cycle.

As noted above, there are several forms of campaign activity that are not subject to the above limits. First, the limits outlined above do not apply to candidates themselves or to their immediate family members. Spending on one's own campaign or that of a family member is essentially unlimited under current campaign finance laws.

Second, independent spending campaigns are not subject to spending limits. Independent spending, defined as advertising done on behalf of a candidate by an outside group (and not coordinated with or directed by the official campaign), can be done with an unlimited amount of money. Given that spending in this manner has been found to be an effective way to sway voters (Engstrom and Kenny), such a loophole can provide a particularly powerful tool for those advocating or opposing a candidate—particularly when spending is not regulated. A few groups have taken advantage of such campaigns in recent years, such as the Wyoming Conservation PAC and the Right to Choose PAC. Individuals, however, have not flocked to the independent-spending loophole to get around contribution limits in Wyoming.

Third, donations to political parties are not subject to contribution limits. In Wyoming, these "soft money" contributions, as is the case in Federal campaign law, can be made in unlimited amounts. Such donations, however, cannot be earmarked for particular candidates for office. If a particular candidate is named in connection with a party contribution, that contribution is considered to be a donation to the candidate's campaign and is subject to the standard limits discussed above.

Finally, an additional item in the Wyoming election code prohibits a particular kind of campaign spending by political parties. Party organizations cannot oppose anybody running under their party banner, either in the primary or in the general election. In other words, elite party members cannot spend party money in an attempt to interfere with the selection decisions made by the public. The public, not the party, decides the party's nominee for office, and the party is not allowed to manipulate that process.

According to Hogan and Hamm, Wyoming's campaign finance laws are slightly more restrictive than the average state's (2001). But the fact that so little money is raised for campaign purposes in Wyoming implies that the "limits" far exceed what most people are contributing. Figure 2 shows the amounts of money contributed to all campaigns in Wyoming between 1990 and 2000, as well as the amount in each year that represents the potential contributions that could have been given, had every donation been given at the maximum legal amount of $1,000. As the figure shows, contributions are nowhere near the maximum amounts, suggesting that, in reality, contributions are far lower than the levels to which the law limits them. For example, according to the

Figure 2
Contributions and Potential Contributions

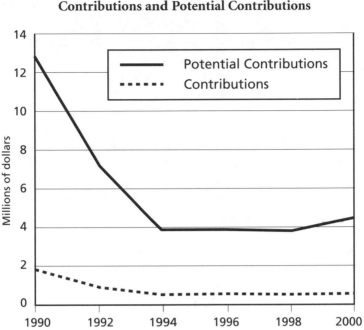

Source: National Institute on Money in State Politics

National Institute on Money in State Politics, 3,273 contributions were made to Wyoming candidates in 1998. If those donations were maximized under the current law, we would find that over $3.2 million was contributed that year in the state. But, in actuality, only $557,000 was raised—which works out to an average donation of only $170.

It seems that, just as Wyoming places a twelve-year term limit on legislators who do not want to serve twelve years, it also places a $1,000 campaign contribution limit on its citizens who do not usually contribute such sums of money. Though it is perhaps the case that the limits do prevent certain very wealthy donors from giving very large amounts, in general, Wyoming politics exists on a scale that is somewhat smaller than the spending rules are designed for.

The Role of Interest Groups

The growing role of interest groups has been implicated in the overall rise of campaign costs in the U.S. Big money interests, it is assumed, infuse big dollars into the system. This, in turn, drives up the costs of campaigning, since challengers have to battle incumbents with huge war chests of campaign funds. Though this may be part of the explanation for why campaign costs have risen nationally, it is clearly not part of Wyoming's story. Campaign spending has not increased here as it has elsewhere. The low amounts of money involved in Wyoming campaigns are not cause for concern that special interests are flooding the political system with money designed to achieve their particular policy goals.

The fact that special interests have not targeted Wyoming in this way is curious. Wyoming's legislature has regulatory and taxing power over huge moneyed interests, given the state's role in the production of energy. The state of Wyoming is an environment where one would expect to find PAC money running rampant and campaign costs skyrocketing. It is interesting that this is not the case and that big money interests do not always lead to big money politics.

However, the fact that the total numbers of dollars donated to political campaigns are low does not mean that special interests do not use what donations they do give to successfully achieve their goals. In order to assess the extent to which interest groups might be altering the legislative process, it is helpful to look at the opinions of those observing the legislative process. Polls conducted over the last twenty years seem to indicate that interest groups are not using their resources to unduly influence policy-making in Wyoming. In a survey conducted in 1979, 96% of Wyoming legislators said that lobbyists helped, more than hindered, the legislative process. This percentage makes sense, given that legislators require a great deal of outside assistance in gathering information on issues and legislation. As Clark and Walter point out in their study of interest groups in Wyoming, the state has a history of strong and active interest groups (1987). Their strength, however, is the result of their lobbying activities and their control of information. They do not make extensive use of PAC contributions to achieve their goals. Indeed, lobbyists are active in the state. A 1983 survey indicated that legislators are contacted an average of 3.3 times per day by interest groups (Cawley et al. 2000).

The opinion held by legislators that interest groups are not a problem in policy-making is also reflected in more recent polling data of Wyoming's citizens. In the 2000 Wyoming Election Study, people were asked whether they felt that state government was run by a few interests or for the benefit of all. Over 56% of Wyomingites answered that state government is run for the benefit of all and not controlled by big interests. Figure 3 shows citizens' responses to the statement that people like them have no say in what the state government does. The fact that over 50% disagree with that statement and another

Figure 3
"People like me don't have any say about what
the state government in Cheyenne does."

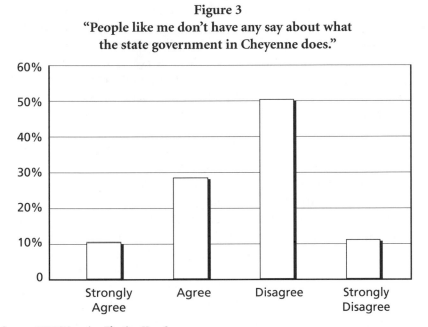

Source: 2000 Wyoming Election Year Survey

11% strongly disagree implies that people in Wyoming are not under the impression that interest groups stand in the way of policy-making in Cheyenne.

In Wyoming, there exist low levels of campaign contributions and the fairly widespread opinion that interest groups are not unduly influential in the state. These two phenomena may well be related to the institutional constraints discussed above. The Wyoming legislature heavily constrains what legislators can accomplish, and it may be that interest groups have found that campaign contributions simply do not pay off in Wyoming's policy-making environment. Overall, the question of whether interest groups have caused campaign spending to rise in Wyoming is easily answered: No. Not only is there a general consensus that interest groups do not wield a troubling amount of influence, but campaign spending in the state has actually gone down over the past decade. Why this is the case is examined below.

Recent Trends

It is obvious that the amount of money involved in winning legislative seats in Wyoming is low in general, but spending has actually (contrary to national trends) decreased from already low levels in recent years. As Figure 1 shows, total spending dropped dramatically between 1990 and 1992, sliding even further after that, and leveling off at about half a million dollars by the late 1990s. Why did it drop so dramatically? This drop does not coincide with any changes in contribution restrictions, nor does it map onto any population patterns. However, overall spending on political campaigns for state office simply dropped by well over half between 1990 and 2000. What occurred in the early 1990s that would lead to such a drop?

Decreased levels of campaign spending after the early 1990s coincide with a change in Wyoming's electoral arrangements. The state changed its system for electing representatives as the result of the *Gorin v. Karpan* decision of 1992. As a result of this ruling, Wyoming abandoned its system of electing representatives from multi-member districts (representatives represented counties, and the number of representatives assigned to each county was based on population) and implemented a single-member district system of elections. As would be expected, changing from a multi-member district system to a single-member district system had consequences for the political system. One consequence that might be expected would be a drop in the number of people running for office. Multi-member systems encourage challengers. When a potential challenger, for example, lives in the same county as a particularly powerful and/or popular legislator he or she will still run, because he or she does not have to unseat the popular incumbent. The challenger can win one of the other seats available in the county. In a single-member district system, potential challengers have no such option. Living in the same district as an entrenched incumbent means that a challenger has no alternative but to unseat that incumbent, something the challenger might well choose not to try.

In fact, the number of candidates running for state office in Wyoming did decrease after the change in electoral arrangements. This decrease in the number of candidates running for office is evident in Table 1. In general, in both the House and Senate, the number of candidates at the end of the decade was lower than before the electoral change that occurred in 1992. The most striking thing about Table 1, however, is the year 1992. In that year, approximately twice as many people ran for House and Senate seats than is usually the case. The new system of elections caused large numbers of new candidates to throw their hats into the ring. Sitting House members figured that, as long as they had been getting votes county-wide in past elections, they might as well run for Senate seats. The number of open House seats left vacant by ambitious new Senate candidates led to a surge in House candidates taking advantage of open seats. But beyond that atypical year, the number of people running for office has been generally lower than was typical before 1992. And, with those

Table 1
Number of Candidates Running for State Office

Year	Senate	House
1988	34	134
1990	26	127
1992	68	201
1994	36	104
1996	23	104
1998	29	96
2000	23	98

Source: Wyoming Secretary of State

lower numbers of candidates, we can expect lower amounts of money to be spent by candidates running for office. As Figure 1 shows, once the anomaly of 1992's election was over, a pattern of between $500,000 to $600,000 in total contributions per year has been the norm.

Conclusion

Wyoming's electoral campaigns for seats in the legislature involve relatively small amounts of money in general, and they involve amounts that have declined even further in recent years. These facts run counter to national trends, a situation that may cause people to wonder if Wyoming's system might be one that should be emulated elsewhere.

The state does have a system of regulating campaign contributions, and that may be part of the reason why there is relatively little campaign money in the state's political system. But it is difficult to ignore the institutional factors that make political contributions to candidates less valuable in the state. The policy-making process is constrained to a remarkably brief period of time, and legislative rules both slow the passage of bills and limit what can be included in a bill. Though legislative procedures commonly stack the odds against the passage of legislation, Wyoming's system is particularly hostile to policy innovation. Thus an investment in a candidate's campaign can be expected to have little payoff in terms of enacting policy. Holding a legislative office in Wyoming is relatively unattractive from a professional standpoint, as evidenced by legislators' low salaries and limited staff support, and the offices are term-limited. Given these characteristics, it is not surprising that prospective officeholders and their contributors spend very little in pursuit of office.

The role of interest groups is often an important part of narratives on money and politics in American political life. However, it is difficult to conclude that interest groups are a prominent part of campaign finance and policy manipulation in Wyoming. Given the small amounts of money they devote to political campaigns and the expressed opinions of both legislators and citizens in the state, it is difficult to conclude that interest groups are using money to manipulate policy to any great degree. Wyoming seems to have done a good job in structuring its institutions so that attempts at such practices are ineffective.

The trend toward reduced levels of campaign contribution activity can also be linked to Wyoming's institutional arrangements. The decrease in contributions coincides with a decrease in the number of candidates seeking public office in the state. Fewer candidates for office can be attributed to a change in electoral arrangements in the state. When Wyoming adopted a single-member district system of elections in place of its county-based multi-member system, fewer people ran for office, and thus less money was raised and spent in pursuit of state office.

If one's goal is to reduce campaign spending and perhaps minimize the role campaign contributions play in the policy-making process, then Wyoming's institutions that promote a "citizen legislature" are certainly worth attention. However, one must understand that the institutions have consequences beyond their effects on money. Wyoming's legislature is particularly constrained in its ability to respond to any interest, whether that interest brings a checkbook or not. Nonetheless, the citizen legislature is popular in Wyoming. As Cawley et al. report: the characteristics of the citizen legislature are "just the characteristics of the legislature that the majority of Wyomingites and, for that matter, most legislators would least prefer to change" (2000).

References

Broder, David. 1999. A state in trouble. *The Washington Post*, 6 October.

Cawley, Gregg, Michael Horan, Larry Hubbell, James King, and Robert Schuhmann. 2000. *The equality state: Government and politics in Wyoming*. Dubuque, IA: Eddie Bowers Publishing.

Clark, Janet M., and B. Oliver Walter. 1987. Wyoming: Populists versus lobbyists. In *Interest group politics in the American West*, edited by Ronald J. Hrebenar and Clive S. Thomas. Salt Lake City, UT: University of Utah Press.

Engstrom, Richard N., and Christopher Kenny. In press. The effects of independent spending on vote choice. *Political Research Quarterly*

Engstrom, Richard N., and Robert Schuhmann. 2001. "Wyoming: Oil and Natural Gas Fuel the State's Economic Bus." In Proceedings: State Budgeting in the 13 Western States. Edited by Robert Huefner. Salt Lake City, UT: Center for Public Policy Administration.

Gorin v. Karpan I. 775. F. Supp. 1430 (D. Wyo. 1991).

Gorin v. Karpan II. 788. F. Supp. 1199 (D. Wyo. 1992).

Government Research Bureau. 2000. Wyoming election year survey. Laramie: University of Wyoming: Government Research Bureau.

Hogan, Robert E., and Keith E. Hamm. 2001. The effects of campaign finance laws on state legislative elections. Paper presented at the State Politics and Policy Conference, Texas A&M University, College Station, TX, 2–3 March.

King, James D. 1993. Term limits in Wyoming. *Comparative State Politics* 14 (2): 1–18.

CHAPTER 5

TEXTILES, TRADITIONS AND SCANDAL: MONEY IN SOUTH CAROLINA POLITICS

Christopher A. Cooper
Anthony J. Nownes

During the 2000 Republican primary, South Carolina was thrust into the national spotlight. George W. Bush was chastised for speaking at Bob Jones University in Greenville, South Carolina, and the major Republican candidates were forced to take a position on the Confederate flag issue. Moreover, the South Carolina primary was considered the key to the Republican presidential nomination. South Carolina's recent experience in the national spotlight points up the growing importance of the South in national politics (Black and Black 1987). More importantly for our purposes, the internal politics of South Carolina provides a fascinating case study of money in politics.

In this chapter, we focus on the role of money in South Carolina politics. South Carolinians have always been suspicious of heavy-handed government regulation. Historically, this suspicion has meant a rather lax set of lobbying and campaign finance laws. However, because of one of the biggest lobbying scandals in American history, the lax laws changed in the 1990s. The 1990s witnessed the adoption and implementation of stringent controls on money in South Carolina politics. These rules have changed forever the role of money in that state's politics. All of this will be discussed in turn. First, however, we will examine the political climate of South Carolina to provide a backdrop for understanding where money fits into the state's politics. We will pay special attention to the state's partisan composition, the preeminence of business in the state, and the state's weak governor/strong legislature political system. Second, we will examine the event that changed the nature of money in South

Carolina politics—Operation Lost Trust, the FBI sting operation that revealed the astounding extent of lobbying corruption in the state. Third, we will explore the specifics of who gets and gives money in South Carolina and how this money affects the state's politics. Fourth, we will discuss the "new" money in South Carolina politics—"soft money" and money spent on independent-issue and candidate campaigns. We will conclude with a discussion of what South Carolina can teach us about the role of money in other states.

Background: South Carolina as a Prototypically Southern State

Before we explore the role of money in South Carolina politics, a bit of background information on South Carolina politics is in order. In this section, we will briefly discuss the partisan composition of the South Carolina electorate, the structure of South Carolina state government, and the role of interest groups in South Carolina politics. Understanding these things is crucial for understanding the role of money in the state's politics.

Partisan Composition: The Rise of the GOP

Over fifty years ago V. O. Key noted, that, like most other Southern states, South Carolina was dominated by the Democratic Party. Boy, have things changed! Today, South Carolina is a remarkably conservative and Republican state. Democrats still hold some power, but Republicans are clearly the majority party. In the clearest example of Republican dominance, South Carolina has supported the Republican candidate for President in the last six elections. Since 1964, the only Democratic candidate for to win a plurality of the South Carolina presidential vote was Jimmy Carter. Carter's victory, attributable mainly to his residence in nearby Georgia, was merely a blip on the radar screen (Graham and Moore 1994). After 1976, South Carolina voters returned to their Republican ways.

While they have dominated presidential politics in South Carolina for some time, Republicans have had less luck in elections for other offices. The first Republican governor of South Carolina in the twentieth century was elected in 1974. Since then, both Democrats and Republicans have elected governors. While Democrats running for president have virtually no chance of winning in South Carolina, Democratic candidates for governor remain viable. For example, Jim Hodges, the current governor, is a Democrat. While Republicans slowly made up ground on Democrats throughout the 1980s and early 1990s,

Table 1
Seats Won by Republicans in the
South Carolina General Assembly, 1964–1996

Year	House	Senate
1964	1 (.8%)	0 (0.0%)
1966	17 (13.7%)	6 (12.0%)
1968	5 (4.0%)	3 (6.0%)
1970	11 (8.9%)	
1972	21 (16.9%)	3 (6.5%)
1974	17 (13.7%)	
1976	12 (9.6%)	3 (6.5%)
1978	16 (12.9%)	
1980	18 (14.5%)	5 (10.9%)
1982	20 (16.1%)	
1984	27 (21.7%)	10 (21.7%)
1986	32 (25.8%)	
1988	37 (29.8%)	11 (23.9%)
1990	42 (33.9%)	
1992	48 (38.7%)	16 (34.8%)
1994	60 (48.4%)	
1996	70 (56.5%)	20 (43.5%)
1998	67 (54%)	
2000	70 (56.5%)	23 (50%)

* 1964–1996 from Broach and Bandy (1999)
* 1998–2000 from SC Legislature Website

the party's breakthrough came in 1994. In 1994, conservative Republican David Beasley was elected governor. In the same year, Republicans took control of the state legislature for the first time since Reconstruction. As Broach and Bandy note, "...the political earthquake that shook the nation that year produced a veritable tidal wave in South Carolina" (1999). Since 1994, Republicans have maintained control of the state legislature. As Table 1 illustrates, the growth of Republican power in the South Carolina legislature is unmistakable. In short, South Carolina has shifted from the lynchpin of the solidly Democratic South to a Republican stronghold.

What explains this sea change? Broach and Bandy suggest that the answer is race (1999). Indeed, "the politics of color," as V. O. Key termed it, has always dominated South Carolina politics. Democratic success in the state (and elsewhere in the South) ebbed as the national Democratic party strayed further to the left on the issue of race. In 1964, longtime U.S. Senator Strom Thurmond defected from the Democratic to the Republican Party. In the same year, Barry Goldwater won the Republican nomination for President, running, like Thurmond, as an opponent of the Civil Rights Act of 1964. In short, through their anti-civil rights stances, Thurmond and Goldwater made it acceptable for white South Carolinians to vote Republican. Today, the state is divided across racial lines. In 1996, only 18% of whites in South Carolina considered themselves Democrats. The corresponding figure for African-Americans was 66%.

Political Structure: Strong Legislature/Weak Governor

States differ dramatically in the relative power of the governor and the legislature. In general, a governor's power is a function of his/her tenure, the extent of his/her budgetary, appointment, removal, and veto powers, and the partisan composition of the state legislature. As is the case in most Southern states, South Carolina's governor has remarkably few formal powers. In fact, Bowman and Kearney point out that South Carolina has the fourth weakest governor in the country (2000) . Moreover, recent figures suggest that South Carolina's governors have traditionally used the veto power quite sparingly (Bowman and Kearney 2000). The weakness of the state's governor led V. O. Key to label South Carolina's government "legislative government." Although a lot has changed since Key coined this label, it remains accurate. The legislature—which comprises 46 legislators in the lower house and 124 legislators in the upper house—remains by far the most important political body in South Carolina.

The Importance of Business Interests

Like all states, South Carolina has its share of organized interests. Ronald Hrebenar and Clive Thomas, the preeminent scholars of interest groups in state politics, categorize states by their level of overall interest group influence (Thomas and Hrebenar 1990; 1996). They define overall group influence as "the extent to which interest groups as a whole influence public policy when compared to other components of the political system, such as political parties, the legislature, the governor, etc." (Thomas and Hrebenar 1990). From here, they classify states as having "subordinate," "complementary," or "dominant" interest group systems. South Carolina is one of only seven states classified as having a "dominant" interest group system (Thomas and Hrebenar 1990; 1996). This indicates that, relative to other political actors in the state, interest groups exert a great deal of power over policy outcomes. The power of organized interests in South Carolina politics is attributable mainly to the numerous points of access provided in the state legislature, the relative power of the state legislature, the generally "business-friendly" nature of South Carolina's political culture, and the relative weakness of South Carolina's lobbying laws (which themselves have been affected by the state's political culture). In short, South Carolina politics provides a political environment ripe for organized interest influence, and there is no evidence that organized interests are becoming less important in the state's politics. Indeed, organized interests set a record in 2000 by spending $11.5 million on lobbying (Associated Press 2001).

The disproportionate influence of interest groups in South Carolina politics begs the following question: Which *types* of organized interests are most active and influential? By all accounts, the types of organized interests that are most active and influential in South Carolina politics are business interests— e.g., individual corporations, trade associations, and professional associations. In contrast, citizen groups and labor unions appear to wield little political power (Botsch 2000; Nownes and Freeman 1998). As for specific types of business interests, one recent study suggests that the South Carolina Chamber of Commerce, which represents 2,500 businesses from all over the state, is the most powerful organized interest in the state (Botsch 2000) As for more specific industries that wield clout, there is little doubt that the textile industry remains the state's "influence kingpin."

While the influence of the textile industry has waned in recent years as more service industries enter the state, the industry remains very powerful in state politics. In addition, utilities—nuclear energy producers in particular— appear to be a fairly strong. Indeed, in 2000, Scana, the parent company of South Carolina's largest utility, spent more on lobbying than any other organization in the state (Associated Press 2001). Other industries that have traditionally been politically powerful in South Carolina include banks, real estate, construction, tourism, insurance, health care, and waste management (Botsch 1992;2000). In recent years, the gambling industry (which spent more than any other industry in 1999) and foreign corporations (buoyed by the recent construction of a BMW plant in South Carolina) have also gained in influence (Associated Press 1999a).

Summary

Our brief summary of South Carolina politics is, of course, in no way definitive. Still, we believe that a bit of background is necessary to understand the role of money in the state's politics. We have highlighted three aspects about South Carolina politics. First, while South Carolina has historically been a heavily Democratic state, it has turned recently into a heavily Republican state. This shift to Republicanism was the result primarily of the politics of race (Glaser 1996). Second, South Carolina state government can be characterized as "legislative government." In other words, the state legislature is relatively powerful, and the governor is relatively weak. Third, South Carolina is quite hospitable to organized interests—especially those representing the interests of businesses. Organized interests are, and always have been, important and powerful players in state politics.

In the end, what is perhaps most striking about South Carolina politics is that it is similar to that of other Deep Southern states. Its recent shift from a solidly Democratic to a strongly Republican state was noticeable throughout the South in the 1990s. Similarly, its governmental structure is similar to that found in many other states of the Deep South. Finally, South Carolina's extreme hospitality to organized interests, especially those representing business interests, is mirrored throughout the Deep South. In many ways, South Carolina is the prototypical Deep Southern state. Indeed, this is one of the reasons we have chosen to focus on South Carolina in this volume. We believe that learning about the role of money in politics in South Carolina can produce many insights about the role of money in Southern politics in general.

Operation Lost Trust and Beyond

Our previous discussion was designed to provide some context for our discussion of money in South Carolina politics. Every observer of South Carolina politics acknowledges that one signal event transformed forever the role of money in the state's politics. That event was the FBI sting operation known as Operation Lost Trust. The sting operation has had profound consequences for state politics in general and the role of money in state politics in particular.

Culture Change

Before 1990, South Carolina government operated under "undefined ethical standards, weak laws, reluctant enforcement, fragmented government authority and an apathetic public" (Associated Press 1999a). In other words, the state government was a free-for-all. There was no limit to how much any person or organization could contribute to a candidate running for statewide office, and politicians were allowed to use surplus campaign funds for personal use. In addition, there were virtually no laws controlling what lobbyists could and could not do, how much money they could spend, and what sorts of gifts and junkets they could provide to government officials. In short, the state of South Carolina was a place where lobbyists operated unencumbered, and individuals and organizations seeking influence could do virtually anything they wanted.

All of this changed in the early 1990s. In the summer of 1990, the FBI conducted a sting operation centering on Rob Cobb, a former state representative turned lobbyist whom the agency caught in a cocaine transaction. When confronted by the FBI, Cobb agreed to take part in a large sting operation. In exchange for leniency and a substantial amount of money, Cobb agreed to pose as a lobbyist offering bribes to policymakers if they voted for a bill to legalize dog racing and horse racing in South Carolina. Cobb's meetings with lawmakers were videotaped, and they eventually led to the conviction of many prominent people. In the end, seventeen members of the South Carolina General Assembly (one tenth of the total!) and nearly a dozen lobbyists were arrested on a variety of charges, including bribery and drug possession (Graham and Moore 1994). All but a few pleaded guilty or were convicted. The corruption uncovered in Operation Lost Trust reached the highest levels of South Carolina government. For example, one of the governor's top aides pleaded guilty to cocaine possession, and the second-ranking member in the state House pleaded guilty to racketeering (Strong 1991). Not surprisingly, Operation Lost Trust led to profound changes in South Carolina politics. Three changes in particular stand out. First, a significant change in the "capital culture" occurred. Second, stringent new lobbying and campaign finance laws were passed. Third, there was a substantial decline in the number of bills introduced in the state legislature.

In the immediate aftermath of the scandal, lobbyists virtually disappeared from the statehouse. Longtime observers of South Carolina politics noted that business interests, long important in South Carolina politics, saw their power decline. Even social meetings between legislators and lobbyists declined in number, as both legislators and lobbyists became aware that the spotlight would be squarely upon them (Graham and Moore 1994). In short, the entire culture surrounding the South Carolina state capital changed overnight. Most noticeable was an increase in professionalism that remains to this day. Lobbying moved out of dank taprooms and into government offices and statehouse hallways. Trips to swanky resorts in Las Vegas were out, and meetings in crowded lobbies were in. Lobbyists and legislators were more careful to cultivate images of professionalism and diligence, and lobbyist-policymaker interactions were low-profile formal affairs. In end, South Carolina came to resemble most other states. As Rosenthal points out, the "good old days" of "good old boy" influence-peddling politics have largely ended in most state capitals as capital cultures have changed from informal and unprofessional to formal and professional (1998).

One apparent effect of this change in capital culture is the introduction of fewer bills in the legislature. While some obvious reasons for this decline could include legislators' growing sensitivity to the appearance of impropriety (Graham and Moore 1994), the reasons could be significantly more complicated. For instance, scholars have established that lobbyists often provide legislators with information that helps them to make decisions (Nownes 1999). The reduced contact between lobbyists and legislators could mean that legislators in South Carolina simply were not aware of as many issues after their contact with lobbyists was reduced. Whether the reduction in bills proposed is positive or negative depends largely on one's own partisan leanings. Nonetheless, the reduction in bills proposed and the change in capital culture mark a significant change in the way government works in South Carolina.

New Laws and Regulations

The most obvious and relevant consequence of Operation Lost Trust was the adoption of stringent new lobbying and campaign finance regulations. On September 23, 1991, an ethics bill was passed unanimously by the state legislature. The legislation contained several major provisions. First, lobbyists were prohibited from spending money on lawmakers unless the lawmakers were part of a specific *group* of lawmakers. For example, under the law, a lobbyist who wished to buy a legislator a meal or a drink could do so only if that legislator was part of a defined group, such as an entire committee or a county delegation (Associated Press 1999a). Second, the law specified that when lobbyists *did* spend money on policymakers, they could spend no more than $25 per lawmaker. Third, the new law limited how much money individuals, parties, and organized interests were allowed to give to candidates for statewide office. Specifically, individuals and organized interests could contribute no more than $3,500 per candidate per election cycle (up to a total of $10,500), and political parties could contribute no more than $50,000 per candidate per election. Fourth, the law limited how much money parties, organized interests, and individuals could give to candidates for local (i.e., non-statewide) offices. Specifically, individuals and organized interests could contribute no more than $1,000 per candidate per election cycle (up to $3,000 total), and political parties could give no more $5,000 per candidate per election cycle. Finally, the law prohibited individual lobbyists from contributing money to any candidate for public office.

In sum, Operation Lost Trust led to the adoption of a set of stringent lobbying and campaign finance regulations that remain in effect today. In fact, it is safe to say that South Carolina now has more stringent and restrictive campaign finance and lobbying laws than all but a few states in the country. These laws, however, emphatically did *not* put an end to big money politics in South Carolina. A number of obvious gaps in the laws remain. First of all, lobbyists are still free to spend as much as they please on lobbying. Second, there are no limits on how much candidates for state or local office can *spend*. Third, there are no limits on so-called "soft money," the virtually unlimited donations from individuals, corporations, and unions to state and national party committees. Finally, there are no limits on independent expenditures—funds spent by an individual or organized interest in support of or opposition to a candidate for public office or a ballot question. In the end, though Operation Lost Trust led to a serious overhaul of South Carolina's once-lax campaign finance and ethics laws, it by no means diminished the role of money in South Carolina politics. We will have more to say about this later.

Money: Spending and Giving

In many respects, South Carolina is an "average" state when it comes to money in politics. When we first consider organized interest non-electoral spending, it is clear that money is as important (if not more important) than ever. As we noted above, despite Operation Lost Trust and the new regulations that it ushered in, 2000 was a record year for lobbyist spending in South Carolina. In all, approximately 750 organized interests (450 of which are corporations) spent $11.5 million on lobbying in 2000. As we mention above, Scana, the parent company of the state's largest utility, spent the most money, $267,677 (Associated Press 2001). Other big spenders included the State Ports Authority ($212,934), and South Carolina State University ($135,478). In sum, organized interests of all kinds spent record amounts to influence policy in South Carolina in 2000.

While the ways that organized interests have gone about their business have changed (i.e., bribery and gift-giving are out) the volume of organized interest activity has not been reduced by recent lobbying laws. One recent study of interest groups in South Carolina noted that state legislators believe that organized interest power has actually increased since Operation Lost Trust (Botsch 2000). In fact, state legislators also suggest that rather than operating "contrary to the public interest," organized interests actually perform either a "necessary and valuable" or "sometimes useful" purpose in state politics (Botsch 2000). In short, the new laws and regulations adopted in the wake of Operation Lost Rust have done nothing to stop big-spending lobbyists.

How Much is Spent and Given?

Did Operation Lost Trust and the new laws and regulations adopted in its wake do anything to stem the tide of rising campaign costs and spending? The answer is an emphatic no. The evidence for the negative is overwhelming and comes from many quarters. Five pieces of information in particular are compelling. First, candidates for state office in 1998 set a record by spending a total of $18,744,967 (Dixon 2000). Second, candidates for state office in 2000 (a year in which the governor's office and other statewide offices were not contested) spent approximately $9 million—also a record (for "off year" election spending). Third, two candidates for the U.S. Senate in 1998 (Ernest "Fritz" Hollings and Bob Inglis) spent more than $6 million—another record. Fourth, the two candidates for governor in 1998 (Jim Hodges and David Beasley) spent a record $9.1 million (Holland 1999). Finally, in late 2000, supporters and opponents of a state-run lottery initiative spent over $2 million (Sheinin 2000). To put these numbers in perspective, a state watchdog group notes that the average cost of winning a state Senate seat rose 100% between 1996 and 2000 (from $51,537 to $102,780), while the average cost of a House seat rose 43% between 1998 and 2000 (from $20,027 to $28,7730). Moreover, the amount spent by gubernatorial candidates more than quadrupled between 1990 and 1998—from approximately $2.3 million to over $9 million (South Carolina Progressive Network 2000). In short, the available data suggests that the reforms implemented after Operation Lost Trust did not in any way reduce the role of money in South Carolina's electoral politics.

Where the Money Comes From: Sources

So where does all this campaign money come from? Though South Carolina's campaign contribution disclosure system is notoriously user *unfriendly*, and a number of reporting loopholes exist that make it difficult to discern precisely how much campaign money comes from which sources, it is possible to discern a few trends. First, as is the case at the national level and in most states, individuals appear to be the most important source of direct campaign contributions for both state and national candidates in South Carolina. One source suggests, for example, that candidates for Congress in South Carolina typically receive well over 75% of their money from individuals (Open Secrets 2000). Another source notes that in the 1998 South Carolina Senate race, the two candidates combined received approximately 75% of their contributions from individuals (Moore and Vinson 2000). As for state races, the picture is a bit cloudier (again, due to loopholes in reporting requirements). A number of sources suggest, however, that individuals remain the most important source of campaign funds for candidates for state office in South Carolina (Open Secrets 2000).

In addition, there is no question that organized interests are an important source of money for candidates for national and state office in South Carolina. Which types of organized interests are the most important sources? Table 2 reports the results of an investigation of South Carolina presented by the Center for Responsive Politics, a campaign finance watchdog group. The figures in Table 2 report what the Center calls the "leading industries" that contribute to PACs, political parties, and candidates within the state. However, it appears (though it is somewhat unclear) that the Center's figures include only donations to PACs, parties, and candidates involved in federal election campaigns. Moreover, the Center includes only those contributions that come from in-state sources. To supplement this table, we have also included Table 3, which lists "top contributing industries" to candidates in the 1998 state elections. While these two sources are far from definitive, they give us a reasonable idea of where the money in electoral politics in South Carolina comes from.

A few trends are noticeable in Tables 2 and 3. First, the tables reiterate that individuals are the preeminent source of campaign money for South Carolina candidates for both state and national offices. Retired people, for example, give large amounts of money to candidates for national office, as do lawyers and health professionals (e.g., doctors and dentists). Similarly, in state races, lawyers and health professionals are important sources of campaign money. Of course, the figures on the contributions from individuals obscure the fact that many individual donors are businesspeople. Nonetheless, they confirm that individuals, rather than PACs and parties, are still preeminent sources of campaign money. Second, Tables 2 and 3 show that lawyers—many of whom work for law firms that engage in lobbying—remain a vital source of campaign money for South Carolina candidates, PACs, and parties. This fact is especially surprising, given that South Carolina's campaign finance laws prohibit lobbyists from contributing money to state election campaigns. They do not, however, forbid law firms from contributing money to candidates, nor do they prevent lobbyists from contributing to political parties or PACs.

Third, Tables 2 and 3 show the economic sectors that are most active in South Carolina electoral politics: textiles, electric utilities, real estate, health care, insurance, construction, contracting, and automotive. Interestingly, these industries are active in supporting candidates for both state and national offices. Fourth, Table 3 indicates that the gambling industry is now a vitally important source of campaign money for candidates for state office. Table 3 does not tell the full story, however. In recent years, the gambling industry has

Table 2
Leading Campaign Contributors to PACs, Parties, and Candidates Involved in Federal Elections, by Industry, 1997–98, 1999–2000, 2000–2001

Rank	Source	Amount
1997–1998		
1.	Lawyers/Law firms	$671,038
2.	Retired	$518,819
3.	Health Professionals	$314,828
4.	Textiles	$254,525
5.	Insurance	$206,669
6.	Real Estate	$193,449
7.	Misc. Manufacturing/Distributing	$139,276
8.	Electric Utilities	$117,757
9.	Automotive	$116,344
10.	Business Services	$109,954
1999–2000		
1.	Lawyers/Law firms	$1,695,201
2.	Retired	$1,077,655
3.	Health Professionals	$ 435,082
4.	Forestry and Forestry Products	$ 316,450
5.	Real Estate	$ 307,656
6.	Textiles	$ 261,785
7.	General Contractors	$ 203,650
8.	Business Services	$ 183,960
9.	Securities and Investment	$ 172,175
10.	Misc. Manufacturing/Distributing	$ 159,410
2001–2002		
1.	Retired	$225,402
2.	Lawyers/Law Firms	$160,894
3.	Health Professionals	$134,904
4.	Real Estate	$ 78,229
5.	Electric Utilities	$ 62,200
6.	General Contractors	$ 48,695
7.	Misc. Business	$ 47,800
8.	Textiles	$ 32,670
9.	Retail Sales	$ 31,500
10.	Insurance	$ 27,365

Source: www.Opensecrets.org/states/summary.asp. Accessed on December 2, 2001.

become one of the biggest spenders in South Carolina electoral politics. In the 1998 gubernatorial election, for example, Democratic challenger Jim Hodges (the eventual winner) collected over $1 million from gambling interests and their supporters (Dixon 2000). Moreover, as we mention above, a recent lot-

Table 3
Leading Campaign Contributors to Candidates for State Office, 1998

Contributing Industry	Amount
1. Candidates	$2,144,016
2. Lawyers	$1,353,726
3. Gambling and Casinos	$808,877
4. Party Committees	$739,464
5. Misc. Manufacturing/Distributing	$681,922
6. Real Estate	$622,656
7. Health Professionals	$573,609
8. Insurance	$459,700
9. Small Individual Contributions (under $200)	$429,708
10. Automotive	$364,451

Source: The National Institute on Money in State Politics, "1998 South Carolina Elections Analysis." Accessed at www.followthemoney.org/reports/sc98 on December 2, 2001.

tery initiative attracted huge amounts of money and attention from the gambling industry. As long as gambling remains an important issue in South Carolina, gambling interests surely will remain important sources of campaign money for state candidates.

A final trend noticeable in Tables 2 and 3 is the virtual lack of big money contributions from non-business groups (e.g., labor unions, citizen groups, etc.). No labor unions or citizen groups crack the top ten in giving. The lack of citizen group and labor union involvement in South Carolina electoral politics was driven home to us during a study that one of us (Dr. Nownes) conducted in 1998. After conducting a survey of 141 groups in South Carolina, we found that 41% of sample organizations made monetary contributions to candidates for office. Table 4, which contains information on which types of

Table 4
Group Type and Monetary Contributions in South Carolina Politics

Type of Interest Group	% making monetary contributions (no./total)	
Labor Union	66	(2/3)
Professional	53	(8/15)
Trade	47	(14/30)
Citizen (i.e., Public Interest)	19	(3/16)
Religious/Charitable	0	(0/3)
Governmental	0	(0/3)
Total	41	(27/70)

Source: Anthony J. Nownes and Patricia Freeman, "Interest Group Activity in the States."

groups provide monetary contributions, emphasizes the dominance of business. Two things in particular stand out. First, business groups (i.e., trade and professional groups) dominate interest representation in South Carolina. Business groups active in South Carolina outnumber other types of groups by a ratio of close to three to one. Especially noteworthy is the lack of labor representation in South Carolina. While a healthy number of citizen (i.e., public interest) groups compete with business groups for power in South Carolina, only a handful of labor unions are active. Thus, while the labor unions that do exist also engage in campaign giving, there simply are not very many of them around. Second, and more important, the data presented in Table 4 illustrate that business groups are far more active than citizen groups in making monetary contributions. While two of three labor unions surveyed said they made monetary contributions, only three of nineteen citizen groups acknowledged making contributions. This stands in sharp contrast to the proportion of business groups that make monetary contributions. As Table 4 indicates, 53% of professional groups and 47% of trade groups make monetary contributions to candidates.

Who Gets the Money?

As we suggested early in this chapter, South Carolina has been transformed from a state dominated by the Democratic Party to one where both parties are active but the Republican Party is in the clear majority. It is not surprising that in the 2000 presidential election George W. Bush received far more money from South Carolina residents than did Al Gore. In all, Bush received more than four times the amount that Al Gore did. The partisan tilt in fund-raising does not end with the presidential race, however. Republican candidates at all levels of government have little trouble raising money. During the two most recent state elections, Republican candidates received almost two-thirds of the total money contributed. There is a clear partisan winner in South Carolina's fund-raising, and it is the Republican Party.

The fund-raising story does not end with partisanship, however. As in other states, incumbent politicians in South Carolina have a considerable fund-raising advantage over challengers. In 1998 South Carolina congressional races, for example, incumbents raised $3,742,865, while their closest challengers managed to raise only $891,918—four times less than the incumbents. The fund-raising advantage, coupled with the other well-documented advantages of incumbency (Herrnson 1998), secured a victory for all five congressional incumbents in South Carolina.

Summary: Who Gives and Who Gets?

South Carolina has relatively strict campaign giving and lobbying laws. When we first examine lobbying laws, it appears that they have in no way decreased the amount of money spent by organized interests. When we examine campaign finance, a number of things seem clear. First, most campaign money comes from individuals. This conclusion must be clarified, however, by noting that many of these individuals are associated with specific organized interests, such as law firms and businesses. Second, organized interests provide a lot of money to candidates in South Carolina. Business groups—especially those in the textile, electric utility, real estate, health care, insurance, construction, contracting, automotive, and gambling industries—dominate giving, while labor and citizen groups are not at all active. In all, the data suggest that, by dint of their campaign giving, business groups have a decided advantage over their labor union and citizen group opponents when it comes to supporting candidates for public office. This seems to be to the advantage of Republicans and incumbents, who receive the bulk of campaign contributions. While we cannot say for certain that the business advantage translates to influence, we can speculate that it puts business groups in a good position to exert influence over state and national office-holders.

The New Money in South Carolina Politics: "Soft Money" and Independent Expenditures

Most treatments of campaign finance in South Carolina and elsewhere focus on direct contributions to candidates and/or candidate spending. However, in recent years political scientists have noted a surge in two other (and relatively new) forms of monetary electioneering—*contributing "soft money"* and *making independent expenditures*. In this section, we will examine "soft money" and independent expenditures in the context of South Carolina politics.

"Soft Money" and Other Party Money

To understand precisely what "soft money" is, we must first understand federal campaign finance laws. The Federal Election Campaign Act (FECA), the main law governing campaign finance in national elections, stipulates that interest groups may not make direct contributions to national party committees. Interest groups may, however, through their PACs, contribute up to $15,000 per year to any national party committee. These rules seem straightforward. But they are not. In the late 1970s and early 1980s, the two major political parties' national committees began to accept direct contributions from organized interests (mostly labor unions and corporations), seemingly in violation of FECA. They also began accepting individual and PAC donations in excess of $15,000. How was this possible? The national Democratic and Republican political parties argued that because FECA applied only to federal elections, FECA did not prohibit them from accepting contributions that defied FECA's guidelines as long as these contributions were not used to finance activities related to federal elections. These contributions, the parties argued, could be used for "party building activities" (such as voter registration drives, voter education, "get out the vote" drives, etc.), and to influence state and/or local elections. Initially, the Federal Election Commission (FEC) balked at the parties' arguments. Eventually, however, the FEC agreed that money that is not spent to affect federal elections is not subject to FECA's rules. In short, the FEC essentially gave the "green light" to national party committees to accept direct interest group and individual contributions "beyond the statutory limits as long as that money is not spent to promote federal candidates. (Dwyre 1996). These extra-statutory contributions are called "soft money," which is best defined as money contributed outside the guidelines of FECA.

"Soft money" can be used to raise more "soft money," to directly support candidates for state and local office, to support state and local parties for "party-building activities that do not promote federal candidates (e.g., slate cards, yard signs, bumper stickers, and sample ballots distributed by volunteers)," to "promote the party or its candidates as a class without mentioning specific names," and to pay for national committees' administrative and overhead costs (Dwyre 1996). Technically, no "soft money" can be used in direct support of candidates running for federal office. But many "soft money" contributions indirectly support federal candidates nonetheless. Covering administrative and overhead costs for national party committees, for example, clearly benefits candidates for federal office by freeing up "hard money" that can be funneled directly to candidates for federal office.

How important is "soft money" in South Carolina politics? Unfortunately, we do not know for sure. One expert on South Carolina notes that a substantial amount of the money spent in South Carolina politics is "soft money," and that "soft money" falls completely outside of South Carolina law and thus is difficult to trace (Botsch 2000). However, we have anecdotal evidence that "soft money" is becoming ever more important in South Carolina politics. As was the case in most states, "soft money" did not become an issue in South Carolina until the 1990s. In the last ten years, however, there has been an explosion of "soft money." In all, the two state parties in South Carolina spent a combined $7 million in 1998 (Moore and Vinson 2000). Not all of this $7 million was "soft money"; some was money contributed directly to the state parties and not funneled through the national parties. Estimates suggest, however, that at least $3 million of this party money was "soft money" (Moore and Vinson 2000).

It is important to note at this point that much of the money spent by the two state parties in South Carolina was contributed directly to the parties and then passed on to candidates for state office, as allowed under South Carolina law. Indeed, one of the major criticisms of South Carolina's campaign finance laws is that they are not particularly harsh on parties. First of all, under South Carolina law, lobbyists, individuals, and organized interests are allowed to donate as much as they want to state party committees. Contributions to state parties in South Carolina are virtually unregulated, and they do not even have to be disclosed! Second, state party committees are allowed to contribute up to $50,000 per election per candidate to candidates for statewide office, and up to $3,500 per election per candidate to candidates for the state legislature. Finally, national party committees are allowed under federal law (and not limited under state law) to make unlimited transfers to state parties. In sum, while the campaign finance laws passed after Operation Lost Trust ostensibly placed stringent limits on interest groups, they did little or nothing to control political parties. Not surprisingly, then, political parties have become extremely important players in South Carolina's electoral campaigns.

Returning to the subject of "soft money," it seems clear that it has played an important role in many recent South Carolina elections. Thus far, "soft money" has been more prominent in elections for national office than in elections for state office. In the 1998 Senate campaign, for example, the state Democratic Party spent a total of $1.7 million, of which approximately $900,000 was "soft money," to try to defeat Republican Senate candidate Bob Inglis. The GOP countered by spending $1.3 million in opposition to Democrat Ernest "Fritz" Hollings, of which approximately $800,000 was "soft money" (Moore and Vinson 2000). Most of this party money was spent on radio and television "issue advertisements," which are nothing more than thinly veiled campaign commercials. Unfortunately, lax disclosure laws make it more or less impossible for us to discern how much "soft money" was spent in other election contests, especially those for state office. There seems no doubt, however, that "soft money" was prominent in other contests as well. Moreover, both parties used some "soft money" to buy generic "pro-party" advertisements.

A great deal of "soft money" was also used on a massive "get out the vote" drive mounted by the state Democratic party (Moore and Vinson 2000). To encourage and increase Democratic turnout in the 1998 election, the national Democratic Party held regional training sessions with party officials throughout the state of South Carolina. The national party also provided political precinct manuals that contained information on how best to register and motivate voters. In addition, the national party contributed money directly to the state party, which then distributed it to county organizations to aid them in voter registration efforts. While Republicans did not ignore "get out the vote" activities, they spent far less money on them. In the end, the Democratic effort seems to have worked. Turnout among Democrats rose in 1998, and increased turnout among African-American Democrats was widely credited with helping Ernest "Fritz" Hollings retain his seat in the U.S. Senate (Moore and Vinson 2000).

Independent Expenditures

One other gaping loophole in South Carolina's campaign finance laws is the following: Under the law, "individuals and groups can spend unlimited amounts in independent campaigns for or against candidates and ballot questions" (Botsch 2000). In other words, if a determined individual or organized interests wanted to help or hinder a certain candidate (for either state or national office) by running a campaign completely separate from that candidate, he/she/it could do so and face virtually no regulation. This kind of spending, which is often referred to as "independent spending," has exploded throughout the country along with "soft money" spending.

How common is independent spending in South Carolina's electoral politics? Again, due to lax disclosure laws, we cannot know for certain. The evidence suggests, however, that independent spending is becoming ever more important in South Carolina elections. For example, one recent account notes that at least fifteen organizations engaged in independent spending during the 1998 South Carolina Senate campaign (Moore and Vinson 2000). Most of this money was spent on television and radio advertisements, direct mail, and newspaper advertisements. Among the most active organizations were national organizations such as the League of Conservation Voters (LCV) and the Christian Coalition, and state organizations such as the South Carolina Education Association. Independent spending was even more prominent in South Carolina's 2000 lottery initiative (because there were no candidates). Organizations of all kinds spent money for or against the lottery, and spending exceeded $2 million. Among the most active groups were pro-lottery "front groups" funded largely by the gambling industry, and anti-lottery groups funded by a variety of lottery opponents, including Christian conservative organizations.

Unfortunately, we have virtually no information on independent spending in other elections in South Carolina. Nonetheless, we are confident that independent spending, because it represents a way around South Carolina's rather stringent campaign finance regulations, will increase substantially in the years to come, as it has done in other states.

Conclusion

So precisely what role does money play in South Carolina politics? At the risk of seeming flippant, we must conclude that the answer is: a big one! For years, lobbyists and their employers had virtually no restrictions on their behavior. Not surprisingly, they exerted substantial influence on policy outcomes and played a large role in elections in the state. Operation Lost Trust changed all this. South Carolinians were outraged by the blatant corruption in their state legislature, and the result was the adoption of strict new lobbying and campaign finance laws designed to reduce corruption as well as the role of money in the state's politics.

If there is one thing that the aftermath of Operation Lost Trust has shown us, however, it is that *money still talks in South Carolina's politics*. On the one hand, it seems clear that state politics in South Carolina have become more professional since Operation Lost Trust, as the state capital became a more formal place where lobbyists and legislators operated "above board" and in the open. On the other hand, lobbyists in South Carolina appear to do more and (more importantly for our purposes) spend more than ever before. As we note, it appears that organized interests operating in South Carolina, like organized interests in other states, may be constricted in precisely *what* they do, but they are in no way constricting in *how much* they can do.

If money remains crucial in lobbying, it remains even more so in campaigning. In short, we have presented a great deal of data, suggesting that, despite new campaign finance laws passed in the wake of Operation Lost Trust, campaigns in the state of South Carolina are big-money affairs. In fact, campaigns in South Carolina became even bigger money affairs after Operation Lost Trust than they were before. By all accounts, campaign spending in South Carolina has skyrocketed in the last ten years—again, much as it has elsewhere. Campaign finance rules notwithstanding, candidates for office in South Carolina still need money, and individuals and organized interests are more than willing to give it to them.

One of the reasons that South Carolina's campaign finance laws have done little to stem the tide of growing campaign spending is that they are riddled with loopholes. While South Carolina's laws are stringent compared to those in many states, there remain many ways for "big money" to find its way into the electoral process. The most glaring loopholes in the state's laws regard the role of parties—both state and national. In short, it is no exaggeration to say that political parties are free to do more or less as they please. If they are careful, parties can collect virtually as much as they want from whomever they want, and they can spend as much as they want on behalf of (or opposition to) whomever they want. "Soft money" and other sorts of party money are becoming an increasingly common part of South Carolina's electoral politics. Another loophole in South Carolina's laws concerns independent spending. Again, it is no exaggeration to state that the lack of independent spending restrictions allows virtually any individual or organized interest to spend as much as he/she/it wants on behalf of (or opposition to) whomever or whatever cause he/she/it wants.

What are the implications of the continued and increasing importance of money in South Carolina politics? Several things occur to us. First, for better or worse, business interests are likely to remain dominant in the state. As is the case elsewhere, business interests in South Carolina are better funded and better organized than other types of interests. This does not mean that business interests always win. It does mean, however, that there are few policy battles or elections in which the interests of the state's largest businesses and business groups are not represented. Second, political party organizations are likely to become more important in election campaigns. Because political party money in South Carolina is virtually unrestricted, parties are likely to continue to be important players in elections (for both state and national office) in the state. In fact, we believe that parties will become even more important in the years to come, as savvy politicians, lobbyists, and organized interests learn that they can utilize parties to get around South Carolina's otherwise strict campaign finance laws. Finally, we believe that campaign finance reform will be an important issue in South Carolina politics in the years to come. Polls show that many South Carolinians are not particularly supportive of their state government institutions. Reasons for this undoubtedly include the rise of "big money" politics and the memory of Operation Lost Trust. Like citizens elsewhere, South Carolinians are suspicious of "big money" politics, and may demand reform before too long. In fact, in 2000 the state legislature passed a serious reform bill that would have required full disclosure of all contributions to parties and expenditures, but the governor vetoed it. We do not believe that this will be the end of the story.

What lessons can we learn from South Carolina? The most obvious lesson is this: *Campaign finance laws that do not seriously constrain political parties and independent spending will have little impact on campaign spending and giving.* In short, as long as loopholes exist, people will exploit them. Despite seemingly strict rules, virtually any person or any organized interest can find a way to insert large sums of money into South Carolina politics. It may take some imagination to circumvent South Carolina's laws. But, make no mistake about it: big spenders can still spend big in South Carolina. In this sense, South Carolina is similar to most states in the country. The fact is that campaign finance laws have not kept up with parties and donors. "Soft money" and independent spending have exploded everywhere in the United States because current national and state laws are ill-equipped to deal with them. Does this mean that campaign finance reform is a waste of time? We think not. It is not hard to envision a law that limits or even prohibits "soft money," or a law that limits what individuals and organized interests can give to parties and what parties can do with the money. It is also not hard to envision some limits of independent spending. However, for new laws to take shape, some politician in South Carolina must provide leadership, much like John McCain has done at the national level.

Another lesson concerns lobbyists: *Lobbying laws do not stop lobbyists and their employers from spending huge sums of money on lobbying.* Nothing short of banning lobbying—which would clearly be unconstitutional—is likely to reduce the throng of lobbyists pressing their demands on South Carolina's policymakers. However, the lobbying restrictions adopted in the wake of Operation Lost Trust have worked in the sense that it is easier than ever for citizens (including us) to figure out who is lobbying, what they are doing, and what they are spending. This is no small matter. Full disclosure is a good way to keep citizens "plugged into" politics and a good way to keep lobbyists and policymakers honest.

References

Associated Press. 1999a. Lobbyists hold on lawmakers has diminished. *The Augusta Chronicle*, 5 May 1999: A01.

Associated Press. 2001. State agencies, universities, corporations spend record setting $11.5 million in 2000. *Associated Press News Wires*, 6 May.

Black, Earl, and Merle Black. 1987. *Politics and society in the South*. Cambridge: Harvard University Press.

Botsch, Robert E. 1992. South Carolina: The rise of the New South In *Interest group politics in the Southern States*, edited by Ronald J. Hrebenar and Clive S. Thomas. Tuscaloosa, AL: University of Alabama Press.

———. 2000. Interest groups in South Carolina. Columbia, SC: Center for Government Studies, University of South Carolina. Retrieved 1 December 2001: www.iopa.sc.edu/scgov/Articles/interest_groups_in_South_Carolina

Bowman, Ann O'M., and Richard C. Kearney. 2000. *State and local government: The essentials*. Boston: Houston Mifflin.

Broach, Glen T., and Lee Bandy. 1999. South Carolina: A decade of rapid Republican ascent. In *Southern politics in the 1990's,* edited by Alexander P. Lamis. Baton Rouge: Louisiana State University Press.

Dixon, Mark. 2000. 1998 South Carolina Elections Analysis. *The National Institute on Money in State Politics* (24 March 2000) Retrieved 24 November 2001: www.followthe money.org/reports/sc98

Dwyre, Diana. 1996. Spinning straw into gold: Soft money and U.S. house elections. *Legislative Studies Quarterly* 21(3): 409–424.

Glaser, James M. 1996. *Race, campaign politics and realignment in the South.* New Haven: Yale University Press.

Graham, Cole Blease, Jr., and William V. Moore. 1994. *South Carolina politics and government.* Lincoln: University of Nebraska Press.

Herrnson, Paul S. 1998. *Congressional elections: Campaigning at home and in Washington,* 2nd Edition. Washington DC: Congressional Quarterly Press.

Holland, Jesse L. 1999. Common cause wants extensive campaign reform. *Associated Press News Wires,* 3 February: 1.

Key, V. O, Jr. 1996. *Southern politics in state and nation, a new edition.* Knoxville: University of Tennessee Press.

Kuzenski, John C. 1998. South Carolina: The heart of GOP realignment in the South. In *The new politics of the Old South,* edited by Charles S. Bullock III and Mark J. Rozell. New York: Rowman and Littlefield.

Moore, Bill, and Danielle Vinson. 2000. The 1998 South Carolina Senate race. In *Outside money, soft money and issue advocacy in the 1998 congressional elections,* edited by David Magleby. Lanham, MD: Rowman and Littlefied.

Nownes, Anthony J. 1999. Solicited advice and lobbyist power: Evidence from three American states. *Legislative Studies Quarterly* 24(1): 113–123.

Nownes, Anthony J., and Patricia Freeman. 1998. Interest group activity in the States." *Journal of Politics* 60(1): 86–112.

Open Secrets. South Carolina. Retrieved 19 September 2001: www.opensecrets.org

Rosenthal, Alan. 1998. *The decline of representative democracy.* Washington DC: Congressional Quarterly Press.

Sheinin, Aaron. 2000. South Carolina lottery camps bet big bucks on television ads. *The State,* 27 October 27.

South Carolina Progressive Network. 2000. Clean elections. Retrieved 1 December 2001: www.scpronet.com/cleanelect

Strong, Tom. 1991. More lawmakers fall in bribery probe: Nearly a tenth of South Carolina's legislators have either admitted or been convicted of wrongdoing. More than 40 cases are still being investigated. *Los Angeles Times,* 18 August: 18.

Thomas, Clive S., and Ronald J. Hrebner. 1990. Nationalization of interest groups and lobbying in the States. In *Interest group politics,* edited by Allan J. Cigler and Burdett A. Loomis. Washington DC: Congressional Quarterly Press.

———. 1996. Interest groups in the States. In *Politics in the American States,* 6th ed., edited by Virginia Gray and Herbert Jacob. Washington DC: Congressional Quarterly Press.

CHAPTER 6

CAMPAIGN FINANCE REFORM IN THE BAY STATE: IS CLEANLINESS REALLY NEXT TO GODLINESS?

Jerold J. Duquette

Introduction

Will clean elections wash in Massachusetts? The Bay State has long been a laboratory of democracy in America. Much of the framework of the U.S. Constitution was developed from the handiwork of John Adams and the design of the Massachusetts Constitution. The state has been at the forefront of innovation in every aspect of political development in America, from the Puritans' attempts to balance liberty and order to the contemporary struggle of governments to deal with the coming information age. But, like the Puritans' efforts, the clean elections experiment will not live up to its promise in the near future.

Massachusetts is not immune from the questionable effects of money on politics. The familiar statistics linking office holders with special interests, the lack of competitiveness in elections, the overwhelming resource advantage of incumbents, and all the other evidence that has inspired individuals and groups around the country to champion campaign finance reform can be found in abundance in Massachusetts.

Current campaign finance laws in Massachusetts, however, are among the most progressive and stringent in the nation. Advocates of reform had considerable success in the early 1990s, pushing the legislature to pass measures intended to control the influence of big donors, powerful lobbyists, and political action committees (PACs). Despite these successful enactments of reform the 2000 election cycle witnessed an escalation of many of the ills reformers had sought to curb. In 2000, 71% of the state's legislators ran for reelection unopposed. Between 1997 and 1999 incumbents in the state raised $20 million. Of that money 80% was raised from people who donated $100 or more. These donors constituted less than 1% of eligible state voters. Incumbent fund raising doubled between 1995 and 1999. The cost of running for office has also steadily increased in the state. In 1998 the average House member, running with opposition, spent nearly $40,000, which represented a 38% increase from the 1996 cycle. Republican A. Paul Cellucci spent a record amount in 1998 to be elected Governor. He spent $6.7 million, which eclipsed the spending of the previous winning candidate, Republican Bill Weld, who spent $3.6 million to get elected in 1994. In 1998, after the legislature failed to budge on the issue of public financing for all of the state's elected officials, reformers took to the ballot box with their "clean elections" initiative.[1]

This chapter will focus on the question of why the goals of reformers cannot be achieved in Massachusetts through the establishment of a comprehensive public financing system for the state's legislators and executive officers. It will examine why the Clean Elections Law faces such an uphill fight despite its easy passage by the voters. After a brief history of campaign finance reform efforts in the state, the chapter will look the provisions of the Clean Elections Law, the fight to enact and implement the 1998 voter-passed law, and the resultant debate on the wisdom of the measure, with an eye toward explaining its likely fate. Despite apparent success with clean elections laws in neighboring states like Maine and Vermont, as well as far away Arizona, full public financing of elections in Massachusetts is not likely to be realized soon due to the effects of the state's professionalized political environment, ambivalent public opinion on the issue, and an increasingly credible argument against full public financing of elections.

Massachusetts may be one of the best test cases for campaign finance reform at the national level. The difficulty of enacting and implementing reform

---

1. More detailed analyses of campaign finance statistics in the state have been published by the Massachusetts Money and Politics Project, which is a program of the Commonwealth Education Project, a 501c(3) non-partisan institute that studies issues of electoral democracy and voter participation in the Bay State. In order to avoid unnecessary duplication of the detailed analyses of money in Massachusetts politics published annually by the project, I will merely reference it here and focus instead on the politics of clean elections and the broader issue of campaign finance reform in the state. Researchers, advocates and policy makers can access the statistical evidence by writing the Money and Politics Project located at 27 Temple Place, Boston, MA 02111, or by phone at 617-422-0017, or by E-mail at massmonpol@aol.com.

in Massachusetts has many parallels to the current struggle to produce meaningful reforms in Washington, D.C. The primary limitations to the usefulness of the Massachusetts case for national reformers, however, are the existence of the ballot initiative and referenda process in the state, and the partisan make-up of the state. Indeed, the capacity to utilize initiative and referenda in many states produces an important caveat to any state-level study purporting to provide useful data to national reformers and policy makers. In Massachusetts, the ability of reformers to utilize the initiative process has been crucial to their prior success as well as their current struggle. While they will probably lose the battle over clean elections for all the state's elected officials, reformers would not even be in the fight without the initiative process. In the absence of this constitutional weapon, the state's campaign finance laws would surely be markedly different.

The partisan environment in the state limits the applicability of the Massachusetts case study to national reforms as well. Massachusetts is a one-party state where, despite the occasional success of Republican gubernatorial candidates, the General Court (state legislature) has been dominated by the Democratic Party since the 1950s. Since 1958 Democrats have had veto proof majorities in both houses of the state legislature. In the 1990s, despite steady Republican dominance of the governor's office, the 40-seat State Senate and 160-seat State House of Representatives have been firmly controlled by the Democrats.

Finally, one area of reform activity important to national policy makers has not been an issue in Massachusetts. While the infamous U.S. Supreme Court decision in *Buckley v. Valeo*, 424 U.S. 1 (1976) created a loophole you could drive a truck through in federal campaign finance laws, independent expenditures have not been significant in Massachusetts. The role of independent expenditures in the state's electoral politics has been so insignificant that neither scholars nor advocates have published significant material on the impact of independent expenditures. When pressed, scholars, activists, and politicians can only site the 1998 gubernatorial campaign of then-Attorney General Scott Harshbarger, who benefitted from nearly three-quarters of a million dollars in independent expenditures by the state's teachers union. Also in 1998, conservative special interest groups attacked a few Democratic state representatives with unfriendly independent expenditures, but, prior to 1998, the issue seems to have been totally irrelevant. Certainly, if the Clean Elections Law is ever fully implemented, it will raise the salience of independent expenditures in state elections.

History of Campaign Finance Reform in Massachusetts

> Of the forty-eight states Massachusetts has been in the forefront with legislation to prevent corrupt political practices.... [T]he treatment of various aspects of the problem is still in the experimental stages in any given state. (Bottomly 1950)

So wrote a Boston University law student more than half a century ago. But for the addition of two states, these words remain just as true today. Although campaign finance reform often seems to be a purely post-Watergate phenomenon, in fact, by mid-century, more than thirty-five states had campaign finance laws on the books. Massachusetts law in this area can be traced to 1892 with the passage of a "corrupt practices" statute. In 1946, Massachusetts overhauled its corrupt practices law. New provisions included prohibitions on vote buying, on undue influence by an employer, on paying for editorial support, and on the purchasing of intoxicating liquors by political committees, among other things (Bottomly 1950).

By 1973, public attitudes about politics and political corruption in America were far more cynical and critical than they had been just a decade earlier. In 1960, Americans saw their President as a hero and generally had faith in their political leaders. By the 1970s presidents were suspect, too powerful, and not accountable enough, and faith in government officials had plummeted. Calls for reform were the order of the day across the country, on Beacon Hill as well as Capitol Hill. In 1973, Massachusetts passed a campaign finance law that imposed strict disclosure rules, record-keeping requirements, and expenditure limitations on state candidates and political committees. Most significantly, the new law created an independent state agency to serve as the depository for all disclosure reports filed by state candidates and committees. The new agency was also charged with the duty to investigate violations of the campaign finance laws.

The Office of Campaign and Political Finance (OCPF) represented a turning point for campaign finance law in Massachusetts, because, prior to the creation of the OCPF, campaign finance laws were not enforced. The Secretary of State administered the law but did not possess the authority to investigate violations. The Attorney General had the authority to investigate and prosecute such violations, but did not have the interest or incentive to do so (Barnhill 1974). The newly created agency's sole mission was the administration of campaign finance reform. The OCPF was more bark than bite in its first decade of operation. When the Ward Commission reported widespread corruption in state government in its 1980 report, the OCPF was singled out as a "do-nothing agency that is overly protective of the public officials it is supposed to police and interested in doing little beyond warehousing the fundraising reports it receives from candidates"(Robinson 1981). Despite the impotence of the office in its early years, its very existence was significant as an institutional acknowledgment of the need for scrutiny of campaign finances. The OCPF has since become a professional investigative unit with the independence and clout to encourage compliance with the laws and the authority to deal with violators.

While several states were setting up similar watchdog agencies at the time, Massachusetts was innovative in its method of choosing an independent director. A committee consisting of the two state party chairmen, the Secretary of State, and a dean from a Massachusetts Law School, who is appointed by the governor for a six-year term, chooses the OCPF Director. The director serves a six-year term and can only be removed by a unanimous vote of the committee. Michael Sullivan, the current OCPF Director, reports that his unique appointment method has allowed him to develop a productive and respectful relationship with the state's elected officials.

In 1975, Massachusetts established a limited public financing system for statewide elective offices. Chapter 55A of Massachusetts General Law, "Limited Public Financing of Campaigns For Statewide Elective Office," provided public funds for candidates for Governor, Lieutenant Governor, Attorney General, Secretary of State, Treasurer, and Auditor, in return for the acceptance of contribution limits as well as full disclosure of campaign contribution sources. For example, a candidate for Governor would have to raise $75,000 in contributions of no more than $250 to be eligible for public money in a primary election. In a general election, gubernatorial candidates would have to raise $125,000 in contributions of no more than $250. The name and address of each contributor had to be reported for the contributions to qualify. In return, candidates could receive up to $250,000 in the primary election and $250,000 in the general election with which to wage their campaign.

The State Election Campaign Fund created by the limited public financing law would be funded by an income tax add-on provision. Bay Staters would have the opportunity to add one dollar to their tax liability annually to be placed in the campaign fund. By the 1990s barely 2% of taxpayers were exercising the add-on option. In 1994, the tax add-on provision was changed to a tax check-off, allowing taxpayers to divert a small portion of their tax payment to the State Election Campaign Fund. Participation jumped to 10%. Nonetheless, the limited public financing law has never raised enough money to fund candidates for all six constitutional offices.

Interest in campaign finance was sparked again in the late 1970s by a high profile scandal in state government. In April 1978, Governor Michael S. Dukakis signed a law creating the Special Commission Concerning State and County Buildings to look into allegations of corruption in the awarding of state building contracts. The commission would be headed by John William Ward, the President of Amherst College, and would become known as the Ward Commission. In an inquiry that took more than two-and-a-half years, the commission found widespread corruption. According to the commission, a well understood but unspoken system of political influence lay at the heart of the public building contract process.

The commission found bribes, payoffs, and kickbacks were a way of life in the state, but particularly disturbing was the connection revealed between "legal" campaign contributions and government contracts. A system of identifying contractors who had contributed to the right campaigns was exposed. In a hearing before the commission, one fund raiser explained how it worked. Essentially, the names of contractors who had been "friends" of the administration were coded with a dot or series of dots as their bids went through the contract award process. The final selection of contractors was made with reference to these codes (Commonwealth of Massachusetts 1980).

The Ward Commission recommendations for reform were dramatic and sweeping. Over the next several years many of the commission's recommendations were enacted into law. Of particular significance was the creation of the Office of the Inspector-General, which the commission recommended. Not enacted, however, were the commission's recommendations on campaign finance reform, which were no less sweeping, and, according to the commission's chairman, no less critical. The commission's final report declared that the public financing system it proposed was so important that "[w]ithout it the thoroughgoing administrative reorganization and the potential for prevention and detection of corruption created by the establishment of an Office of Inspector General...will be seriously weakened" (Commonwealth of Massachusetts 1980). Central to the commission's recommendations was a plan to strengthen the limited public finance system then in place by including legislative candidates and providing a more reliable funding mechanism than the existing tax add-on system. This recommendation was dead on arrival on Beacon Hill.

The 1980s saw only minor technical adjustments to the state's campaign finance laws. But, more than a decade after the Ward Commission detailed its stark conclusions and critical recommendations for reform, the campaign finance reform movement got another shot in the arm from political scandal. The headline in the *Boston Globe* on May 23, 1993, made it clear that money in politics was back on the front burner. The banner read, "Beacon Hills' Money Game: A Hidden World of Tropical Junkets, Easy Cash, and Sweet Deals"(McDonough 2000). In a book about his experiences as a state legislator, former State Representative John McDonough skillfully chronicles the scandal and its impact on the campaign finance debate. He writes, "The *Globe* had wanted to set off a fire storm, and it got its wish"(McDonough 2000).

The scandal broke when a group of legislators, including the Speaker of the House, were accompanied surreptitiously by a *Globe* photographer on a trip to a conference of the Council of State Governments in San Juan, Puerto Rico. As it turned out the legislators never made it to the conference and were instead photographed with lobbyists from several industries, having fun at a beach side resort. The voters paid for the trip, and the lobbyists picked up the food and bar tabs. The *Globe* reports documented the links between the lobbyist partygoers and pending legislation, and the relationships between legislators and lobbyists became the focus of numerous investigations from the State Ethics Commission to the FBI.

The scandal focused the public's attention on the corrupting influence of money in politics once again. It also provided a boost for attempts by public interest groups in Massachusetts who had been trying to push the state legislature into enacting campaign finance reform. Common Cause Massachusetts was spearheading an effort to pass reform that would dramatically lower contribution limits and limit the aggregate amounts candidates could raise from private sources. Groups like Common Cause have been active in the state for decades, but never before had these groups been able to wield so much influence on Beacon Hill. The scandal gave momentum to the group's effort to get their brand of reform on the November 1994 ballot. Armed with enough signatures to bypass the legislature, Common Cause negotiated a campaign finance reform package that would move the state far beyond its previous efforts. Legislators did not want voters weighing in on such a complex issue with the memory of the *Globe* series so close at hand.

The legislation, negotiated and shepherded through the legislative process by Election Laws Committee Co-Chairmen Senator Stanley Rosenberg and Representative John McDonough, was far-reaching and among the most aggressive in the country. A report prepared by the Massachusetts Public Interest Research Group (MassPIRG) claimed the law stacked up quite well when compared to other states' laws. (See Table 1.)

"An Act Further Regulating Public Financing of Political Campaigns" was signed into law on June 15, 1994. The law reduced the amount that individuals and political action committees (PACs) can contribute to individual candidates from $1000 to $500 per calendar year. Lobbyists can only give candi-

Table 1
Other States' Campaign Finance Reform Laws Compared to Massachusetts

	Provisions Stricter than MA	Provisions Similar to MA	Provisions Less Strict / MA
Individual Contribution Limits	1	4	44
Aggregate Individual Limits	4	0	45
Individual PAC Limits	0	1	48
Aggregate PAC limit for Candidates	1	1	47
Lobbyists Contributions	1	6	42
Spending Limits	4	3	42
Public Funding	1	3	45

Source: MassPIRG, "Campaign Finance Reform: Proposed Law Stacks Up Well," Boston, 1994.

dates $200 as a result of the law. Common Cause had sought to reduce individual and PAC contributions to $100. The aggregate amount of money that candidates can take from all PACs combined was also limited for the first time by the Act. These limits range from $150,000 per year for Governor to $7,500 per year for a State Representative. The law also sets an aggregate limit on political donations allowable by individuals of $12,500 per year. On the other hand, the law actually increased the amount of money that PACs can contribute to political parties from $1000 per year to $5000 per year. Most observers have speculated that this move was intended to strengthen the role of political parties in the state on the theory that parties serve an important public information and voter mobilization function (Becker 1995).

The 1994 measure also increased disclosure requirements. In addition to having to provide information on contributors of more than $50, candidates would now have to provide the name of the contributor's employer and occupation on any donation of $200 or more. Lobbyists and PACs were required by the measure to disclose more. Executive branch lobbyists would be required to register with the state and report all political donations. Lobbyists would have to file reports quarterly with the state, rather than bi-annually. PACs were required to report their names, purposes, interests, and major sources of funds (Becker 1995).

The law made subtle but significant changes to the state's limited public financing system. Previously, the State Election Campaign Fund received voluntary contributions from taxpayers who chose to add one dollar to their tax bill to pay for public financing of elections for state constitutional officers. The 1994 legislation changed this to a tax check-off, rather than an add-on. This allowed taxpayers to contribute to the fund without increasing their tax bill. The public financing system was also changed by the imposition of spending limits on candidates who seek monies from the fund. These limits were $1.5 million for Governor, $625,000 for Lieutenant. Governor and Attorney General, and $375,000 for Secretary of State, Auditor, and Treasurer. Until 1994 the state's public financing system only required contribution limits and disclosure of contribution sources.

Negotiations over the 1994 reform package illustrated the profound impact which that state's initiative and referenda laws can have on public policy formation. Armed with the resources to get on the ballot, public interest groups like Common Cause can compel legislators to act. Despite the passage of the 1994 law, campaign finance reformers in the state were eager for more reform. They felt that the 1994 changes were good, but not good enough. State Senate Minority Leader Brian Lees characterized the 1994 package as mere "record-keeping" improvements, rather than comprehensive reform. It left untouched candidate war chests, which allow incumbents to stockpile funds in non-election years in order to ward off potential challengers. Furthermore, the contribution limits passed were set for calendar years, rather than election cycles, which makes the $1000 individual contribution limit actually $2000 per election cycle.

The reformers had negotiated for half a loaf and, in the aftermath, began to experience buyer's remorse. In the meantime, a so-called "Clean Money" (read "public financing") movement had begun to gain momentum around the country in the mid-1990s. In the fall of 1995, more than 1,200 clean elections volunteers in Maine collected 65,000 signatures to put the "Maine Clean Elections Act" on the 1996 ballot. That measure passed and took effect for the 2000 elections (Donnelly, Fine, and Miller 1999). The success of that ballot question, which was approved by Maine voters by a margin of 56 to 44 percent, re-energized the Massachusetts reform groups who immediately went to work on a public financing initiative of their own. According to the national campaign finance reform group Public Campaign, many of the leaders who had fought for and won the clean elections fight in Maine moved to Massachusetts to set up shop for a similar fight in the Bay State. In the fall of 1997, nearly 3,000 volunteers collected over 100,000 signatures to put clean elections on the Massachusetts ballot in 1998. The Vermont legislature also gave hope to the reformers when in 1997 they enacted a public financing system for statewide offices in the Green Mountain state.

The Massachusetts Clean Elections Law

Ballot question #2 in 1998 asked Massachusetts voters to decide whether the state should institute public campaign financing for all state candidates,

Table 2

Office	Primary: Pub. Funds	Primary: Sp. Limits	Gen: Pub. Funds	Gen: Sp. Limits
Gov.	$1,500,000	$1,800,000	$1,050,000	$1,200,000
Lt. Gov.	$383,000	$450,000	$255,000	$300,000
Atty. Gen. or Treasurer	$360,000	$450,000	$240,000	$300,000
Sec. of State or Auditor	$120,000	$150,000	$80,000	$100,000
Gov. Councilor	$19,000	$24,000	$13,000	$16,000
Senator	$43,000	$54,000	$29,000	$36,000
Representative	$15,000	$18,000	$9,000	$12,000

Source: 1998 Massachusetts Voter Guide.

both legislative and executive. The law would allow candidates to receive public funds for their campaigns in exchange for limiting their contributions and spending. A thorough explanation of the proposed initiative appeared in the state's 1998 voter guide. An easy-to-read table explained how much public money candidates could receive and how much money, public or private, they could spend under the law. (See Table 2.)

The law set the maximum individual contribution for participating candidates at $100. Non-participating candidates before and after the law's passage were limited to $500 worth of individual contributions. To qualify for public funding under the new law candidates have to prove their viability by raising a minimum number of individual contributions of between $5 and $100 dollars. Gubernatorial candidates have to raise 6000 such contributions. Lieutenant Governor candidates, as well as candidates for Attorney General and Treasurer, are required to collect 3000 qualifying contributions. Secretary of State and Auditor candidates need 2000 contributions, while Governor's Council candidates need only 400. State Representative candidates are required to obtain 200 contributions between $5 and $100, and State Senate contenders need 400 qualifying contributions. The law requires these qualifying contributions to be raised during a limited time period. Statewide candidates can begin raising the contributions on August 1 of the year before the election, while other candidates can start on January 1 of the election year. For all candidates the money must be raised by the last day to file nomination papers with the Secretary of State. The Clean Elections Law also eliminates the unlimited transfers of soft money from the national political parties to the state parties, and requires timely electronic disclosure of all contributions to candidates and political committees on the Internet.

In order to help participating candidates remain competitive with well-financed non-participating opponents, the law provides matching funds to participating candidates over and above the amount for which they are eligible. If non-participating candidates exceed the spending limits of the participating candidates, then the participating candidates would receive matching funds equal to the amount of excess spending by their non-participating opponents. Matching funds are capped, however, at two times the statutory spending limit. This provision was intended not only to foster equal resources among candidates but also to encourage more candidates to participate by removing the advantage of using only private money in a campaign.

Noticeably absent from the measure was any language dealing with limitations on independent expenditures. David Donnelly, Executive Director of Mass Voters for Clean Elections, indicated that an independent expenditure provision was not included in the Massachusetts initiative in order to reduce the threat of legal and political challenges to the measure. Similar measures in other states had been and were being challenged in court. In Minnesota, in *Day v. Holahan*, 34 F.3d 1356 (8th Cir. 1994) an independent expenditures provision was struck down by a federal court, and a similar provision of the Maine Clean Elections Law was being challenged in court as the Massachusetts law was being drafted. A federal judge in Maine has since upheld the independent expenditures provision of that state's law, leaving a conflict between federal districts that remains unresolved.

The Fight for Clean Elections

Despite passage of the clean elections initiative by Massachusetts voters in 1998, it has yet to be fully implemented. The fight for passage has become the fight for implementation, and this fight is proving to be a much tougher one for the proponents of public financing in the state. The initiative cannot be meaningfully implemented without sufficient appropriations from the state legislature. As of this writing, the state legislature has not provided the necessary funds, despite a ruling by the state's Supreme Judicial Court upholding the law.

In early 1998, supporters of public financing, facing solid opposition in the state legislature, put all their eggs in the ballot initiative basket. The initiative campaign was spearheaded by an organization formed for that purpose. The Mass Voters for Clean Elections was an organization staffed by veterans of the clean elections fight in Maine. Led by Executive Director David Donnelly, they were ready to do battle in the Bay State. Donnelly's organization was and is strongly supported in the state by the better established and battle-tested state chapter of Common Cause. Common Cause was the organization that had negotiated the 1994 package of reforms armed with enough voter signatures to take their case to the ballot if necessary.

The campaign to get the clean elections initiative on the ballot was easily successful. Once on the ballot, supporters were assisted mightily by two factors. First, the popular name of the initiative made vocal opposition costly, because it required explanation. Second, the proponents were very well organized with a seasoned and professional core staff organization, while opponents were never well organized. Most opponents of the measure seemed unwilling to exert much energy in opposition due to fear of being labeled "dirty." While some legislators spoke out against the use of tax dollars to fund private campaigns, no significant statewide organization used its resources to fight the initiative. A statewide "No on 2" committee was created, but was badly outspent and out-organized by the proponents of the initiative. Opponents seemed content in the knowledge that, even if the initiative were passed. the legislature would surely not fund it. Powerful Speaker of the State House of Representatives Thomas Finneran made no secret of his intention to scuttle the law legislatively if necessary.

When the clean elections initiative passed at the ballot box in November 1998, very few people were surprised, although the two-to-one margin of victory was unexpected. The real fight had only just begun. Because the law required technical corrections in order to implement it, the legislature began debating how to structure the law in 1999. In the 2000 and 2001 budgets, the legislature appropriated $10 million to the Clean Elections Fund. With interest, the fund had about $23 million as of November 2001, but it is significant to note that, despite having appropriated the monies to the Clean Elections Fund in the 2000 and 2001 budgets, the legislature must still release the entire amount in the 2002 budget for the 2002 election cycle.

Each year since passage of the initiative, debate on the issue has been heated and controversial, with opponents pushing hard to eviscerate the law. In an outside section (rider) of the FY2000 state budget, the legislature created a study commission to examine every aspect of the law in order to determine the best way to implement it. While all sides recognized that the voter-passed law needed technical corrections, proponents of the measure saw this as an attempt to gut the law. The fourteen-member commission included three members of the House, three members of the Senate, and eight citizen representatives. The commission was to return to the legislature by October 1, 2000 with recommendations (State House News Service, January 1, 2000). To date the commission has produced no recommendations or reports. In an outside section (rider) of the FY2001 budget the legislature postponed the start date for clean elections candidates to begin complying with the law from December 8, 2000 to March 31, 2001. The then-Governor Cellucci's veto of the change was overridden by one vote in the House (State House News Service, April 27, 2001). The battle lines were drawn. Common Cause, Mass Voters for Clean Elections, and a handful of sympathetic legislators were bucking up against the Election Laws Committee chairmen in both houses of the legislature, as well as the very powerful and pugnacious Speaker of the House, whose open defiance of the voter-passed initiative has never dimmed. Debate on the law in 1999 and 2000 was heated, including some very confrontational hearings held by the study commission and a failed attempt in the House to put another question on the ballot to clarify voters' understanding of clean elections (Crowley 1999).

The 2000 elections in Massachusetts set the stage for the bitter fight over funding the Clean Elections Law. Clean elections systems similar to the one passed by the state's voters in 1998 were in effect for the 2000 elections in Maine, Arizona, and Vermont. While clean elections advocates in these states were trumpeting the success of their reforms, Massachusetts reformers were busy highlighting the continued lack of competition in the Commonwealth's elections. Mass Voters for Clean Elections reported in several of their publications and public statements that Massachusetts ranked second in the nation, behind Arkansas, on a list of states with the least competitive elections. The group's web site is replete with statistics about the state's poor record on competitiveness. The highest spender wins over 90% of competitive races in the state. Less than one third of legislative races in 1998 and 2000 were contested. And less than 1 % of the state's registered voters contribute 80% of the money for election campaigns. Despite being armed with these sobering statistics, advocates of the new law have been fighting an uphill battle against opponents in the state legislature.[2]

The 2000 elections made the job of clean elections advocates even harder and served to embolden the opponents. On the 2000 state ballot were eight questions to be decided by the voters. One in particular would unintentionally impact the momentum for clean elections. The voters overwhelmingly passed an income tax reduction. The tax cut, combined with a slowing national economy, provided clean elections opponents the opportunity to make an argument about priorities. Less tax revenue would make it harder to fund

2. These statistics and more are available at the Mass Voters for Clean Elections web site. Retrieved 17 July 2001: http:// www.igc.org/massvoters/.

needed and popular programs and easier for foes of public financing to attack it as a drain on the treasury. Proposals surfaced in the legislature to divert the funds currently in the Clean Elections Fund to more pressing concerns. Opponents of clean elections in the State House of Representatives proposed using the money from the Clean Elections Fund to provide salary increases for human service workers in the state. While no such diversions of funds were actually passed out of the House in 2001, they did bring some credibility to the arguments against clean elections (State House News Service, April 27, 2001).[3]

In February 2001, the Office of Campaign and Political Finance filed a technical corrections bill necessary for that agency to administer the law. The bill languished in committee and has yet to be acted on by the full House. The Election Laws Committee chairman in the House, Joseph Wagner, an outspoken critic of the law, has publicly called for the law's repeal (State House News Service, April 27, 2001). The increasing leverage of clean elections opponents was evidenced in early March 2001 when supporters of the law offered some concessions to lawmakers if they would allow the law to be implemented. The concessions included raising the amount of money in qualifying contributions that would need to be collected, the elimination of public funding in uncontested elections, allowing incumbents to spend up to $6,000 of their war chests in non-election years for constituent services, and increases in the spending limits for Secretary of State and Auditor's races (State House News Service, April 27, 2001). Unfortunately for the reformers, the concessions were not enough. In April 2001 the Committee on Ways and Means failed to recommend funding for the Clean Elections Law. Chairman John Rodgers indicated that the uncertainty of the actual costs of the law made it impossible for the committee to recommend a funding level (State House News Service, April 27, 2001).

On May 1, 2001 the House passed its FY2002 budget without appropriating a specific amount of money to the Clean Elections Law. Instead, the House voted to fund the law with a tax check-off, allowing taxpayers to elect to divert between $1 and $100 to the Clean Elections Fund. This move was seen by supporters of the law as a clever way to kill the measure. Such a funding mechanism is very unlikely to produce enough money to effectively implement the law. Defenders of the provision noted that if those who voted for the law choose to divert $100 to the Clean Elections Fund, there would be sufficient funds.

---

3. Bills diverting clean elections funds were passed out of both houses of the state legislature in February 2002 in response to the Supreme Judicial Court's decision in *Bates v. Director of OCPF*, No. SJC-08677.

Table 3

Office	# of Contributions	Minimum Qualifying Amount
State Representative	200	$3,000
State Senator	450	$9,000
Governor's Council	400	$6,000
Secretary of State	2,000	$40,000
Auditor	2,000	$40,000
Treasurer	3,000	$60,000
Attorney General	3,000	$60,000
Lt. Governor	3,000	$60,000
Governor	6,000	$120,000

Source: Summary of Lees-Rosenberg Amendment on Clean Elections (Prepared by Senate Staff)

In the State Senate the Clean Elections Law had a much smoother ride. After intense negotiations between key Senators and supporters of the law, the Senate amended the Clean Elections Law. The Lees-Rosenberg amendment, named for the two Western Massachusetts legislators who crafted it, addressed the major concerns of legislators without gutting the spirit of the measure. The law as passed by the voters failed to account for the need of legislators, particularly Western Massachusetts legislators whose districts are far from the state capital, to spend funds on district offices and constituent services. Most legislators rely on campaign funds for this purpose because the legislature only appropriates a small amount for these expenses. The Senate amendment addressed this by permitting incumbents an exemption from the matching funds provision of the law for funds raised for constituent services. Without this exemption money spent during non-election years on constituent services would count against incumbents' campaign spending limits, turning incumbency advantage into disadvantage.

A second issue addressed by the Senate amendment was the fund-raising threshold to qualify for public money. Legislators felt this threshold was too low, too easy to achieve, regardless of political viability. The amendment adds an additional test of viability. Not only must a candidate raise a specific number of contributions of between $5 and $100, he or she must also raise a minimum-qualifying amount of contributions. This prevents, for example, a fringe candidate for the House from collecting two hundred $5 contributions and becoming eligible for public financing. Such a candidate would have to raise at least $3,000 in contributions of between $5 and $100 as a result of the amendment. (See Table 3.) Other issues addressed by the Senate amendment included an increase in the amount of matching funds available to participating candidates in statewide elections when their non-participating opponents spend beyond the statutory limits, streamlining of the reporting requirements for non-participating candidates, and the establishment of a role for local elections officials in certifying qualifying contributions.

The amendment also included language giving candidates a second chance to opt-in to the system. Because of all the confusion about the law's implementation and the impact of such confusion on candidates trying to decide how to proceed, the Senate amendment moved the opt-in date to ninety days after the passage of the FY2002 budget. Some observers saw this seemingly innocuous provision as a product of the gubernatorial aspirations of the State Senate President, who had nearly $3 million in the bank. The ninety-day window would allow the Senate President to spend his funds freely for three months and then opt-in on an equal footing with his competitors. The Senate's FY2002 budget package included the amended Clean Elections Law, $20 million for the Clean Elections Fund, and a provision that would remove annual funding of the law from the appropriations process, making it automatic and therefore safe from legislative maneuvering. Clean elections advocates said initially that they were pleased with the Senate compromise and pushed hard for its adoption in the House. As weeks, then months, passed without action in the House, the reform advocates amended their position by withdrawing their support for delaying the opt-in date until ninety days after the budget's passage.

Despite the favorable treatment of the law in the Senate, supporters' fears that the opponents in the legislature would scuttle the law seem to have come true. House Minority Leader Francis Marini predicted that the Senate version would not fare well in the House and he was quite right. Marini said that while he is philosophically opposed to public financing, he respects the voters' wishes and would vote for a good bill. He predicted at the time, however, that opponents in the House were too strong and that the bill was in serious trouble. Opponents had long hinted that the House would kill the law and the Senate funding would disappear in the conference committee on the FY2002 budget, which is exactly what happened. Acting Governor Jane Swift pledged her support for the law and promised to veto any attempts to gut it. However, because the law was simply left without funds, there was nothing the Acting Governor could do. Like the House Minority Leader, the Acting Governor claims to be philosophically opposed to public financing but respectful of the voters' wishes. She tried positioning herself as a defender of the measure in order to bolster her chances in the 2002 Governor's race. The President of the Senate, Thomas Birmingham, a leading Democratic contender for Governor in 2002, has pledged to fight for full funding of the law, but the measure's chief opponent, Speaker of the House Thomas Finneran, continues his bold opposition to the law.

Ironically, serious public debate and analysis of publicly financed campaigns in the state did not commence until after passage into law of this sweeping new public financing system. Prior to its being placed on the ballot, when the Joint Committee on Ways and Means of the state legislature reviewed the proposed initiative, they summarily rejected it as totally without merit. The committee's majority report on the clean elections initiative makes clear that the members of the committee felt the 1994 reforms were both dramatic and sufficient. The report noted that only one in ten taxpayers choose to contribute a dollar to the campaign fund currently, and that the proposed initiative would be an unwelcome drain on the treasury that could threaten vital programs. The state legislature gave no serious consideration to additional reform (House Report, May 5, 1998).

A report issued by the Special Commission on Public Financing of Political Campaigns two years earlier was also emblematic of the climate of debate on this issue prior to the fight to implement the Clean Elections Law. The 1994 reform legislation included the establishment of a commission to study ways to improve and/or amend the state's limited public financing system. The commission, Chaired by Office of Campaign and Political Finance Director Michael Sullivan, issued a report to the legislature in the spring of 1996. The major recommendations of the commission included increasing the tax check-off from one to three dollars and a public education campaign to boost participation in the check-off. No significant changes to the limited public financing system were recommended (Senate Report, June 10, 1996).

Massachusetts voters had little opportunity to seriously consider the pros and cons of public financing before the proponents took to the streets to get signatures for a ballot initiative. The campaign to get the initiative on the ballot was certainly not one that included a serious public debate about the merits of public financing. Volunteers bragged about how easy it was to get people to sign the petitions. Just the mention of "getting money out of politics" prompted voters to sign. Leaders of the reform drive refer to politicians who have "converted" to their position as having "gotten religion." In other words, it was a matter of faith, not reason. Once on the ballot, the campaign for passage was understandably biased. It was not until the law passed and had to be implemented by the legislature that a serious discussion of the pros and cons of public financing has been undertaken in the state. With no other choice but action, state legislators have been forced to deal with the substance of the reform. In doing so, many legislators have provided valuable critical analysis of the measure.

Despite the faith of the reformers, public financing is not universally advocated. In a recent study of campaign finance in state legislative races,

Thompson and Moncrief concluded that the prospects are unclear at best. They recommended further research, specifically case studies of states grappling with reform (1998). The fight for clean elections in Massachusetts may be a perfect case to look at because, unlike in other states, a genuine debate about public financing is underway. This has happened because advocates have forced the legislature to deal with the issue. If legislators do not want public financing, they will have to make a substantive case against it. Many legislators are doing just that. Attempts to push it off, or under-fund it will eventually give way to the need to deal directly with the law. By that time both advocates and opponents will be armed with serious substantive arguments. Despite the onslaught of recent events on the world stage and changing economic fortunes in the state and nation in the fall of 2001, this substantive debate has quietly begun.

The Debate on the Clean Elections Law

There are only two things that are important in politics. The first is money…and I can't remember what the other one is.
— Mark Hanna, Ohio political boss, 1895[4]

Clean elections proponents have marshaled a powerful and professional indictment of the current system of campaign finance in the state and the nation. Well-financed public interest organizations have, since the mid-1990s, worked tirelessly to promote public campaign financing measures at the local, state, and national levels. The prestigious McArthur Foundation, in the early 1990s, began funding studies of public financing at the state level that have produced a strong portfolio of statistical data in support of public financing measures. The national organization Public Campaign claims to be working closely with activists in thirty-five states to push toward public financing laws. New public financing laws are on the books in Massachusetts, Maine, Vermont, and Arizona. And proponents have commissioned surveys of public opinion showing strong support in the states and the nation for campaign finance reform, especially in the wake of Arizona Senator John McCain's national campaign for reform at the federal level. Several recent court decisions have also helped reformers rebut political and constitutional arguments against public financing.

---

4. Quoted in a report published by the Massachusetts Money and Politics Project titled "Capitol Gains" (Boston: 1998).

In Massachusetts, reformers have relied on research findings from an organization called the Massachusetts Money and Politics Project, which is a program of the Commonwealth Education Project, a 501c(3) organization. In a report published in December 2000, titled "On the Eve of Reform" the group summarized and interpreted statistics on campaign contributions and candidate spending by state legislators from 1997–1999. Their findings, while not surprising, were quite compelling. Overall, the report concluded that "the pool of political donors…is smaller, gives more money, represents narrower interests more closely tied to state lawmaking and appears less interested in giving for elections—and more in giving for access and goodwill—than ever before."

Specific findings reported included the following: Less than one percent of eligible voters contributed $100 or more to legislative candidates, and these contributions accounted for over 80% of the money raised by incumbents between 1997 and 1999. More than one third of the $100 or more contributions given to incumbents came from lobbyists, PACs, lawyers and government employees. Incumbents raised 59% of their money during the first six months of each year, when the legislature is in the midst of budget debates and committee hearings. Finally, the study lists the finding that has been most prominent in the fight for clean elections: that the state ranked second to last in contested general elections for the state legislature. The only state with a worse record was Arkansas.

An earlier report prepared by the Massachusetts Money and Politics Project included information about the money picture in statewide races as well as legislative races. The conclusions of the 1999 report titled, "The Money Threshold," were familiar. Winning candidates for all offices spent on average twice as much as their losing opponents. Only three in ten new candidates raised enough money in 1998 to run competitive races. In 1998, the candidate who spent the most money won every statewide race.

The findings of the studies of the Massachusetts Money and Politics Project have fueled the arguments of clean elections reformers, who make essentially seven arguments about the pathologies of the current system of campaign finance in the state. 1) The system causes an escalating "arms race" in fund raising. In 1998, candidates for the Massachusetts House of Representatives spent 38% more as a group than they did in 1996. The winner in the 1998 governor's race spent a record amount to win office in 1998, which was 43% more than the previous winner. 2) The system establishes a "money primary," where viability is measured purely by fund-raising prowess. 3). It increases the time candidates must spend on fund raising and decreases the amount of time spent on public policy issues. 4) New candidates are discouraged by the daunting task of fund raising to be competitive. 5) The lack of competition encouraged by the system leaves voters with fewer choices. 6) Fewer competitive races mean fewer opportunities to hear substantive debate about public policy issues. And finally, all of these things are said to contribute to a seventh problem–cynicism and declining participation rates by the state's voters. Since 1980 the costs of campaigns have outpaced inflation, while voter turnout in the Bay State has dropped 20%.

Reform opponents are not nearly as well organized as proponents, and their arguments are not nearly as well coordinated. Credible policy-based arguments against public financing are often drowned out by extreme ideological rhetoric. Charges that public financing would create "government controlled speech," and "socialism for politicians," and further empower the "liberal" media tendency to detract from reasoned arguments about unintended consequences.[5]

Many legislators, however, have been willing to voice serious concerns about the Clean Elections Law. Although outright opposition is rare, many legislators have sought to expose weaknesses in the law. Many of the problems perceived by legislators were dealt with in the State Senate amendment to the law. The law failed to insulate campaign funds used by legislators for district offices and constituent services from campaign spending limits. Prior to the Senate compromise, clean elections proponents argued that such funds should be appropriated from the legislature, not derived from campaign funds. Now they have conceded that point by supporting the Senate amendment, which insulates such funds from the spending limits.

The law, according to several legislators, gives electoral opportunities to fringe candidates who lack genuine public support by setting the bar too low in terms of qualifying contributions. Republican State Representative Paul Frost was quite candid on this point, telling *The Massachusetts News* "that the law will be an opening for wackos"(Moreno 2001). One legislator, speaking on the condition of anonymity, argued that the law unfairly disadvantages incumbents by funding multiple challengers equally, with little regard for their actual electoral viability. Rather than create the opportunity for substantive debate, the measure would finance an escalation of personal attack campaigning, leaving incumbents as prime targets unable to adequately defend themselves. The Senate compromise sought to address this problem by increasing the amount of money candidates must raise privately to qualify for public money.

---

5. A conservative electronic newspaper called *The Massachusetts News* has devoted considerable ink to articles about the defects of the Clean Elections law. The publication can be accessed at www.massnews.com.

Many state legislators also dispute some of the reformers' assumptions about the current system. One State Senator argued that fund raising does not dominate his time, that, while it may be a problem at the federal level, state legislators are easily able to meet their fund-raising goals without compromising their policy-making efforts. No state legislator interviewed for this study indicated having trouble raising money, or that their fund-raising efforts crowded out more important activities. Further, some legislators expressed anger at the implicit suggestion of reformers that legislators are easily bought and sold. Legislators are also quick to point out that the law does nothing to stem the tide of independent expenditures, which, while not currently significant in state elections, would surely take on greater significance if the Clean Elections Law were fully implemented. Opponents are also happy to mention the irony of the fact that the law does not limit expenditures in ballot initiative campaigns.

The debate on clean elections in the state does not focus on technicalities for long, however. Both friend and foe of the voter-passed law quickly turn their attention to public opinion, arguing alternately that the public is or is not truly supportive of the measure. Opponents of the law in the state legislature have argued consistently, since the initiative passed in 1998, that the voters did not understand what they were voting for. The popular name of the initiative, they argue, clouded the issue, and voters uncritically voted for "clean elections" without appreciating the fact that it was a taxpayer financed system. This argument motivated the House of Representatives on May 7, 1999, to pass a bill placing a non-binding referendum about the Clean Elections Law on the 2000 ballot. Supporter of the bill and House Minority Leader Francis Marini said on the floor that day, "Lets make sure that this is really their [the voters] priority with their tax dollars, instead of roads or education" (State House News Service, May 7, 1999). The bill was passed overwhelmingly in the House. Although the measure did not see the light of day in the State Senate, the underlying argument of its sponsors remained and remains viable.

Opponents further argue that voters' dislike for public financing has been proven clearly by their lack of participation in the current tax check-off system for funding statewide elections. Participation in this program has never risen above 10%. The disparity between the 67% of voters who voted for clean elections and the 10% of taxpayers who were willing to fund it with their tax dollars illustrates, according to opponents, the disconnect between the initiative and voters' true intentions.

Countering the assertion that Massachusetts voters were tricked into supporting the Clean Elections Law and do not actually support public financing, clean elections advocates cite public opinion surveys of both state and national voters. A poll, commissioned by clean elections advocates and conducted by the polling firm of Kiley & Company in February 2001, purports to show a steady level of support for public financing. Voters are said to have favored implementing the Clean Elections Law as passed by a margin of 74% to 18%. The same study refuted the voter ignorance argument by asking the state's voters if they would continue to support the law, knowing that it would cost the state $10 million a year. According to the survey, voter support, when voters were so informed, remained high at 66%. The survey went further, reporting that, even when voters are presented with a balanced presentation including both positive and negative assessments of the law, they continue to support it by a margin of 72% to 20%, with 8% undecided or unwilling to comment. National polling data also seems to indicate a general feeling of support for campaign finance reform among Americans. However, close examination of polling on this issue does reveal ambivalence on the part of voters in the Bay State, as well as the country at large. In addition, the continued strong opposition of elected officials, many of whom claim to have seen private polling on the issue, seems to indicate that the level of current public support for the Clean Elections Law is unclear.

Findings from a survey commissioned by the national clean money organization Public Campaign in 1997 actually showed lower levels of support for significant changes to campaign finance law in Massachusetts, although the overall findings were supportive of reform. Only 37% of Massachusetts voters surveyed felt that "major change" was required. The same survey indicated that only a bare majority of 51% favored the use of public funds for political campaigns. Forty-three percent opposed public funding and 6% reported being undecided or without an opinion.[6]

Another poll that was not commissioned by advocates, conducted by the University of Massachusetts' McCormick institute in May 2000, also showed less than overwhelming support for public financing in the state. Sixty percent of respondents indicated little or no knowledge about the Clean Elections Law. Fifty-three percent could not remember if they had supported or opposed the measure at the polls. Twenty-one percent claimed to have voted for it, while 14% claimed to have opposed it. Thirteen percent said they did not vote at all. On the abstract question of campaign finance reform, 78% reported that it was either very or somewhat important to undertake. When asked specifically about public financing, however, support dropped twenty points to 58%. The UMASS researchers hypothesized that the drop indicates

---

6. Public Campaign's polling can be accessed at www. publicampaign.org/stpoll. html

less support for public financing than for so-called "clean elections." The same study showed that 60% of voters polled felt the estimated costs of publicly financing elections for all state offices was too high. The UMASS poll also called into question voters' support for funding the new law from general revenues. More than half (57%) of respondents who said they favored public financing preferred the law be funded by a voluntary tax check-off. Only 23% of the same group favored using general revenues.

The debate about clean elections has not been limited to the halls of the State Legislature and the press; several court cases have had, and will have, an impact on the fight for clean elections in the state and around the country. In Maine and Arizona, two states where clean elections systems were in effect for the 2000 elections, courts upheld voter-passed public financing laws. A federal district judge in Maine upheld that state's law despite the existence of a controversial provision that counted independent expenditures against the campaign spending limits of the candidates benefitting from the expenditures. Plaintiffs argued that counting such expenditures against candidates, who had no control over the spending, was unfair, and that it would discourage independent groups from exercising their First Amendment right to political speech. Judge D. Brock Hornby ruled in *Dagget v. Webster*, Civ. No. 98-223-B-H (D.ME., Date Issued: 11/5/99) that the provision was reasonable and that the First Amendment guarantees unfettered speech, not uncontested speech.

The Maine decision was significant to the Massachusetts law because it gave judicial sanction to many of the provisions of the Massachusetts law that opponents hoped to challenge, such as the reporting requirements imposed on non-participating candidates and the matching funds provision. The constitutionality of independent expenditure provisions, however, remains an issue because the Maine decision contradicts an earlier federal court decision in Minnesota. In *Day v Holahan*, 34 F.3d 1356 (8th Cir. 1994), the court ruled that a similar independent expenditures provision was unconstitutional. This conflict creates an inconsistency in the law between federal districts that may have to be settled ultimately by the U.S. Supreme Court.

In Arizona, the State Supreme Court ruled that that state's Clean Elections Law could go forward for the 2000 elections despite some constitutionally problematic technicalities that the Court severed from the law. While this case had no specific impact on the provisions of the Massachusetts Clean Elections Act, it did provide further judicial endorsement for voter-passed public financing systems.

The most significant judicial fireworks, however, have happened right here in the Bay State. Because the funding of the law was tied up in the legislature's negotiations on the FY2002 budget, Massachusetts gubernatorial candidate and former State Senator Warren Tolman filed a federal lawsuit against the State. Tolman argued that the state's failure to fund his clean elections candidacy had harmed his ability to run for Governor. While Tolman did not prevail in his federal case, another lawsuit in which he was a party did go his way. A number of plaintiffs, including Mass Voters for Clean Elections, Mr. Tolman, and several individual voters sued the State in State Court (*Bates v. Dir. of the Office of Campaign and Political Finance*, No. SJC-08677). They were looking for injunctive relief from the Office of Political and Campaign Finance. They wanted the office's director, Michael Sullivan, to disburse funds to clean elections candidates, despite the lack of a legislative appropriation. The State Court suit was based on Article 48 of the amendments to the Massachusetts Constitution, which requires the legislature to provide the necessary funds to implement legislation passed by the voters, or to repeal such laws.

On January 25, 2002, the Massachusetts Supreme Judicial Court ruled for the plaintiffs. In their "memorandum and order" the Court found that Article 48 of the amendments to the state constitution does require the state legislature to either fund or repeal measures passed by ballot initiative, despite the defendants argument that the Clean Elections Law's language, which includes the phrase "subject to appropriation," makes clear that appropriation of funds is at the discretion of the legislature. Defendants further argued, and were supported by the Court's dissenting opinion, that the Constitution's language in Article 48 must be understood in the context of the intent of its Framers.[7] Such consideration, combined with another constitutional provision prohibiting direct appropriation of funds by ballot initiative, makes clear that the legislature cannot be hamstrung by ballot initiatives. The legislature's prerogative and power to wield the purse strings in state government cannot, from this perspective, be delegated to the voters directly.

The Court's 5–2 decision did not include extensive argument or a remedy. The dissent, however, was extensive and compelling. Legal analysts speculated widely about the reasons for the Court's unusual decision, which was not predicted by any objective commentators. The Court hoped to avoid having to fashion a remedy that could ignite a constitutional firestorm. The Court's hope

---

7. The discovery of legislative intent is not usually possible in cases arising out of Massachusetts law because state legislative debates are not transcribed or recorded. However, in this case the intent being examined was that of the delegates to the 1917-18 State Constitutional Convention and the provision in question is a constitutional amendment, not a statute.

of coaxing the legislature into funding the law produced, instead, passage in both houses of the legislature bills gutting the Clean Elections Law and transferring the clean elections funds to other more pressing concerns. These bills did not garner enough support to override the Acting Governor's promised veto, but they did make clear to one and all that the legislature would not cave in to the Court's pressure.

Having had the Court's bluff called, the Court's decision on a remedy, handed down on February 25, 2002, stopped short of ordering the legislature to appropriate the funds. Instead, the Court found that candidates who complied with the law, and who therefore have been or would be hurt by its lack of funding, were entitled to monetary damages. In other words, the Court placed itself in the position of funding the law by handing down individual damage judgments to qualified candidates. To accomplish this difficult task efficiently, the Court remanded all further proceedings in the case to a single Justice, who would have broad discretion in her efforts to obtain funds to satisfy present and future judgments on the matter. As of this writing, Justice Martha Sosman had not yet ruled on any petitions to her by qualified clean elections candidates other than the original plaintiff, Warren Tolman, who has received a portion of the money for which he was eligible under the Clean Elections Law.

As of this writing, the question remains: where will the plaintiff, the Director of the Office of Campaign and Political Finance, get the funds? The Court did not find that clean elections funds were deemed appropriated as a matter of law despite legislative inaction, and, without an appropriation, the OCPF Director has no money to give to the plaintiffs. The only funds available for the payment of damages without a legislative appropriation are held in a specific account created for that purpose, which, at the time of the decision, did not even have enough funds to pay Tolman the total amount he was due. Justice Sosman issued a clarifying opinion shortly after the February 25, 2002 decision, stating that if the legislature did not cooperate with the Court by transferring sufficient funds into the legal judgments account, the clerk of the court could authorize a county sheriff to seize state property, which would then be sold to produce revenue that could be used to satisfy the legal judgment against the state (Ring 2002).

The battle over clean elections has moved from the ballot box, to the legislature, to the Courts. Having failed to extract funding from the legislature, advocates of the Clean Elections Law are counting on the Supreme Judicial Court to salvage and sustain their effort. It remains to be seen, as of this writing, who will prevail in this escalating game of constitutional chicken. Reform advocates are hoping the courts can save their reform measure for the 2002 elections. Otherwise, they will have to ramp up for another battle at the ballot box.

Conclusion

The Clean Elections Law in Massachusetts is mortally wounded for three very good reasons. 1) The state's elected officials are professional politicians whose political careers are their careers. 2) Public support for clean elections is not nearly as clear as the advocates claim. 3) the arguments of opponents of the Clean Elections Law have gotten considerably stronger since the initiative passed. The constant presence of the issue forced elected officials to formulate serious counter arguments for which clean elections advocates were not prepared. Advocates had counted on using the unreflective cynicism of the public to extort reform from a gun-shy legislature, but the law's opponents in the legislature have not rolled over, and, despite the failure of the legislature to fund the Clean Elections Law, as well as a high profile decision by the State's highest court excoriating the legislature, the threatened public outcry has not materialized.

Politics on Beacon Hill is a highly professional, full-time activity. The state's legislature (and by implication its politics) is classified by the National Conference of State Legislatures as highly professional, with full-time elected officials and staffs, long legislative sessions, high legislator pay, and stable membership. The electoral stakes for these professionals are high. All of the states in which clean elections laws have been successfully implemented are considerably less professionalized in this respect.

Maine and Vermont are purely part-time legislatures. The National Conference of State Legislatures classifies both northern New England states as "part-time," with low legislator pay, small staffs, and high member turnover. Clean elections advocates also tout the success of Arizona's Clean Elections Law, but there, too, the comparison is inappropriate. Arizona is classified by the National Conference of State Legislatures as "in-between, hybrid," meaning not strictly part-time or full-time. Arizona's legislators earn $24,000 per year. Only the majority and minority leadership have full-time staffs, and, due to term limits in the state, turnover in the legislature was relatively high even before the enactment of the Clean Elections Law. Furthermore, most Arizona state legislators maintain outside employment due to the relatively low pay they receive as legislators.

Elected officials whose livelihoods depend on their re-election weigh the costs and benefits of campaign finance reform differently than part-time, or non-professional elected officials do. The high material stakes of re-election for professional politicians provide increased incentive to resist measures intended to enhance electoral competition, and they change the calculus regarding how much public outcry can be resisted. Also, full-time elected officials, with their increased resources, are better able to communicate with their constituents and are therefore less vulnerable to single-issue attacks.

Public support for campaign finance reform is widespread, but very soft. Frequent references by advocates to the two-to-one margin of victory at the ballot box are intended to highlight the breadth of support, without revealing how shallow it is. The bravado of some of the law's opponents, like House Speaker Tom Finneran, may stem from their careful reading of public opinion. While advocates brag about the margin of victory at the polls, legislators realize that it's not quite that simple. In fact, out of 3,378,165 registered voters in 1998, less than one third voted for the clean elections initiative. The two-to-one margin only accounts for the ratio of yes to no votes. Ballots cast without a vote on the question, totaling 282,867, or 12.03%, are not accounted for. Also unaccounted for by advocates is the nearly 47% of registered voters who stayed home on Election Day in 1998.

Despite numerous efforts to understand public opinion on campaign finance reform at the state and national levels, researchers are divided on the public's level of support. The case of the Massachusetts Clean Elections Law, however, seems to be providing compelling evidence that, at least in the Bay State, voters are not terribly energized by campaign finance reform. There is very little evidence that voters are upset about the failure of the state legislature to fund clean elections. The lead advocacy group, Mass Voters for Clean Elections, has not been able to generate significant levels of public outcry about the apparent scuttling of the public financing measure. While it is easy to argue that the recent terrorist attacks have distracted the public from process issues like campaign finance reform, it should be noted that the law had been bottled up in the state's budget conference committee for two months before that fateful day in September. Protests organized by advocates at the state house before and after September 11, have not attracted much attention.

Two prominent elected officials who intended to run for governor as clean elections candidates, State Treasurer Shannon O'Brien and Secretary of State William Galvin, recently announced in the fall of 2001 that they could not continue to adhere to the fund-raising requirements of the Clean Elections Law because of the uncertainty of its fate and the need for them to be competitive with the candidates who are not running as clean elections candidates. O'Brien and Galvin were the highest profile elected officials committed to the public financing system. Their decision not to run "clean" did not bode well for the law. Both candidates blasted the legislature for scuttling the law as they announced their decision to back out of the law's regime, and still no great public outcry was audible. Not even a very high profile decision of the state's highest court berating the legislature and upholding the Clean Elections Law has generated any significant public dissatisfaction with the law's opponents.

The virtual neutralization of public opinion on the Clean Elections Law cannot be attributed simply to voter apathy, or lack of enthusiasm. The opponents of the measure have increasingly been willing to make substantive arguments against to the law. Virtually every elected official, regardless of their position on clean elections has prefaced their remarks about it by saying that they are "not fans" of government by referenda. Even supporters of the law admit that it was not carefully drafted, and that it requires technical corrections. In other words, the fact that the law was enacted by ballot initiative instead of the regular legislative process has provided opponents with a substantive argument against the law that seems to be resonating with the public.

Arguments against initiative and referenda, such as David Broder's recent offering, *Democracy Derailed* (2000), make a compelling case against this Progressive Era innovation. Clean elections opponents in the Bay State have argued with increasing political confidence that direct legislation is not an effective way to make public policy. Opponents argue that, unlike the legislative process, ballot initiatives are straight up or down votes that are not amenable to negotiation. The bargaining in the legislature that is often the target of the reformers' ire actually produces the compromises necessary for workable public policies. Even the Supreme Judicial Court's decision on February 25, 2002, that upheld the Clean Elections Law contained some good news for opponents. The two justices in the minority wrote a compelling dissent that will provide opponents of the measure with some credible and authoritative arguments. One such argument is that the Massachusetts Constitution's requirement that only the legislature can appropriate money is effectively violated if the Clean Elections Law is funded without legislative approval. This line of argument fits nicely with Broder's in that preserving the power of the purse exclusively for the legislature provides a valuable check on the state's initiative process.

Clean elections advocates anticipated that the public would discount any attempt to argue against the law on the merits, seeing such arguments as thinly veiled attempts to thwart the will of the people for personal gain. In the wake of a slowing economy in the state, and the national focus on international events and domestic security concerns, voters are not playing along. Arguments about the flaws of "government by referenda" and about funding other priorities first, like education and airport security, are not being dismissed as politics as usual. Supporters of the Clean Elections Law are themselves on the defensive.

Clean Elections activists are very energetic and quite committed. Unfortunately for them, their passion far exceeds the public's. Legislators know that, while clean elections advocates are very active and visible around the state, when push comes to shove, their electoral coalitions will not be severely weakened by this single issue. Constitutional officers, on the other hand, may have more to fear from the clean elections advocates. Candidates for statewide office should avoid raising the anger of clean elections advocates because they are well funded and well organized and could be marshaled by a friendly statewide candidate very effectively. In fact, one of the reform components missing from the Clean Elections Law is the regulation of independent expenditures. Clean elections activists are likely to utilize this loophole in their reform regime to help friendly statewide candidates and punish unfriendly ones in the 2002 elections.

In numerous public statements about the 2002 budget, which ultimately left the Clean Elections Law unfunded, David Donnelly, Executive Director of Mass Voters for Clean Elections, promised (read "threatened") those who conspired to thwart the will of the people that his supporters will get their revenge at the ballot box in 2002. It is clear that the clean elections advocates intend to mount a serious campaign for their measure and against those they see as "law breakers, not law makers."[8] While they will have considerable difficulty weakening the local electoral coalitions of legislators, they may have a marginal impact on the elections for statewide offices. Ironically, that may be bad news for clean elections supporter and Senate President, Tom Birmingham, whom reformers have pledged to hold responsible for the legislature's failure to fund the law, but not for House Speaker Tom Finneran, who has always opposed the reform openly and energetically. The clean elections advocates will complicate Birmingham's run for governor, while Finneran's seat in the legislature is beyond the reach of the reform's proponents.

In the final analysis, campaign finance law in Massachusetts has had very little impact on the conduct of politics for some of the same reasons that reforms at the national level have not realized their promise. Professional politicians, ambiguous public opinion, and reasonable objections have spelled de-

---

8. Donnelly used this phrase in several public statements referring to the Senate President, Tom Birmingham, and to the Speaker of the House, Tom Finneran.

feat for comprehensive campaign finance reform on Beacon Hill and Capitol Hill. Reforms in both the states and Washington happen incrementally, and usually only in the wake of a high profile scandal. The impact of reasonable arguments against various incarnations of campaign finance reform is often underestimated. In Massachusetts, substantive objections to the Clean Elections Law have gotten a hearing and have had an impact on the debate. Because Massachusetts voters were able to force the issue through the initiative process, unlike the nation's voters, the experience of the Bay State has elevated the terms of the debate about campaign finance reform. At the national level, rational incentives of professional politicians and the juxtaposition of conflicting public opinion data have always over shadowed reasonable debate about the merits of reform. Only high profile scandals, such as Watergate and Enron, produce movement on campaign finance reform in Washington. In Massachusetts, which mirrors the national government in professionalism, and where public opinion is equally open to interpretation, the same logic applies. But in Massachusetts reasonable debate has reared its ugly head despite the absence of a recent scandal. This is the case because the debate is not merely about proposed policy; it is about the implementation of current law.

Logical argument having been long the province of academics, suddenly activists and politicians in the state have been confronted with the need to marshal substantive arguments for their views. Advocates for reform cannot merely repeat familiar statistics about the alleged defects of the current system. They have to defend and advocate for an existing law. The reformers have been confronted with the difficulty of translating voter cynicism into workable public policy. Clever slogans will not cut it in this arena. When fashioning workable public policy, the simple classification of good versus evil, or clean versus dirty, losses its usefulness. Equally out of their comfort zone, the state's politicians have been forced to put up or shut up on campaign finance reform. They cannot continue to claim the voters have not spoken, nor do their claims of voter confusion have much political resonance. They have had to formulate substantive objections. The Supreme Judicial Court's involvement in this case has kept the issue alive, and, regardless of how this potential constitutional showdown is resolved, clean elections will be an issue in the 2002 elections and beyond.

Social scientists have long struggled to understand how and why change occurs in American politics. Academics, activists, and politicians have long understood that change happens incrementally in American politics, and yet, repeatedly, this seemingly simple lesson is forgotten. Gingrich Republicans tried to dismantle the welfare state and were chastened. President Clinton tried to overhaul the health care industry and was rebuked. The advocates of clean elections in Massachusetts overplayed their hand and are learning a hard lesson about hardball politics. Despite these short-term miscalculations at the national level, changes in welfare and health care were forthcoming. In the fight for campaign finance reform in Massachusetts, the over-reach of the clean elections advocates will also likely advance the ball on campaign finance reform in the long run.

The Achilles heel of virtually all reforms that seek to change our allegedly broken political system is the failure of the reformers to appreciate the participatory part of our participatory democracy. Effective citizenship requires more than merely following the law and voting on Election Day. Reformers tend to let the voters off easy in exchange for mere support for change at the ballot box, and they don't spend enough time cultivating the activity of the voters between elections. Reformers seem to focus too much on the effects and not enough on the root causes of systemic problems. Money's influence on politics is the effect of the problem, a symptom of the disease. The root cause is voter apathy and ignorance. Money cannot control elections or policy decisions if the voters care enough to stay informed. No doubt, reformers understand this but see it as an inescapable reality. Improving effective participation is seen as a worthwhile, but different, fight. Campaign finance reform seeks to ameliorate the symptoms of the disease, and this is certainly a worthwhile, even necessary, pursuit. Unfortunately, the failure to acknowledge the culpability of the voters encourages the very cynicism that makes real systemic change impossible. It is the resignation and cynicism of the voters that allows politicians to find and exploit the inevitable legal loopholes in reform measures. When the loopholes are exploited, voters are once again reminded of the futility of reforms, the advocates of which always promise more than they can deliver.

In Massachusetts, because of the hard work of the reformers, politicians will have to make voters think about the consequences of the clean elections remedy. To do so will require arguments on the merits. The reformers need to make the voters think more comprehensively about the problem in order to credibly and productively participate in the debate. To do so they will have to shelve their focus, group-tested slogans, and acknowledge that hard problems require hard solutions, solutions that cannot be effected by legislative fiat or court orders, but rather must be accomplished with the ongoing vigilance and participation of the state's citizenry. Finally, all sides would be well advised to revisit the memoir of one of the state's favorite sons, Larry O'Brien. The title of the book by the Kennedy and Johnson administration insider is *No Final Victories* (1974). O'Brien understood well that success in American politics comes not with election or the enactment of legislation, but with the improvement and continuance of the debate, both of which require expanding the efforts of the many, not restricting the efforts of the few.

References

Barnhill, James H. 1974. Massachusetts political finance laws—an overview. Massachusetts Law Quarterly 59: 239–67

Becker, Lawrence A. 1995. Regulating politics: Election laws in Massachusetts. Unpublished paper.

Bottomly, John S. 1950. Corrupt practices in political campaigns. *Boston University Law Review* 50: 331–64

Broder, David S. 2000. *Democracy derailed: Initiative campaigns and the power of money.* New York: Harcourt, Inc.

Commonwealth of Massachusetts. 1980. *Final Report to the General Court of the Special Commission Concerning State and County Buildings*, 31 December: 1 and 8. Boston.

———. 1996. *Report of the Special Commission on Public Financing of Political Campaigns*, 10 June: Report #S2313. Boston.

Crowley, Michael. 1999. Clean elections efforts blocked. *Boston Globe*, 19 October, A1

Donnelly, David, Janice Fine, and Ellen Miller. 1999. *Money and politics: Financing our elections democratically.* Boston: Beacon Press.

Malbin, Michael J., and Thomas L. Gais. 1998. *The day after reform: Sobering campaign finance lessons from the American states.* Albany: Rockefeller Institute Press.

Massachusetts General Court. 1998. Joint Committee on Ways and Means. *Clean elections initiative petition report.* (5 May): 2. Boston.

Massachusetts Money and Politics Project. 1998. *Capitol gains: Big donors in the state legislature.* Boston.

———. 1999. *The money threshold: A summary of campaign spending, competition, and choice in the 1998 Massachusetts state elections.* Boston.

———. 2000. *On the eve of reform: An inside look at legislative fund raising in Massachusetts 1997–1999.* Boston.

McDonough, John E. 2000. *Experiencing politics: A legislator's stories of government and health care.* Berkeley: University of California Press.

Moreno, Paul. 2001. Did mass voters understand clean elections law? *The Massachusetts News*, 2 July.

O'Brien, Lawrence F. 1974. *No final victories: A life in politics from John F. Kennedy to Watergate.* Garden City, NY: Doubleday & Company, Inc.

Ring, Dan. 2002. Candidates shy from "clean" funding. *Springfield Union-News*, 28 February, A1, A6.

Robinson, Walter V. 1981. Campaign watchdogs portrayed as toothless violations often went undetected. *Boston Globe*, 1 January, A1

Thompson, Joel A., and Gary E. Moncrief. 1998. *Campaign finance in state legislative elections.* Washington, DC: Congressional Quarterly Press.

Interviews

Thomas F. Birmingham, President of the Massachusetts Senate

David Donnelly, Executive Director, Mass Voters for Clean Elections

Thomas M. Finneran, Speaker of the Massachusetts House of Representative
Brian P. Lees, Senate Minority Leader of the Massachusetts Senate
Rep. Francis L. Marini, Minority Leader of the Massachusetts House of Representatives
Linda J. Melconian, Majority Leader of the Massachusetts Senate
David Nyhardt, Executive Director, Public Campaign
Stanley C. Rosenberg, Assistant Majority Leader of the Massachusetts Senate
Michael Sullivan, Director of the Massachusetts Office of Campaign and Political Finance
Warren Tolman, 2002 Candidate for Governor of Massachusetts
Rep. Joseph F. Wagner, Co-Chair, Election Laws Committee, Massachusetts House of
    Representatives
Michael J. Walsh, Budget and Policy Advisor to the Massachusetts Senate Majority Leader
Ken White, Executive Director, Common Cause Massachusetts

CHAPTER 7

Iowa's Experience with Limited Regulation

Ed Mansfield
Charles Smithson[1]

Introduction

In our digital world, we like to see things in absolutes. It's "1" or it's "0."
You're a survivor or you're off the island. Something is all good or all bad. We
have trouble accepting shades of gray, uncertainties, imponderables, and
trade-offs. This applies to the current campaign finance reform debate.

Proponents of campaign finance reform view contribution limits as a moral
imperative. Without them, expenses spiral out of control; candidates spend
too much time raising funds; legislators become the captive of special interests; and elections become uncompetitive.

To campaign finance reform opponents, however, limits are both unconstitutional and undesirable. In their opinion, an absence of limits fosters fluid
races with unpredictable outcomes, heavy involvement by ideologically motivated donors, and a better informed electorate.

Our research of Iowa state legislative campaigns over the last ten years
shows that neither generalization quite captures the Iowa experience. Campaign finance in Iowa is largely unregulated. Public financing does not exist.
Individuals may contribute to candidates without limit. Significantly, as we
shall see, Iowa also permits free transfers of campaign funds from candidates

1. The authors wish to express their deep appreciation to Joan Lucas and Katy Gam-
mack of Money & Politics Iowa (MAP Iowa) for their assistance in providing source materials for this chapter. The conclusions herein are solely the personal views of one or both
of the authors and do not represent the positions of any governmental agency.

to political parties and from political parties to candidates. Additionally, private-sector labor unions (but not corporations or public-sector unions) may donate funds from their treasuries to political action committees, which in turn may transfer them to candidates.

Our analysis[2] suggests that Iowa's relatively unregulated system has had both positive and negative effects. Campaign contributions and expenses in Iowa are escalating rapidly, although the numbers derived from official disclosure reports may overstate the aggregate level of expenditures, because some of the money is simply circulating between candidates by way of the political parties and thus gets counted twice. On the other hand, races do not seem to be getting less competitive. A significant concern, however, is the growing pool of funds, particularly PAC and other special interest money, which flows into the campaign committees of state legislative candidates who belong to the leadership.

More generally, it may be appropriate to distinguish the *campaigning* effects from the *governance* effects of campaign finance. It is conceivable that Iowa's deregulated system may promote more lively, informed, and competitive races from a campaigning standpoint, while also having adverse consequences for governance, such as a greater potential for special interests to influence the legislative agenda or, perhaps, freeze the respective positions of each political party concerning pending legislation.

An Overview of Iowa and Its Campaign Finance Laws

Iowa likes to consider itself a stalwart of the farm economy and a picture of balance and moderation, and some of the statistics bear this out. Iowa ranks thirtieth in population, with just under three million residents, but the largest metropolitan area, Des Moines, contains only 456,022 residents and ranks ninety-first in population among the nation's metropolitan areas. Iowa leads the nation in production of corn, soybeans, and pork.

In recent history, Iowa has been a closely divided two-party state. While demographic statistics might lead one to predict that Iowa would be predominantly Republican, in the last several decades Democratic views on foreign

2. Unless credit is specifically given to another source, the data used in this chapter come from the *Iowa Official Register* ("the Red Book"), published by the Iowa Secretary of State's office, or from newsletters and databases assembled by Money and Politics Iowa (MAP Iowa) and available on the MAP Iowa website at www.MAP Iowa.org.

policy and on agriculture have found favor in the state (Barone 1998). In 1990 and 1994, Iowans elected a Republican governor. In 1998, for the first time since the 1960s, they elected a Democrat.

Currently, both the State Senate (50 members) and the State House of Representatives (100 members), which together make up the "General Assembly," have Republican majorities. The Republicans gained control of the House in 1992, and the Senate in 1996. However, Republicans had not previously controlled both houses since the early 1970s. The average Senate district contains slightly less than 60,000 residents; the average House district slightly less than 30,000.

As of October 2001, there were 564,692 registered Republicans and 537,779 registered Democrats in Iowa. However, as recently as 1992, Democrats had a registration edge (Keefer 1999), and Iowa has supported the Democratic candidate for president in every election since 1988. In 2000, the Democratic nominee, Al Gore, carried the state by less than 5,000 votes. Iowa is a right-to-work state, but approximately 16.1% of the workforce consists of union members, which is above the national average (Dalbey 2001).

Iowa has a part-time legislature that generally meets from January to late April each year, except for special sessions. Senators are elected to four-year terms, with half the Senate up for election in each even-numbered year. Representatives serve two-year terms. Decennial redistricting in Iowa occurs through a mainly nonpartisan process (*Iowa Code* ch. 42). An independent office draws the new district lines based on neutral criteria, such as compactness and preservation of political subdivision boundaries. This tends to result in significant turnover at the state legislature following the start of each decade.

Another distinguishing feature of Iowa is its first-in-the-nation presidential caucuses. To succeed in these caucuses, a presidential campaign generally needs to be well-organized, with local allies throughout the state. Some argue that these caucuses have strengthened Iowa's political parties (Barone 1998). What is undeniable is that they have increased the flow of money into Iowa political campaigns, as would-be presidential candidates try to enlist supporters among Iowa officeholders. Committees such as the Campaign for a New American Century (Lamar Alexander), the Campaign for Working Families (Gary Bauer), and Americans for Hope Growth & Opportunity (Steve Forbes) have contributed substantially to Iowa campaigns.

Iowa's campaign finance laws, like those of many other states, date back to the Watergate era. In June 1973, the legislature enacted the Campaign Disclosure-Income Tax Check-off Act, which required disclosure of contributions and expenditures and also severely limited campaign expenditures (65 G.A.

ch. 138). The expenditure limit was $.30 times the numbers of voters in the district who voted for President in the last election. If in effect today, the law would limit a candidate's spending to about $4,000 on a House race and $8,000 on a Senate race. During the debate over the legislation, limitations on contributions were proposed but defeated.

The 1973 campaign finance legislation passed the state House of Representatives by a 77–16 margin, passed the Senate unanimously, and was promptly signed by the Governor. In 1975, the legislature added a ban on corporate contributions (66 G.A. ch. 57). In 1976, the legislature repealed the expenditure limit in the wake of *Buckley v. Valeo* (66 G.A. ch. 1078).

In 1986, the state was rocked by a scandal known as "Mingo-Gate." Lobbyists funded a stag party, which included two nude female dancers, for a legislator in Mingo, Iowa. Twenty-one legislators attended at the lobbyists' expense. Partly as a result of the publicity surrounding this event, there was a further push to reform campaign finance laws (Bruner 1998). In 1987, both houses of the General Assembly (then controlled by the Democrats) approved a measure on a largely party-line vote that would have provided public financing for legislative and statewide candidates who agreed to abide by expenditure limits. However, the Republican Governor vetoed the legislation. Hence, the basic structure of Iowa's campaign finance laws has not changed over the last twenty-five years and, as with federal campaign finance law, that structure differs from what the legislature originally intended.

The Iowa Disclosure Requirements

The Iowa campaign finance laws apply to individuals seeking any state, county, or local elected public office (*Iowa Code* ch. 56). Thus, candidates for township trustee through governor must follow the same requirements. However, any candidate who receives contributions, makes expenditures, or incurs indebtedness of $500 or less does not have to register with the government and file public disclosure reports. Subject to that one exception, every candidate for state or local elected office must comply equally with the campaign laws.

Candidates for statewide office and the General Assembly who cross the $500 threshold must register with the Iowa Ethics and Campaign Disclosure Board within ten days. The Campaign Board, established by legislation in 1993 and based in the state capital of Des Moines, is an independent agency whose members are appointed by the governor. By law, it has six members, of which no more than three may be from the same party. In addition to enforcing Iowa's campaign finance laws, it also investigates ethics complaints against public officials. (A predecessor entity, the Campaign Finance Disclosure Commission, was structured differently and had more limited authority.)

Candidates for county and local office who pass the $500 threshold must register with the auditor of the county where the office sought is located. The county is then responsible for providing copies of filings to the state's Campaign Board, which has authority over the campaign finances of all candidates for public office in Iowa.

Not only candidates, but also organizations that advocate the election of a candidate or the passage of a ballot issue, must register when they cross the $500 threshold. These are known as "political committees" or, in common parlance, PACs. Registration is either central (with the Campaign Board) or local (with the county auditor), depending upon whether or not the political committee intends to be involved in a statewide (or state legislative) race. Any organization that is certified as a "political party," based on results of federal and statewide elections, also is required to register. A certified "political party" is then permitted to have a local organization in each county that registers as a "county central committee."

Every candidate's committee and every political committee must have a treasurer who is an Iowa resident and has reached the age of majority. All campaign funds must be maintained in an Iowa bank account segregated from any other funds of the candidate or the committee.

The committee treasurers play a pivotal role in the campaign finance process in Iowa. The treasurer is required to keep a detailed and exact account of the contributions made to or for the committee. The name and mailing address (but not the occupation or employer) of every person contributing in excess of $10 to the committee must be recorded along with the date and amount of the contribution. Not surprisingly, all contributions must be made in the name of the person actually making the contribution. The use of pseudonyms is prohibited. All disbursements made by the committee, including the name and mailing address of every person to whom an expenditure is made, must be recorded. The treasurer is not permitted to spend campaign funds without the approval of the candidate, or of the chairperson, in the case of a political committee.

By far the most important duty placed on the campaign treasurer is to file campaign disclosure reports that disclose publicly the money taken in and spent by the committee. Although the treasurer is required to file the report, the law places the ultimate burden of responsibility on the candidate, or on the chairperson, in the case of a political committee. A report that is not filed on or before the required reporting date subjects the candidate or political committee chairperson to possible civil and criminal penalties.

Candidates for statewide office and the General Assembly file reports directly with the Campaign Board. Candidates for county and local office file their reports with the county auditor, who then provides copies to the Campaign Board. Political committees that advocate for or against statewide or General Assembly candidates or for or against passage of a statewide ballot issue file reports with the Campaign Board. All other political committees file with the appropriate county auditor, who then provides copies to the Campaign Board. Political parties file with the Campaign Board, while county central committees file with both the Campaign Board and their county auditor.

Reports may be hand-delivered, faxed or mailed. To be considered filed on time, a mailed report must be postmarked on or before the due date; other methods of filing require the report to be received by the due date. The state's Campaign Board has developed a voluntary electronic filing program that permits reports to be filed by computer disk or modem. The Campaign Board is also developing a system that would allow committees to file reports via the Internet. However, there remains substantial opposition in the Iowa legislature to mandatory electronic filing, on the ground that this would unfairly penalize rural legislators with limited technological resources.

At present, members of the public have to travel to the appropriate repository to view reports, or they may obtain copies by mail or fax. Beginning in 2002, state legislative and statewide reports will be available for public viewing on the Campaign Board website.

Due dates for reports depend on the office sought by the candidate, on whether it is an election year for the candidate, and on the amount of money raised by the candidate. Candidates for statewide office and the General Assembly are required to file reports by January 19 of every year (the approximate date when the legislature convenes). During election years, candidates for these offices also must file reports by the 19th of May, July and October.

Additionally, in an election year, candidates for statewide office and the state legislature must file supplemental reports the Friday before the primary and the general election if they have received contributions in excess of a certain amount since the previous reporting deadline. That threshold is $10,000 for gubernatorial candidates, $5,000 for other statewide candidates, and $1,000 for state legislative candidates.

Political committees, party organizations, and candidates for county and local office are subject to similar, but not entirely identical, reporting deadlines. They do not have to file supplemental reports.

Each regular report must disclose the amount of cash in the campaign account at the beginning of the reporting period. In addition, the report must disclose the name, mailing address, and amount of each contribution to the committee exceeding $25 in a calendar year, the name, mailing address and market value of donated services or goods in excess of $25 (these are known in Iowa as "in-kind" contributions and include coordinated expenditures), the name, mailing address, and amount of any loans received, and the total proceeds from any fund-raising event. Contributions of $25 or less during a calendar year are lumped together and reported as a total of "un-itemized" contributions.

Each report also must disclose the name, mailing address, and amount of all campaign expenditures and loan repayments of $5 or more. Expenditures of less than $5 may be reported as "miscellaneous" so long as they do not exceed $100 to any one person during the calendar year.

Furthermore, each committee must report the nature of debts and obligations owed by the committee and the names and mailing addresses of any consultants and other entities with which the committee has entered into contracts. Finally, the committee must list all campaign property that was originally valued at more than $500 and must continue reporting the value of the property until it falls below $100. However, this separate listing is not required for "consumable" campaign property, such as stationery, yard signs, and other campaign materials that have been permanently imprinted to be specific to a candidate.

A committee must continue to file reports until all funds are expended, debts and loans are repaid or forgiven, and the committee files a statement of dissolution.

In 1986, the legislature enacted a second prong of public disclosure (71 G.A. ch. 1023). In its current form, that legislation requires a "paid for by" attribution statement to be placed on many materials that advocate the outcome of an election. Any individual, organization, or committee that pays for a political advertisement, brochure, mailer, poster, billboard, or outdoor advertising facility must disclose who paid for the costs of producing and distributing the material. In addition, the words "paid for by" must be included. The attribution statement must be "conspicuous" on all materials except for posters. The attribution statement is not required on yard signs (interpreted as any sign sixteen square feet or less), buttons, bumper stickers, or other small items where the inclusion of the statement would be impracticable.

Contribution Limits in Iowa

Even though Iowa does not limit the *amount* of money that can be contributed to a committee from any one source, certain entities are prohibited from making contributions to candidates, political committees, or political parties and their central committees.

In particular, Iowa parallels federal law in prohibiting contributions by insurance companies, banks, and for-profit and non-profit corporations in elections involving candidates for public office. These entities also are barred from using their funds to engage in independent expenditures expressly advocating the election or defeat of candidates.

Corporations and similar entities may establish sponsored PACs analogous to the "separate segregated funds" permitted by the Federal Election Campaign Act. Iowa law permits corporate treasury funds to be used to pay for administrative and solicitation expenses of these PACs. Additionally, stockholders, administrative officers and members of corporations may be solicited for contributions to the PAC. No other corporate employees may be solicited, although they are permitted to contribute.

Interestingly, Iowa law does *not* prohibit private sector unions from making candidate contributions. It is not clear, however, that this "loophole" has much practical significance. Although some private-sector unions reportedly make direct transfers from their treasuries to their PACs, others rely on a separate PAC checkoff. In any event, public-sector unions are prohibited by law from making contributions out of their treasuries to parties or candidates (Iowa Code ch. 20.26). Historically the teachers' association (the Iowa State Education Association) has had the most active labor PAC in Iowa (Smith 2001).

Candidates for statewide or state legislative office may not be officers, or otherwise direct, maintain, or control any PAC. Also, a PAC may not be established to advocate for only one candidate. The corollary to this prohibition is that a candidate may establish one and only one campaign committee.

In 1991, the General Assembly enacted several restrictions on the use of campaign funds by candidates (74 G.A. ch. 226). Candidates are prohibited from using campaign funds to make contributions to other candidates; likewise, they may not receive campaign funds from other candidates. Candidates may use campaign funds only for campaign purposes, educational expenses, and other expenses associated with the duties of office or with constituency services. Significantly, as will be discussed below, candidates *are* permitted to make contributions to political parties, county central committees, or partisan political committees (but not PACs). Candidates may, if they are so inclined, make contributions to charitable organizations or a state or county general fund—or return contributions to contributors on a pro rata basis. However, campaign funds may not be used for personal expenses or personal benefit. No committee may transfer funds in an attempt to circumvent any of these restrictions on the use of campaign funds.

In addition, since 1992, registered lobbyists and PACs have been prohibited from making contributions, arranging contributions, or acting as an agent or intermediary for contributions to an elected state official, member of the General Assembly, or candidate for state office during the regular legislative session (74 G.A. ch. 1228). For the governor and gubernatorial candidates, the ban extends to the 30-day bill-signing period after the close of each legislative session.

The Iowa campaign finance laws also contain an income tax checkoff. Every Iowa taxpayer may direct that $1.50 of his or her income tax liability be paid to the Iowa election campaign fund. These tax dollars are then turned over to the taxpayer's designated political party, or if no designation is made, are divided equally among all certified political parties. The checkoff has had only a modest impact. For the 1999 tax year, the most recent year for which statistics are available, it raised a total of $137,735. The political parties may use funds received from this program only in general elections.

As might be expected, given Iowa's relatively modest level of campaign finance regulation, there have been relatively few significant court challenges. In 1998, a federal court entered an injunction against the enforcement of Iowa's prohibition on corporate contributions (*Iowa Right to Life Committee, Inc. v. Williams* 1999). The plaintiff, Iowa Right to Life Committee, had argued that the statute was unconstitutional because it purported to ban some forms of corporate issue advocacy. The district court agreed but also, somewhat surprisingly, did not adopt a narrowing construction. Instead, it declared the entire provision invalid. This temporary "loophole" was closed by the legislature in the following legislative session (78 G.A. ch. 136) so that corporate contributions or expenditures for the benefit of candidates are now outlawed but issue advocacy is permitted.

Some General Observations

As can be seen from the foregoing review, Iowa law imposes few restrictions on the amount of money that flows into political campaigns. Rather, the law focuses more on public disclosure and the regulation of certain campaign activities. Whether or not the regulatory system is working is subject to debate.

A non-profit organization named Money & Politics Iowa (MAP Iowa) and funded by the Joyce Foundation has been the most durable and active private watchdog over campaign finance in Iowa. Using information derived from official disclosure reports, MAP Iowa publishes six newsletters a year, detailing where campaign money comes from and how it is spent. The print media, more typically, focus on the overall level of campaign fund-raising and spending. For example, in October 2000, following the October 19 reporting deadline, the *Des Moines Register* ran two articles that noted the rapid rate at which legislative campaigns were raising and spending money (Roos 2000a and

2000b). This mirrored a similar article which had appeared in October 1998, following the same reporting deadline (Roos 1998). However, in none of these articles was there discussion of the sources of campaign funding. The media in Iowa tend to become more interested in specific candidates and contributors when a formal complaint has been filed with the Campaign Board.

The general attitude of Iowans concerning campaign finance is difficult to measure. As noted earlier, in 1987, the General Assembly passed legislation providing for public financing in state campaigns, legislation was vetoed by the governor. More recently, however, there appears to be little impetus in the state toward more stringent regulation of campaign finances. According to a 1998 survey, most Iowa legislative and statewide candidates agreed that "money plays too big a role in influencing election outcomes and public policy," but few considered campaign finance reform to be a legislative priority (League of Women Voters of Iowa 1997).

Neither the leadership in the state legislature nor the governor has advocated greater regulation. In the case of the governor, this may be partly because his 1998 come-from-behind victory was widely perceived to have benefitted from timely, large campaign contributions that enabled him to get his message out. In any event, whether the general public cares deeply about these issues is uncertain, since there has not been a statewide poll that has contained campaign finance reform as part of a question. Unlike many states, Iowa does not have an initiative process that allows propositions to be placed on the ballot without having been endorsed by the state legislature. Thus, Iowa's Constitution does not allow voters to bypass the legislature—a route to enactment of campaign finance reform that has been available in some other states.

Moreover, Iowa has not had a campaign finance "scandal" in recent years that might test the public's acceptance of the current system and energize efforts for reform. Nonetheless, significant amounts of money flow through the system. In 1998, contributions to legislative candidates, with all 100 House seats and 25 of the 50 Senate seats up for election, totaled $6,141,058. In 2000, contributions reached $9,800,515.

Trends in Iowa Campaign Finance 1992–2000

Based on our review of state legislative races, campaign finance in Iowa has displayed the following trends over the past decade:

1. A dramatic growth in campaign fund-raising and spending. Total contributions to state legislative campaigns have increased from $3,606,739 in 1994 to $9,800,515 in 2000. In Iowa, the average successful State Senate

candidate spent $111,363 (not counting primary spending) to get elected to an office that pays a base salary of $20,758 per year. The average State House candidate spent $42,866.

2. Significant involvement by PACs, which regularly have accounted for over 30% of all campaign contributions to legislative candidates in Iowa.
3. A rough balance in PAC contributions to both Democrats and Republicans.
4. An apparent advantage to the Republicans in campaign fund-raising from non-PAC sources.
5. An increase in the role of political party contributions, which have gone from being 9% of all contributions (in 1994), to 12% (in 1996 and 1998), to 14% (in 2000).

Perhaps, most importantly, a perception has arisen in Iowa that legislative leaders are the gatekeepers for campaign funding. Increasingly, large PAC contributions are being made to legislative leaders, who in turn transfer that money to party committees, which then spread their funding around to rank-and-file candidates. This development, facilitated by Iowa's lack of monetary limits on contributions, arguably has several effects. First, it appears to have resulted in some competitive races, as each party jockeys for control of the legislature in a competitive two-party state. Second, it has produced a seemingly high degree of party loyalty, because many legislators indirectly are indebted to their leaders for a large percentage of their campaign funding. Third, one can argue that this party cohesion has been deployed to further a fairly narrow "special interest" agenda. All this suggests that, while the lack of campaign contribution limits or public financing in Iowa may have produced lively *campaigns*, it may have adversely impacted the quality of *governance*.

Sources of Campaign Money

Rapid Increases During the 1990s: the Role of Parties

Although Iowa is a relatively rural state with no major media markets and, indeed, prides itself on the old-fashioned "retail" politics exemplified by the Iowa Presidential Caucuses, the costs of legislative races have jumped tremendously in the last decade. Table 1 shows the trends.

Meanwhile, party contributions to legislative races have increased both in absolute terms and as a percentage. See Table 2.

Compared to party organizations in other states, Iowa's state parties do rather well at raising campaign funds. A recent study ranked Iowa 14th nationally in the amounts raised by its state parties in 1999–2000, even though Iowa is only the 30th most populous state (Okamoto 2001). Iowa's standing may be the re-

Table 1
Contributions Received by Legislative Candidates from All Sources

1993	$421,159
1994	$3,606,739
1995	$800,645
1996	$5,264,006
1997	$1,039,205
1998	$6,141,058
1999	$1,799,622
2000	$9,800,515

Table 2
Party Contributions to Legislative Races

1993	$11,205	(3%)
1994	$331,376	(9%)
1995	$9,696	(1%)
1996	$608,398	(12%)
1997	$17,011	(2%)
1998	$738,811	(12%)
1999	$130,358	(7%)
2000	$1,333,989	(14%)

sult of several factors, including its presidential caucuses, which act as a magnet for campaign funds, and the ongoing battle in the 1990s for control of the state legislature. Nonetheless, it seems likely that the absence of monetary contribution limits in Iowa is also a significant consideration, as is the channeling of funds from legislative leaders through the political parties to other legislative candidates.

Table 3, which combines both independent expenditures and candidate contributions by the parties (for both legislative and statewide races), demonstrates the increased spending by the two major state parties.

While it is clear that the state parties have spent more money and that many of their expenditures are not coordinated with candidates, their true influence in the campaign process is difficult to measure. Independent expenditures by a party that are not done in "coordination" with a candidate are difficult to track. Until *Iowa Right to Life, Inc. v. Williams* was decided, a party was required to provide notice of an independent expenditure to the benefitted candidate within twenty-four hours of the expenditure. The candidate then had seventy-two hours to either "disavow" the expenditure or "accept" it. Copies of both the notice and the candidate's decision had to be filed with the Campaign Board. If the candidate "disavowed" the expenditure, the party reported it as an independent expenditure. If the candidate "accepted" the expenditure,

Table 3
Party Spending (Excluding Loan Repayments)

	Democrats	Republicans
1992	$891,013.78	$416,817.81
1994	$1,056,598.66	$829,380.69
1996	$3,125,255.80	$1,868,427.79
1998	$2,332,631.45	$2,327,484.54
2000	$6,016,233.36	$4,910,302.78

it was reported as an in-kind contribution. However, the controlling statute was suspended by a federal court injunction in October 1998. Thus, Iowa currently does not have a statute governing independent expenditures, and parties are not required to identify the candidates on whose behalf they make expenditures. Accordingly, if the Iowa Democratic Party pays for the production and distribution of a brochure advocating the election of a candidate, but does not coordinate that expenditure with the candidate, its report will only disclose payments to a printing company and for postage.

The PACs

During the 1990s, PAC contributions to Iowa General Assembly candidates have increased significantly in absolute terms but declined slightly as a percentage. See Table 4.

PAC contributions in Iowa tend to be distributed fairly evenly between the parties. For example, in 2000, the ten largest PACs included a conservative group that gave almost exclusively to Republicans, four industry PACs that gave predominantly to Republicans, three union PACs that gave overwhelmingly to Democrats, and the trial lawyers' PAC that gave almost entirely to Democrats. Republican candidates received $653,338 and Democratic candidates received $612,650 from these top ten PACs. From all PACs, Republican leg-

Table 4
PAC Contributions to Legislative Candidates

1993	$195,119 (46%)
1994	$1,688,777 (47%)
1995	$321,210 (40%)
1996	$2,481,127 (46%)
1997	$375,937 (36%)
1998	$2,408,174 (39%)
1999	$658,273 (37%)
2000	$3,172,687 (32%)

Table 5
Largest Recipients of PAC Contributions in 2000

Senate Majority Leader	$148,050
Senate Minority Leader	$148,584
House Minority Leader	$134,095
House Speaker	$98,150
House Majority Leader	$91,200

islative candidates received $1,682,306 in 2000 and Democrats $1,497,881. Since Republicans controlled both houses of the legislature both before and after the 2000 elections, it would be difficult to view this 53% to 47% disparity in PAC funding as reflecting a significant "PAC advantage" to either party. Indeed, it appears that PAC-giving may have somewhat different patterns now than it did in the 1980's, when trade association PACs predominated and incumbents were the primary beneficiaries of their contributions (Bruner 1990).

The Leadership Phenomenon

PAC contributions, however, are *not* evenly distributed among candidates. In 2000, the Speaker of the House and the House Majority Leader (both Republicans) received $98,150 and $91,200 respectively in PAC contributions. This was nearly $60,000 more than the next Republican received (in terms of overall PAC contributions). Likewise, the House Minority Leader and the House Minority Whip received $134,095 and $53,200 in PAC contributions; the next Democrat received only $31,323.

The Iowa Senate told the same story. The Senate Majority Leader (a Republican) received $148,050 in PAC contributions, exceeding his closest Republican competitor (the Senate President) by nearly $90,000, who in turn outdistanced her nearest Republican competitor by nearly $25,000. The Senate Minority Leader, along the same lines, received $148,584 in PAC contributions, which was over $85,000 more than the next Democrat received. Table 5 summarizes this information. Significantly, the Senate Majority Leader was not even up for election in 2000.

Additionally, each of these leaders was at the top of the list of party donors. That is, except for the cash raised by one leader, most, if not all, the cash they raised in 2000 was turned over to their party. See Table 6.

Perhaps significantly, the only legislative leader above who did not turn over all, or nearly all, his cash contributions to his party in 2000 was the House Minority Leader, even though he had a relatively easy contest, winning 60% of the vote. He was unseated as Minority Leader by his colleagues prior to the

Table 6
Transfers to Party Committees by Legislative Leadership in 2000

Senate Majority Leader	$240,800	(92% of cash raised in 2000)
Senate Minority Leader	$284,000	(126% of cash raised in 2000)
House Minority Leader	$99,000	(58% of cash raised in 2000)
House Speaker	$199,314	(107% of cash raised in 2000)
House Majority Leader	$185,814	(125% of cash raised in 2000)

start of the 2001 legislative session. Another representative, who did not have major party opposition in 2000 but who, nonetheless, raised $60,950 in cash and made $60,500 in party contributions, replaced him.

One other potentially significant trend was noted in a 1997 study. According to that report, contributions to hold-over senators (those not up for re-election) increased at a rate of 56.32% from 1993 to 1995, faster than the rate of increase in contributions to legislative candidates in general (League of Women Voters of Iowa).

Patterns in Individual Contributions

While party and PAC dollars play a significant role in Iowa campaigns, individual contributions still account for about half of reported contributions. Drawing broad conclusions about individual contributors can be difficult, because Iowa law does not require disclosure of the contributor's business or occupation.

Nonetheless, several observations can be made. First, despite the absence of contribution limits, most individual contributors make relatively small contributions. For example, for 1998, only 17% ($517,015 out of $2,994,073) of the money contributed to state legislative campaigns was in blocks of $1,000 or more. This was the high-water mark for individual contributions during 1993–99.

Second, it does appear that some of the large contributors are ideologically motivated. For example, a study of the 1997–98 election cycle performed by MAP Iowa and the National Institute on Money in State Politics classified ten of the forty-five top individual contributors as "party" or "ideological." Even a number of the large contributors who had discernible ties to specific businesses may be considered "ideological" donors. According to a MAP Iowa analysis of the top five individual contributors to Iowa legislative campaigns from 1993 to 2000, each of them gave overwhelmingly to candidates of only one political party.

Third, it appears that, while PAC money is more or less evenly divided between the parties, individual contributors may favor Republicans. Four of the five top individual contributors mentioned in the previous paragraph gave predominantly to Republicans. During the 1999–2000, there were 829 individual contributions of $500 or more to Republicans, for a total of $711,693, and 522 individual contributions of $500 or more to Democrats, for a total of $425,308.

A Republican Advantage?

One last point should be made about campaign dollars in Iowa. In recent years, Republican candidates have had an overall edge over Democratic candidates in raising money for Iowa legislative races. In the 1996 and 1998 election cycles, Republican candidates for the House reportedly accounted for 62% and 67% of campaign spending (Keefer 1998; 1999). Similarly, during the 1996 and 1998 combined election cycle for the Senate (half the Senate was up for election in 1996, the other half in 1998), the Republicans had a 61% to 39% overall spending advantage in contested races (Keefer 1999).

Given the relative balance in PAC funding, these figures probably reflect a Republican advantage in individual contributions as well as a concerted effort by the national Republican Party during the 1990s to wrest away control of Iowa's legislature from the Democrats. For example, when the Republicans took control of Iowa's Senate in 1996, the national Republican Senatorial Committee provided $273,000 in last-minute money to the Iowa State Victory Committee, a partisan committee that supported fourteen Republican Senate candidates.

On the other hand, as Table 3 indicates, Democratic Party organizations have had an overall spending advantage in Iowa over the Republicans during the 1990s. Thus, the contribution data alone, which do not account for independent party expenditures, may exaggerate the degree of any Republican advantage.

Competitiveness of Races

An important question is whether this largely unregulated regime and the resulting increase in money flow (particularly to the legislative leadership and the parties) have led to a decline in the competitiveness of races during the last decade.

To examine this question, we looked first at the correlation between candidate fund-raising and victory in the last five Iowa election cycles, beginning with 1992 and ending with 2000. Each election cycle was broken down into races for the State Senate and State House, and races for statewide office (Governor, Attorney General, Secretary of State, State Treasurer, Secretary of Agriculture, and State Auditor). For a race to be considered, there had to be at least two candidates in the race, each of whom raised a minimum of $50 in campaign contributions.

In 1992, using these criteria, the success level for State Senate candidates who did not raise as much money as their opponents in 1992 was 20% (5 out of 25). In addition, those five of the twenty-five candidates had the distinction of being successful despite being also outspent by their opponents. A sixth candidate won by taking in more money but spending less than the opponent did.

For the House elections, the 1992 data are similar to those for the Senate. Out of seventy-seven races, sixty-one candidates won their elections while raising more money than their opponents. Fifty-seven of those candidates also outspent their opponents. Thus, the success rate for House candidates who did not raise as much money as their opponents was 21%. Out of those sixteen successful candidates, fifteen were also outspent.

In the 1994 election cycle, there were sixteen races for State Senate that met the standards for consideration set forth above. The success rate for State Senate candidates who did not raise as much money as their opponents was 19% (3 out of 16). In addition, two of the three candidates prevailed in their races despite being outspent by their opponents. On the other hand, two other candidates won by raising more money but spending less.

In the Iowa House, the 1994 success rates were nearly identical to those of the Senate. There were sixty-four contested races, and twelve successful candidates raised fewer funds than their opponents. Thus, the victory rate for candidates who did not raise as much money as their opponents was 19%.

There were twenty eligible races for the State Senate in 1996. Four of the races were won by candidates who raised more money than their opponents for a 20% success rate. One of these four candidates outspent the opponent despite raising less money.

In the House, there were seventy-six contested races in 1996. Seventeen of those were won by the candidate who raised less money. Thus, House candidates who did not raise as much money had a success rate of 22%. All of those candidates were also outspent, yet they still came out on top.

In the 1998 election cycle, six of seventeen successful Senate candidates raised more money and spent more money than their opponents did, for a 35% success rate. Another candidate won despite being outspent by the opponent.

Less-well-funded House candidates also had more success. Seventeen out of sixty-two 1998 House races were won by candidates who raised less money than their opponents, for a victory rate of 27%. All seventeen also were outspent by their opponents.

Table 7

Cycle:	Races:	Winner Raised Less:	Winner Spent Less:
State Senate			
1992	25	5	6
1994	16	3	4
1996	20	4	3
1998	17	6	2
2000	21	4	2
State House			
1992	77	16	19
1994	64	12	14
1996	76	17	17
1998	62	17	17
2000	65	11	14
Statewide Races			
1994	6	2	2
1998	5	2	2

The 2000 elections saw a return to previous numbers. In the Senate, four out of twenty-one contested races were won by candidates who raised less money for a 19% success rate. Two of the four outspent their opponents.

For the 2000 House elections, there were sixty-five contested races. Eleven were won by candidates who had a fund-raising deficit, for a success rate of 17%. Ten of the eleven were outspent by their opponents, while four other candidates were successful raising more and spending less than their opponents.

In 1994, there were contests for all six statewide offices in Iowa. Two were won by candidates who raised and spent less than their opponents. In 1998, five of the six elections were contested. Again, two of those five were won by candidates who raised and spent less than their opponents. Table 7 summarizes these results.

Another possible measure of competitiveness is the number of close election races. For the five election cycles from 1992 to 2000, we totaled the number of state legislative races where the winner defeated the loser by less than 10% (55%-45%). As we indicate above, Iowa has a largely apolitical redistricting process that favors existing political subdivisions (particularly counties) and gives no consideration to places where incumbents reside. Thus, the first election after each decennial census (e.g., 1992) tends to be a free-for-all. However, a steady decline in close races thereafter—particularly in light of the ever-larger sums of money being pumped into campaigns—might suggest that campaign funding is having an adverse effect on election competitiveness.

Table 8
Elections Where the Winner Prevailed by
Less than 10 Percentage Points (1992–2000)

House	1992	25 out of 100	(25%)
	1994	15 out of 100	(15%)
	1996	17 out of 100	(17%)
	1998	20 out of 100	(20%)
	2000	17 out of 100	(17%)
Senate	1992	11 out of 32	(34%)
	1994	4 out of 25	(16%)
	1996	8 out of 25	(32%)
	1998	5 out of 26	(19%)
	2000	5 out of 25	(20%)

We did not observe such a trend in Iowa, however. The data for House and Senate elections are compiled in Table 8. By way of comparison, it should be noted that in at least half of Iowa's House and Senate districts during recent years, either the Republicans or the Democrats have held at least a ten-point advantage in party registration (Keefer 1998; 1999).

Nor does it appear that incumbents were able to entrench themselves with increasing success during the 1990s. Table 9 shows the trend on defeated incumbents.

Yet another indicator of competitiveness is the funding gap between incumbents and challengers. A significant difference in the availability of campaign funds might suggest that the existing system is making it difficult for would-be candidates to mount adequately funded challenges. Yet the differential is not that great. According to one study of the 1998 election cycle, the average incumbent raised $42,348, the average challenger $24,709 (Dixon 1999). Another study found that incumbents raised more money than challengers in the 1994 and 1996 cycles, by an average of $20,562 to $13,711 and $29,379 to $20,433, respectively (League of Women Voters of Iowa 1997). While the reported differences of 71% (1998), 44% (1996), and 50% (1994) may appear large, these figures include undeniably popular incumbents.

Table 9
Defeated Incumbents

1992	1 Senate	22 House
1994	0 Senate	3 House
1996	5 Senate	9 House
1998	2 Senate	3 House
2000	2 Senate	6 House

An analysis performed by MAP Iowa of the 2000 state legislative races provides additional corroboration, in our view, that Iowa has not yet fallen into a pattern where incumbents consistently raise and spend more money than their challengers and, thus, defeat them. MAP Iowa concluded that the average amount of money available to winners in contested House races was $50,677; the average available to losers was $54,354. The Senate figures were similarly close: $115,038 available, on average, to winners, and $108,430 to losers. An earlier study of the 1994 and 1996 election cycles showed that losing legislative candidates were actually closing their fund-raising gap in comparison to winners (although winners still had an absolute advantage raising money) (League of Women Voters of Iowa 1997).

Conclusions and Proposals for Reform

Iowa's recent experience provides little evidence that a lack of contribution limits or public financing has diminished the competitiveness of campaigns. At least in this state, with its part-time legislature and no major media markets, legislative races appear to remain competitive. Although campaigns became significantly more expensive during the 1990s, it does not appear that either party had a large fund-raising advantage, or that incumbents were unduly favored. Iowa's experience does show, however, that problems can emerge when, for political reasons, it becomes impossible to update laws and regulations to changing circumstances.

To begin with, although Iowa relies heavily on disclosure, that disclosure is imperfect and incomplete. Individual contributors are not required to disclose their employer or their occupation. As a result, this information does not appear on official reports filed with the Campaign Board. This makes it very difficult to spot trends in individual contributions or the existence of "bundling." For example, when presidential candidate Al Gore decided to build his Iowa organization by asking wealthy supporters outside Iowa to contribute to Iowa Democrats running for the state legislature, this practice went unobserved until an aggressive reporter ran an article in the *Waterloo Courier* (Stern 1999).

Moreover, Iowa does not have mandatory electronic filing. Given the increasing prevalence of computers and the use of the Internet, the rationale for electronic filing has become ever more powerful, at least when a committee is above a certain threshold in assets and expenditures. When contributions and expenses are being maintained on a computer, as is almost invariably the case for a legislative or statewide campaign, the data should be transmitted to the Campaign Board in electronic form.

Nonetheless, improving the quality of disclosure would not by itself resolve the serious issues raised by the cycling of money from PACs to legislative leadership and, from there, to parties and then to rank-and-file candidates. Some might favor placing discretionary campaign funds in the hands of legislative leaders, on the theory that the practice enhances party discipline and leads to a quasi-parliamentary system. But Iowa decided to go in a different direction in 1991, when the General Assembly and the governor approved a ban on transfers of campaign funds between candidates, based on a perception that rank-and-file members had become too beholden to party leaders (74 G.A. ch. 226). Over the course of the past decade, however, what was prohibited in one form has surfaced in another. The only difference is that legislative leaders now transfer campaign funds to party committees rather than directly to other candidates.

Extending the 1991 ban to prohibit transfers of funds from a candidate's committee to a party might make it more difficult for special interests to influence the legislative agenda through contributions to leaders. Large donors would have to give to party committees or directly to the candidates who are involved in tight races. As a matter of logic, it is difficult to see any public-policy interest that is served by large PAC or individual contributions to legislative leaders. Since Iowa has no dollar limits on contributions, individuals or PACs that are truly concerned about *electing* candidates (as opposed to *influencing* their behavior once elected) can achieve all of their goals by contributing to the party or directly to the affected candidates. By contrast, a donor who makes a campaign contribution to a legislative leader, knowing that the leader will transfer the contribution to another candidate, wants to affect *how* legislators act in addition to *which* legislators are elected.

Indeed, it seems unlikely that a serious First Amendment challenge can be raised against strict limits, or even an absolute ban, on contributions by candidate committees to party committees. The recent decision, *Federal Election Commission v. Colorado Republican Campaign Committee*, 121 S. Ct. 235, (2001) (*Colorado Republican II*), which upheld limits on contributions from political parties to candidates, amplified the dangers of "subtle circumvention" when an "affluent nominee" uses the party to route campaign funds to "needier candidates." Sharply restricting, or even entirely prohibiting, the indirect flow of money from one candidate to another seems fully consistent with the rationale of *Colorado Republican II* and the legislative intent behind the 1991 amendments to Iowa's campaign finance laws. This limitation, or ban, might mitigate the governance effects of Iowa's current system, while preserving vibrant political campaigns.

In 1990, a participant in Iowa's legislature published a study, complaining that narrow special interest bills were pervading the legislative agenda (Bruner

1990). More recently, a somewhat different critique has emerged; deadlock and partisanship have become the worries of the day. Observers of recent legislative sessions have expressed concern that Iowa's elected officials have failed to take action on the more important issues confronting the state, leaving them for the following year's agenda (Lee 2001; Roos and Zeleny 2000; Zeleny and Roos 1999). For example, tax policy and regulation of hog confinements appear perennially on lists of things "undone" by the legislature. These are also areas where PACs have contributed heavily. One might draw the conclusion that recent trends in campaign finance, particularly the increasing flow of contributions from PACs to legislative leaders to political parties to rank-and-file, are partly to blame for this development.

There is no reason to believe that campaign spending in Iowa will moderate in the future. As the state remains politically competitive, the flow of money should continue to escalate. One irony is that Iowa's relatively clean reputation, and the relative absence of major scandals, may have hindered the prospects for further regulation of campaign finances in the state. Given the lack of an initiative process, a large public outcry probably would be needed to convince political leaders in Iowa to enact campaign finance reform. Yet public concern is likely to remain low as long as Iowa's residents perceive it as a "good government" state.

References

Barone, Michael, William Lilley III, and Laurence J. DeFranco. 1998. *State legislative elections, voting patterns and demographics.* Washington, D.C.: Congressional Quarterly, Inc.

Bruner, Charles. 1990. Lobbying, interest groups, PACs, and the Iowa General Assembly. In *Issues in Iowa Politics,* edited by Lee Ann Osbun and Steffen W. Schmidt. Ames, IA: ISU Press.

Dalbey, Beth. 2001. Has organized labor lost its clout? *Des Moines Business Record,* 3 September.

Dixon, Mark. 1999. 1998 Iowa elections analysis. National Institute on Money in State Politics. 27 September.

Keefer, Joseph D. 1999. *Iowa political guide 1999–2000.* MegaStats Corporation.

———. 1998. *Iowa political yearbook 1998.* MegaStats Corporation.

State of Iowa, *Iowa Code (2001).*

Iowa Right to Life Committee, Inc. v. Williams. 1999. Civil No. 4-98-CV-10399, *aff'd,* 187 F.3d 963 (8th Cir.).

League of Women Voters of Iowa. Spotlight on campaign finance reform, more sunlight for Iowa. Retrieved [November 3, 2001]: www.lwvia.org/reform.html.

Lee, Jennifer Dukes. 2001. Rancorous rerun feared in 2002. *Des Moines Register,* 10 May.

Okamoto, Lynn. 2001. Iowa ranks 14th in "soft money" collection for 2000 election. *Des Moines Register,* 27 July.

Roos, Jonathan. 1998. Politicians' coffers fill faster this year," *Des Moines Register*, 20 October.

———. 2000a. Money pours in for candidates for legislature. *Des Moines Register*, 25 October.

———. 2000b. Cash pours into races for office. *Des Moines Register*, 26 October.

Roos, Jonathan, and Jeff Zeleny. 2000. Session's worth in contention. *Des Moines Register*, 27 April.

Smith, Mark. 2001. Interview by Ed Mansfield and Charles Smithson. 13 November.

Stern, Eric. 1999. Gore was behind donations to Iowa legislative candidates last year. *Waterloo Courier*, 7 February 7.

Zeleny, Jeff, and Jonathan Roos. 1999. Issues already loom for legislature 2000. *Des Moines Register*, 1 May.

CHAPTER 8

Campaign Finance in Florida: Who Gave It, Who Got It, Who Knows?

Darryl Paulson

Introduction

Manning Dauer, one of the most renowned scholars of Florida politics, thirty years ago described Florida as "the different state"(1972). Florida is different in many ways. It is a Southern state geographically, but bears few similarities to the rest of the political South. Part of Florida resembles the South politically and culturally, but most of the state resembles the Midwest more than Mississippi. The political maxim in Florida is that "the farther north you go, the farther south you get." Florida's northern panhandle, or "Redneck Riviera," varies little from neighboring Alabama and Georgia. Miami's political culture is a melting pot of New York Jews, Cubans, Haitians, African-Americans, and many other ethnic groups. Its liberal Democratic politics is closer to that of New York City, Philadelphia, and other large metro areas than it is to that of the rest of Florida.

Florida is "different" in many other ways. It is one of the nation's fastest growing states. In 1900, Florida was the least populated southern state. One century later, only Texas had a larger population in the South, and Florida's 15.9 million residents made Florida the nations fourth largest state. Florida is the most urbanized southern state, with 85% of its residents residing within ten miles of the Atlantic Ocean or Gulf of Mexico (Dye 1998).

Much of Florida's population growth is due to rapid in-migration, particularly from New York, Massachusetts, Ohio, and Michigan. The new residents' lack of attachment to Florida has created numerous problems for the state's politics and public policy. If you ask Floridians where they are from, a majority will name their place of origin rather than Orlando, Tampa, Miami, or St. Petersburg. This "rootlessness" increases the cost of political campaigning since so many residents lack familiarity with the state's politics and political leaders. Florida's rapid in-migration means that its candidates have to consistently appeal to a new and constantly changing electorate. Only Nevada has fewer native-born residents than Florida.

The composition of Florida's population also makes Florida "the different state." In one respect, the ethnic composition of Florida is substantially different from the rest of the South. On the other hand, Florida's demographics make it a microcosm of the nation. African-Americans and Hispanics each comprises 15% of the state's population, and the 2000 census found Hispanics had become the largest and fastest-growing ethnic group in the state. The diversity of the state's population reflects the ethnic diversity of the United States. Florida has become the "bellwether state," as the 2000 presidential election so clearly demonstrated. Florida is quickly becoming the new Peoria of the nation, as all types of political, cultural, and economic trends are first test-marketed in the Sunshine State (MacManus 1996).

Another way that Florida differs is in its elderly population. Florida ranks first among the fifty states in both the median age of its population and the percentage of residents sixty-five years or older (Dye 1998). Seniors are the state's most consistent voters, with three out of four voting regularly. The problem for statewide politicians is that the senior voters are not monolithic. They are certainly not all politically conservative, as any politician who has had to tangle with the "condo commandos" of Dade, Broward, and Palm Beach Counties has learned. In fact, voters over age sixty were the only age group in Florida that was more Democratic than Republican, according to a Florida State University Annual Policy Survey.

Finally, Florida differs in one other way that directly impacts the cost of political campaigning—the abundance of media markets. Unlike Illinois and the media dominance of Chicago, or Georgia and the dominance of Atlanta, Florida has nine major media markets. In the panhandle the *Pensacola News Journal* dominates, while in the state capital the dominant medium is the *Tallahassee Democrat*. *The Florida Times-Union* is the paper of record in Jacksonville, while, in north central Florida, candidates must appeal to the *Gainesville Sun* and *Ocala Star Banner*. In the Tampa Bay area, the *St. Petersburg Times* and *Tampa Tribune* compete for dominance. Further south, on the west coast, candidates must reach the readers of the *Bradenton Herald* and *Sarasota Tribune*. In southwest Florida, one of the fastest growing areas in the state, the *Naples Daily News* and *Fort Myers News Press* are the papers of record. The *Orlando Sentinel* is the paper of central Florida, while the *Fort Lauderdale Sun Sentinel*, and the *Miami Herald* and its Spanish edition, *Nuevo Herald*, are dominant newspapers in southeast Florida. Any candidate running for statewide office will find the cost of campaigning has escalated due to the plethora of media markets.

This chapter will provide a brief review of political parties and interest groups in contemporary Florida politics. After examining the impact of partisan realignment and legislative turnover in interest group politics, we will examine the history of campaign finance regulation in Florida. We will then examine some of the controversial issues in campaign finance, along with the impact of state and federal court decisions. Finally, we will observe the role of money in political campaigns and determine what, if anything, can be done to make the system work.

Political Parties in Florida

Florida, like the rest of the South, was a one-party Democratic state from the end of Reconstruction in the 1870s until the early 1950s. The 1950s saw the emergence of "Presidential Republicanism" in Florida. From 1952 through 2000, Republican presidential candidates carried Florida's electoral votes in nine out of the twelve elections. Only Lyndon Johnson in 1964, Jimmy Carter in 1976, and Bill Clinton in 1996 were able to break the Republican monopoly in presidential elections.

While Republicans were dominating presidential campaigns in Florida, the Democrats maintained a stranglehold on state and local elections. Two important factors in the 1960s began to alter the state's political makeup. One was immigration. Along with the rapid population growth of Midwestern Republican migrants, the Cuban Revolution led to the arrival of hundreds of thousands conservative Cubans into south Florida. The second factor was the civil rights movement, which led many white conservative Democrats to abandon their party. In 1996, Claude Kirk became the first Republican governor since Reconstruction and, two years later, Republican Edward Gurney defeated the legendary LeRoy Collins to win one of the U.S. Senate seats.

Table I shows voter registration in Florida from 1970 to 2001. Two things are readily apparent. First, the huge increase in voter registration illustrates the state's rapid population growth. Second, the 3-to-1 Democratic voter registration advantage of 1970 has almost completely disappeared . By 2001, Republican voter registration only slightly lagged behind that of the Democrats.

Table I
Florida Voter Registration, 1970–2001

Year	Republican	Democratic	Other	Total
1970	711,090 (25.4%)	2,024,387 (72.4%)	61,523 (2.2%)	2,797,000
1980	1,429,645 (29.7%)	3,087,427 (64.2%)	292,649 (6.1%)	4,809,721
1990	2,448,488 (40.6%)	3,149,847 (52.2%)	432,926 (7.2%)	6,031,261
2001*	3,494,139 (39.0%)	3,853,524 (43.1%)	1,605,313 (17.9%)	8,957,824

* Figures are for August 2001   Source: Florida Dept. of State, Division of Elections

Democrats can only take solace in the fact that the rapid Republican gains in the 1990s have slowed to a trickle.

Republican advances in voter registration are directly related to Republican gains in political power. Republican Bob Martinez was elected governor in 1986, and Republican Connie Mack captured a U.S. Senate seat in 1988. The following year Florida became the first southern state to elect a majority of Republicans to its Congressional delegation. Republicans and African-Americans joined forces in 1992's reapportionment battle. As a result of this coalition, both blacks and Republicans experienced a huge increase in elected legislators. Three African-Americans won congressional seats, the first to do so in more than 120 years.

As Table II indicates, Republicans went from obscurity in the 1960s to political control of the legislature by the 1990s. The GOP seized control of the state Senate in 1994, the state House in 1996, and captured the governor's office in 1998. Florida became the first southern state in which Republicans controlled both the legislative and executive branches.

Table II
Partisan Control of State Legislature, 1960–2000

Year	House (Number of seats)		Senate (Number of seats)	
	Democrat	Republican	Democrat	Republican
1960	88 (92.6%)	7 (7.4%)	37 (97.4%)	1 (2.6%)
1970	81 (68.1%)	38 (31.9%)	33 (68.94%)	15 (31.2%)
1980	81 (67.5%)	39 (32.5%)	27 (67.5%)	13 (32.5%)
1990	74 (61.6%)	46 (38.3%)	23 (57.5%)	17 (42.5%)
2000	43 (35.8)	77 (64.2%)	15 (37.5%)	25 (62.5%)

Source: *Journals of the House of Representatives and Journals of the Senate (Florida)*

Table III
Legislators' and Lobbyists' Choice of Most Influential Interest Groups
(Dye 1998)

Interest Group	Percentage of Legislators/ Lobbyists Mentioning These Groups
Associated Industries of Florida	61.9%
Florida Association of Realtors	52.2
Florida Home builders Association	34.1
Florida Bankers Association	32.1
Florida Association of Trial lawyers	31.9
Florida Association of Insurance Agents	31.6
Office of the Governor	30.9
Florida Chamber of Commerce	29.5
Florida Power & Light	29.4
Florida Medical Association	24.3

Source: Data from Anne E. Kelly and Ella L. Taylor, "Florida: The Changing Patterns of Power," in Ronald J. Hrebenar and Clive S. Thomas (eds.), *Interest Group Politics in the Southern States* (Tuscalossa: University of Alabama Press, 1992).

Interest Groups and Lobbyists in the Sunshine State

For most of Florida's history, powerful economic interests, including citrus, cattle, gambling, phosphate, electric power, and the liquor lobby, have dominated the state. While still influential in the state, the traditional interest groups have been joined by lobbyists representing tourism, building and construction, banking, insurance, health care, environment, senior citizens, and trial lawyers. As a "right to work" state, unions exert little influence on the politics of Florida. Only the teachers unions and public employee unions have sufficient membership and money to be important political players.

Florida has an extremely powerful interest group structure. Ziegler and van Dalen found that Florida had the highest number of registered lobbyists among the states they examined (1971). A 1995 study found that there were fourteen lobbyists for every legislator, or three times the national average (Rosenthal 2001).

Table III lists Florida's most influential interest groups as ranked by members of the legislature. Although the list fluctuates from year to year, these are the groups that dominate the process, year to year.

Consistently heading the list as Florida's most powerful and effective interest group is Associated Industries of Florida (AIF). AIF's $4 million office is conveniently located midway between the Capitol and the Governor's Mansion. With over 6,000 members, AIF represents such powerful economic interests as Publix, Lykes, Eckerd Drugs, Winn-Dixie, U.S. Sugar and Disney. AIF maintains a sophisticated computerized record of state legislative committee hearings, member's voting records, bill tracking and monetary contributions by all groups to all legislative candidates (Florida's Superlobby 1995).

Certain factors make Florida's legislature more susceptible to interest group pressure. First, the low legislative salaries, about $26,000, provide lobbyists with an opportunity to assist legislators with travel, meals, entertainment, and other financial expenses during the session. Second, the short sixty-day annual legislative session creates legislative logjams at the end of the session which provide a unique opportunity for interest group pressure. Third, political power in the legislature is concentrated in the Speaker of the House and President of the Senate. These individuals control the legislative agenda, assign members to committees and appoint all committee chairs. This concentrated power allows interest groups to focus their resources on these key power brokers. Finally, in 1992, Florida voters passed the "Eight is Enough" amendment to the constitution. House members are now limited to four two-year terms and Senators to two four-year terms. A majority of the state legislature had to give up their positions in the 2000 election. The new class of inexperienced legislators is far more likely to be influenced by the more experienced lobbyists.

Lobbying firms have turned to "team lobbying" on the major issues such as health care and deregulation. Up to fifty lobbyists will collaborate on the key piece of legislation. Republicans lobby Republicans, Democrats are hired to lobby Democrats, African-American lobbyists will lobby black legislators, and women will lobby women. Specialization is the name of the Tallahassee lobbying game (Silva 1998).

Many of Florida's legislators have been caught in the act of lobbying while in office. In 1995, Rep. John Thrasher (R-Orange Park) was admonished by the House for lobbying the state medical board to reject increased regulations on doctors performing surgery in their offices. Thrasher was the general counsel for the Florida Medical Association and served as Speaker of the House in 1999 and 2000. After leaving the legislature, Thrasher signed a lucrative contract with Du Pont Pharmaceuticals to lobby against passage of a bill that would have allowed the substitution of generic drugs for eleven brand-name drugs. Florida law prohibits lawmakers from lobbying their legislative colleagues for two years after leaving office. Thrasher's efforts were directed at persuading Governor Bush to veto the bill. His efforts failed.

Also, in 1995, Senator John McKay was forced to resign from the chairmanship of the powerful Ways and Means Committee when he was found to be having an affair with a lobbyist for Sprint. This was at the same time that McKay's committee was considering a telecommunications bill. McKay went through a divorce, married the lobbyist, and was elected President of the Senate for 2001 and 2002. His new wife continues as a lobbyist, but is only registered to lobby the House.

A third major scandal developed in 1995 when Senator Alberto Gutman (R- Miami), Chair of the Senate Health Care Committee, was accused of accepting fees for brokering the sale of an HMO. Gutman resigned his chairmanship and agreed to pay the state $4,200. He would later be found guilty of pocketing $2 million from a $15 million Medicare fraud and was sentenced to prison. This was the same person who in 1988 mailed out a questionnaire to 1,000 lobbyists. Supposedly seeking their input, Gutman especially sought their money. "As this year is an election year," he wrote, "your early financial help is also needed. Please send your maximum contribution so that an early strong financial showing can be achieved." (Legislative Ethics 1988).

In addition to the Florida Elections Commission's duty to monitor campaigns, The Florida Commission is charged with scrutinizing the conduct of elected officials and public employees. Unfortunately, Florida is one of only two states that does not allow its Ethics Commission to initiate investigations. The legislature considered granting the Commission this power in 2000, but the law never passed. The nine members of the Commission are appointed by the Governor, the House Speaker, and the Senate President. Also the Commission can merely recommend punishment. The ultimate responsibility of punishing their own colleagues resides with the legislature. Once again, the legislature has created the illusion of regulation against the reality of "every man for himself" (Morgan 2001).

Most Floridians believe that interest groups and their lobbyists exert too much influence on the political process. The annual Florida State University Policy Survey found that three out of four Floridians believe that "the country is pretty much run by a few big interests looking out for themselves." Only 18% contended that the country "is run for the benefit of all people" (Florida Annual Policy Survey 2000). Floridians also have an increasingly unfavorable view of the performance of the legislature. In 1980, 44% thought the Florida legislature was doing a good job. By 2000, the percentage had fallen to 27%.

Campaign Finance In Florida

The first regulation of campaign finance in Florida occurred in 1897, when the Florida legislature passed a law prohibiting corporations from using money for political purposes. The first major limits on campaign spending were adopted in 1913 and adjusted several times in later years. 1951 marked a turning point, as the Florida legislature passed the "Who Gave It, Who Got It" law. The National Municipal League was so impressed with the "Who Gave It, Who Got It" law that it used it as the basis for its model reporting law (Roady 1962).

The 1951 law required candidates to report all contributions and expenditures and limited campaign contributions to $1,000. Stringent reporting requirements were a key part of the law. Gubernatorial and U.S. Senate candidates were required to submit weekly reports. All other candidates had to file monthly reports. The intent of the law was to allow voters to see who gave money to each candidate and how the candidates spent the money.

Like so many laws, the "Who Gave It, Who Got It" law was stronger in theory than in practice. The real problem was a lack of enforcement. A 1972 study by the *Miami Herald* discovered that candidates had collected and spent more money than the law allowed. Three victorious candidates had not submitted reports a full five months after the election, far beyond the forty-five day reporting deadline (Mansfield 1976).

The 1973 legislature passed the Campaign Finance Act to limit contributions and expenditures and, most importantly, to add an enforcement mechanism. Candidates for statewide office could accept contributions of up to $3,000 from individuals, while all other candidates were limited to $1,000 per election. Expenditures in the governor's race were capped at $250,000 in the primary and runoff and $350,000 in the general election. All other statewide races had a $550,000 limit. Candidates for the State House were limited to $55,000 and State Senate candidates to $65,000. All candidates had to sign the quarterly reports and were held responsible for their accuracy. The most important feature of the 1973 law was the establishment of the Florida Elections Commission to hear violation complaints and recommend civil fines. Stephen O'Connell, a former Supreme Court justice and University of Florida President, was named to head the Commission (Mansfield 1976). Chapter 106 of the Florida Statutes contains Florida's campaign finance laws, including provisions on contributions, expenditures, and reporting requirements for individuals and PACs.

The Campaign Finance Act of 1973 also regulated political action committees for the first time. Florida law made a distinction between political action committees (PACs) and committees of continuous existence (CCEs). PACs were conceived of as ad hoc committees whose primary function was to support or oppose ballot issues. CCEs were viewed as permanent committees. Both PACs and CCEs could make the same contributions as individuals (Kerstein 1987).

The 1973 law was amended in 1991, with the new provisions taking affect on January 1, 1992. Individuals, corporations, PACs, and CCEs found their contribution limits lowered to $500 per election. Payment by check is required for all amounts greater than $100 and contributors must provide their names and addresses and, for contributions over $100, their occupations. Donations must be deposited in the campaign account within five days of receipt, and no contributions can be accepted on the day of the election or less than five days prior to an election. The campaign treasurer must file quarterly reports no later than the tenth day following the end of the quarter (January, April, July and October). Following the last days of qualifying for office, the reports must be filed on the 32nd, 18th and 4th days preceding the first primary and the 18th and 4th days preceding the second primary and general election. The penalty for late reports preceding each primary and the general election is $500 per day (State of Florida 2000).

The Florida legislature approved partial public financing for gubernatorial and cabinet races. There was no public financing for state legislative races in 1986. To qualify for public financing, gubernatorial candidates must first raise $150,000 in contributions and agree to limit total spending to $5.8 million. Cabinet candidates must first raise $100,000 in contributions and agree to limit total spending to $2.3 million. In one of the more unusual disputes on public financing, the Florida Court of Appeals ruled that Republican Jim Smith was entitled to receive public funding in his race for governor. The Court said Smith followed Florida law in his gubernatorial race, and nothing in state law prevented him from running for a second office in the same election cycle and receiving public funding. (*Jim Smith v. Bob Crawford, et al*, 645 So. 2d 513, 1994). The spending totals are adjusted each campaign cycle. Once the Florida Office of Public Campaign Financing has certified that a candidate qualifies for matching funds, the candidate will receive $1 for every $1 they raise for all contributions of $250 or less (Haughee 1986). If any candidate rejects public funding and spends more than the spending caps, their opponent will receive a dollar for every dollar exceeding the cap. This was a major issue in both the 1994 and 1998 gubernatorial races.

In 1994, incumbent Democrat Governor Lawton Chiles agreed to the then $5 million limit, while his opponent, Jeb Bush rejected public financing. Bush raised over $9 million for his campaign. For every dollar in private funds that Bush raised over the $5 million cap, the Chiles campaign received an equal amount in public funds, effectively giving Chiles $4 million in matching funds. Chiles had the best of both worlds. He could claim he was supporting public financing in order to keep campaign costs down and, at the same time, he received public funds allowing him to match Bush's expenditures dollar for dollar. Chiles managed to edge Bush in one of Florida's closest gubernatorial elections.

Bush and the Republicans learned from their mistake. As GOP State Chairman Tom Slade noted, "There is no education in the second kick of the mule"(1999). Republicans and Democrats both took advantage in loopholes in Florida's campaign laws. In the 1998 election, the cap on gubernatorial spending had risen to $5.8 million. Expenditures beyond that limit would trigger the state to provide matching funds to Bush's opponent, Democrat Buddy Mackay. Bush quickly raised the $5.8 million and then advised supporters to make unlimited "soft money" contributions to the Florida Republican Party. Taking advantage of the recent Colorado *Republican Federal Campaign Committee v. Federal Election Commission* case, 516 U.S. 604 (1996), Republicans raised and spent millions of dollars in "independent expenditures" on the Bush campaign. The Republican Party collected around $13 million in contributions which were used for overhead costs and advertising for the Bush campaign. By limiting contributions to his own campaign at the $5.8 million set by state law, Bush made sure his Democratic rival, Buddy MacKay did not receive a nickel of public financing (Nickens 1998).

Democrats accused Republicans of violating the spirit of the public finance law. Rick Dantzler, a Democratic state legislator and one of several Democratic gubernatorial candidates in the 1998 primary, accused Bush and the Republicans of "money laundering. It's nothing more than a way around the contribution limit and to keep his campaign from spending more than the $5.7 million cap." Sally Harrell, Bush's campaign manager, said the law applied equally to both parties and reiterated Bush's opposition to public financing. She argued that Democrats wanted to "use negative campaigning against Jeb Bush and use taxpayer money to do it" (Nickens 1998). Bush easily defeated his Democratic opponent in the 1998 campaign.

In recent years, Republicans have continued to attack public financing. In 1997, Republican Secretary of State Sandra Mortham challenged the law by arguing that the legislature had eliminated the trust fund made of candidate failing fees and other tax dollars that was to be the source of public financing. Florida Circuit Court Judge Nikki Clark ruled against the Secretary of State and held that other state revenue sources could be used. Clark's ruling would be upheld by the Florida Court of Appeals (*Chiles v. Department of State, Division of Elections*, 711 So. 2d 151 1998). Florida's Constitutional Revision Commission proposed incorporating public financing into the State Constitution, and 64% of the voters approved the change in the 1998 election. As a part of Florida's "must-pass" election reform bill in the aftermath of the 2000 presidential election, House Republicans added an amendment to destroy public financing. The provision was dropped from the final bill.

Critical Issues In Campaign Finance

What do individuals and PACs expect in exchange for their campaign contributions? The usual response is access, assistance, and influence. Access means contributors expect legislators to be attentive to their views. Phone calls will be returned, and meetings with legislators or government officials will be scheduled. Assistance refers to the expectations that elected officials will help contributors when problems arise or red tape needs to be cut. Finally, influence is the desire of contributors to help shape public policy. There is nothing inherently illegal about any of these expectations of campaign contributors.

Lobbyists continue to offer hospitality suites, football tickets, and free trips as part of their enticements to legislators. In 1988, eight lobbyists for U.S. Sugar, the railroads, Georgia Pacific, and other business interests hired three private planes to fly legislators for a week of relaxation in the Florida Keys. The legislators developed collective amnesia when asked questions about who attended or what may have been discussed (Morgan 1998).

In 1997, Florida legislators investigated free plane trips for Governor Chiles that he failed to disclose at the same time they were themselves taking trips and not reporting them. A loophole in Florida law allows legislators to disclose nothing if the trip was arranged by their political party. This loophole allows legislators and lobbyists to bypass Florida's public records law, supposedly one of the strongest in America. Barbara Peterson, executive director of the Florida First Amendment Foundation, argues that "claiming these records are not public because they don't fall under the definition of legislative business is so narrowly defining legislative business as to be ludicrous" (March and Talev 1997).

A significant fund-raising scandal shook the Chiles administration in 1998, relating to Florida's $11.3 billion settlement with the tobacco industry. A team of attorneys was selected by Chiles to represent Florida's interests. Most of the members of this legal "dream team" were longtime personal friends of Chiles as well as campaign contributors. The $11.3 billion settlement was quickly agreed to by the tobacco industry and, as a result, the attorneys were paid almost $3 billion in fees. The day after the settlement, the Democratic party's chief fund-raiser, Jeff Ryan, contacted Chiles' Chief Inspector General Harold Lewis for help. According to Lewis' notes, Ryan told Lewis that Democratic Party Executive Director Scott Falmlen "wanted to call PTA for money" (Talev and Cox 1998; Pellemens 2000). The PTA or People's Trial Advocates, as the dream team was known, contributed $100,000 at a 1996 fund-raiser attended by Vice President Gore. The Florida Senate investigated fund-raising activities conducted out of both Governor Chiles' and Attorney General Bob Butterworth's office. Lewis was forced to resign and Democratic Party officials acknowledged making illegal fund-raising phone calls in government offices and at public expense.

On February 18, 1999, former state House Speaker, Bolley "Bo" Johnson (D-Pensacola) was indicted for failing to pay income taxes on more than $500,000 in income received during his speakership. Johnson was also charged with extorting a $15,000 kickback from a campaign aide. Johnson was paid $176,000 in "consulting fees" during his last year in the legislature from a casino chain seeking legalized casino gambling in Florida. The Speaker and his wife Judy received an additional $341,000 from other businesses and lobbyists seeking to do business with the state. Although nothing the couple did violated existing state law, both were found guilty of federal income tax evasion charges and both were sentenced to prison terms (Wark, et al. 2000).

After a U.S. District Court ruling that prohibited state officials from requiring political committees to register with the state and report contributions and expenditures, numerous interest groups in Florida formed committees to raise money to support friendly candidates. The case was brought by the Florida Right to Life Committee which contended that forcing it to report contributions and expenditures violated its First Amendment Rights. Florida law required reporting by groups whose focus was to primarily influence government. The Right to Life Committee successfully argued that political involvement was a secondary and not a primary purpose. As a result of the Right to Life decision, many Florida interest groups created PACs. John Sebal, President of AIF, created the Alliance for Florida's Economy. The Alliance operates one of the most sophisticated approaches to track the vote of every legislator, in committee and on the floor, as well as tracking their opinions on a diverse range of issues. The Alliance even tracks where candidates get their money from to determine whether they get it from business-friendly groups or their adversaries. Since 1994, Associated Industries has seen 90% of the candidates it backs win their elections (Wasson 2000). "That's our stealth money," said Shebal. "We'll use it to defend friends and go after those who try to upset our people and take them out" (Morgan 2000). People for a Better Florida was set up by the Florida Medical Association to support their interests. "The purpose of this type of committee is precisely the fact that you don't have to disclose who is giving you the money," said Dr. Miguel Machado, treasurer of the new committee. "The trial lawyers, Associated Industries, everyone is doing it. All we are doing is trying to keep pace" (Morgan 2000).

Florida Right to Life (FRL) won another important court victory in November, 2001. In *Florida Right to Life v. Lamar* (2001), the 11th U.S. Circuit Court Appeals in Atlanta struck down a section of Florida's campaign finance law that prohibited candidates from making charitable contributions to or soliciting charitable contributions from "any religious, charitable, civic, or other causes or organizations", established primarily for the public good (Fla. Stat. 106.08). Secretary of State Katherine Harris wanted to make a contribution to FRL, but refrained out of concern that her contribution would violate the law. The Court found it "likely that FRL again will lose donations from candidates who fear prosecution, especially given that the Florida election Commission has taken action against candidates who have made charitable donations." This section of the law "is on a collision course with the First Amendment."

Florida and California legislators utilize Leadership PACs to a greater extent than most legislatures. Leadership PACs allow influential legislators to raise money for their own personal PACs. Funds are then distributed to legislative candidates with the expectation that legislators receiving funds will be indebted to the individual distributing the funds. This might include supporting the donor's attempt to secure a position of legislative leadership or supporting certain legislative issues.

Johnnie Byrd, a Republican House member from Plant City, established his PAC, The Committee for Responsible Government. The committee has spent $230,000 in its two years of existence to support fellow House Republicans. Although leadership funds were banned in 1989 by the legislature, the new PACs are structured as committees of continuous existence, which were authorized by the 1973 Campaign Finance Act. Critics complain that there is no way to know who gives money or where it goes. Supporters, such as Byrd, argue that the committees are constitutional. "If you're telling me my constitutional right to freedom, to associate with like-minded people and have those people join together to spend money to promote ideas is somehow a loophole, you're talking about a loophole of what?" said Byrd. "The U.S. Constitution and the Bill of Rights?" (Varian and Goffard 2001) Byrd, who has locked up enough votes to become speaker in 2003, has released the names of contributors and the amount contributed, even though he is not required by law to do so.

A wildly popular annual event in Tallahassee draws repeated criticism from journalists and government reform advocates. It is the annual party thrown by lobbyists to kick off the legislative session. At a cost of $50,000, the 5,000 attendees enjoy free food and drink. The hosts include Anheuser Busch, AT&T, Coca-Cola, Philip Morris, U.S. Sugar, and Walt Disney World, to name a few. State Senator James Hargrett (D-Tampa) compared attending the party to merely attending another meeting. "If I'm concerned about my constituents having jobs, I'm concerned about the employers giving the jobs," said Hargrett. "And lobbyist is not a dirty word" (Talev and Cox 1998). Most legislators see the function as merely a welcome back event. Rep. Sandy Murman (R-Tampa) argues that "any good legislator will look at legislation on its merits. I do" (Taley and Cox 1998). Florida Common Cause director Sally Spencer made an analogy between a date and the annual dinner. "When a man pays, what does he expect in return? I think that applies to the legislative process" (Taley and Cox 1998).

The Florida Money Tree

A 1995 study by the *Tampa Tribune* discovered more than $3 million in special interest cash was reported spent in trying to influence the legislature in 1994. Unfortunately, more than half of the lobbyists required to file the reports failed to do so by the deadline, so the $3 million figure is certainly a gross estimation of lobbying costs.

Penalties for failing to file include fines of up to $5,000 and up to a two-year ban on lobbying, but someone must file a complaint (Lavelle 1995). Table IV lists the major donors to the Republican and Democratic Party in 1998. Contributing more than a million dollars to Republicans were real estate and development interests ($2.2 million), insurance ($2.2 million), health companies ($2.0 million) and telecommunications ($1.2 million). Far and away the leading contributors to the Democrats were lawyers, primarily the state's trial lawyers ($2.2 million).

Between 1990 and 1999, $140.4 million was contributed to the Florida Republican and Democratic Party (Pellemans 2000). Republican Party Chair Tom Slade boasted of raising $35 million for the 1998 campaign, "more money than any state political party has ever raised in history"(Dyckman1999). Slade and Republicans looked at this accomplishment with pride, while critics saw it as an indication of the weakness of Florida's campaign finance laws.

Florida law prevents political parties from pumping unlimited funds into commercials for any one candidate, but the parties have evaded this by creating "three-pack" ads. In 1998 the Republican Party spent millions on ads for Jeb Bush that briefly mentioned two other candidates. In one of the more confusing assessments of the "three-pack" ads, Democratic candidate Buddy MacKay noted: "Had I understood the system I was in, I probably would not have run. This is not sour grapes. I understand the game" (Dyckman1999).

In *Republican Party of Florida v. Florida Election Commission*, 658 So. 2d 653 (1995), the Florida Court of Appeals reversed a FEC ruling banning a political ad because it constituted an illegal campaign contribution. "We con-

Table IV
Major Donors to Republican and Democratic Parties, 1998

Republican Donors of $5,000 or more		Democratic Donors of $5,000 or more	
Real estate and development	$2,249,527	Lawyers and law firms	$2,576,888
Insurance	2,238,639	National, state	
National, state		Democratic committees	1,393,607
Republican committees	2,103,449	Insurance	895,550
Health companies and		Health companies and	
professionals	1,988,238	professionals	790,785
Occupation unidentified	1,573,850	Unions	605,276
Telecommunications	1,207,260	Real estate and development	602,365
Construction	861,206	Contributions from candidates	459,086
Hotels, restaurants, tourism	836,844	Telecommunications	429,598
Contributions from candidates	756,759	Electric and water utilities	371,434
Parimutuels and other gambling	756,342	Financial, including	
Electric and water utilities	728,144	loan companies	341,000
Lawyers and law firms	692,320	Agribusiness, including	
Financial, including		citrus, phosphate, sugar	263,700
loan companies	686,007	Transportation companies	237,630
Business groups and		Parimutuels and other gambling	210,888
individual lobbyists	611,038	Business groups and	
Agribusiness, including		individual lobbyists	189,900
citrus, phosphate, sugar	534,614	Environmental interests	184,000
Manufacturing	498,166	Hotels, restaurants, tourism	181,000
Banking	416,817	Banking	142,580
Transportation companies	411,749	Information technology	130,000
Private prison companies	368,500	Tobacco	123,900
Wayne Huizenga and companies	334,800	Beverage	97,799
Automobile sales	324,519	Automobile sales	91,678
Oil and energy	300,940	Construction	63,000
Information technology	289,250	Wayne Huizenga and companies	53,500
Consultants and engineers	282,524		
Tobacco	278,250		
Unions	265,250		
Investors	253,750		
Merchandising	245,956		
Media companies	223,864		
Car rental other than Huizenga	152,100		
Outdoor advertising	141,482		
Waste management companies	120,000		
Jack Eckerd	100,000		
Accountants	96,500		
National Rifle Association	95,000		

Source: Division of Elections

Table V
Campaign Contribution in Statewide Races, 1998

Race Candidate	Total Contributions	Number of Contributions	Election Result
Governor			
Jeb Bush (R)	$9,125,443	22,963	Won
Buddy McKay (D)	$6,350,805	16,834	Lost
Commissioner of Education			
Tom Gallagher (R)	$975,042	2,317	Won
Peter Rudy Wallace (D)	$662,791	2,072	Lost
Treasurer			
Bill Nelson (D)	$2,805,069	5,658	Won
Tim Ireland (R)	$1,533,167	3,048	Lost
Attorney General			
Bob Butterworth (D)	$916,446	2,171	Won
David Bludworth (R)	$287,217	936	Lost
Comptroller			
Bob Milligan (D)	$567,245	1,837	Won
Newall Daughtrey (D)	$86,128	936	Lost
Secretary of State			
Katherine Harris (R)	$16,000,832	4,197	Won
Karen Gievers (D)	$545,128	606	Lost
Agriculture Commissioner			
Bob Crawford (D)	$1,129,948	2,747	Won
Rich Faircloth (R)	$7,435	32	Lost

Source: Florida Division of Elections

clude," said the Court, that "the issuance of an injunction under such circumstances constitutes an unconstitutional prior restraint of speech."

An examination of campaign spending in the 1998 Florida election found that contributions to all candidates totaled $55,841,108. This did not include "soft money" contributions to the parties that were spent on the candidates' behalf. Table V shows total contributions in the 1998 gubernatorial and cabinet races. Voters in 1998 also approved a restructuring of Florida's unique cabinet system by reducing the six cabinet officers to three—Attorney General, Chief Financial Officer, and Commissioner of Agriculture. The three other positions will be eliminated with the 2002 election. That is one unplanned way to lower campaign costs.

Table VI provides a breakdown in contributions by economic interest. Party contributions and money from lawyers and lobbyists were two of the top three sources of funds. According to the National Institute on Money in State Pol-

Table VI
1998 Contributions by Economic Sector*

Economic Sector	D%/R%	Total Contributed	% of Total
Party	41/59	$8,445,397	16 .6%
Finance, Insurance & Real Estate	38/62	$7,684,516	15.1%
Lawyers & Lobbyists	58 /42	$6,470,937	12.7%
Non-Contributions	60/40	$4,986,321	9.8%
General Business	39/61	$4,380,547	8.6%
Health	36/64	$4,328,299	8.5%
Construction	36/64	$2,449,135	4.8'%
Other	42/58	$2,242,913	4.4%
Agriculture	46/54	$2,118,839	4.2%
Candidate	56/44	$1,697,237	3.3%
Communications & Electronics	40/60	$1,411,721	2.8%
Transportation	39/61	$1,330,222	2.6%
Labor	79/21	$1,312,492	2.6%
Energy & Natural Resources	38/62	$1,309,433	2.6%
Small Contributions	47/53	$640,509	1.3%
Ideology & Singe Issue	49/51	$59,983	0.1%
Defense	30/70	$20,850	0.04%
TOTALS	**46/54**	**$50,889,352**	**100%**

Source: Division of Elections

itics, Florida's political parties received $53,692,769 in "soft money" during the 1999-2000 election cycle. Only New York parties received more ($91.7 million), a fact attributed to the Hillary Clinton U.S. Senate race (Drinkard 2001).

The National institute on Money in State Politics, a nonpartisan organization, discovered that candidates running in 1998 in contested races for the Florida House raised $79,976 on average. Contested Florida Senate races found candidates raising $194,110. Total expenditures in the 120 member House, where all seats are up for election every two years, were $18,505,767. Ninety-six incumbents raised $10 million, compared to $2.8 million by sixty-five challengers and $5.7 million by eighty-four candidates in open-seat races. On the Senate side, where only one-half of the forty seats are contested every two years, total expenditures, amounted to $6,774,943. Sixteen Senate incumbents raised $4 million, thirteen challengers raised $1.2 million, and $1.6 million were raised by eleven candidates for open seats (National Institute 2001). Former legislator Robert Trask Mann best expressed the influence of money on the political process: "We all agreed that no member of this chamber can be bought. But I have seen some on loan for a whole session of the legislature" (Kelley and Taylor 1992).

During the eight years of the Clinton Administration, the President made frequent fund-raising visits to Florida, pulling out millions of dollars from the

Sunshine State. Florida Democrats privately criticized the White House for draining much needed funds out of the state for the exclusive use of the Clinton-Gore ticket. During the 2000 presidential race, President Clinton made several forays into Florida to raise money for the Gore campaign. Nothing, however, energized Democratic fund raising more than the Florida election controversy in 2000 and the election of George Bush as President. Democrats blamed Governor Jeb Bush, his brother, and Secretary of State Katherine Harris for purging black voters and orchestrating George Bush's 537-vote victory. The Democrats believed that they had found the "hot button" issue that would mobilize partisans to financially back the party. The objective—defeat Jeb Bush in 2002. The goal—raise $15 million for the Democratic Party, with at least half of the money coming from outside Florida. As state Democratic Chair Bob Poe commented, "Jeb is going to be the poster child for getting this done"(Kleindienst 2001). The Democrats were focused and motivated. At their annual Jefferson-Jackson Day dinner, Connecticut Senator Joe Lieberman, the Democratic Party's Vice Presidential candidate in the 2000 election, was the featured speaker. "If you show Jeb the door in 2002," said Lieberman, "together we'll show George the door in 2004"(March 2001). All 1500 seats were sold out, and the dinner raised $750,000 for the Democratic Party.

Realizing that the Democrats were energized, the Bush campaign began to take the challenge seriously. A half dozen Democratic challengers stepped up to take on the incumbent governor, led by former Clinton Attorney General Janet Reno. Then, along came September 11. The terrorist attack on the Twin Towers and the Pentagon transformed America in so many ways. It also transformed Florida politics. As President Bush's popularity soared from the 50% to the 90% range, it also lifted the campaign of Governor Jeb Bush. Democratic optimism plunged, as did Democratic fund raising. All fund-raising was suspended temporarily after September 11, and few of the Democratic candidates have been able to recover their fund-raising momentum.

Making The System Work

Florida's "Who Gave It—Who Gets It" law of 1951 was once considered the model for the nation. It may have been on paper, but there was a glaring lack of enforcement, a problem characteristic of most state and federal campaign finance laws. But critics of campaign finance legislation argue the problem is the law itself. Laws requiring disclosure violate freedom of association according to critics. People who contribute money to unpopular candidates, groups, or causes may find themselves out of a job or socially ostracized. The

U.S. Supreme Court, in a number of cases, ruled against forcing certain groups to turn over membership lists. In *NAACP v Alabama*, 357 U.S. 449 (1958) and *Gibson v Florida Legislative Investigating Committee*, 372 U.S. 539 (1963), the Supreme Court refused to force the NAACP to turn over membership lists and financial contributor lists to state authorities. As the Court said in the Alabama case, "Invisibility of privacy in group association may in many circumstances be indispensable to preservation of freedom of association, particularly where a group espouses dissident beliefs." Disclosure of members of the NAACP was not required because disclosure would mean members would be subjected to economic and political pressures. Would this not also be true for individuals from unpopular groups who contribute money to unpopular causes?

Critics also maintain that most campaign finance reform proposals are designed to place a cap on contributions and expenditures. This, they argue, amounts to nothing more than incumbent protection legislation. Since incumbents have name recognition, as well as all of the perquisites of incumbency, the only way for challengers to win is to spend large sums of money to counter the incumbent's natural advantages.

Critics of campaign finance reform and contribution and spending caps point out that the law is on their side. The U.S. Supreme Court's *Buckley v Valeo*, 424 U.S.1 (1976) decision equated money with speech. Attempts to limit campaign expenditures amounted to stifling political speech. Although the *Buckley* decision has been widely criticized, as long as it stands, it will constrain what the states and federal government can do to regulate campaign financing.

Let us examine some of the campaign finance reforms that have been offered and examine the likelihood of their adoption in Florida. The 1998 Report of the Task Force on Campaign Reform found little national support for public financing of congressional elections. Only 26% strongly favor "public funding of all congressional and presidential campaigns, at a cost of about $5 a person"(Report 1998). There is also little public support for public financing in Florida, which may be surprising, since Florida does have partial public financing. In response to a question whether citizens favored using public funds to pay part of the cost of campaigns in exchange for limits on contributions from individuals and political action committees in order to reduce the influence of special interests, "46 percent were in favor and 50 percent were opposed (*Polling Report* 1996). If there is little support for public financing in Florida, why did 64% of the electorate in 1998 support including a public financing section in the Florida Constitution? My view is that voters were asked if they supported public funding in state races, and they said yes, because they wanted to diminish the power of special interest groups. If voters had been asked if they supported public financing either through their personal contributions or with tax revenue, the measure would have failed.

The Task Force Report recommends "a combination of partial public financing, modest increases in basic contribution limits with subsequent indexing for inflation, and new efforts to plug the two most egregious loopholes in the current system of campaign finance: 'soft money' and 'issue advocacy'"(Report 1998). Soft money was intended to assist in party-building activities, but much of the money has been used to support party candidates through issue advocacy ads. Such ads tout all of the virtues of a candidate without specifically urging voters to vote for or against a particular candidate. Florida law specifically prohibits soft money ads in support of a candidate, but the "three-pack" ads have emerged as the loophole of choice. Parties in Florida have created ads for a particular candidate and then quickly flashed the name and photos of two other candidates. The "three-pack" is "legal" under Florida law.

Florida is one of only thirteen states that does not limit contributions to political parties. In 1998, the Bankers Insurance Group was in a bitter dispute with Democrat Bill Nelson, Insurance Commissioner. Although the amount that Bankers Insurance could give to Nelson's opponent was limited by the law, there was no limit to what they could give to the Republican Party. Bankers Insurance gave $440,500 to the Republican Party, and the Party then funneled money to Nelson's opponents. Republican Party Chairman Tom Slade candidly described what happened: "What they wanted to do was whip Bill Nelson, and I was a willing partner" (*St. Petersburg Times* 1999).

Two weeks after the 1998 election, in which the Republican Party pumped in over $10 million to the Jeb Bush campaign, Florida Senate President Toni Jennings (R-Orlando) denounced the soft money loophole and called for a $5,000 limit per year on donations to a party. "What is important," said Jennings, "is that elections became more about community than about contributions. Because there are some things money can't buy. Like public trust" (Dyckman 1999). In exchange for limiting contributions to a party, Jennings proposed raising the ceiling on donor contributions in gubernatorial and cabinet races to $1,000 per election or $1,500 for an entire campaign. Jennings' proposal also called for closing the "three-pack" loophole.

Jennings' proposal immediately was attacked, mostly by members of her own party in the legislature and Republican Party Chairman Tom Slade. "There are two ways for us to lose the current advantage we have," said Slade. "Number one is to let Democrats change the rules, which has now been proposed by Sen. Jennings, or for us to self-destruct on the horns of our own inappropriate conduct" (Dyckman 1999). Republicans argued that limiting contributions to the party not only violated free speech, but also would handcuff

Table VII
Major Fund-Raising Recipients in 1998
in Period Preceding Legislative Session

Between February 1 and March 2, 114 sitting legislators collected a total of $2.2 million. They got $286,000 on February 27 alone. Most $6 of every $10 came in during the week leading up to the session. Here are those who raised the most money that week.

Amount	Legislator	Party/hometown
$84,000	Sen. John McKay	R-Bradenton
$68,000	Sen. Steven Geller	D-Hallendale
$53,000	Sen. Kendrick Meek	D-Miami
$44,000	Sen. Jim Horne	R-Orange Park
$33,000	Sen. Alberto Gutman	R-Miami
$32,000	Rep. J.D. Alexander	R-Frostproof
$31,000	Rep. Carlos L. Valdes	R-Miami
$30,000	Rep. Elaine Bloom	D-Miami Beach
$29,000	Sen. John Laurent	R-Bartow
$27,000	Sen. Don Sullivan	R-Seminole

Source: *Tampa Tribune*

the parties. They argued that interest groups who could make unlimited independent expenditures would become the new political parties. "They're asking for the parties to disarm and leave the arena to interest groups," said Slade. "Haven't they told us that "special interests" are bad?" Slade also wondered "Why is it OK for these newspapers to take unlimited advertising dollars and then spend as much as necessary to exercise their free speech rights through editorials, but wrong for political parties to do the same thing?" (Slade 1999) Jennings' proposals passed the Senate, which she controlled as President, but were torpedoed by her Republican colleagues in the House. Minor changes were adopted, but massive campaign finance reform lacked both public and political support.

A constant issue confronting state legislatures is: When may legislators receive campaign contributions? Can they receive contributions while the legislature is in session? Until 1994, legislators could receive campaign contributions during the legislature's annual sixty-day session. At the urging of Democratic House Speaker Peter Wallace, the House passed a rule preventing members from accepting or soliciting funds during the sixty-day session. Lobbyists are quick to adjust to changing circumstances. Fund raising is now at a frenetic pace immediately prior to the sixty-day session. As Table VII indicates, massive amounts of money exchange hands right before the session begins.

$286,000 was given in 1998 on the day preceding the opening of the legislature, and $126,000 was given the day before the 1999 session. Much of the money, in $500 maximum contributions, exchanged hands at the annual $50,000 pre-session party hosted by Florida's leading interest groups and lobbyists.

One of the significant issues involving campaign finance is the appearance of regulation versus the reality of non-regulation. Legislators constantly boast of their state's stringent campaign finance laws, while journalists constantly bemoan the "toothless," unenforceable laws. As usual, the truth is probably somewhere between the two extremes. The point is that the public may be deceived into believing strong campaign finance laws exist when, in reality, the laws are more symbolic than substantive. I would argue that Florida and all other states might want to reassess all of their campaign finance laws and remove those that are symbolic, and step up enforcement of those that are substantive.

For example, Florida law clearly specifies that candidates and parties need to record the names and addresses of all contributors, and also the occupation of contributors giving over $100. The law also says the occupations must be specific so the media and public can track the flow of campaign contributions from different economic interests. In 1998, the Republican Party of Florida failed to disclose occupations for $6.6 million in contributions. Another $1.6 million was attributed to donors whose occupations were listed as "corporation," "chairman," "businessman," and "executive." This is hardly the "specific occupation" required by law. The public does have the right to know who is trying to influence the political process. As Martin Dyckman, Associate Editor of the *St. Petersburg Times*, argues, enforcement of this position is easy. Simply require candidates to return all contributions lacking full disclosure (Dykman 1999). Unless the legislature does this, the public will perceive the law does one thing when, in reality, it is a "paper tiger."

Occasionally, a legislator will run so blatantly afoul of the law that it becomes a public issue. I have already mentioned former House Speaker "Bo" Johnson, who accepted over $500,000 in fees from interest groups and lobbyists during his tenure as speaker. Johnson is in prison, but not for violating Florida law. He was convicted of failing to pay federal taxes on this undeclared income. State Senator Alex de la Portilla (R-Miami) was fined $311,000 by the Florida Elections Commission in November, 2001, for violating state election laws 311 times during his 1999 campaign. In a 4-3 vote, the Commission said de la Portilla accepted $10,000 in cash, when state law limits cash contributions to $100. They also said he failed to report $144,000 in contributions and $68,000 in expenditures. Senator Portilla contended the errors were made by staff and corrected in amended reports. He accused the Election Commission of "political shenanigans," and has introduced a bill to abolish the twenty-eight-year-old Commission and transfer its power to the state Division of Administrative Hearings in the Attorney General's Office (Hauseman 2001).

Conclusion

Florida's experience with campaign financing has run the gamut from no regulation, to model regulation, to its current symbolic legislative approach. It took over fifty years after statehood before Florida passed its first campaign finance law in 1897, banning corporate contributions. The first fifty years of statehood was essentially a libertarian, hands-off approach. The next fifty years saw the emergence of a modest legislative approach, where some contribution and expenditure caps were adopted. 1951 marked the passage of Florida's "Who Gave It, Who Got It" law that was the model of the nation. The post-World War II population growth completely transformed Florida's politics. Florida became less southern and more urbanized and cosmopolitan. Politics and politicians played a more critical role in both the state and the nation. The rapid urbanization also created pressures for growth management, and politicians were expected to balance the pressures for growth with the preservation of the state's natural resources. As politicians played a more critical role, the volume of campaign funds expanded. As a two-party system developed out of the previous one-party Democratic politics, the pressures built on both parties to be the dominant political force in Florida. As money has flooded Florida politics, the legislature has responded with symbolic legislation designed to assure the state's residents that campaign spending has been properly regulated.

It is also apparent that Republicans and Democrats in Florida and in the nation take fundamentally different approaches to campaign finance. Most Republicans oppose public financing and also oppose limits on contributions and expenditures. Most Democrats favor public financing and favor caps on contributions and expenditures. Finally, most incumbents, whether Republican or Democrat, favor the status quo. They all won with the current system and are not very supportive of rocking the boat.

What should Florida do with respect to campaign finance? That depends on whether you are a Republican or Democrat, or you support other views on the political left or right. Florida was on to something when it passed its famous "Who Gave It and Who Got It" law in 1951. A simple system that reports who is making contributions, whether limited or unlimited in amount, is better than the current system which is not enforced. A simple system that reports how candidates spent their contributions is better than the current system that is not enforced. Give voters and the mass media accurate information about contributions and expenditures, establish a strong enforcement component, and let everyone draw their own conclusions.

References

Dauer, Manning. 1972. Florida: The different state. In *The changing politics of the South*, edited by William C. Havard. Baton Rouge: Louisiana State University Press.

Drinkard, Jim. 2001. State, local parties rake in "soft money" millions. *USA Today*, 27 August, 4A.

Dye, Thomas. 1998. *Politics in Florida*. Upper Saddle River: Prentice Hall.

Dyckman, Martin. 1999. Know your contributors. *St. Petersburg Times*, 28 February, 4D.

———. 1999. The money pit. *St. Petersburg Times*, 28 February, 1D.

Florida Annual Policy Survey. 2000. Tallahassee: Florida State University.

Florida's superlobby. 1995. *Palm Beach Post*, 29 November, 6B.

Haughee, Chris. 1986. The Florida election campaign financing act. *Florida State University Law Review* 14 (Fall): 586-605.

Legislative ethics: An oxymoron. 1988. *St. Petersburg Times*, 17 April, 12A.

Kelley, Anne. 1981. *Modern Florida government*. Temple Terrace: MDA Publications.

Hauseman, Julie. 2001. Senator wants election rules panel abolished. *St. Petersburg Times*, 30 November, 3B

Kelley, Anne, and Ella Taylor. 1992. Florida: The changing patterns of power. In *interest group politics in the Southern states*, edited by Ronald Hrebenar and Clive Thomas. Tuscaloosa: University of Alabama Press.

Kerstein, Robert. 1987. *An analysis of Florida's election law*. Tallahassee: Policy Studies Clinic, Florida State University.

Kleindienst, Linda. 2001. Florida Democrats seek donations nationwide. *Florida Sun-Sentinel*, 1 June, 3B.

Lavelle, Louis. 1995. The money machine. *Tampa Tribune*, 14 March, 1A.

MacManus, Susan. 1996. An American microcosm. *The World and I* 11 (August): 36-41.

Mansfield, William. 1976. Florida: The power of incumbency. In *Campaign money*, edited by Herbert Alexander. New York: Free Press.

March, William. 1998. GOP, Democrats milk spending limit loophole. *Tampa Tribune*, 10 March, 1A.

———. 2001. Democrats aim at Bush brothers. *Tampa Tribune*, 24 June, 1A.

———, and Margaret Talev. 1997. Loopholes let lawmakers fly without telling. *Tampa Tribune*, 10 December, 1B.

Morgan, Lucy. 1988. *Legislators have amnesia over junkets to Keys. St. Petersburg Times*, 25 May, 1B.

———. 1998. *Public campaign financing upheld. St. Petersburg Times*, 10 December, 1B.

———. 2000. Election could see unlimited spending. *St. Petersburg Times*, 6 August, 1A.

———. 2001. Ethics law lets foxes guard the henhouse. *St. Petersburg Times*, 15 December, 1B.

National Institute on Money in State Politics. 2001. 1998 Florida election analysis. Retrieved [March 6, 2002]: http://www.followthemoney.org

Nickens, Tim. 1998. In money, Bush leads in more ways than one. *St. Petersburg Times*, 23 February, 1A.

Pellemans, Michelle. 2000. Do lobbyists buy more than lawmakers' time? *Tampa Tribune*, 29 February, 1A.

Report of the task force on campaign reform. 1998. *Campaign Reform.* Princeton: Princeton University.

Roady, Elston. 1962. Who gave it and who got it law. *Laws and Contemporary Problems* 27 (Summer): 431-439.

Rosenthal, Alan. 2001. *The third house: lobbying and lobbyists in the States,* 2nd ed. Washington, D. C.: Congressional Quarterly Press.

Silva, Mark. 1998. Florida's legislature. In *Almanac of Florida politics, 1998,* by Tom Fiedler and Lance de-Haven Smith. Dubuque: Kendall-Hunt.

State of Florida. 2000. *Candidate handbook on campaign financing.* Tallahassee: Division of Elections.

Slade, Tom. 1999. Should Florida limit contributions to state parties?" *Wall Street Journal,* 10 February, F4.

Talev, Margaret, and David Cox. 1998. Food, booze, money flow as party kicks off session. *Tampa Tribune,* 8 April, 1B.

Talev, Margaret and Michelle Pellemans. 1998. "Fundraiser targeted attorneys," Tampa Tribune, April 8, 1D,

Varian, Bill. and Christopher Goffard. 2001. Committee fuels campaign for speaker. *St. Petersburg Times,* 21 May, 1A.

Wark, John, et al. 2000. Ethics legislation not a high priority item. *Tampa Tribune,* 3 March, 1A.

Wasson, David. 2000. Lobbyists extending reach to elections. *Tampa Tribune,* 10 July, 1B.

Ziegler, L. Harmon, and Hendrick van Dalen. 1971. Interest groups in the States. In *Politics in American states,* edited by Herbert Jacob and Jack Vines. Boston: Little, Brown.

CHAPTER 9

THE FUEL BEHIND OKLAHOMA'S POLITICS— THE ROLE OF MONEY

Jan Hardt

When one thinks of Oklahoma, one typically pictures oil and gas fields, Native American reservations, and cowboys riding the plains. Unfortunately, Oklahoma is also a state with a reputation for corruption. From 1965 to 1993, Oklahoma suffered numerous scandals, including three Oklahoma Supreme Court Justices convicted of bribery or impeached in 1965, a former Oklahoma House Speaker sent to jail for bribery in 1975, Okscam from 1980 to 1984 that resulted in 220 felony convictions involving county commissioners and suppliers in most of the state's counties taking kickbacks, and the Stifel scandal where public education bonds were misused in the late 1980s and early 1990s. Then came the Governor Walters scandal in 1993, and several different accusations against Governor Keating in the late 1990s.

As a result of these scandals, Oklahomans have very populist tendencies. Oklahomans want to control how their government is run, and they generally have a strong distrust of politicians and government. Consequently, Oklahomans have taken several actions to ensure that they can continue to have power in government. Oklahomans have joined interest groups. Oklahoma is a relatively small state with only about three and a half million people, but Oklahoma is one of the more active interest group states in the nation, with oil and gas, Native American, and gun groups leading the way. Oklahomans also have made great use of initiatives, because they allow citizens the opportunity to put legislative measures directly on the ballot. Another sign of Oklahoma's populist tendencies is the fact that it was the first state in the country to pass term limits on its state legislators. These term limits, which will not be fully effective until 2004, were designed to make state legislators more accountable to the public. But Oklahoma did not stop there. During the 1980s, many Oklahomans campaigned to get an Oklahoma Ethics Commission created and added to the Constitution. As of 1990, Oklahomans have had their wish granted. Oklahoma does have an Ethics Commission and although Oklahoma sometimes does have problems with corruption, it also has some of the more detailed ethics laws of any state in the country.

This chapter examines campaign finance in Oklahoma by exploring several key components: 1) the early history of campaign finance in Oklahoma, the creation of the Oklahoma Ethics Commission and the laws governing campaign finance in Oklahoma; 2) changes in the ethics laws since 1990, resulting from court cases, state legislative decisions, and application of those laws from individual cases of corruption; 3) the role of money in recent elections, particularly the election of 2000, including its use in both federal-level races in Oklahoma as well as state-level races; 4) how political action committee money is spent in Oklahoma, including the amounts spent, the types of PACs that spend, the most active PACs, and the amount spent per different types of candidates; 5) interest group lobbying in Oklahoma and how lobbyists can influence the making of public policy; and 6) some concluding thoughts, including how Oklahomans feel about reform and recent efforts to achieve reform.

Campaign Finance Laws in Oklahoma

In the United States there is a two-tier system for regulating campaign money. The federal government passes laws and makes decisions for federal candidates, specifically the U.S. House, U.S. Senate, and presidential candidates. The states regulate the campaigns of all other candidates. In the early 1970s two decisions by the federal government had a major impact on the creation of state campaign finance systems. The first decision was by the U.S. Congress. In 1971 and 1974, the Congress passed the Federal Election Campaign Act (FECA) of 1971 and 1974. This law set limits on campaign spending and contributions for federal election candidates. It also required disclosure of campaign contributions and expenditures and set up penalties for not abiding by the regulations. The second decision came from the U.S. Supreme Court in 1976 with *Buckley vs. Valeo*. The court ruled that limits on overall campaign spending were unconstitutional because they prevented candidates from speaking about their own campaigns. Candidates after the Buckley decision thus are allowed to spend as much as they want on their campaigns. The only exception is a situation when public funding is established, as with presidential candidates. If they accept public funds, the government can place limits on overall spending.

The end result of these two decisions was the creation of a campaign finance model for the states, showing them what they could and could not do in terms of regulating campaigns. At this point, the individual states had three choices: 1) they could implement finance regulations stronger than that of the federal government; 2) they could require state-level candidates to abide by the same regulations as federal candidates; or 3) they could enact weaker requirements. These federal-level decisions thus created a guideline for the campaign finance laws of Oklahoma and the forty-nine other states. States could enact limits on individual or group contributions, and they could specify who could donate to campaigns. They could also enact disclosure laws, requiring candidates to file reports to indicate who gave money, how much was given, and exactly how it was spent. But, after the Buckley decision, states could not enact limits on overall campaign spending, unless state funding was somehow involved. Eight states have made the decision to either enact the FECA laws or to make them tougher in their states. Florida has devised the toughest state law, placing $500 limits on both individual and group contributions to candidates. Only a handful of states currently have no limits on contributions, including Oklahoma's neighbors New Mexico and Colorado (Council of State Governments 1996).

Oklahoma's road to creating strong ethics laws has been a slightly bumpy one. A palpable tension exists between the need for strong ethics laws and the recognition that members of the legislature are reluctant to pass laws that could damage their re-election chances. The first two attempts by the state legislature, in 1968 and 1986, were very modest efforts, with only the Oklahoma Ethics Commission Act in 1986 producing any real reform. That act generated rules governing the reporting of campaign expenditures and contributions, but did not place any real limits on contributions, nor did it deal effectively with the issue of lobbyists. In the late 1980s, many had the strong perception that the Oklahoma legislature would attempt to weaken the ethics rules even further. To prevent that from happening, Governor Henry Bellmon used his Constitutional Revision Study Committee to promote the creation of a constitutional ethics commission. It was placed on the ballot in 1990 as an initiative and passed overwhelmingly after a publicity campaign was launched through the media.[1] Found in Article XXIX, the Oklahoma Ethics Commission is a constitutionally established body whose goal is to ensure "rules of eth-

---

1. Don Maletz and Jerry Herbel, "The Oklahoma Ethics Commission 1997–98." In *The Almanac of American Politics, 2000.* Stillwater, Oklahoma: OPSA Press, 2000.

ical conduct for campaigns for elective state office and for campaigns for initiatives and referenda." The Ethics Commission consists of five unpaid commissioners, each serving a term of five years and appointed by a different source. The Governor, the Attorney General, the Speaker of the House, the Chief Justice of the Supreme Court, and President Pro Tempore each make an appointment to the commission, and they must ensure that no more than three of the commissioners may be from one political party, and each must be from a different congressional district.

The Oklahoma Ethics Commission has made several achievements. First, candidates and initiative campaigns now have to file quarterly and annual reports, stating both their contributions and expenditures. Failing to file means that there could be substantial fines, or at the very least, unfavorable publicity. Second, contributions to campaigns are now limited to $5,000 per calendar year. All contributions over $50 in the aggregate now have to be reported. Candidates or initiative campaigns must now report the name, address, and occupation of each contributor, and the amount and type of each contribution. Third, campaigns must report all expenditures, whether they are paid or in-kind expenditures. Fourth, state officials are now subject to financial disclosure rules, meaning that they now have to state their sources of income and any potential conflicts of interest. This requirement, combined with strict definitions on what constitutes a conflict of interest, makes it easier to determine if a state official is being unethical. Fifth, lobbyists must also disclose their financial activities. Finally, the Ethics Commission must respond when questions about ethical behavior are raised, typically by holding hearings, seeking testimony, issuing advisory opinions, conducting investigations, or issuing official "ethics interpretations."

Oklahoma's laws are at times stronger than the federal laws, but at times they are also comparatively weak, as shown in Table I. The best example of this is Oklahoma's limit on campaign contributions. Oklahoma's law is weak compared to the federal law, because corporations are allowed to create political action committees to donate to campaigns under Oklahoma law. Under federal law, they are expressly prohibited. Yet the limit for political action committees in Oklahoma is $5,000 per campaign in a calendar year, while in federal elections individuals can donate $5,000 per campaign per election. Since most candidates will typically compete in two (or even three) elections—a primary, a general, and maybe a runoff election, political action committees in Oklahoma can donate less than under federal law. Yet Oklahoma's contribution limit is the same for both individuals and political action committees, $5,000 per calendar year, and as result, Oklahoma has a weaker individual contribution limit than the federal law which is $1,000. Oklahoma also has stricter laws on who can donate. State highway patrol officers and supernumerary tax

Table I
Oklahoma Campaign Laws Compared with the Federal Law, FECA

	Oklahoma Law	Federal Law	Which is tougher?
Individual Contributions	$5,000 per calendar year	$1,000 per candidate per election	Federal
PAC Contributions	$5,000 per calendar year	$5,000 per campaign per election	Oklahoma
Corporation donations allowed	Yes	No—only as soft money	Federal
Who can donate?	Specific restrictions	Few restrictions	Oklahoma
Use of public funds	No	Yes, presidential elections only	Oklahoma

consultants are prohibited from making contributions, and the early law indicated that state officials, state employees, judges, and classified employees *should* not make contributions (CSG 1996). Moreover, the state legislature also passed a law in 1979 that created a state campaign fund for distribution to political parties and candidates, thus creating state funding similar to that of the federal law. The campaign fund would have been created through a $1 voluntary contribution from state income taxes. No money was ever put aside in this fund, however, because the Attorney General of Oklahoma ruled in 1979 that the law violated the constitutional prohibition against making gifts of public funds to private entities for non-public purposes. In 1982, the Oklahoma Supreme Court refused to rule on the Attorney General's opinion, effectively killing the state campaign fund and dashing the hopes of the Oklahoma Democratic Party that had hoped for this fund to be enacted.

The end result is that the Oklahoma Ethics Commission is quite active. In FY 2000 alone, the Commission held forty-four administrative hearings on assessments, assessed late fees against 236 persons or entities, processed 3173 campaign contribution and expenditure reports, received 562 statements of financial interest, processed 511 designation of agent forms, received nineteen complaints or messages of other information, and issued eight informal opinions and four official ethics interpretations. From lobbyists alone, the Ethics Commission processed 466 lobbyist registrations, 737 lobbyist expenditure reports, fourteen lobbyist termination reports, and 1,737 pieces of lobbyist related correspondence.[2]

2. Source: "2000 Annual Report published by the Oklahoma Ethics Commission." Oklahoma Ethics Commission.

Yet the Oklahoma Ethics Commission also faces several important limitations, resulting from tension between the state legislature and the commission. On several occasions, including the Political Subdivisions Ethics Act (1995), the legislature has made it clear that while the Ethics Commission can conduct investigations upon a complaint and prevent possible violations, it does not have jurisdiction to enforce criminal penalties. Thus, the Ethics Commission has few options when it finds that a campaign has violated ethics laws. Fines can be issued, although sometimes the threat of the fine is worse than the actual fine. For example, the penalties for filing late reports are automatically $100 per day, and can reach a maximum of $1,000. Yet when the Ethics Commission assessed $73,625 in late fees in FY 2000, appeals reduced that amount to $61,590. The total amount collected in FY 2000 was only $10,459. The commission can also hope that the publicity surrounding an ethics violation is sufficient to render compliance. Most of the time, the publicity comes from the violator's opponent, who can make a campaign issue out of late reports or other ethics violations. But the opponent can do this only if the violation occurs during the course of the campaign. The Ethics Commission can also issue public reprimands. This option apparently is not used very often, because in 1999 the first such public reprimand was issued when a statewide candidate received an in-kind contribution from a local restaurant in the form of food, supplies, and restaurant space for a campaign rally. Under the law, corporations are explicitly prohibited from making this kind of contribution to candidates. The second limitation of the Ethics Commission is a direct result of its constitutional authority. The commission only has jurisdiction over state and county campaigns, but not local elections or municipal officials. While the Political Subdivision Ethics Act authorizes the commission to provide reporting forms for municipalities and school boards, those forms are not filed with the Ethics Commission. Instead, municipal and school board clerks, as well as local district attorneys handle the forms, and they are given the responsibility of enforcing the ethics rules.

Changes to the Ethics Laws Since 1990

The bumpy road of the Ethics Commission continued, even after its overwhelming passage by the public in 1990. From its very inception, the state legislature determinedly challenged the commission's authority. In the 1991 legislative session, the state legislature passed the Ethics Commission Act. This act, while seeming to recognize that a Ethics Commission must exist, also placed on it additional limits. The legislature required that all rules proposed by the Commission must be presented to the legislature by the second date of the legislative session. If not disapproved by joint resolution, they then take effect at the beginning of the following July. Yet, members of the state legislature not only rejected the commission's first set of rules in 1992 but even created their own substitute rules. The Ethics Commission then went to court, arguing that the state legislature was trying to undermine the constitutional authority of the Ethics Commission. In 1993, the Oklahoma Supreme Court agreed in *Ethics Commission v. Cullison* et al., 850 P. 2d 1069 (Oklahoma 1993). The court ruled that the action by the Legislature unconstitutionally encroached on the powers of the Ethics Commission and the commission had the right to create ethics rules for the state of Oklahoma. In 1994, the Oklahoma Ethics Commission faced a smoother path; the 1994 rules were allowed to go into effect on July 1, 1994.

The 1993 case of Governor David Walters clearly revealed the weaknesses of the Ethics Commission when investigating illegal acts by public officials. The charges against Governor Walters stemmed from his 1990 campaign for governor when he raised $2.7 million. This figure was stunning for two reasons: 1) it was a record for a gubernatorial campaign in Oklahoma at the time, and 2) it was later learned that donors paid more than 10% of the total in cash. Walters was accused of accepting donations larger than the $5,000 limit and of promising jobs in exchange for contributions, among other charges. The FBI started an investigation of his campaign in 1991, but it was dropped that year for insufficient evidence. The FBI files, however, were given to State Attorney General, Susan Loving, a Walters appointee, in March 1992. By October 1993, that investigation led a multi-county grand jury to come forth with twenty indictments, including a multi-count indictment against Walters himself, with eight felony counts and one misdemeanor count.

The Oklahoma Ethics Commission became involved only because Walters challenged the grand jury probe in the Oklahoma Supreme Court, arguing that the Ethics Commission should have jurisdiction in investigating campaign irregularities, and not the attorney general. The Ethics Commission responded with a friend of the court brief, citing that the Ethics Commission had limited staff (one investigator and one attorney) and limited resources compared with the Oklahoma State Bureau of Investigation. Thus, Walters' challenge could have seriously weakened campaign finance rules if successful because the Ethics Commission was effectively conceding that it could not conduct the investigation on its own. In October 1992, the Supreme Court ruled against Walters, allowing the grand jury probe to continue. Within a few weeks, a plea agreement had been reached that allowed Walters to plead guilty to the misdemeanor charge of accepting a contribution in excess of the $5,000 limit. He also had to agree to a $1,000 fine, a promise not to claim innocence in future speeches, a one-year deferred sentence, and a "donation" of $135,000 to the Ethics Commission, which effectively cleaned out his 1994 reelection fund. He chose not to seek reelection for governor that year.

Another challenge to the Oklahoma Ethics Commission came in the late 1990s when Oklahoma became the first state to require electronic filing from most statewide candidates and large political action committees. The Oklahoma Ethics Commission's electronic filing system was launched on July 1, 1997, with $700,000 spent on the system. Ironically, $135,000 of that money came from former Governor David Walter's campaign as part of his 1994 plea agreement for ethics laws violations. Any statewide candidate with more than $5,000 in contributions and any political action committee contributing more than $10,000 was required to file electronically, making those reports instantly available to the public online. But alas, the state legislature became involved, and in the last days of the 1998 legislative session, voted to end mandatory electronic filing, making it voluntary instead. This essentially made the law useless; most candidates have decided not to file electronically, and politically, there is no incentive for them to do so unless their opponent is also required to file. The Executive Director of the Ethics Commission stated publicly that this move by the state legislature made Oklahoma the "laughing stock" of other states because it moved backwards in electronic filing.

Yet the Ethics Commission does have the power to file complaints against public officials when questions are raised by outside parties about their ethics practices. In 1997, the Commission filed the first such complaint against the subsequent Governor, Frank Keating. Democrats charged that Keating used state vehicles for political fund-raising trips on thirty-two separate occasions. They also argued that his use of state funds to purchase an airplane violated ethics rules. But Keating, anticipating the complaint to be filed with the Ethics Commission, launched his own attack. He charged that there was a conflict between two state rules. While state law demands that the Commissioner of Public Safety provide security and transportation for the governor, Ethics Commission rules forbid the use of public property or funds for support of political activities. Keating argued that the state law had priority over that of the Ethics Commission, and the Oklahoma Supreme Court agreed in May 1998, effectively ending the investigation. Governor Keating has also faced questions concerning $250,000 given to him by Jack Dreyfus over an eight-year period. Those complaints ended Keating's chances to be named as a cabinet nominee by President George W. Bush in early 2001.

The Oklahoma Ethics Commission also has the power to issue ethics interpretations, which allow the Commission to have a profound impact on ethics policy. In FY 2000, the Ethics Commission issued four such interpretations.

The first interpretation allowed not-for-profit corporations to use corporate funds to advocate the election or defeat of candidates/initiatives so long as corporate money was not used to make independent expenditures. Independent expenditures expressly advocate the election or defeat of a clearly identified candidate or candidates. The second interpretation said that candidates did not have to file electronically so long as they included their last-minute financial activity on the appropriate report. The third interpretation said that corporate entities are allowed to use corporate funds to create campaign literature, so long as that literature does not qualify as an independent expenditure by including some sort of express advocacy. The fourth interpretation resulted from the gubernatorial campaign of Representative Steve Largent (R-OK). When he began to campaign for governor in 2002, he inquired as to whether his federal election campaign fund could be transferred to his state gubernatorial campaign fund. With this fourth interpretation, the Ethics Commission rejected that request, saying that funds cannot be transferred from a federal committee to a state committee, nor they could be transferred from one state candidate committee to another state candidate committee.

The Ethics Commission can also influence campaign finance policy by making rule change proposals to the legislature. Unless both houses of the legislature reject the proposals, they take effect. In 2000, the Ethics Commission considered changing the amount that a political party could donate to certain campaigns in Oklahoma. The commission appointed a ten-member task force to study the issue, and that task force recommended that political parties be allowed to give $50,000 to candidates for governor and $25,000 for candidates for statewide office, instead of the $5,000 per candidate currently permitted under the law. The task force, however, declined to raise the political party limit for state legislators, claiming that candidates in statewide races need to raise more money because of the greater number of constituents. These proposals, however, were withdrawn in February 2001 before they went to the state legislature because of the need for further study.

The end result is a campaign finance system in Oklahoma that has some strengths, but also has some weaknesses. The Oklahoma Ethics Commission has ensured since 1990 that all but municipal-level campaigns must file timely reports detailing their contributions and expenditures. It also has placed limits on individual, PAC, and political party contributions. Yet, the commission does not have jurisdictional authority over enforcement and thus has been left with an enforcement system that is very weak at best. Recent moves to make the electronic filing system voluntary have only weakened the Oklahoma Ethics Commission's ability, and attempts to raise the contribution limits of PACs and political parties will only weaken Oklahoma Ethics law as it currently stands.

Campaign Finance in Oklahoma—
The Federal Races

Oklahoma's political culture reveals some clues about how money will be spent in Oklahoma. In Oklahoma, there are more registered Democrats, but this state typically votes Republican, particularly for the more significant races. Thus, since the 1950s, Oklahoma has voted only once for a Democratic president, and as of August 2001 five out of its six members of Congress are Republicans. Yet, the picture at the state level is much more competitive. The Oklahoma state legislature is currently split, with Democrats having a three-seat edge in the House, although a greater advantage in the Senate. But, typically, Democrats have dominated the state legislature. Party registration also favors the Democrats, with 59% Democrat and 34.9% Republican in 1997.[3]

Campaign finance in Oklahoma tends to mirror this dichotomy. At the federal level, with most Oklahomans voting for Republicans, Republicans raise and spend more than the Democrats, with 75% of all contributions going to Republicans, and only 24.5% going to Democrats.[4] But the reverse is true at the state level. Democrats raise and spend more money than Republicans. Nowhere is this true than with PAC receipts. Republicans were 52.9% of the candidates in 2000, but only received 30% of the PAC money. Democrats, on the other hand, constituted 47.1% of the candidates, but received 71.8% of the PAC money. Democrats also did better overall. Democratic legislative candidates in 2000 raised $41,046 on average and spent an average $39.621.[5] Republicans, on the other hand, only raised $30,481 and spent $27,339 on average. The worst fund raisers in 2000 were most Corporation Commissioner candidates and all third- party legislative candidates. With the exception of the eventual winner, Bob Anthony, who raised $275,625.20 and spent $254,644.55, the other Corporation Commissioner candidates did not fare as well. Combined, the four challengers raised only $13,772 and spent only $14,386. Third party candidates did the worst, raising only $275.75 on average, and spending only $251.70 on average.

Spending on Oklahoma congressional races tends to be mostly under national averages. The national averages for the 1999–2000 congressional races

---

3. Figures from the Oklahoma Election Board, 1997, in an interview by the author.

4. Congressional campaign finance information was taken from www.opensecrets.org, September 2001, unless otherwise noted.

5. All Oklahoma state campaign finance information is from the Oklahoma Ethics Commission. Contributions and expenditures were reported as summary information, but all PAC information had to be calculated by the author.

were $809,713 for incumbents, $357,956 for challengers, and $1,139,974, for open-seat candidates. Only three Oklahoma congressional candidates were able to surpass these averages: Representative Brad Carson (D-OK), spending $1,209,242 in the second district open seat, incumbent Representative J.C. Watts Jr., spending $1,546,659 in the third district, and challenger Randy Beutler (D), spending $414,786 in the sixth district. With the exception of Beutler, challenger spending was particularly low, with three challengers spending less than $25,000 and one of those spending nothing. Thus, candidates in Oklahoma typically spend under the national average. This is not a surprise, given the size of the state. What is a surprise is that occasionally there will be candidates who spend way beyond the expected in order to win. Representative J. C. Watts (R-OK) typically outspends his opponents by a clear margin. In 1998, for example, he spent $1.46 million, while his opponent, Ben Odom (D-OK) only spent $356,373. The same was true in 1996, with Watts spending $1.36 million, and Odom spending $350,073.[6]

Federal election races in 2000 were fairly predictable. As expected, Oklahomans voted for George W. Bush, and returned five of the six congressional incumbents back to Congress. But the most exciting federal race in Oklahoma that year was for an open seat in the second district, a race which has been unpredictable in the past. This was a seat where in 1994 Virgil Cooper, a relatively unknown seventy-one-year-old retired school principal, beat Representative Mike Synar (D-OK) in a primary runoff despite being outspent. Cooper spent only $75,202, campaigning as a "Will Rogers Democrat," while Synar spent over $300,000.[7]Cooper eventually lost in the general election to Representative Tom Coburn (R-OK) who spent $604,924. Coburn promised his constituents during his campaign that he would abide by self-imposed term limits; he would only be in office for his six-year term. Thus, in 2000, his seat became an open seat, hotly contested by Democrats and Republicans alike. The two eventual party nominees were Brad Carson and Andy Ewing, respectively. Carson in his race spent $416,000, while Ewing spent $508,000. Because this was seat "up for grabs," though, the two political parties outspent both candidates, with Democrats spending $525,000 and Republicans spending $440,00. Carson eventually won, becoming the only Democrat in the eight-member Oklahoma congressional delegation.

Despite their predictability, Oklahoma's federal election races offer several clues about campaign spending in Oklahoma. First, candidates for Congress

6. *The Almanac of American Politics, 2000.* Washington, D.C.: National Journal, 1999.
7. Jim Meyers, "Synar Defeat Sets Off Warning." *Tulsa World,* 22 September 1994.

in Oklahoma mostly received their money from Oklahomans. In the 2000 elections, Oklahomans contributed 31% of all contributions; the next largest state contributor was Oklahoma's neighbor, Texas, with only 2%. Most contributions (74.9%) went to Republicans, ranking Oklahoma sixth in the nation in its percentage of Republican contributions. Thus, what's important in Oklahoma is not voter registration, but which political party wins seats in office. With Republicans holding seven of the eight congressional seats, the high percentage of Republican contributions is easily understood, but it does show how difficult it will be for Democrats to win those seats. Second, soft money in Oklahoma mostly went to Republican candidates for Congress, with much of it coming from oil and gas companies. Phillips, BP Amoco, Kerr-McGee, and Chesapeake Energy were the top four donors of soft money in the 1999–2000 election cycle, and 100% of their money went to Republicans. In fact, the top ten soft money donors gave $933,918 to Oklahoma candidates, and only $70,000 of that went to Democrats, or only 7.5%. $65,000 of that came from one company, Sonic Corporation, a fast-food chain, which gave 100% to Democrats.

Campaign Spending in the State Races

Collecting comprehensive campaign finance information in Oklahoma is very difficult, despite the existence of an active state ethics commission. The good news is that candidates and PACs are required to report their campaign contributions and expenditures to the Ethics Commission. The bad news is that information is not very accessible to the public. There are several factors that limit public accessibility. First, as discussed previously, campaign finance information is not available online and won't be for several years until kinks in the software are solved. Thus, in order for the public to get campaign information, they have to travel to the state capitol building, where the Ethics Commission is located. Once this hurdle is past, gathering the information then becomes a problem. Collecting information on an individual race is not difficult; one just needs to locate the paperwork for those candidates. The problem arises when one tries to get comprehensive finance information, i.e., gathering all campaign expenditures so comparisons can be made across candidates. By law, the Ethics Commission is not required to collect comprehensive information. As a result, the Ethics Commission only has reports of the last two election years (1998 and 2000) where the name of the candidate, race, district, contributions, and expenditures were reported on a single form. Thus, some types of campaign finance information are difficult to find in Oklahoma:

Table II
Average Money Raised and Spent by Type of Seat Sought—2000 Elections

	Mean $ Raised	Mean $ Spent
Corporation Commissioner	$58,279	$53,806
Senate	$53,572	$47,349
House	$27647	$26,495
County Sheriff	$7304	$8876
County Commissioner	$3555	$4658
County Clerk	$2402	$2871
County Assessor	$1414	$2217
County Treasurer	$313	$750

how much PAC money is raised, how the PACs spend their money on candidates, how individuals give to candidates, how candidates spend their money, etc. Without this information, it is very hard for reporters and the public to find out how candidates are spending money on their campaigns, one of the most important goals of any campaign finance legislation.

Once the information is gathered, campaign spending in the state races is fairly predictable. As shown in Table II, the higher the level of the race, the more money is spent on average. In the 2000 elections, for example, Senate legislative candidates received more contributions and spent much more than their counterparts in the House. Candidates for Senate seats raised $53,572 and spent $47,349 on average, while House candidates raised $27,647 and spent $26,495 on average. It is important to note that sometimes candidates accept more in contributions than they can spend. For many incumbents, this is the start of their war chests, or the money that they hold over to use for the next election. One of the more recent trends in Oklahoma elections is for candidates to begin their races earlier and earlier. This matches a trend at the federal level that some have called the "permanent campaign," where candidates are raising funds and seeking the wisdom of consultants year round, whether it is an election year or not.[8] Since 1996, for example, House Democrats have held birthday parties for House Speaker Loyd Benson (D) that became fund raisers. The 1999 party raised over $125,000 and included ninety hosts who gave $1,000 or more, and sixty sponsors who gave $500 each. The hosts included lawyers and lobbyists, bankers, and union members.

These war chests make it much more difficult for challengers to compete with incumbents because challengers are typically outspent by incumbents. In the 2000 state legislative races, incumbents raised an average of $46,450, while

---

8. Sidney Blumenthal, *The Permanent Campaign*. New York: Touchstone Press, 1982.

challengers raised only $16,225. The same is true for spending; incumbents spent $43,932 while challengers spent $14,951. Incumbents in Oklahoma thus have a tremendous advantage. Not only do they normally already have the many advantages of incumbency (constituency service, name recognition, etc.), but one of the most important ways to gain name recognition is to spend money so that campaign leaflets can be given to constituents (Pomper 2001). Campaign leaflets are very important in Oklahoma because much of the campaigning in Oklahoma occurs by knocking on doors and dropping off information. This is particularly true in state legislative races and those for city and county seats. Challengers are thus at a distinct disadvantage; they can knock on the doors, but won't have the money to spend on the leaflets. Incumbents also typically send follow-up mailings to their constituents, an activity that obviously cannot be done by challengers. As seen with the federal races, it is in the open seat races where candidates really spend the money, whether for House or Senate seats. These seats are very competitive because potential candidates know that this seat represents a window of political opportunity (Schlesinger 1966). In 2000, open seat candidates spent an average of $57,031 and raised $51,422.

But does spending money mean victory? The assumption made throughout this discussion is that if a candidate spends more money, he/she will win. With money, candidates can not only buy those leaflets, but they can also host fund raisers, buy consultants, attend rallies, put up signs, and perform all the other activities of a modern campaign. Yet spending more money might be a curse. Spending money beyond what is expected could be a sign of candidate vulnerability. Sometimes, candidates raise more money than expected not because they are having a good year, but because they are facing tough races and they do not want to be unprepared. In Oklahoma, this was not the case. The winning candidates raised and spent more money than the losers. Candidates who won raised $51,214 and spent $47,071, while candidates who lost raised only $19,307 and spent $18,584.

PAC Money in the 2000 Elections

Contributions and expenditures are important, but they don't tell us much about *how* the money is spent in particular race. What percentage of a candidate's contributions come from PACs and what percentage came from individuals? Do these percentages vary if incumbents or challengers are examined? What about Democrats or Republicans? Did Republicans get more from oil and gas companies or did Democrats? Did PACs give differently to leaders than non-leaders? What type of PAC gave more to incumbents, challengers, and open seat candidates? These are the types of questions that can only be examined by gathering comprehensive campaign finance data. In Oklahoma, to do this one needs to look at every single candidate and compile the information by hand.

In the 2000 Oklahoma elections, 416 PACs gave $3,490,313 in contributions to 293 candidates, for an average candidate contribution of $11,912. PAC money represented 36.4% of all money raised at the state level, and most of that money went to incumbents. Traditionally, at both the federal and state levels, incumbents have received more PAC money than challengers because the PACs know that incumbents are more likely to win seats. PACs want to give money to candidates they know will be in office because those are the legislators who will vote on public policies. With open seat candidates, PACs are usually willing to take the chance, typically giving heavily to those candidates (Pomper 2001). Election 2000 data seems to confirm this. Incumbents raised an average $17,448 in PAC contributions, while challengers only raised $5050. The open seat candidates did the best of all; they raised $20,416. PACs definitely give to winners, giving $19,436 to winners, while giving only $6,547 to the losers. Female legislative candidates also did well with PACs, receiving $15,690, compared with the males who raised $11,434.

The activity of individual PACs can be measured in several different ways: the total money spent by the PAC, the number of contributions, and the average contribution made. All three measures yield different results about the most active PACs in Oklahoma. When looking at overall spending, party does matter. Of the top eleven PACs, seven of the PACs are either connected with a party or are ideological in nature, but they give only to one party. The two most active PACs are the Oklahoma House of Representatives Democratic Campaign Committee and the Republican Majority Fund, which gave $184,200 and $109,500 on average, respectively. The other five PACs are WIN-PAC (which gives only to Democrats), the Oklahoma Republican Party, House GOP, the Oklahoma State Republican Senate Committee, and The New Oklahoma (only giving to Republicans). Other PACs in the top ten include Chickasaw Nation (ranked #3 and giving $97,675), two labor PACs, OK AGC, a contractor association (ranked #5 and giving $80,850), as well as the OK AFL-CIO (ranked #10 and giving $71,700), and the Working Oklahomans Alliance (ranked #7 and giving $78,100).

In looking at the amount of contributions, there is almost an entirely different list of PACs. While there are 149 state legislators in Oklahoma, most PACs do not give to both parties' candidates, so it should be expected that the number of contributions should be less than 149, even if a PAC gave more

Table III
PAC Money by Type of PAC, 2000 Elections

Type of PAC	Sum	Percent	Count	Average
Agriculture	$42,200	1.24	221	$190.95
Banking	$138,225	4.08	517	$267.36
Business	$122,450	3.61	399	$306.89
Insurance	$92,575	2.73	310	$298.63
Oil and Gas	$271,805	8.02	774	$351.17
Telecomm.	$110,127	3.25	451	$244.18
Utilities	$151,862	4.48	576	$263.65
Education	$72,964	2.15	351	$207.87
Health	$375,020	11.05	1377	$272.35
Professional	$82,550	2.43	234	$352.78
Senior	$24,100	0.71	81	$297.53
Labor	$410,360	12.10	698	$587.91
Construct	$156,825	4.62	320	$490.08
Pub Employee	$59,500	1.75	118	$504.24
Party	$889,895	26.24	738	$1205.82
Ideology	$168,250	4.96	135	$1246.30
Guns	$19,450	0.57	95	$204.74
Environment	$2,400	0.07	9	$266.67
Indian	$147,775	4.36	212	$697.05
Other	$26,902	0.79	23	$1169.65
Unknown	$25,690	0.76	52	$494.04

than one contribution to a candidate. This is borne out by looking at the numbers. Only four PACs in Oklahoma gave to 149 candidates or more, including the Oklahoma Optometric Association, the OKC Firefighters Association, the OKIE PAC (a utility PAC), and the Chickasaw Nation. There were sixteen PACs that gave more than 100 contributions, but most of PACs gave only to a small number of legislative candidates. For example, of the 416 PACs, a whopping 280 PACs gave to only five candidates or fewer. The list of single-contribution PACs included many of the smaller county parties, but also some noteworthy PACs, and some not so noteworthy. American Home Products, Ford Motor Company, Nations Bank PAC all gave a single donation, but so did HAMPAC.

The most active PACs in terms of average donation yield a third distinct list. The top of this list is heavy with those who gave large amounts, but only gave a small number of contributions. Of the top twenty-five PACs, only twelve gave to more than five candidates. It is important to remember that the largest donation legally possible by a PAC is $5,000. The largest contribution was made by the CFRC to a single candidate— $4,000. Much more noteworthy, though, is that the PACs with the largest number of donations in the top twenty-five average donation list were party or ideological PACs, including the Republican Majority Fund, the Democratic Candidate Campaign Committee, the Oklahoma State Republican Senate Committee, the OK State Republican Candidate Committee, Democrats of the OK State Senate, and OK House of Representatives Democratic Campaign Fund. Thus, party and ideological PAC contributions make a big difference. Not only do they give a lot of money per candidate, but they also spread their wealth, giving to numerous candidates. Of the party/ideological PACs in the top twenty-five, the average contribution was $2,269, providing candidates with a substantial boost to their campaigns, particularly since many received money from more than one party/ideological PAC. Yet overall, the average contribution from a PAC was fairly small, only $486, far under the $5,000 maximum. Many PACs gave small contributions; of the 416 PACs, 185 PACs gave $250 or less. The most noteworthy contributions were from the Phillips 66 Company's PAC, which typically gave either a $500.66 donation or a $250.66 donation to candidates.

Since 416 PACs gave to state legislative candidates, it makes sense to attempt to classify them in order to see if any patterns emerge. One of the standard ways to classify PACs is to sort them by corporation, association, labor, party/ideology, and other. Under this classification, 27.4% of the PAC money came from corporate PACs, 16.4% came from association PACs, 18.5% came from labor PACs, 36.2% came from party/ideology PACs, and 1.6% came from other PACs. This classification does show one fact. The party/ideology PACs were active, giving large contributions to most candidates. When candidates received money from only one or two PACs, that PAC was typically a party or ideology PAC. These candidates were usually poorly funded challengers who faced well-funded incumbent opponents. Even the candidates that were well funded, though, received money from party/ideology PACs. But these candidates received money also from two party/ideology sources. They typically received money not only from state party PACs but also from the national party/ideology PACs. Several members of Congress in Oklahoma have established candidate or leadership PACs so that they can give to other candidates. Senator Don Nickels (R-OK), for example, created a Republican Majority Fund, so that he could help Republicans regain the state legislature. The New Leadership Fund and the Democratic Congressional Campaign Committee are other examples of national PACs that gave to legislative candidates.

Although this classification is useful when examining the political parties, it does not say much about many of the special interests that are important in Oklahoma. Do Native Americans, oil and gas companies, and agriculture interests help the campaigns of state legislative candidates? Of course, the only way to answer this question is to divide up the classifications even further.

Table IV shows the different categories of PACs, the total of their donations, the percentage of all PAC donations, the number of donations, and the average donation. This table reveals that not only do the parties and labor give money, but so do health and oil and gas companies. Surprisingly, however, the percentage for oil and gas companies was only 8.0%. That seems fairly small, given the significance of oil and gas as one of main industries in Oklahoma. Other surprises include the low numbers for agriculture, banking, business, and utilities. The low percentage for education (2.2%) was not unexpected. Although common and higher education are always substantial agenda items in the legislature, the salary for educators in this state typically ranks below the national average.

Even more information can be gained from Table IV by looking at the number of contributions and the mean contribution per candidate. What should be obvious is that the party/ideological PACs are very important to candidates because they give very large contributions on average, slightly over $1,200 each. Considering that some candidates only raised $7,000 or $8,000, candidates thus depend heavily on these PACs to conduct their campaigns. Another large source of money is the Native American PACs; they only gave 212 contributions compared to the 738 from the parties, but they gave fairly large contributions, averaging $697. The various labor PACs, AFL-CIO, public employees, and the construction workers, etc., also gave large average contributions. The low contributions from agriculture and gun interests, however, were unexpected. Yes, the agriculture PACs did include associations of individual farmers, not known nationally for their campaign generosity, but they also included the major tobacco groups—Phillip Morris and RJ Reynolds—as well as some of the large-scale farm interests. Yet, the average donation was a measly $192. Similarly, one of the gun PACs was the National Rifle Association. Oklahoma has the reputation of being a "gun and pickup" state, and it is confirmed by the fact that even most Democrats in Oklahoma are against gun control laws. Yet, here again, the average contribution from the NRA was only $205. Perhaps, in both of these cases, the PACs were trying to make "appearance" contributions. In other words, they spread their wealth among many candidates so that they could maintain their access and influence.

Once contributions are divided into smaller categories, it becomes very easy to sort those contributions by characteristics of the candidates. The percentage of contributions from each PAC can be compared to the percentage of that characteristic in the population. One of the most obvious distinctions between candidates is party affiliation—Democrat or Republican. Democrats did better with most PACs than Republicans. The Democrats were 47.1% of the candidates but received 99.0% of the money from telecommunications compa-

Table IV
PAC Contributions by Incumbent, Challenger & Open Seat,
2000 State Legislative Elections

Type of PAC	Challengers				Incumbents				Open Seats			
	Sum	Count	Avg. Contrib.	% of Total	Sum	Count	Avg. Contrib.	% of Total	Sum	Count	Avg. Contrib.	% of Total
Agricult	2575	14	183.93	6.10	38825.00	203	191.26	92.00	800	4	200.00	1.90
Banking	10850	42	258.33	7.85	102025.00	380	268.49	73.81	6100	17	358.82	4.41
Business	23800	49	485.71	19.44	89800.00	336	267.26	73.34	8850	14	632.14	7.23
Insurance	8975	31	289.52	9.69	80550.00	270	298.33	87.01	3050	9	338.89	3.29
Oil & Gas	19250	47	409.59	7.08	244854.52	712	343.90	90.08	7700	17	452.94	2.83
Telecomm	5171	25	206.87	4.70	100726.87	413	243.89	91.41	4850	11	440.91	4.40
Utilities	13700	55	249.09	9.02	130362.21	501	260.20	85.84	4900	14	350.00	3.23
Education	10000	46	217.39	13.71	56994.00	276	206.50	78.11	7800	20	390.00	5.14
Health	25325	96	263.80	6.75	340245.00	1245	273.29	90.73	5700	29	196.55	7.81
Professl	5000	11	454.55	6.06	72700.00	212	342.92	88.07	9450	36	262.50	2.52
Senior	1600	7	228.57	6.64	0	0	0	0.00	0	0	0	0.00
Labor	75635	112	675.31	18.43	308125.00	551	559.21	75.09	0	0	0	0.00
Construc	10975	30	365.83	7.00	137225.00	270	508.24	87.50	26600	35	760.00	6.48
Pub Emp	10550	17	620.59	17.73	42250.00	91	464.29	71.01	8625	20	431.25	5.50
Party	404038	341	1184.86	45.40	386431.13	325	1189.02	43.42	6750	10	675.00	11.34
Ideology	92900	73	1272.60	55.22	46850.00	41	1142.68	27.85	98566	71	1388.25	11.08
Guns	1550	13	119.23	7.97	17900.00	82	218.29	92.03	28500	21	1357.14	16.94
Environ	500	2	250.00	20.83	1700.00	6	283.33	70.83	0	0	0	0.00
Indian	25650	22	1165.91	17.36	102175.00	78	1309.94	69.14	200	1	200.00	8.33

nies, 90.6% from Native Americans, 89.9% from labor, and 86.5% from education. These percentages were all expected; Democrats nationwide typically fare well among those groups. The biggest surprise was that Democrats received large percentages from some of the other PACs, including 85.1% of the money from gun organizations, which were almost all pro-gun organizations. They also received 67.1% of the money from banking interests, 78.8% from professionals, and 66.4% from health personnel. In fact, the only two types of PACs where Democrats did not fare well were party PACs and ideology PACs. The ideology PAC percentage is certainly notable, with Democrats receiving only 2.9% of the money there, while Republicans received a whopping 97.1%. What becomes obvious from these figures is that Democrats get a far larger percentage of the PAC money (71.9% overall, compared with 29% for Republicans), yet Republicans are competitive in campaigns because they receive the bulk of the party/ideology money as well as money from individual contributors.

Another distinction arises between House and Senate PAC contributions. In the 2000 election, 81.4% of the candidates competed for House seats, while only 18.6% competed for Senate seats. Senate candidates did very well, however, in receiving contributions from PACs. In every category, but environmental PACs, Senate candidates got more than their share of the money (29.8%), with business, banking, insurance, most professional groups, and Native Americans contributing the most. The Native Americans were the largest contributors, giving 43.6% of their PAC contributions to Senate candidates. Moreover, the average donation to Senate candidates was typically much larger than to House candidates, for all types of PACs, except utilities and ideology. Senate candidates, for example, received an average donation of $884 from labor, while their House colleagues received only $497. Similarly, the party PACs gave only $1,157 on average to House candidates, but $1,410 to Senate candidates. Part of this distinction necessarily lies in the differences in the seats. Senate seats cover more geographic area, are more prestigious, and are up every four years in Oklahoma, instead of the two years for House seats. Yet Senate candidates still did fairly well even considering these differences.

Political action committees tend to give to winners. Thus, it is expected that winners will receive more in PAC contributions than losers. Generally, this was the case. For all PACs except for the political parties, the PACs gave more in overall contributions to winners rather than losers, despite the fact that only 42.6% of the candidates were winners, while 57.4% were losers. The political parties gave $411,027 to winners, but $478,867 to losers. For candidates, though, overall contributions are not the most important factor. What they care about is that they are getting more money than their opponents. This is particularly true for candidates who might think that they are losing their races. Fortunately, for the losers, several PACs gave more in average contributions to losers than to winners. Business, insurance, professional, public employee, labor, and Native American PACs all gave more heavily to losers than to winners. These are also PACs that favored Democrats over Republicans. The most notable difference is with the professional PACs who gave only $300 on average to winning candidates, but almost $600 to losing candidates. Labor PACs gave a substantial difference, with $505 going to winners, but $705 going to the losers. The political parties too favored the underdogs. They gave $1,304 to losing candidates, but only $1,090 to winning candidates. Many financially challenged candidates only received party money; thus, it is not surprising that many of them would lose. Ideology PACs, however, were a source of substantial money for many winning candidates. Although there were many other PACs, including agriculture, health, and guns, that gave more to winning candidates, none did with the generosity of the ideological PACs. Ideology PACs gave 97% of their money to Republicans, with $1,336 to winners, but only $1,083 to losers.

Much of the findings with winners and losers were confirmed by looking at the differences between incumbents, challengers, and open seat candidates. Since most challengers in the 2000 Oklahoma election were losers, it is not a surprise that incumbents should receive more money overall from PACs than challengers. PACs tend to give more to incumbents because incumbents are more likely to win and thus more likely to be there when public policy decisions are made. With every PAC, except party and ideology PACs, incumbents received more overall money than challengers. As Figure I shows, in some cases the differences were quite substantial. Banking PACs gave $102,025 to incumbents, but only $10,850 to challengers. Oil and gas companies were particularly worried about taking a risk by giving to challengers, with only $19,251 given to challengers, compared with the $244,204 to incumbents. There are two notable exceptions to this rule, however. The political parties and ideology PACs both gave more to challengers than incumbents in overall spending. These exceptions are not unexpected. Party money often serves as "seed money" during a campaign; they are the initial dollars that give campaigns fund-raising momentum so that individual donors and other PACs will be more likely to contribute.[9] The ideological PACs were especially generous, giving $92,900 overall to challengers, compared with $46,850 for incumbents.

---

9. Mick Hinton, "Early Starts Help State Parties Court Campaign Money." *The Tulsa World*, 27 April 1999.

Figure I
Spending on Oklahoma Congressional Seats, 1990–2000

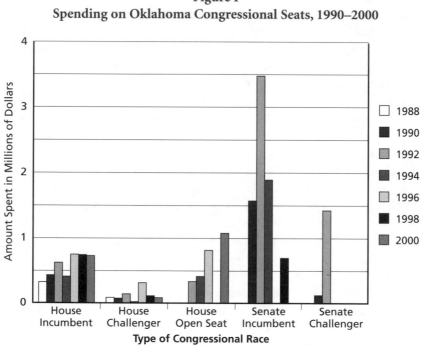

But once again, looking at overall spending does not provide a full picture. PACs can give more overall to one type of candidate, but then can give less on average. What the candidates care about is the amount the PACs donate to them, not how much they spend overall on other candidates. Looking at averages removed many of the differences shown above, with most PACs. including the political parties. giving approximately the same amounts on average to both incumbents and challengers. This indicates that once challengers climb over the initial hurdle of encouraging PACs to give to them, they do fairly well in terms of the amount given. This is not the case with all PACs, however. Challengers actually did better on average with banking, labor, and construction, receiving about $200 more on average from these PACs. Challengers also received more from ideology PACs, getting $1,272 on average, instead of $1,142 given to the incumbents. Incumbents did particularly well with Native American groups, getting about $150 more on average than challengers. Examining the party money from party PACs also reveals some interesting results. The Republican Party PACs tended to give more to their incumbents than their challengers, averaging $1,353 for incumbents and $1,294 for challengers. Democrats, though, were inclined even more to donate to their incumbents, giving $1,137 to incumbents but only $849 to challengers.

Open seat races need to be looked at differently. They are more competitive and usually feature more activity than races that include an incumbent.[10] Open seat candidates were only 4.8% of all candidates, but received 9.7% of the PAC money, indicating that the PACs gave a bit more importance to these races, knowing that either party could take the seat. Thus, it is not surprising that party and ideology PACs, which give only to one party, were the most likely to give PAC money, with 11.3% and 11.1%, respectively, of their money going to open seats. Open seat candidates also did fairly well with business, health, and Native American PACs. Yet once again, average donations reveal a more interesting picture. The most surprising by far is the average donation given by the political parties. They only gave $675 on average to open seat candidates, compared with the $1,189 given to incumbents and the $1,184 given to challengers. With the competitiveness of these races, parties should have given more to these seats, thinking that a few extra dollars might be enough to take the seat, particularly given the close seat distribution in the Oklahoma legislature. In fact, this is exactly what the Republicans did with their ideology PACs, giving $1,386 to open seat candidates, but only $1,142 to incumbents, and $1,272 to challengers. Thus, Democrats clearly missed an important political opportunity in 2000, one that could have made a difference given the closeness of these races and the seat distribution in the legislature. Most other types of PACs followed this trend, giving open seat candidates larger contributions than they gave to other candidates. Native Americans were a notable exception, giving only $200 on average to open seat candidates, but $1,309 to incumbents, and $1,166 to challengers. The relatively small contribution could be explained by the fact that there were few open seat candidates and perhaps many of these open seats were not located in heavily Native American portions of the state.

Do leaders in the state legislature get more PAC money than non-leaders? The expectation would be yes, since by definition leaders are more likely to be incumbents than are non-leaders. Yet, the results are somewhat surprising. Of the 2000 candidates, 12% were leaders, and 88% were non-leaders. Leaders did do well with most of the business and association PACs, including agriculture, banking, insurance, oil and gas, telecommunications, utilities, etc. They also did well with the ideological PACs, getting 24.2% of the funds. Yet,

---

10. Open seat candidates received only 51% of the vote, compared with incumbents who had 71.9% of the vote and challengers who had 28.1% of vote. Thus, open seat races are much more competitive.

the leaders did not do well with the political parties, getting only 8.8% of their funds. Looking at average donations, again a truer picture emerges. While the leaders did not get a high percentage of the overall party funds, on average they received about the same donation as non-leaders, with $1,170 going to leaders and $1,164 going to non-leaders. It is again with ideology where a big difference emerges. Ideological PACs gave a substantial $1,938 to leaders, but only $1,394 on average to non-leaders. This makes sense given that many of the ideological PACs are leadership or candidate PACs formed by the most Republican members of Oklahoma's congressional delegation to keep their party in control of the Oklahoma legislature. All three of the labor classifications, however, tended to support non-leaders in office by giving them about $100 more on average.

There might also be some gender differences in PAC contributions. Some studies have suggested that females are more likely than males to support the so-called "soft" issues, such as labor, health care, family leave, the environment, etc., whereas men would support the "hard" issues, like guns, national defense, and foreign policy. Others have debunked this notion, arguing that both male and female politicians care about these issues (Carroll 1994). Looking at PAC contributions, thus, might be a way to tell if there are gender differences in the public policy concerns of state legislators. Males represented 87.6% of the candidates, while females represented 12.4%. Females did the best with environmental PACs, but also did well with education and different labor PACs, except construction workers. Females did significantly better with party and ideology PACs than expected, receiving about 21% of their contributions from these PACs. Where females had the most trouble, somewhat surprisingly, was with groups dealing with seniors. Only 4.6% of senior money went to females. As expected, females did poorly with both gun organizations and agriculture, yielding only 8.2% and 6.2% of their money respectively. The average donations for males and females were fairly equal across the range of PACs, with the exception of ideology PACs who gave $1,278 on average to males, but only $1,147 to females.

One controversy surrounding PAC contributions is the percentage of out-of-state contributions. This is particularly true with congressional races, as judging by the furor that surrounded Hillary Clinton's successful bid to become a New York Senator. Although part of the concern was that her residency in New York barely predated her campaign announcement, she and her opponent, Republican Rick Lazio, relied heavily on out-of-state funds. In state legislature races, most of the PAC funds should be from in-state contributors, particularly in Oklahoma, given its limited public policy impact on other states. This indeed turned out to be the case. 87% of the PAC contributions were from in-state PACs, while only 13% were from out-of-state. With several PAC categories, there were no out-of-state contributions, including public employees, education, professional, senior, construction, environmental organizations, and Native Americans. The largest percentages came from gun organizations (82.5%), oil and gas companies (49.3%), telecommunications (29.4%), and labor (22.8%). Oklahoma's competitive state legislature was apparently not even a concern to the national parties, who only gave 2.6% of the party money. However, these national party organizations, when they did get involved, contributed heavily, with an average contribution of $2,091 as compared with $1,149 for the in-state parties. These findings, though, fit in with other trends reported nationally for the political parties. Their involvement in most state and non-competitive federal races is typically minimal, averaging about 2 to 4%. Yet their activity is not insignificant. When they do get involved, they usually try to maximize their impact by giving heavily in targeted competitive races. Their goal is to provide the financial boost that might get them an extra seat or two in the legislature (Pomper 2001).

Elections of 2000 Compared with Other Races

In many states, there seems to be a consistent trend. Political campaigns have become more and more expensive. In Oklahoma, this is true to some extent, but sometimes the cost of races can be difficult to predict. Typically, open seats tend to be very expensive. Candidates know that these seats represent a "window of political opportunity" that cannot be wasted because they know that there is no incumbent (Schlesinger 1966). Unfortunately, both parties know this and, as a result, these seats tend to be the most competitive, with the winner getting only 51% of the vote in the 2000 open seat elections, compared with an incumbent's 71% of the vote to a challenger's 29%.

As a result, open seats tend to be very costly, but this is not always the case. Oklahoma's gubernatorial elections are a perfect example. In 1986, the candidates spent only $5.12 per vote. Yet in 1990, Oklahoma had one of its most expensive gubernatorial races ever, costing $9.2 million, or slightly over $10 per vote. The 1990 race featured an open seat, because incumbent Governor Henry Bellmon unexpectedly decided to retire. His opponent in 1986, David Walters, was the successful candidate for Governor in 1990, beating former federal prosecutor Bill Price and Independent Wes Watkins. In 1994, David Walters decided not to run after being indicted for violating campaign finance laws in his 1986 and 1990 campaigns. This created a second open seat. Governor Frank Keating faced Lieutenant Governor Jack Mildren and Watkins again, winning with 47% of the vote in a three-way-race. Yet, this race was not as costly, with the three candidates spending about $3.5 million, or about $4 a vote. There are several reasons why this race was probably not as expensive. After the campaign finance abuses of the Walters campaign, candidates were probably reluctant to raise excess funds. Moreover, this was the second open seat gubernatorial election in four years, and one of the major candidates, Jack Mildren, had faced an unexpectedly tough contest in his Democratic primary. In 1998, Governor Keating out-raised Laura Boyd, a Democratic State legislator, spending over $2.7 million to her $582,187, or about $4 per vote, about the same as in 1998.

Oklahoma congressional races have been much more predictable over the years, with candidates spending more in the competitive races. Figure I shows spending in the 1990–2000 congressional races, with divisions made between incumbents, challengers, and open seats. The more significant the race, the more money that will be spent, and open seat races tend to be more expensive than those featuring an incumbent. Senator Don Nickels (R-OK) is a good example of this tendency. In 1986, with a tough challenger in James Jones, Nickels spent just over $3.2 million to get 55% of the vote. That race cost an expensive $6.5 per vote, as Jones spent just over $2.5 million. Yet more recent contests have been less expensive, typically costing between $3 and $4 a vote, regardless of whether the race featured an incumbent or was an open seat. Senator Don Nickles raised under $3.5 million in his 1992 campaign and $2.6 million in his 1998 campaign. These US Senate races averaged out to about $3.8 per vote and $3.0 per vote, respectively. In 1994, the open seat race between Representative David McCurdy (D-OK) and Jim Inhofe (R-OK) was about as nasty as they come, but even in this race the money spent was $3.86 per vote, with Inhofe raising $1.92 million and McCurdy raising $1.87 million.

Spending on state-level elections has been fairly consistent over the years, with over $8.9 million spent by House and Senate candidates in 1998, and over $8.7 million spent in 2000. Again, the trend of spending the most in the higher-level races continued. In the 2000 elections, only state legislative seats, a Corporation Commissioner seat, and county posts were contested. The Corporation Commissioner candidates spent the most, but state Senate and House candidates spent less, spending $53,806, $47,349, and $26,495, respectively. For the county posts, candidates generally spent under $10,000, unless they were in the major counties, like Tulsa or Oklahoma City.

The 1998 elections are a better demonstration of how the type of race makes a difference, because in this election numerous state level posts were contested. Besides the posts for Governor and Lieutenant Governor, Oklahomans elected a State Auditor, Superintendent of Public Instruction, Labor

Table V
Spending in 1998 Oklahoma Elections by Type of Race

Race	Average Contribution	Average Expenditure	Winner Spent
Governor	$611,388.43	$577,095.90	$2,895,054.71
Lieutenant Governor	985,321.88	843,953.50	856,787.69
State Auditor	231,166.39	224,756.10	220,422.39
Superintendent, Public Instruction	99,373.11	2,724.92	93,325.94
Commissioner Of Labor	84,346.89	102,746.50	377,764.99
Insurance Commissioner	146,061.89	168,056.8	244,240.09
Justice OK Supreme Court	67,264.59	67,220.59	
District Attorney	30,456.60	32,340.20	
District Judge	20,811.73	19,467.66	
Associate District Judge	4,184.84	4,424.78	
State Senate	57,593.35	57,082.29	
State House	24,307.62	25,969.55	

and Insurance Commissioner, as well as numerous judges. As shown in Table V, the Governor and Lieutenant Governor races were the most expensive, with the Lieutenant Governor race actually being more expensive. But average numbers can be misleading, because they include several candidates in these races who spent very little. Much more impressive are the winners' total spending for some of the state level races. Governor Keating clearly outspent all the other winning candidates, spending $2.89 million to win his seat. Most of the other state-level candidates spent a few hundred thousand dollars, including Insurance Commissioner Carroll Fisher, who beat the incumbent John Crawford in an upset. For the judicial candidates, the level of race was clearly a factor, with Supreme Court candidates spending the most and Associate District Judge candidates spending the least. Once again, Senate candidates outspent House candidates, $57,082.29 to $25,969.55, or just slightly more in 1998 than in 2000.

Lobbying in Oklahoma—A Tale of Influence?

Some of the earliest lobbying groups in Oklahoma were identified by American journalist John Gunther in 1948, who found that the most active groups were the Baptist Church, oil interests, the elderly, the education lobby, and county rings. The number of lobbyists for PACs has grown steadily, with eighty-three registered lobbyists in 1976, 343 lobbyists in 1986, 410 in 1997,

Figure II
Lobbyists in Oklahoma, 1986, 1997, and 2000

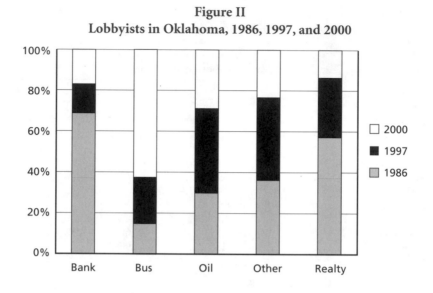

and 466 in 2000.[11] In 2000, 676 organizations had registered lobbyists working for them. As shown in Figure II, more lobbyists are working for non-petroleum business interests, including 60% of all lobbyists in 2000. The second and third largest organizations in 2000 were oil organizations and other organizations, respectively. This represents a decline in the number of realty lobbyists, as seen in Figure II. Again, however, breaking down some of these PAC categories provides information. Of the 676 organizations, the largest two groups were business organizations and health organizations, each with 16.6% of all registered lobbyists. Oil organizations represented 7.5% of all lobbyists, while professional and telecommunications organizations were next, each with 6.9% of all lobbyists. Just counting up the registered lobbyists for each organization, though, can be misleading because it does not recognize that some organizations are more powerful than others. For example, the Oklahoma State AFL-CIO is only counted once, yet as we have seen, it is very generous in terms of its PAC contributions. Looking at just numbers, education and professional groups are also underestimated in terms of their power. This seems to be confirmed by a study of Oklahoma legislators who were asked to identify the most influential interests in 1991. They named education, labor,

---

11. All lobbying statistics from 1997 and 2000 were calculated by the author from the "Oklahoma Registered Lobbyists" report, published by the Oklahoma Ethics Commission. Statistics from earlier years come from Morgan et al 1991.

and professional groups at the top of their list, with banking, public employees, oil, and business groups rounding out the list (Morgan et al. 1991).

When campaign finance rules were tightened in 1990, those concerning lobbyists got particular attention. There are specific statutes to regulate the activities of lobbyists. Any person who spends in excess of $250 in a calendar quarter for lobbying activities, who receives compensation in excess of $250 in a calendar quarter for lobbying services rendered, and /or whose employment duties in whole or in part require lobbying is considered to be a lobbyist. Every quarter lobbyists must file expenditure reports with the commission when an expenditure on any one member of the legislative, executive, or judicial branch exceeds $37.50. PAC money is given to candidates by lobbyists and their PACs for a reason. They hope that they can influence who gets into office and more importantly, their public policy decisions. Yet there is some disagreement as to whether PAC money buys votes. Many consumer interest groups, like Common Cause and Public Citizen, would say, "Yes, of course it does!" Yet, numerous studies by political scientists suggest that PAC money does not buy votes directly, but it can buy access. In today's busy world, access to a state legislator may be just as important. State legislators remember PAC contributions, and they may allow those lobbyists to get their views heard.

Yet the appearance of impropriety may be just as important to state legislators, particularly since improper PAC contributions could return to haunt state politicians in future elections. Given the extensive history of corruption, along with the great distrust of politicians by Oklahomans, improper PAC contributions have been a recurring election issue in recent years. Governor Frank Keating, for example, raised questions in 1996 when the Senate Democrat's political action committee accepted contributions of $5,000 by three Indian nations, and then Democrats voted immediately afterward to pass Indian fuel tax legislation. But Senate Pro Tempore Stratton Taylor (D) responded by suggesting that Keating's criticism should also include his own contributions from gasoline interests in the state.[12] Keating again raised questions in 1998 when two Democrats accepted contributions from Tulsair owner Tom Clark, even though a legislative committee spent most of the 1997 session investigating Clark's sale of the $2.9 million airplane to the state. The Democrats responded, saying that they received numerous contributions over the years, and the issue is not the contribution itself, but the timing of that contribution before a vote.[13] At the

---

12. Paul English, "Campaign Contributions' Link to Legislature Actions Cited." *The Daily Oklahoman*, 19 April 1996.

13. Paul English, "Donations Can Raise Questions on Motive, Keating Says." *The Daily Oklahoman*, 31 March 1998.

same time, Democrats were also criticizing Keating, particularly for his use of state vehicles for political fund-raising trips and for his vacation with several Conoco executives, despite ongoing legislation at the time.

Another controversy concerns the question of the government lobbying itself. Some of the lobbyists listed by the Ethics Commission include state workers in Oklahoma municipalities, government agencies, colleges, and school districts, who use taxpayer money to lobby for increases in appropriations. Relying on taxpayer funds (paid in the form of dues), the Oklahoma School Boards Association, for example, lobbied against a state question that would have limited property taxes. The Ethics Commission doesn't require state employees who lobby to register as lobbyists, and some of the lobbyists even give themselves titles other than "lobbyist," such as "legislative consultant." That, combined with the fact that some of them only lobby part time, makes it very difficult to tell how much money the state of Oklahoma spent on lobbying itself.[14]

The Future of Campaign Finance in Oklahoma

The picture of Oklahoma that has been created so far is one of intense Oklahoman populism in the face of political scandals, increasing campaign spending, a larger role for PACs, and more lobbyists. As Oklahoma has moved closer toward reform, it also seems to take several steps back, as seen with its initial attempts to create the Ethics Commission and then more recently, creating greater public access to campaign finance information. Given these events, it is not a surprise that Oklahomans want campaign finance reform. In September 1999, six interest groups joined together to conduct a statewide campaign called, Oklahoma Citizens for Campaign Finance Reform. These groups included Common Cause, the Family Farm Alliance, the Interfaith Alliance, the League of Women Voters, the Oklahoma's Conference of Churches, and the Sierra Club. The campaign's goal was to concentrate on reform at the state level.[15] One of this campaign's first major activities was to join with the national Study Circles Resource Center to conduct study circles on campaign finance in several cities throughout Oklahoma during 2001. Moreover, a group called Norman Citizens for Campaign Finance Reform is pushing for a $125 cap on individual campaign contributions to candidates running for mayor or

---

14. Robby Trammell, Randy Ellis, and John Greiner, "Taxpayers Pay 'Lobbyists' to Promote Public Causes." *The Daily Oklahoman*, 27 February 2000.

15. John Greiner, "State Coalition Pushes Election Finance Reform." *The Daily Oklahoman*, 28 September 1999.

city council, and a $250 maximum from families, or a sharp reduction from the $500 limit for city council and the $1,000 limit for mayor currently allowed. Norman candidates faced pressure to abide by these limits during the 2000 election and, even though none were obliged to do so since they were not yet part of the city charter, only one individual contribution to the ten candidates' campaigns during that election exceeded $250. That donation was $500. The group believes that their success in putting campaign finance reform on the agenda led candidates to abide by these restrictions voluntarily.

What these and other efforts show is that Oklahomans clearly do want campaign finance reform. This was confirmed in March 26–29, 2001, when Oklahomans were surveyed in response to the US Senate's consideration of the McCain-Feingold federal campaign reform bill.[16] Oklahomans said, for example, that they think campaign contributions buy access to members of Congress and influence their decisions. 71% also said that sweeping reforms in the federal campaign finance system were necessary. Oklahomans also clearly want to put limits on campaign spending. The greatest support came for putting limits on the money labor unions and business can donate to political parties, or soft money. A majority, though, want to limit how much people can give to candidates and how much candidates can spend on their own campaigns. This is despite the fact that the Supreme Court has ruled spending limits unconstitutional, unless there are public funds involved. Currently, both Oklahoma and the congressional campaign finance laws do not have spending limits.

Oklahomans can take heart in the fact that Oklahoma has not succumbed to the spiraling campaign cost nightmare that has plagued some other states. Campaigns do not cost that much in Oklahoma, with the costs of most congressional races and of most state races still under the national average. Many candidates do receive PAC contributions, but few receive the maximum contribution of $5,000, and there are hundreds of PACs that just give four to five donations per election year. But there are some ominous signs. The Second District open seat race in 2000 clearly opened some eyebrows, not just because of what the candidates spent, but because the two national parties contributed over $1 million. Another race that got some attention was Kirk Humphrey's campaign for Mayor in 1999. He spent $157,492 during just a primary to win a job that pays only $2,000 per year. As a result, he spent $6.98 per vote in the primary alone.

Other ominous signs for those wanting campaign finance reform came from the Oklahoma Ethics Commission and the state legislature. Efforts in

---

16. Chris Casteel, "Oklahomans Want Restrictions on Campaign Finances, Poll Says— Most in State Believe Money Buys Influence," *The Daily Oklahoman*, April 2, 2001.

2000 by the Ethics Commission to weaken existing ethics laws are a step in the wrong direction, most notably the suggestion that campaign contribution limits should be increased for the political parties from $5,000 to $25,000 or $50,000. This reform was suggested by two prominent figures in Oklahoma politics, Republican Helen Cole and Democrat Pat Hall in January 2000, who called for the creation of a task force to study and recommend campaign finance reform in Oklahoma.[17] Yet increasing the political party limit could make it very difficult for challengers to compete against incumbents and seems to buck the national trend for lowering campaign contribution limits, not raising them. Moreover, Oklahoma was the first state in the nation to require mandatory electronic filing of campaign reports, but also the first state in the nation to retract that requirement just over a year later. As a result, the public has very limited access to campaign finance information in Oklahoma. Almost all serious efforts require a trip to the Oklahoma Ethics Commission, and it has only limited summary information. Anyone who wants to find out how much legislators are spending on their campaigns during an election season must examine each legislator's file by hand, a very time-consuming process. Even after the election is over, only the name of the candidate, the office, the total contributions, and the total expenditures are produced on a summary report, which has only been available for the 1998 and 2000 elections. Thus, finding comprehensive individual contributor, PAC, and/or expenditure information can only be viewed as a major undertaking, and not for the faint at heart.

In addition, the examples of corruption in Oklahoma just don't seem to go away. Despite a very strong populist sentiment where Oklahomans openly cite their distrust of politicians, corruption still continues. Many Oklahomans had hoped that with the advent of a strong Ethics Commission in 1990 that many of the ethics scandals that have plagued state politicians over the years would simply end. Yet the case of former Governor Walters in 1993 and the numerous ethics scandals that have centered on Governor Frank Keating (the airplane, the Dreyfus gifts, etc.), seem to justify Oklahoma's reputation. Oklahoma's image was not enhanced in the 2000 elections when it made national headlines for two events. First, voters faced an unfortunate circumstance. One of their candidates died before her name could be removed from the primary ballot. Yet, despite some publicity, she won the race anyway, encouraging many national commentators to make fun of Oklahomans for their lack of po-

---

17. Paul English, "Campaign Finance Target of Reform." *The Daily Oklahoman,* 29 January 2000.

litical knowledge. Fortunately, an even greater publicity campaign ensued, and she did not win the general election. Second, two candidates became embroiled in controversy when one campaign printed and sent numerous brochures featuring the other campaign's candidate in very suggestive pictures. For a state trying to establish its image, these events do not help. Nor do the stories circulating about other state politicians. Accusations of buying votes, accepting improper gifts and loans, ghost employees, and complaints about weaknesses in the ethics laws were rampant in last few years, raising some questions about the effectiveness of the reforms.

Thus, there are some success stories, and the public clearly wants campaign finance reform. Yet, the tales of corruption, the attempts to reduce limits on political party contributions, and the lack of extensive public access to campaign finance information all raise serious questions about the state's ability to reform its campaign finance laws. So what will it take to achieve campaign finance reform in Oklahoma? One of the trickiest issues will be the current tension that exists between the Oklahoma Legislature and the Ethics Commission. Not surprisingly, state legislators have been reluctant to pass legislation or rules that could put their political careers in jeopardy. Given the history between these two institutions, one should not hold out much hope. Yet, this is what it will take if Oklahoma is to rid itself of the reputation for political corruption.

References

The almanac of American politics. 2000. Washington, D.C.: National Journal.

Blumenthal, Sidney. 1982. The permanent campaign. New York: Touchstone Press.

Carroll, Susan. 1994. Women as Candidates in American politics. Bloomington, IN: Indiana University Press, 2nd edition.

Congressional Races, Oklahoma. Retrieved September, 15, 2001: www.opensecrets.org

Council of State Governments (CSG). 1996. Book of the states. Lexington, KY: Council of State Governments.

English, Paul. 1996. Campaign contributions' link to legislature actions cited. The Daily Oklahoman, 19 April.

———.1998. Donations can raise questions on motive, Keating says. The Daily Oklahoman, 31 March.

———. 2000. Campaign finance target of reform. The Daily Oklahoman, 29 January.

Greiner, John. 1999. State coalition pushes election finance reform. The Daily Oklahoman, 28 September.

Hardt, Jan. 2000. Political parties and elections in Oklahoma. In Oklahoma Government and Politics: An Introduction, edited by Christopher L. Markwood. Dubuque, IO: Kendall/Hunt Publishing Company.

Hinton, Mick. 1999. Early starts help state parties court campaign money. The Tulsa World, 27 April.

Maletz, Don, and Jerry Herbel. 2000. The Oklahoma ethics commission 1997–98. In *The Almanac of American Politics*. Stillwater, Oklahoma: OPSA Press.

Meyers, Jim. 1994. Synar defeat sets off warning. *Tulsa World*, 22 September.

———. 1995. Races costly reports show. *Tulsa World*, 15 February.

Morgan, David, Robert England, and George Humphreys. 1991. *Oklahoma politics and policies: Governing the Sooner State*. Lincoln, NE: University of Nebraska Press.

Oklahoma Ethics Commission. 2000. Fiscal year 2000 annual report.

Pomper, Gerald M., ed. 2001. *The election of 2000: Reports and interpretations*. New York: Chatham House Publishers.

Schlesinger, Joseph A. 1966. *Ambition and politics: Political careers in the United States*. Chicago: Rand McNally.

Trammell, Robby, Randy Ellis, and John Greiner. 2000. Taxpayers Pay "Lobbyists" to Promote Public Causes. *The Daily Oklahoman*, 27 February.

CHAPTER 10

Special Interest Money in State Politics: Lessons from the Minnesota Experiment

David Schultz

Special interests—including political action committees (PACs), lobbyists, and wealthy individuals—play an important and often adversely described role in American politics, such that limiting their influence is a recurrent goal of campaign finance reform legislation (Warren 2001; Baumgartner and Leech 1998; Drew 1999; Gais 1998; Sorauf 1992; Birnbaum 1993; Magleby and Nelson 1990). This is true even at the state level (Thompson and Moncrief 1998; Salmore and Salmore 1996; Loftus 1994). Minnesota represents one example of a state adopting the types of laws advocated by many reformers as necessary to curb the impact that PACs, lobbyists, and wealthy individuals have upon state elections and policy formation.

This chapter examines efforts in Minnesota to curb the impact of special interests, most notably PACS and lobbyists, in state politics. It does that by presenting a detailed analysis of money in Minnesota politics from 1994 through the 2000 elections, documenting the total amount of money spent by individuals, political parties, lobbyists, political action committees, and interest groups in terms of direct candidate contributions, soft money contributions, independent expenditures, and lobbyist disbursements. The argu-

Special thanks and acknowledgments go to the Campaign Practices and Public Disclosure Board for making this data available, and to Senator John Marty who commented on this chapter. All errors here are mine.

ment will be that Minnesota's experiences in campaign finance reform provide important lessons to advocates in other states or in Washington, D.C., as they debate specific policy proposals.

In assessing the Minnesota model, this chapter briefly describes the history of campaign finance reform in the state and provides an overall analysis of the way money is spent in the state both in terms of campaigns and elections and for lobbyist activity.

One conclusion will be that, to understand how money influences the political process, one needs to look beyond simply direct contributions to candidates and instead realize that political actors have at least four different ways that money may be disbursed to secure political objectives. Hence, individuals, organizations, and sectors of the economy mix and match their use of money, suggesting that any successful campaign finance reform needs to address all four types of spending options.

Second, a major goal of recent Minnesotan efforts has been to regulate the amount of money and influence PACs and lobbyists have on the state's political and legislative processes. Minnesota has been successful in regulating the flow of campaign contributions from lobbyists and PACs to candidates through its voluntary public financing system, demonstrating that the state's partial-public financing of elections may be a model for other states and federal races. Yet, third, it has been less successful or willing to regulate contributions to political parties and legislative caucuses and to prevent money previously given to candidates from shifting elsewhere. Thus, these alternative avenues to direct money to influence state elections and policy making have effectively undermined efforts to place limits on the amount of money lobbyists and PACs can contribute. Finally, Minnesota's campaign finance reform system has been successful in securing many important goals, such as producing a higher percentage of competitive races, but other goals have not been obtained.

Minnesota's Campaign Financing System

Daniel Elazar (1984) classifies Minnesota's political culture as moralistic, suggesting that the impetus for political reform, including regulation of money in politics, is rooted in public intolerance for corruption. Some writers such as Elazar, Gray, and Spano (1999) claim that Minnesota's political culture is the explanation for many of its reforms. While perhaps true, in part, close party competition and the location of the state capital in the main media market in the state offer better explanations for public attitudes and legislative action on this subject. Minnesota's exceptionalism, as many attribute to the state (Atkins 1988), clearly has cultural roots, but many of its reforms and practices can also be traced to specific institutions and practices that define its political culture.

Like most states, Minnesota enacted few regulations or restrictions on money in state campaigns prior to the 1970s. Notable among the pre-Watergate reforms was a prohibition on corporate involvement in state electoral activity that was adopted in the Progressive Era. That ban continues to this day, although it extends only to corporate political activity in terms of direct advocacy for or against the election of a candidate for state office. Corporations are free to engage in issue advocacy as a result of *First National Bank v. Bellotti*, 435 U.S. 765 (1978). However, prior to that decision, the ban had extended to even issue advocacy. Even today, there is a total prohibition on corporate express advocacy, including the formation of corporate PACs, although this ban is somewhat weakened by the laws permitting non-profit corporate associations to sponsor PACs. Interestingly, this ban on corporate political activity does not extend to labor unions, and they remain free to make political contributions directly from treasuries and to form PACS.

Since the 1970s, there have been two waves of reform in Minnesota, one in 1974 and another in 1993. Both were precipitated by political scandals. In 1974, Minnesota, like many other states, legislated numerous reforms after Watergate (Donnay and Ramsden 1998). Here, the state adopted numerous changes to its laws, including its unique partial public financing system for all state constitutional and state legislative races. Under the 1974 statute, the state adopted both contribution and expenditure limits (including independent expenditures) to candidates for state offices, and it instituted a $1.00 tax check-off to pay for the publicly funded campaigns. This check-off would either go to the Democratic Farmer Labor (DFL) or the Independent Republican (IR) party (Donnay and Ramsden 1998). Money from the check-off would be awarded to each party based upon how much each raised statewide. Because DFLers outnumbered IRs by two to one, the Republicans insisted on special formulae that gave challengers a 10% increase in their spending limit, an idea not adopted until 1993. In addition to these provisions, the state also secured disclosure rules for contributions, lobbyist disclosure rules that remain almost unchanged to this day, and the creation of an Ethical Practices Board (now called the Campaign Practices and Public Disclosure Board) to implement and oversee the 1974 Minnesota Ethics in Government Act.

Subsequent court decisions forced several changes in the 1974 reforms. First, the constitutionality of a publicly financed campaign system and a tax check-off to finance it was a question mark at the time Minnesota enacted its reforms. The Supreme Court's *Buckley v. Valeo*, 424 U.S. 1 (1976) upheld the federal tax check-off to finance the public funding of presidential races and it also upheld contribution limits. However, it struck down expenditure limits and also stated that a publicly funded campaign system must be voluntary. *Buckley* foreshadowed the fate of the Minnesota law, and, in *Bang v. Chase*, 442 F. Supp. 758 (1977), affirmed in *Bang v. Noreen*, 436 U.S. 1 (1978), the courts invalidated the state expenditure limits. This decision also struck down the distribution mechanism under the check-off, with the Court arguing that it needed to reflect check-off within districts, not statewide.

Round two of Minnesota's campaign finance reforms came in 1993. After media accounts of state legislators accused of using their state phone card for personal business, a scandal called "Phonegate," and after other legislators had been seen taking excessive gifts from lobbyists—including DFL Speaker of the House Dee Long shown on television golfing at a conference—DFL State Senator John Marty pushed through several important modifications to the Ethics in Government Act (Elazar, Gray, and Spano 1999).[1] In addition, these reforms sought also to lessen the impact of lobbyist, PAC, and big donor contributions in the state, as well as to reduce of the cost of campaigns and equalize spending between challengers and incumbents.

In describing the aim of these reforms, Senator Marty stated: "Our goal is to make elections fairer and remove the influence of special interests" (Coffman 1993). Elsewhere Marty indicated that "Money talks in politics…And that leads to a disenfranchised majority of the public and the expanded power of wealthy people and power interests" (Smith 1993). The then-state senator and later U.S. House member Bill Luther at one point argued that it was "time to accept the challenge and eliminate contributions from all PACs and lobbyists" (Coffman 1993), and Steve Sviggum, then House minority leader and subsequently Speaker of the Minnesota House of Representatives, declared that "Special interests are tending to dominate the legislature" (Coffman 1993).

The state adopted a total prohibition on lobbyist gifts to state officials, both elected and appointed, and to staff employed by the state, as well as a ban on gifts to officials in may local jurisdictions. Minnesota thus joined Wisconsin as only the second state to this day to have a total prohibition on lobbyist gifts. Despite repeated efforts in 1995, 1997, and 1999 (notably all non-election years) by some legislators to weaken various parts of the gift ban, the law remains intact without amendments. In addition, Minnesota also raised the income tax dues check-off to $5.00, permitted citizens to designate this check-

---

1. The current campaign finance reform laws are codified in MINN. STAT. §§ 10A.01-51 (2000).

off to go either to the DFL or IR parties, a state general political fund, or, in some cases, to minor parties if they qualify either by petition or by a showing of popular vote at the ballot. As of 2001, the state DFL and former IR (now the RPM or Republican Party of Minnesota) parties, as well as the Green Party and the Independence Party, all qualify as major parties and for the check-off.[2] The 1993 reforms also specified the formula for the general fund, whereby 21% goes to the gubernatorial races, 23.3% to state senate races, and 46.6% to state house races.

The act modified the political contribution refund program, whereby each Minnesota adult could contribute up to $50 per year to eligible candidates and political parties and get that contribute rebated (not a tax credit) to them. Minnesota is unique in having this rebate system. Originally the law sought to off-set independent expenditures by permitting a candidate who participated in the public financing system to receive a public subsidy from the state, once notified that he or she was the target of such an expenditure or his or her opponent was a beneficiary of the same. Along with allowance, the law lifted the expenditure limits for candidates participating in the public financing system when their non-participating opponents exceeded the spending limits. Finally, all independent expenditures over $100 had to be documented, named, and reported to the state.

Subsequently, several portions of the 1993 reforms were attacked in Court. In 1994 the Minnesota Education Association (MEA), a traditional DFL supporter, and the Minnesota Citizens Concern for Life (MCCL), a Republican supporter, challenged the independent expenditure disclosure and public subsidy law. In *Day v Holahan*, 34 F.3d 1356 (8th Cir. 1994) the Eighth Circuit Court of Appeals invalidated that provision, arguing that the public subsidy chilled free speech. In light of the Supreme Court's *Colorado Republican Federal Campaign Committee v. Federal Election Commission*, 518 U.S. 604 (1996), the RPM successfully challenged the state ban on party independent expenditures on behalf of candidates in *Republican Party of Minnesota v. Pauly*, 63 F.Supp. 2d 1008 (D. Minn. 1999). However, in *Rosenstiel v. Rodriguez*, 101 F.3d 1544 (8th Cir. 1996), the court upheld the lifting of the spending caps provision for a candidate participating in public financing when the non-participating opponent exceeded the spending cap.

As currently amended, the regulatory system for campaign finances in the state includes several components.

---

2. The Independence Party consists of Governor Jesse Ventura and one former Republican state legislator who switched to this party. The Green Party of Minnesota holds no state elected office.

If one accepts partial public financing in Minnesota, a candidate must agree to several requirements.

Spending limits. In 1998, the last year when the state's constitutional offices held elections, the state's mandated spending limits were: Governor/Lieutenant Governor, $1,926,127; Attorney General, $321,023; Secretary of State, $160,514; State Auditor, $160,514; and State Treasurer, $160,514, while, for the 2000 legislative races, for State Senator the limits were $$50,630 and, for a House of Representatives race, $25,320. Spending limits are adjusted by June of election years (they are indexed for inflation) and 10 % additional spending is available to a candidate running for the office the first time, and, when a candidate wins by less than 2–1 in a contested primary, 20% additional spending. These spending limits are now indexed for inflation, and candidates are freed from the limits if they face an opponent who does not participate in the voluntary public financing program.

Contribution limits. There is a limit on the amount of money a candidate can accept from PACs, lobbyists, and large contributors (over $250)—20% of the candidate's total spending limit.

Individual contribution limits. In general, individual contribution limits vary by office and by whether it is an election year or not. These limits to candidates are in place regardless of whether one accepts public financing, and they also extend to limits on contributions by political committees and political funds. The limits in 2000, for example, an election year, were $500 per individual, and $100 in a non-election year for State House and Senate races. Political parties, including the state party and local party units, as well as the legislative caucuses, are limited to $5,000 total aggregate contributions in an election year and $1,000 in an non-election year for the state Senate and House, $5000 aggregate for any year for the Governor, $2,000 aggregate any year for the Attorney General, and $1,000 aggregate per year for the Secretary of State, State Auditor, and State Treasurer.[3]

Candidate contribution limits. Candidate contributions to one's own campaign are limited to ten times the individual contribution limit for that office, if one accepts public funding. Thus, a candidate for Governor would be limited to $50,000 per year.

To be eligible for the public subsidy, a candidate must receive contributions in $50 chunks (or only the first $50 is counted) for a total of: Governor/ Lieutennant Governor, $35,000; Attorney General, $15,000; Secretary of State,

---

3. In 1998 voters amended the Minnesota Constitution to eliminate the State Treasurer office at the end of 2002.

$6,000; State Auditor, $ 6,000; State Treasurer, $6,000; State Senator, $3,000; and State Legislator, $1,500. Candidates not agreeing to the public subsidy must notify the Board of Elections and opposing candidate of their intent not to participate in the public subsidy and also must inform them when they have exceeded the spending limit. Candidates who agree to the public subsidy and are running against a person who does not agree to the public subsidy are freed from spending limits (but still eligible for the subsidy) under certain conditions.

As noted earlier, in 1998, 100% of all incumbents and 99% of all challengers participated in the public subsidy program, while in the 2000 legislative races, virtually all candidates opted to participate in the voluntary program. Since 1990, participation in the program has been consistently over 90%, with 99% in the 1998 and 2000 election cycles (Donnay and Ramsden 1998).

To pay for the partial public subsidy, there are several sources of funds. First, $1,500,000 is transferred every election year from the State General Fund to the State Election Campaign Fund. Second, Minnesota residents may use a check-off on their state income tax or homeowner or renter fund ($5 check-off per taxpayer), and this check-off or homeowner/renter fund must be set aside for a specific party or for placement in the general campaign fund. Since 1974, the percentage of taxpayers participating in the check-off program has dropped from 22.3% to 9% in 1997. For a party to be eligible for money from the general fund, it must receive at least 5% of the vote in a statewide office or 10% in a legislative office. Third, parties and candidates who agree to participate in the public subsidy and abide by the spending limits are also eligible to participate in a public rebate program. Every adult in Minnesota may contribute up to $50 total per year and have the money rebated to them by the state.

The total public subsidy (excluding the contribution refund program) cannot exceed 50% of the candidate's expenditure limit, and many receive significantly less than this 50%. However, public funding could approach near 100% if the rebates and subsidies are added together. Many candidates do not even reach the spending or expenditure limit, sometimes spending only about half of the permitted amount. This results in a scenario where, for many candidates, the real or effective amount of money that they receive from public sources is far in excess of the 50% limit, often approaching 75% or more. Hence, many candidates need not solicit very much money from private sources, producing in many cases, a near total public financing of races. There is no evidence that one major party is given an advantage by the funding system. In fact, Republicans generally raise more money from the rebate system than do Democrats.

Table I
Campaign Spending Costs in Minnesota and Wisconsin

State	Minnesota*	Wisconsin**
1990 Population	4,375,099	4,891,769
Number of Senators	67	33
Senate size	69,030	148,235
Senate Race spending	$49,114	$306,375
Senate per capita cost	$0.71	$2.07
Number of Representatives	134	99
House size	34,530	49,411
House cost	$24,083	$145,885
House per capita cost	$0.70	$2.95
Governor's race	$1,926,127	$7,094,248
Governor per capita cost	$0.44	$1.45

* Minnesota spending figures based upon the statutory maximum expenditure limits.
** Wisconsin spending figures based upon the most amount money expended by any candidate in the most recent race for that office.

There are several other features in the regulation of Minnesota's political system that should be noted.

Easy voter registration. One can register to vote in several ways, including at the polls on election day. It is this easy registration that contributes both to the high voter turnout in the state and, according to some, for Jesse Ventura's victory in 1998, when first-time and disaffected voters were able to show up on election day and vote.

Spending costs are lower and not growing as fast as other states. In general, the cost of running for office in Minnesota is less than that of comparable states, according to per capita analysis.

For the purposes of comparison, campaign spending in Minnesota and Wisconsin may be contrasted. Wisconsin was included for comparison because of the similarities to Minnesota in terms of political culture, voting demographics, and geographic location. Also, like Minnesota, Wisconsin has a partial public financing system but, unlike Minnesota, a very small portion of the average campaign costs are available through public funds (generally less than one-third of the state spending limit) and therefore most candidates for office opt not to participate in the public financing system.

Using 1998 as a basis of comparison, Table I provides a contrast between the two states. Perhaps the most relevant comparison between the two states is the per capita cost of an election. The per capita cost is the amount of money spent per candidate per voter in the most expensive and most recent election for that office. As the above comparison demonstrates, Minnesota's system is by far the less expensive overall. Moreover, if one keeps in mind that candidates for office in Minnesota only need to raise a maximum of 50% of the expenditure limit from private funds, then the public cost per office per campaign for the Senate, House, and Governor is $0.36, $0.35, and $0.22, respectively (this is also the maximum cost per voter in terms of private funds also).[4]

Finally, there are limits on when registered lobbyists may give. Registered lobbyists may not give contributions to state legislators during session, and candidates may not solicit or accept contributions while the Legislature is in session. However, there is no ban on the aggregate amount of money that party or legislative caucuses may spend. There are no "friends of" committees or permitted transfers from one candidate to another. There are no limits on independent expenditures or issue advocacy in the state, and there is no limit on, or disclosure for conduit funds. Finally, there are no limits on contributions, either to political parties or the House and Senate Legislative Caucuses.

Overall, four basic goals seem to have been the aim of the 1974 and 1993 reforms: 1) strengthen political parties; 2) weaken the influence of lobbyists, PACs, and larger givers (Malbin and Geis 1998); 3) lessen incumbent electoral advantages (Donnay and Ramsden 1995); and 4) increase party competition (Donnay and Ramsden 1998).

Given the novelty and goals of Minnesota's partial public financing system, how well have the reforms secured these objectives, especially that of containing the impact and influence of lobbyist and PAC money? This is the subject of the remainder of the chapter.

Methodology

This chapter documents political spending in Minnesota since 1994. The goal is to see how well Minnesota's partial public financing system limits the impact of lobbyist and PAC money on state politics and also to investigate what impact the 1974 and 1993 reforms have had on the flow of money in the state.

---

4. Factors other than the campaign finance reform laws may also account for differences in spending. For example, Minnesota has 67 State Senators and 134 members of the House of Representatives, whereas Wisconsin has 33 Senators and 99 Members of the State Assembly. In addition, while Minnesota is dominated by one major media market in the Twin Cities, Wisconsin has several media markets. Both the size of the legislatures and the location of media markets thus may influence campaign spending.

All of the campaign finance data presented in this study was obtained from the Campaign Practices and Public Disclosure Board. The information was made available in electronic format and Access 2000 and Excel 2000 were used to perform the analysis.

In classifying PACs, special interests, and lobbyists, the categories used by the Campaign Practices and Public Disclosure Board were employed as much as possible.

In tracking lobbyist political contributions, when they represented more than one association or group and where special identification of an interest group or industry was required for this study, lobbyist disbursements or contributions were credited to every interest that the lobbyist was associated with. In a few cases this might mean that some money was counted more than once in this section. Yet, because the law could legally attribute that money to any of those interests represented by that lobbyist, there is no reason not to count that money as being traced back to more than one group.

Finally, there are some reasons to think that parts of this study may both be under-counting and over-counting the amount of money in Minnesota politics.

First, there may be under-counting money because some lobbyists who expended money in terms of political contributions could not be identified because they were no longer registered lobbyists in 1999. Additionally, this study does not count wealthy individuals who give on behalf of a specific cause, special interest, or in lieu of their corporation or association. Were they identified and counted, the money that could be traced to specific interests would be even greater throughout this report.

In terms of over-counting, this is again a problem where efforts to identify the influence of specific industries are made. Here, all groups categorized as registered to lobby on special issues such as liquor, insurance, or health care are included. While many of these groups may not have actually lobbied on these specific issues, current law does not require groups to make specific identification or accounting of whom they are lobbying for in terms of specific legislation or how much they have spent on their behalf.

Overall, while there may be some over- and under-counting, the dollar amounts given there are reasonable estimates under current disclosure laws.

Historical Data

This section provides historical data on the flow of money in Minnesota politics over the last few years.

Contributions to Candidates

The Minnesota State Legislature is a part-time body. It generally meets two times every biennium. The odd years, 1995, 1997, and 1999, mark the long sessions that go from early January until the third week of May. During the long session, the Legislature puts together a two-year state budget. In the even years, there is a short session from the end of January until late May. Generally during this session the state capital budget is produced. The even years are also election years in partisan elections. What all this means is that in even years there generally is an increase in political contributions. while in the long session-years there is a decrease in contributions and an increase in lobbyist activity.

The Minnesota House of Representatives is composed of 134 members who serve two-year terms. All 134 members stand for reelection at the same time. The Minnesota Senate is composed of sixty-seven members who serve four-year terms. All sixty-seven members stand for reelection at the same time. The state has six constitutional officers who serve four year terms, and all stand for reelection at the same time. In 1994, there were elections for the constitutional officers and members of the House. In 1996 and 2000 there were elections for the House and Senate, while in 1998 there were elections for the constitutional officers and the House. Both of the parties in each house have a legislative caucus. This caucus sets policy and the agenda for the party in that body. The caucuses are entitled to raise and dispense money, with no dollar amount restriction on contributions. Caucuses may not accept or solicit lobbyist money while the legislature is in session. Until 1998, both legislative houses were held by the DFL, while the RPM held the Governor's office. In 1998 the RPM took control of the House and retained it in 2000, while Jesse Ventura, running as the Reform Party candidate, was elected governor in 1998.

There was a significant rise in political contributions made by lobbyists and PACs to state legislative and constitutional office candidates from 1994 to 2000. These years are used as benchmarks, because in both 1994 and 1998 there were State House and constitutional office elections, 1995 and 1997 being long-session years. Additionally, 1996 was a year when both the House and the Senate faced elections.

The total amount of money contributed to candidates in 1994 and 1998 for elections increased by 168%. However, the amount of money contributed by lobbyists tripled, and the amount contributed by PACs and political funds increased by 42%. While PAC contributions decreased when the 1996 and 1998 elections are compared, these are not fair comparisons because of the types of elections occurring in those years.

Table II
Political Contributions to Candidates: 1994–2000

Year	Total C	Total P/L	Total L	Total P
1994	$ 3,169,665.00	$ 641,359.00	$ 62,710.00	$ 578,649.00
1995	300,807.00	26,994.00	7,965.00	18,029.00
1996	2,970,919.00	1,072,200.00	51,140.00	1,021,060.00
1997	1,138,316.00	78,696.00	19,356.00	59,340.00
1998	8,496,247.00	1,010,519.00	186,324.00	824,194.00
1999	8,900,621.00	1,083,045.00	203,855.00	879,189.00
2000	7,852,290.00	3,537,514.00	184,021.00	3,353,493.00
Total	$32,828,865.00	$7,450,327.00	$715,371.00	$6,733,954.00

Total C = Total political contributions made to candidates
Total P/L = Total political contributions made by lobbyists, PACs, and political funds to candidates
Total L = Total political contributions made by lobbyists to candidates
Total P = Total political contributions made by PACs and political funds to candidates

Contributions to Political Funds

Lobbyist and PAC contributions to political funds rose significantly from 1994 to 1998. These are contributions to political parties, the House and Senate majority and minority caucuses, and other political groups. Lobbyists' contributions to political funds increased by 87% when 1994 and 1998 are compared, and PAC contributions increased by 32%.

Another trend to examine is how soft money has become an increasingly important problem in Minnesota politics. Data is available from 1994 to 2000. Over the last few years, soft money contributions have increased dramatically. Over a six-year period, soft money contributions totaled over $76 million, al-

Table III
Total Lobbyist and PAC, Cash and In-Kind Contributions to Political Funds: 1994–2000

Year	Lobbyist	PAC	Total
1994	$71,247.14	$2,116,965.87	$2,188,213.01
1995	$57,350.00	$351,388.70	$408,738.70
1996	$136,992.06	$2,693,522.08	$2,830,514.14
1997	$38,153.00	$812,341.35	$850,494.35
1998	$133,173.65	$2,797,683.47	$2,930,857.12
1999	$230,142.00	$3,669,520.00	$3,899,662.00
2000	$215,603.00	$3,702,109.00	$3,917,712.00
Total	$882,660.85	$16,143,530.47	$17,026,191.32

Table IV
Hard and Soft Money Contributions: 1994–2000

Year	Total Soft Money	Total Hard Money	Total Soft/ Hard Money	Soft/Hard Money Difference
1994	$5,948,423	$3,169,665	$9,118,088	$2,778,758
1995	$2,232,879	$300,807	$2,533,686	$1,932,072
1996	$8,883,377	$2,970,919	$11,854,296	$5,912,458
1997	$4,046,273	$1,138,316	$5,184,589	$2,907,957
1998	$14,120,407	$8,496,247	$22,616,654	$5,624,160
1999	$21,188,267	$8,900,621	$30,088,888	$12,287,646
2000	$20,104,560	$7,852,290	$27,956,850	$12,252,270
Total	$76,524,185	$32,828,865	$109,353,051	$43,695,321

All contributions include cash and in-kind contributions.

most $44 million more than the total for hard money during the same five year period.

According to Table IV, soft money contributions reached a seven-year and, presumably, an all time record high in Minnesota in 1999. Total soft money contributions exceeded $21 million in 1999. At the same time, hard money contributions in Minnesota approximated $9 million in1999, producing total contributions of over $30 million. Oddly, in 2000, an election year, hard and soft money were down from the year before. However, viewing 1999 and 2000 as an election cycle, the total amount of hard and soft money was dramatically higher here than in previous cycles, with many contributors seeming to prefer to give money in a non-election year, perhaps representing efforts to curry favor with the new RPM majority in the House while still giving money to the DFL in the Senate.

Comparing 2000 to 1994, there was a 338% increase in the total amount of soft money contributions in Minnesota. Since 1994, over $76 million in soft money has been raised, compared to $32 million in hard money.

Another way to chart the growth in soft money contributions over time is to compare two parallel years, 1995 and 1999. Both of these were budget session years in the State Legislature that occurred immediately after gubernatorial and Minnesota House of Representative races.

In 1995, both soft and hard money contributions decreased after the 1994 election years. Presumably parties and candidates in 1995, in a non-election year, would not be receiving or needing as much in contributions as they would have in 1994 and, therefore, it makes sense that contributions would have gone down that year.

This same pattern was not evident in 1999. Instead of contributions going down in 1999 after the 1998 elections, contributions increased dramatically. The $21 million in soft money contributions in 1999 represented approximately a $7 million or a 50% increase from the $14 million figure in 1998, and hard money contributions increased by $500,000, or about 5%.

Along with an absolute dollar amount increase in soft money in Minnesota, the percentage of all contributions coming from soft money increased. In 1998, 62.5% of all contributions were soft money. In 1999, soft money accounted for over 70% of all contributions.

Another soft money trend in 1999 was the transfer of money from out-of-state or national party units to the state parties. In 1999, the Republican National State Committee was the largest soft money contributor overall, and it made over $1 million in soft money transfers to the Republican Party of Minnesota. The Democratic National Committee was the overall second largest soft money contributor in 1999, and it transferred $545 thousand to the Minnesota DFL party.

Contributions to Parties, Caucuses, and Political Funds

Soft money contribution patterns in Minnesota changed over a three-year period, from 1998 to 2000. These changes reflect a shift in political control among the state's parties. In the 1998 election year, both houses of the state legislature were controlled by the DFL, with the incumbent Republican governor retiring. In 1998, Jesse Ventura, then a Reform Party member and now an Independence Party member, became governor while the Republicans took control of the House for the first time in over a decade. In 2000, the RPM retained control of the House. Overall soft money contributions, but especially from lobbyists and PACs, reflected that shift in power.

For example, according to Table V, there was an increase in soft money contributions to all political funds in 1999 as compared to 1998. There was a 31% increase to parties and political funds, but the biggest increase in contributions went to the RPM and its legislative caucuses. The Democratic and Republican Senate Caucuses demonstrated a 131% and a 299% increase, respectively.

Comparing the state Democratic and Republican parties and their legislative caucuses (but excluding county party units), soft money contributions to the Democrats increased by about $780,000 from 1998 to 1999, but Republican contributions increased by $1,724,000. Republicans raised more soft money contributions than the Democrats in 1999, but in 2000, the DFL again took in far more soft money contributions than the RPM.

Why have soft money contributions increased so dramatically? There are several reasons. First, unlike hard money, there are fewer restrictions on soft

Table V
Soft Money Contributions to Political Parties,
Caucuses, and Political Funds: 1998–2000

Political Fund	1998 total	1999 total	2000 total
All Political Funds	$14,120,407.11	$21,188,266.50	$20,104,560
State DFL Party	$2,978,872.70	$ 3,432,159.78	$4,642,675
Republican Party Minnesota	3,332,002.61	4,418,417.29	$1,883,318
Independence Party	$0	9,873.31	$0
DFL House Caucus	1,006,562.96	1,134,468.78	$1,323,521
RPM House Caucus	585,513.81	1,093,045.74	$993,106
DFL Senate Caucus	158,305.89	365,597.78	$915,287
RPM Senate Caucus	43,535.00	173,902.09	$237,051
Total State Party and Caucus	$8,104,792.97	$10,627,464.77	$9,994,958

Includes cash and in-kind contributions.

as opposed to hard money. Soft money is unregulated money in terms of the amounts that may be given as campaign contributions to political parties, caucuses, and other political funds. This money may be used for a variety of political activities including party building, voter registration, get out the vote campaigns, and independent expenditures on behalf or against candidates. In fact, soft money has become the main source for negative attack ads.

Wealthy individuals, political action committees, and lobbyists, while restricted in how much they may give in terms of hard money contributions to candidates, can give virtually unlimited amounts to parties and political funds. Political parties interested in raising a lot of money, or individuals or groups interested in using money to influence elections or gain access, use soft money contributions.

In addition, under the Minnesota public subsidy or public finance system, candidates are limited in how much money they can accept from large donors, PACs, and lobbyists. Soft money contributions are a way to circumvent or avoid these hard money restrictions by making donations to parties and leg-

Table VI
Soft Money Contributions to State Parties and Caucuses: 1998–2000

	1998	1999	2000	3 Year Total
State DFL and Legislative Caucuses	$4,143,741	$4,932,226	$6,911,483	$15,987,450
State RPM and Legislative Caucuses	$3,961,051	$5,685,365	$3,113,475	$12,759,891
Totals	$8,104,792	$10,617,591	$10,024,958	$28,747,341

islative leaders who can then use this money for a variety of purposes. Thus, the explosion of soft money undermines Minnesota's public financing system and efforts to restrict the influence of large donors, PACs, and lobbyists, or to otherwise contain the cost of running for office.

Second, soft money donations have dramatically increased because of the relative success of the state partial public financing system in producing more competitive races. As Donnay and Ramsden (1995) demonstrated, there is increased competition in the state's legislative races. Despite the fact that the public financing still favors incumbents (Donnay and Ramsdem 1998), more money is now available to challengers, producing very few uncontested races (Malbin and Gais 1998). With increased competition, there is a demand to raise more money, including raising it through the parties.

One result of that increased competition was evident in 1998. As noted above, the Democrats retained control of the Senate, the Republicans took control of the House, and Jesse Ventura, an independent, took the governorship. This resulted in what Minnesotans call "tripartisan" government. Yet this tripartisanship has it costs: Lobbyists and interest groups need to contribute even more to gain access or protect themselves. Proof of that, in part, is that in 1999 data that reveal the money following the election returns, House Republicans were the beneficiaries of increased soft money largess!

Finally, soft money contributions have increased dramatically because political parties can now make independent expenditures on behalf of individual candidates. On September 29, 1999, a federal court declared unconstitutional a Minnesota law making it illegal for political parties to make independent expenditures on behalf of candidates. The case, *Republican Party of Minnesota v. Pauly*, 63 F. Supp. 2d 1008 (D. Minn. 1999) was brought by the Republican Party of Minnesota. As a result of this lawsuit, soft money contributions are even a more valuable tool to circumvent hard money and public finance restrictions.

Overall, soft money contributions have risen dramatically in Minnesota to the point where the total amount of soft money dwarfs that of hard money. Because it is unregulated, soft money can be used as way to undermine hard money and campaign finance restrictions.

Lobbyist Disbursements

Minnesota requires all individuals who serve as lobbyists—individuals engaged for pay or authorized to spend more than five hours in any month or more than $250 in a year for the purposes of influencing legislation, admin-

Table VII
Lobbyist Disbursements: 1996–2000

Year	Legislative	Administrative	Met Council	Total
1996	$3,196,328.29	$654,759.41	$249,974.35	$4,101,062.05
1997	$6,378,340.00	$447,145.50	$183,058.65	$7,008,544.15
1998	$4,501,926.92	$828,559.33	$204,572.83	$5,535,059.08
1999	$5,077,986.00	$826,439.00	$286,008.00	$6,190,433.00
2000	$5,430,218.00	$443,805.00	$302,743.00	$6,176,766.00
Total	$24,584,799.21	$3,200,708.24	$1,226,356.83	$29,011,864.28

istrative action, or action of a metropolitan government[5] to register with the state and to file three reports on their disbursement. Approximately 1,300 individuals are registered as lobbyists, and they are required to report their disbursements, excluding political contributions, on January 15, March 15, and July 15. The reports must stipulate whom they are lobbying for and how much they spend in the aggregate to lobby. However, they do not have specify how much money they disburse on behalf of which client, what legislation they are specifically lobbying on, whom they have lobbied, or how much they are paid (and their pay typically far exceeds the amount of disbursements they report). Lobbyists are prohibited from giving gifts to any state officials or staff.

Using a baseline of 1996 to 2000, Table VII indicates that lobbyists spent over $29 million dollars to influence public policy. Over $24 million alone was spent simply to lobby the state legislature. Using 1998 and 2000 as comparative years (both were non-budget years), lobbyists spent $900,000 more just two years later to influence the state legislature. This was a 41% increase in just two years.

Summary

The historical trend from 1994 to the present demonstrates a significant increase in lobbyist, PAC, and special interest contributions to candidates, political funds, and to influence the state governing process. In addition, it also demonstrates significant increases in hard and soft money contributions, with soft money contributions constituting the bulk of the political contributions.

---

5. MINN. STAT. § 10A.01, subd. 21 (2000).

Case Study: 1998

The 1998 election year is a good case study to examine the role of money in Minnesota politics. In 1998 the state House of Representatives and all of the constitutional offices were up for reelection.

Contributions to Candidates

According to Table VIII, by far the largest source of contributions to candidates for political office was from individuals who represented 64% of all the donations directly to candidates. The second largest amount of money was from candidates. Of the over $1.4 million from candidates, $1,315,000 was

Table VIII
1998 Political Contributions to Candidates

Source	Amount	Percentage
Candidate	$1,438,929.26	16.90%
Committee Member	$61,851.66	0.70%
Political Party	$514,948.65	6.10%
Lobbyist	$186,324	2.20%
PACs	$824,194.00	9.70%
Individual	$5,458,077.30	64.20%
Other/unclassified	$11,922.13	0.10%
Total	$8,496,247.00	99.90%

Percentages have been rounded and therefore do not add up to 100%.

Table IX
Political Contributions to Candidates, Including Mark Dayton

Source	Amount	Percentage
Candidate (excluding M. Dayton)	$123,929.26	1.50%
Candidate Mark Dayton	$1,315,000.00	15.50%
Committee Member	$61,851.66	0.70%
Political Party	$514,948.65	6.10%
Lobbyist	$186,324	2.20%
PACs	$824,194.00	9.70%
Individual	$5,458,077.30	64.20%
Other/unclassified	$11,922.13	0.10%
Total	**$8,496,247.00**	**100.00%**

Mark Dayton's contribution to his own campaign for governor. In fact, Mark Dayton's contribution to his own campaign for governor constituted 15.5% of all the contributions to candidates in 1998. If his individual contribution is excluded, contributions from PACs represent the next largest source of political contributions to candidates. All told, almost 12% of all the contributions made directly to candidates came from PACs and lobbyists.

Contributions to Political Funds

Lobbyists and PACs are one of the most important contributors to political funds. In fact, lobbyists and special interests have a pervasive influence and impact upon the funding of many of the primary political organizations in Minnesota and most citizens do not see this influence or impact.

Before describing this influence, two points are worth noting. First, the term "political funds" refers to a large scope of political organizations in the state, ranging from political parties to other private organizations set up for political purposes. Political funds also include the party caucuses set up by both the majority and minority parties in the Minnesota House and Senate.[6]

Second, money given to these caucuses is unregulated in terms of the amounts given. Thus, while contributions to candidates are limited in amount, there are very few restrictions on money given to political parties and caucuses. As a result, the money given to these organizations is enormous both because this money can influence the parties or caucuses and because this money can be spent on behalf of candidates. Hence, money given to these funds is every bit as influential as direct contributions to candidates, but, because it is less visible and less directly tied to candidates, it is often ignored by observers. Yet this unregulated money, a form of soft money (Malbin and Geis 1998), is a choice means for special interests because contributions to political funds can be a means to funnel influence and escape regulation and public scrutiny. As a result, groups and individuals do an end-run around the hard

---

6. Technically there are no political action committees in Minnesota. State law instead allows for the creation of political committees and political funds. MINN. STAT. §10A. Subd. 27, defines a political committee as "an association whose major purpose is to influence the nomination or election of a candidate or to promote or defeat a ballot question, other than a principal campaign committee or a political party unit."

MINN. STAT. §10A. Subd. 28 defines a political fund as "an accumulation of dues or voluntary contributions by an association other than a political committee, principal campaign committee, or party unit, if the accumulation is collected or expended to influence the nomination or election of a candidate or to promote or defeat a ballot question."

Table X

1998 Cash and In-Kind Political Contributions to Political Funds

Political Fund	Total Contributions	Lobbyists	PACs/ Political Funds	Total Lobbyist/PAC
All Political Funds	$14,120,407.11	$133,173.65	$2,797,683.47	$2,930,857.12
State DFL Party	$2,978,872.70	$1,350.00	$794,152.48	$795,502.48
Republican Party Minn.	$3,332,002.61	$6,000.00	$49,750.00	$55,750.00
DFL House Caucus	$1,006,562.96	$46,299.49	$661,343.57	$707,643.06
RPM House Caucus	$585,513.81	$27,908.00	$267,000.00	$294,908.00
DFL Senate Caucus	$158,305.89	$11,150.00	$83,700.00	$94,850.00
RPM Senate Caucus	$43,535.00	$1,350.00	$10,800.00	$12,150.00
Total Party and Caucus	$8,104,792.97	$94,057.49	$1,866,746.05	$1,960,803.54

money contribution limits by giving to the parties, caucuses, and other political funds. As Malbin and Geis correctly note, the result has not been to strengthen parties but instead to weaken them as they have become dependent upon these groups (1998). Contrary to the assertion that parties serve to filter contributions and contributor influence, Minnesota demonstrates the contrary.

Looking at the data in Table X and Graph I, there is no question that PAC and lobbyist money has a pervasive and significant impact upon all political funds in the state, having a particularly powerful influence upon the Republican and Democratic parties and caucuses. Almost 25% of all the money that is contributed to political funds comes from PACs and lobbyists, with a high of over 70% of their money pouring into the House DFL caucus. However, even these figures may underestimate special interest influence because local parties are also major contributors to state parties, and these local or county party units also receive significant percentages of their money from special interests.

Generally, DFL organizations are more dependent upon PAC and lobbyist money than the Republican Party of Minnesota (RPM).

Finally, comparing 1994 to 1998, overall soft money contributions increased by 34%, with contributions by lobbyists increasing by 87% and PACs by 32%.

Lobbyist Expenditures

In addition to direct contributions to candidates and political funds in 1998, lobbyists spent an enormous amount of money lobbying the state government to secure public policy objectives. This money was spent to lobby the state legislature, the administration or executive branch, or the Met Council, a seven county regional governing board for the Minneapolis-St. Paul area, as

Graph I
1998 Political Funds: Percentage of Total Contributions from PACs/Lobbyists

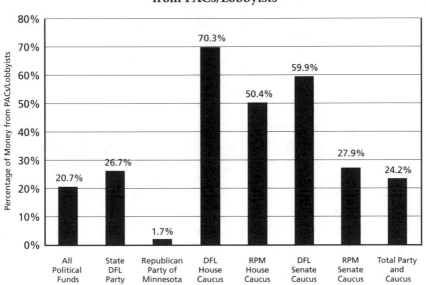

well as Minneapolis, Saint Paul, and some of the other local governments in the Twin Cities area.

In 1998, lobbyists spent over $5.5 million to influence the state, with $4.5 million of it directed towards the state legislature alone. To put this $4.5 million into perspective, compare it to the $31,141 annual salary of a state legislator. A disbursement of $4.5 million in 1998 means that lobbyists spent an

Table XI
Total Lobbyist and PAC Cash and In-Kind Contributions to Political Funds: 1994–2000

Year	Lobbyist	PAC	Total
1994	$71,247.14	$2,116,965.87	$2,188,213.01
1995	$57,350.00	$351,388.70	$408,738.70
1996	$136,992.06	$2,693,522.08	$2,830,514.14
1997	$38,153.00	$812,341.35	$850,494.35
1998	$133,173.65	$2,797,683.47	$2,930,857.12
1999	$230,142.24	$3,669,520.31	$3,899,662.55
2000	$215,603.00	$3,702,109.00	$3,917,712.00
Total	$882,661.09	$16,143,530.78	$17,026,191.87

Table XII
1998 Total Lobbyist Disbursements

Period	Type of Disbursement			
	Legislative	Administrative	Met Council	Total
1/1–3/31	$1,661,149.17	$189,849.61	$51,133.72	$1,902,132.50
4/1–6/30	$1,001,697.17	$168,945.16	$64,644.74	$1,235,287.07
7/1–12/31	$1,839,080.58	$469,764.56	$88,794.37	$2,397,639.51
Total	$4,501,926.92	$828,559.33	$204,572.83	$5,535,059.08

average of $22.398 per legislator to influence the legislative process. If one adds the amount spent on lobbying the administration to the $4.5 million on the assumption that lobbying the executive branch is another way of seeking to influence the law making process, then an average (mean) of $26,520 per legislator was spent. These two amounts mean that lobbyists spent the equivalent of 72% (at $22,398) or 85% (at $26,520) of a legislator's salary to influence the legislative process.

Independent Expenditures

The last way that interests can disburse money to influence elections and public policy is by making independent expenditures. These are expenditures that urge the election or defeat of specific candidates or urge the voters to support or defeat specific issues. Corporations cannot make disbursements for political candidates, but they can escape this legal limitation by making independent expenditures in terms of what is known as issue advocacy whereby they urge support or opposition to an issue but not a candidate.

In 1998, the fifty largest independent expenditures totaled approximately $1.4 million.

Total 1998 Special Interest Spending

Bringing together money spent on direct contributions to candidates, contributions to parties and political funds, lobbyist disbursements, and independent expenditures, special interests spent $9.7 million dollars in 1998 to influence state elections and public policy.

Comparing this figure to the $31,141 salary for state legislators, that $9.7 million works out to $48,333 per state legislator. However, if we exclude lobbying expenses for the Met Council (keeping in mind that this all includes Twins Cities local governments) and the administration, and, if we focus simply upon the remaining amount, that still works out to an average of $33,438

Table XIII
Total Spending by Special Interests: 1998

Total Lobbyist Disbursements	$5,535,059.08
Total Lobbyist/PAC Contributions to Candidates	$824,194.00
Total Lobbyist/PAC Contributions to Political Funds	$1,960,803.54
Total Independent Expenditures	$1,394,912.72
Total 1998 Spending	**$9,714,969.34**

spent per legislator to influence the state policy process. This average is almost $2,300 more than the average salary of a state legislator.

Examining just lobbyists alone, they account for over $5.8 million dollars in Minnesota in 1998. This works out to $29,127 per legislator in comparison to the $31,141 salary for a state legislator.

Another way to examine special interest money is to look at what percentage of PAC and lobbyist money comes from what source. One finds that only 8.5% of all this money in state politics is sourced in contributions to candidates. Over 20% is located in soft money contributions to the parties, caucuses, and political funds, with 14% located in independent expenditures and the bulk found in lobbyist disbursements. What this pattern of special interest spending reveals is that less than 10% of the money is limited in terms of the amounts given and less than 10% of the money can tie special interests directly to a candidate. This means that examining special interest influence by looking at only contributions to candidates misses approximately 92% of the money spent by PACs and shows that special interests escape limits or serious disclosure.

Case Study: Eight Industries

A second case study that demonstrates the role of money in Minnesota politics examines how much money is spent in specific policy areas to influence elections and policy outcomes. While many lobbyists and political observers would deny that money influences policy deliberations, one has to ask if that is true, why would lobbyists and special interests expend all these resources? Spending money to influence public policy should be viewed as another form of a business investment decision where the choice to invest is made when the benefits associated with the expenditure outweigh the costs.

In 1998 Common Cause Minnesota carried out a study—*Where There is Smoke, There is Funding*—examining the impact of tobacco money upon legislative efforts to pass youth access legislation (Paulson and Schultz 1998). The study concluded that between 1994 and 1996 tobacco concerns spent between $1 million and $2.4 million to successfully halt the passage of laws that would have made it more difficult for juveniles to buy tobacco products. This study sought to connect tobacco contributions to members of the state legislature, and it demonstrated dramatic voting differences between those who took and rejected tobacco money. The Common Cause study, along with papers released by the tobacco industry as a result of state litigation, revealed a pervasive pattern of influence that included lobbyist disbursements, illegal contributions, and significant pressure politics. As a result of the documented influence of the tobacco industry, attention turned to other businesses and interests to see if they had similar patterns of influence.

The eight industries selected for this case study include those interests and organizations that represent issues of concern to firearms, gambling, health care, insurance, liquor and beer, medicine, public utilities, and real estate.[7]

Candidate Contributions

In 1998, interests in all eight areas made contributions directly to candidates for the House of Representatives or to a candidate for a constitutional office. For example, in examining data presented in tables XIV to XVI, in 1998, lobbyists for gambling interests made a total of $5,067 contributions to legislative candidates and an additional $23,685 to candidates for constitutional offices. In addition to lobbyist contributions, PACs and political funds representing gambling interests made $19,500 in contributions to House candidates and $9,700 in contributions to constitutional office candidates. In sum, gambling interests made $57,952 contributions directly to political candidates in 1998. Contributions of other interests, ranging from a low of $2,787 from firearms interests to a high of $90,332 from real estate interests, were made in 1998. Overall, these eight interests alone contributed $439,795 directly to Minnesota House and constitutional office candidates in 1998.

Two observations are in order. First, contributions came from both lobbyists and PACs. In the case of lobbyists, their political contributions are on top, regarding the money, the time, and the other resources they expend to influence legislation. Hence, political contributions serve as an added tool, weapon, or reward to elected officials, thereby augmenting lobbyist skills. Clearly lobbyists would not be making these contributions unless they found it to their

---

7. The classification of organizations representing these interests was based upon information and categories provided by the Campaign Practices and Public Disclosure Board. The year 1998 was selected as the year to study.

Table XIV
1998 Lobbyist Contributions to Political Candidates: Eight Industries

| | Contribution Total per Office | | |
	Legislative	Constitutional	Total
Firearms	$887	$400	$1,287
Gambling	$5,067	$23,685	$28,752
Health Care	$3,487	$44,910	$48,397
Insurance	$3,887	$21,750	$25,637
Liquor	$750	$13,750	$14,500
Medical	$2,962	$26,050	$29,012
Public Utilities	$2,287	$54,462.50	$56,750
Real Estate	$3,037	$42,870	$45,907

Table XV
1998 Political Contributions to Candidates by PACs and Political Funds

| | Contribution Total per Office | | |
	Legislative	Constitutional	Total
Firearms	$1,500	$0	$1,500
Gambling	$19,500	$9,700	$29,200
Health Care	$20,797	$550	$21,347
Insurance	$10,750	$2,500	$13,250
Liquor	$14,634	$4,350	$18,984
Medical	$29,942	$10,900	$40,842
Public Utilities	$12,855	$7,150	$20,005
Real Estate	$31,700	$12,725	$44,425
Total	$141,678	$47,875	$189,553

Table XVI
1998 PAC and Lobbyist Political Contributions to Candidates: Eight Industries

| | Contribution Total per Office | | |
	Legislative	Constitutional	Total
Firearms	$2,387	$400	$2,787
Gambling	$24,567	$33,385	$57,952
Health Care	$24,284	$45,460	$69,744
Insurance	$14,637	$24,250	$38,887
Liquor	$15,384	$18,100	$33,484
Medical	$32,904	$36,950	$69,854
Public Utilities	$15,142	$61,613	$76,755
Real Estate	$34,737	$55,595	$90,332
Total	$164,042	$275,753	$439,795

Table XVII
1998 Contributions to Political Funds: Eight Industries

Industry	Contribution
Firearms	$5,000
Gambling	$153,953.48
Health Care	$64,825
Insurance	$15,950
Liquor	$83,950
Medical	$103,536
Public Utilities	$34,420
Real Estate	$94,250
Total	**$555,884**

political advantage to do so. Even if lobbyists do not make political contributions explicitly for political purposes, there is no denying that giving money to elected officials and candidates for office helps their ability to gain access and influence.

A second observation is that many lobbyists represent multiple interests. When receiving a contribution from a lobbyist, a candidate or elected office does not know which interest that contribution represents. Hence, contributions from lobbyists serve to benefit all of the interests and principals that the lobbyist represents.

While there are some restrictions on the time and amount of money lobbyists may give, there is no prohibition on a lobbyist's making a contribution. Moreover, lobbyists are not required to report contributions under $100 and, thus, the data collected represent an under-reporting of the actual contributions made by them.

Contributions to Political Funds

Lobbyists and PACs representing these eight industries also made significant contributions to political funds, political parties, and caucuses in 1998. First, lobbyists representing these eight sets of interests contributed amounts ranging from a low of $1,750 from firearms to a high of over $57,000 from real estate.

Another way to look at the influence of these eight sets of interests is to ask what percentage of all the contributions from lobbyists were represented by contributions from one of them. In the case of both the state DFL and Republican parties, 100% of the money each received from lobbyists came from one of these eight interests. Lobbyist contributions from these eight industries

Table XVIII
Total Lobbyist Disbursements: 1998*

Industry	1/1–3/31	4/1–6/30	7/1–12/31	Total
Firearms	$19,359.00	$13,557.90	$18,160.85	**$51,077.75**
Gambling	$149,018.02	$24,411.97	$16,006.88	**$189,436.87**
Health Care	$117,909.04	$226,037.24	$132,804.65	**$476,750.93**
Insurance	$144,050.67	$213,781.56	$92,647.37	**$450,479.60**
Liquor	$5,041.44	$24,139.16	$10,289.59	**$39,470.19**
Medical	$62,777.43	$76,448.05	$27,807.02	**$167,032.50**
Public Utilities	$69,139.18	$110,043.32	$40,451.72	**$219,634.22**
Real Estate	$10,878.86	$14,258.32	$7,445.36	**$32,582.54**
Total	**$578,173.64**	**$702,677.52**	**$345,613.44**	**$1,626,464.60**

* Dates refer to the lobbyist reporting reports.

seemed to dominate the caucuses and political funds of both parties. What this suggests is that lobbyists representing these interests give rather significantly to both parties, and such a pattern of giving indicates that contributions are not being made for ideological reasons but for political influence.

In addition to contributions directly from lobbyists, organizations representing these eight interests also contributed heavily in 1998, with amounts ranging from a low of $5,000 from firearms to over $150 thousand from gambling. Overall, PACs and political funds representing these organizations contributed heavily to the major political parties, House and Senate Caucuses, and other political organizations in the state, occupying an important financial influence on these groups.

This pattern of giving also indicates contributions to political funds can be a way to hide influence on a candidate. A candidate can forswear money from alcohol, yet her party may still take that money and spend it on behalf of that candidate. Hence, a candidate can hide from special interest money by rejecting acceptance of its money in terms of direct contributions but still benefit from the money in other ways.

Lobbyist Disbursements

These eight industries invested heavily in lobbying the state legislature in 1998. In total, the eight spent over $1.6 million to lobby the state legislature, the high being almost one-half million dollars from the health care industry alone. Excluded from this study is what these eight set of interests spent on lobbying the administration and the Met Council. Were those figures added in, total lobbyist disbursements would perhaps be another $750,000 to $1,000,000.

Table XIX
1998 Independent Expenditures: Eight Industries and Total for all PACs and Political Funds

1998 Independent Expenditures	Total
Firearms	$10,534.32
Gambling	$9,007
Health Care	$26,502.34
Insurance	$0
Liquor	$43,500
Medical	$19,783
Public Utilities	$8,000
Real Estate	$0
Total for 8 Industries	$117,326.66
1998 Total for all PACs and Political Funds	$1,394,912.72

Independent Expenditures

Finally, organizations representing these eight industries also spent varying amounts on independent expenditures to influence elections or the legislative process. Liquor interests spent the most at $43,500, with insurance and real estate spending nothing.

Overall Industry Spending

Putting it all together, these eight industries spent a significant amount through lobbyists and PACs to influence the legislative process in 1998.

Table XX
1998 Disbursements to Influence Legislation and Elections: Eight Industries

Industry	Lobbyist Disbursements	Contributions to Candidates	Contributions to Political Funds	Independent Expenditures	Total Expenditures
Firearms	$51,078	$2,787	$6,750	$10,534	$71,149
Gambling	$189,437	$57,952	$193,885	$9,007	$450,281
Health Care	$476,751	$69,744	$115,346	$26,502	$688,343
Insurance	$450,480	$38,887	$49,073	$0	$538,440
Liquor	$39,470	$33,484	$112,825	$43,500	$229,279
Medical	$167,033	$69,854	$126,618	$19,783	$383,288
Public Utilities	$219,634	$76,755	$91,092	$8,000	$395,481
Real Estate	$32,583	$90,332	$151,589	$0	$274,504
Total	$1,626,466	$439,795	$847,178	$117,326	$3,030,765

Table XXI
Legislative Lobbyist Disbursements: 1996–1998

Name of Industry	1996 Total	1997 Total	1998 Total	3 Year Total
Firearms	30,127.21	49,436.75	51,077.75	130,641.71
Gambling	37,843.73	140,993.66	189,436.87	368,274.26
Health Care	444,263.90	503,373.47	476,750.93	1,424,388.30
Insurance	348,976.98	509,603.63	450,479.60	1,309,060.21
Liquor	21,536.94	28,459.17	39,470.19	89,466.30
Medical	118,650.45	293,370.01	167,032.50	579,052.96
Public Utilities	142,113.98	274,870.07	219,634.22	636,618.27
Real Estate	39,427.73	29,474.90	32,582.54	101,485.17
Total	$1,182,940.92	$1,829,581.66	$1,626,464.60	$4,638,987.18

Firearms interests spent only $71,000, while interests representing health care spent over $600,000 to influence the legislative process. Overall, the eight collectively spent over $3 million to influence elections and legislative deliberations. Again, if administration and Met Council expenses were added, perhaps the number would easily top $3.5 to 4 million.

The expenditure patterns suggest that there are several different ways for these industries to have an influence at the state legislature: hard and soft money contributions, lobbying, and independent expenditures—several tools to achieve objectives.

Cumulative Effects: Eight Industries Over Time

Influence and money do not operate in a vacuum but are located within a web of contexts and patterns that are historical. In examining the impact that money has upon the political process, one should not simply look at how much money was spent in one year on one type of activity. Instead, as this study has attempted to point out, the influence of money upon the Minnesota political process must be seen in light of how several different sources of money bear to exert pressure upon the policy process and how the different ways to use money augment and complement one another. Similarly, one needs also to examine the cumulative impact of money over time and how over a period of several years the use of money can pressure and influence the political process.

In examining the eight subject areas noted above, the focus was simply upon the use of money in 1998 to achieve policy objectives. However, the interests represented in these eight areas have been using money over a period of several years to further their interests. Reviewing Table XXI, from 1996 to

1998, over $4.6 million was collectively spent by lobbyists alone in these eight subjects. Health care and insurance interests alone disbursed well in excess of $1 million each just to lobby the state legislature during this three-year period. For those who say that lobbying has no impact, one has to wonder why so much money was spent by these interests to curry legislative favor or secure objectives unless those interests felt that the expenditures paid off in some way.

In addition to money spent lobbying, all of these industries spent money in terms of candidate contributions, contributions to the political parties, caucuses, and other political funds, and perhaps in independent expenditures. While this study was unable to gather all of this data for 1996 through 1998, including these figures here could possibly have pushed up the amounts spent by these groups by one or two million dollars.

2000 Election Data

Many of the trends demonstrated by PACs and lobbyists from 1994 to 1999 continued into the 2000 election and off-budget year. One way to clarify these trends is by comparing the years 1996 and 2000. Both were election years for the entire legislature; they were also non-budget or short session years and, even though beyond the scope of analysis for this chapter, both were presidential election years where all of Minnesota's United States House of Representatives were up for election and an incumbent United States Senator also faced a close contest. Thus, 1996 and 2000 are good years to compare.

However, 1996 also saw the presence of the Independence and Green Party of Minnesota as major political parties under Minnesota law. Both were eligible to participate in the state's partial public financing, rebate, and checkoff systems. Yet neither party elected candidates (although Ralph Nader did get more than 5% of the popular vote in the state as a presidential candidate) nor did either receive PAC or lobbyist contributions.

According to tables XXII and XXIII, both hard and soft money contributions increased significantly when the 1996 and 2000 elections are compared, with soft money contributions up 226% and hard money up by 264%. However, lobbyist and PAC contributions increased by 360% and 328% respectively, thereby outstripping significantly the overall contribution increases.

Similarly, lobbyist and PAC soft money contributions also increased dramatically, although not as great as overall soft money increases or in comparison to hard money. Lobbyist soft money contributions increased by 157% and PAC contributions by 137%. Turning specifically to how those soft money contributions were allocated, Table XXIV reveals how the state DFL and its leg-

Table XXII
Growth of Hard and Soft Money In Minnesota Elections: 1996 and 2000

	1996	2000	Percent Increase
Total Soft Money	$8,883,376	$20,104,560	226%
Total Hard Money	$2,970,919	$7,852,290	264%
Total Hard & Soft Money	$11,854,295	$27,956,850	235%

Table XXIII
Lobbyist and PAC Hard Money Contributions: 1996 and 2000

	1996	2000	Percent Increase
Lobbyist	$51,140	$184,021	360%
PAC/Political Fund	$1,021,060	$3,353,493	328%
Total	$1,072,200	$3,537,514	330%

islative caucuses again emerged as the chief beneficiary of lobbyist and PAC money. Surprisingly, the DFL House caucus, still a minority, surpassed the RPM caucus. In addition, as shown in Table XXV, another trend examined in 2000 was lobbyist and PAC contributions to local party units and to other PACs and political funds. Often overlooked is the role that Lobbyists and PACs play in contributing to these local party units or political organizations. Not only does this giving extend financial influence to these other organizations; it also hides or masks their role in state politics. In Minnesota, lobbyist contributions to local party organizations are recorded as contributions to lobbyists. However, once that money is then transferred to a third organization, it is listed as a contribution not from a lobbyist but the intermediate organization. Thus, about $457,000 in PAC and lobbyist contributions went to other political organizations, with almost another $200,000 going to local party units.

Significantly, the soft money contributions increased for many of the reasons noted earlier—such as split control of the legislature and tightness of legislative electoral competition. But also the newly liberated ability of parties

Table XXIV
Lobbyist and PAC Soft Money Contributions: 1996 and 2000

	1996	2000	Percent Increase
Lobbyist	$136,992	$215,603	157%
PACs/Political Funds	$2,693,522	$3,702,109	137%
Total	$2,830,514	$3,917,712	138%

Table XXV
Lobbyist and PAC Soft Money Contributions to Parties and Caucuses: 2000

Political Fund	Soft Money Contributions			
	Total	Lobbyists	PACs/Political Funds	Total Lobbyists/ PACs
State Totals	$20,104,560	$215,603	$3,702,109	$3,917,712
All DFL Party/ Caucus Units	$7,157,326	$85,000	$2,872,535	$2,957,535
ALL RPM Party/ Caucus Units	$3,237,854	$108,264	$394,391	$502,655
Contributions to other PACs/Funds	$9,709,308	$22,339	$435,183	$457,522
State DFL	$4,642,675	$0	$1,614,367	$1,614,367
Republican Party Minn.	$1,883,318	$0	$500	$500
DFL House Caucus	$1,323,521	$35,800	$520,469	$556,269
RPM House Caucus	$993,106	$93,675	$294,400	$388,075
DFL Senate Caucus	$915,287	$47,275	$294,400	$388,075
RPM Senate Caucus	$237,051	$13,700	$84,850	$98,550
State Party/Caucus Total	$9,994,958	$190,450	$3,072,286	$3,262,736
DFL State Party/Caucus	$6,911,483	$83,075	$2,692,536	$2,775,611
RPM State Party/Caucus	$3,113,475	$107,375	$379,750	$487,125
Local DFL	$245,843	$1,925	$179,999	$181,924
Local RPM	$124,379	$889	$14,641	$15,530
Local Party Totals	$370,222	$2,814	$194,640	$197,454

Table XXVI
Total PAC and Lobbyist Spending: 1998–2000

Expenditure Type	1998	1999	2000
Total Lobbyist/PAC Contributions to Candidates	$1,010,519	$1,083,045	$3,537,514
Total Lobbyist/PAC Contributions to Political Funds	$1,960,804	$2,930,857	$3,917,712
Total Lobbyist Disbursements	$5,535,059	$6,190,435	$5,430,218
Total Independent Expenditures (Non Party)	$1,394,913	$1,472,863	$2,318,419
Total Lobbyist/PAC Spending	$9,901,294	$11,677,200	$15,203,863
Total Lobbyist/PAC Spending Per Legislator	$49,260	$58,095	$75,641

and caucuses to make independent expenditures on behalf of candidates indicated a new-found effort on the part of parties and caucuses to secure soft money for this purpose.

Table XXVII
Party and Caucus Independent Expenditures: 1998–2000

Party	1998	1999	2000	Percentage Increase 1998 to 2000
Democrats	$323,596	$402,887	$2,020,143	624%
Republicans	$592,855	$775,515	$2,003,348	338%
Total	$916,451	$1,178,402	$4,023,491	439%

Party total is computed by adding together all independent expenditures by the state party and House and Senate Caucuses.

The year 1998 was the last full year that parties and caucuses were barred from making independent expenditures on behalf of candidates before a September 1999 court decision freed them to engage in this type of spending. Thus the 2000 election was the first to see the impact of this decision. Comparing party and caucuses independent expenditures from 1998 to 2000 in Table XXVII, one sees an overall 439% increase, with the DFL's expenditures increasing by over 600%. In some cases, party and other independent expenditures totaled over $310,000 for a state house race (Lorenz 2001), definitely making the real cost of running for that office way more than the official candidate spending limits for it. Clearly the court decision has lead to an explosion in party independent expenditures, serving as a way to circumvent candidate spending and contribution limits.

Finally, in 2000, overall lobbyist disbursements generally increased by 151%. But, perhaps adding support to Governor Ventura's claims that he is not open to lobbyist influence, expenditures to influence the administration surprisingly decreased by almost one-third.

Putting all of the 2000 data together in Table XXIX, from 1998 to 2000 lobbyists and PACs dramatically increased their spending in Minnesota, but specifically to influence the legislative process. If in 1998 the total lobbyist/PAC per legislator spending was approximately $49,000, on 2000 it was increased by over 50%, exceeding $75,000.

Table XXVIII
Lobbyist Disbursements: 1996 and 2000

	1996	2000	Percent Increase
Legislature	$3,196,328	$5,430,218	170%
Administration	$654,759	$443,805	−33%
Met Council	$249,974	$302,743	121%
Total	$4,101,061	$6,176,766	151%

Table XXIX
Total PAC and Lobbyist Spending: 1998–2000

Expenditure Type	1998	1999	2000
Total Lobbyist/PAC Contributions to Candidates	$1,010,519	$1,083,045	$3,537,514
Total Lobbyist/PAC Contributions to Political Funds	$1,960,804	$2,930,857	$3,917,712
Total Lobbyist Disbursements	$5,535,059	$6,190,435	$5,430,218
Total Independent Expenditures (Non Party)	$1,394,913	$1,472,863	$2,318,419
Total Lobbyist/PAC Spending	$9,901,294	$11,677,200	$15,203,863
Total Lobbyist/PAC Spending Per Legislator	$49,260	$58,095	$75,641

Conclusion: Assessing the Impact of Minnesota's Campaign Finance Laws

There is no question that the amount of money spent in Minnesota politics—both across the board and by PACs and lobbyists—has increased dramatically since the 1993 reforms took effect in 1994. What does that say about the efficacy and effectiveness of the Minnesota campaign finance reform laws?

First, while the partial public system has been successful in weakening the impact of certain types of money in terms of direct candidate contributions, it has not eliminated that money from Minnesota politics or otherwise weakened interest groups and strengthened political parties. The amount of soft money and money spent by lobbyists and PACs in Minnesota politics is significantly higher than many would estimate, given the scope of the 1993 reforms aimed at diminishing their monetary influence. While these reforms and Minnesota's campaign finance system have generally lessened the amount of money lobbyists and PACs can give directly to candidates, data through the 2000 elections indicate that soft money contributions and lobbyist expenditures, and especially since 1999, independent expenditures, are alternative avenues for this money. Moreover, as the 2000 data show, even PAC contributions are dramatically rising in the area of hard money. What all these suggests is that the monetary influence of lobbyists and PACs has not disappeared; the lobbyists and PACs have simply shifted to new outlets. Thus, Minnesota's campaign finance regime has been slipping further from its objectives of reducing special interest money, as more and more loopholes and end runs are created to get around the system. The campaign finance regime failed to secure one of its core 1993 objectives, as it has become possible to do an end-run around hard money restrictions.

With the failure to address the growth of lobbyist and PAC monetary influence, the effort to impose spending limits on races is effectively being eviscerated by the presence of soft money and party-caucus independent expenditures. While there are spending caps for candidates, when the soft money contributions and independent expenditures for races are included, the real cost for running for election in Minnesota is dramatically higher than the caps would suggest. Thus, another one of the goals of the 1993 reforms and the state campaign finance laws is being undermined.

Second, when, on average, more money is spent per legislator per year to achieve influence than an average legislator makes (approximately $32,000 per year), one has to wonder what impact this money has on policy deliberations and political behavior in the state. Besides simply making it more expensive to run for office than previously thought, there is evidence that this money has had an impact upon public policy in the state.

For example, a Common Cause Minnesota study (Paulson and Schultz 1998) examined the impact of tobacco money upon state politics and legislation that would make it more difficult for minors to obtain tobacco products. In examining three key 1997 votes on this youth access legislation, the study found that legislators who took tobacco contributions were far more likely to oppose this legislation than those who voted for it. There may be some questions regarding whether the tobacco money changed votes or reinforced preexisting voting patterns. However, because of the settlement reached between the State of Minnesota and the tobacco industry, millions of pages of tobacco industry documents corroborate the scope of the influence the industry had on state politics in terms of granting tobacco lobbyists access and in setting the legislative agenda on youth access. While similar access to documents of other industries does not exist, there is ample evidence that money spent by the Minnesota Twins has kept the decision to publicly finance a new stadium on the agenda despite clear public opposition to such an arrangement. Also financial contributions by the gaming and gambling industry has produced changes in the state's laws in this area (Schultz 1999).

Yet money has also had a real impact upon politics in the state in terms of influencing citizen attitudes and civic engagement. In the Fall of 1997, Common Cause Minnesota, in conjunction with St. Cloud State University (SCSU), surveyed 602 Minnesota adults regarding their views on the role of money in politics (Paulson and Schultz 1998). The survey asked a series of questions about voter behavior and attitudes towards money in politics. These questions were asked as part of the annual survey performed by SCSU. The margin of error for the survey was +/- 5%. The SCSU survey team looked at a variety of political questions focusing on issues and on candidates for the upcoming 1998 gubernatorial race. The aim of these questions was to ascertain how political campaign contributions influenced public attitudes and political participation.

When asked: "Do you think elected officials are more likely to respond to individuals and organizations that contribute to their campaigns than to voters who do not contribute to their campaigns," 88% responded yes. The survey ran cross-tabulations, using age, education, gender, income, and party affiliation to find out if there would be any difference within these categories. In all of these categories, over nine out of ten (90%) Minnesota adults believe that elected officials respond to individuals or organizations that contribute money more than they respond to voters who do not contribute.

When asked a second question: "Are you personally less likely to vote or participate in politics because you believe that those who give political contributions have more influence over elected officials than you do," 33% responded yes. Finally, when this question was cross-tabulated with whether the respondent had voted in 1996, there was a clear difference between the attitudes and behavior of voters and non-voters. While only 32% of those who said they voted in 1996 said that they were less likely to vote or participate in politics because of the influence of contributors, 53% of those who said they did not vote responded yes. This percentage is over double the response, suggesting that among those who did not vote, the role of money in politics is significant to their political attitudes and their non-participation in the Minnesota political process.

Finally, 75% of those surveyed indicated that they supported limits on political spending by individuals and organizations as a way to make elected officials more responsive to voters.

Overall, the results of these questions demonstrate that, even in a state such as Minnesota, there is a strong belief regarding the adverse impact of money on the political system. Hence there is evidence that this money inhibits citizen activism, and there is strong support for restrictions on political spending. Whether it be the appearance or reality of corruption, Minnesotans believe money has an impact on politics, and it has an effect on their political behavior.

Third, another important conclusion indicates that if one wishes to understand how money is disbursed for political purposes, one needs to realize that there at least four ways actors can disburse money to achieve influence. How money is spent, depends on numerous factors, including perhaps the laws governing each type of use of money, the type of influence desired, and the character of the political actor, among other issues. How and when money is disbursed is akin to an investment decision by a firm seeking to maximize revenues. Here, the goal is to maximize influence, and disbursing money to achieve that objective can be done in several ways. Thus, in ascertaining influence, one should not look only to correlations between money given to an elected official and how that official votes, because direct contributions to elected officials is only a small piece of the money trail. Such an analysis under-counts influence. Instead, a more appropriate way to measure the impact of money is to examine how money sets the political agenda, how money produces certain winners and losers in the policy process, and how money undermines the moral legitimacy of the political process.

Finally, Minnesota's experiences with regulating political money reveal some successes and failures, suggesting that other jurisdictions, be they other states, cities, or even the federal government, need to appreciate the many ways money can be used to leverage influence if it hopes to achieve any of its reform objectives.

References

Atkins, Annette. 1988. Minnesota: Left of center and out of place. In *Heartland: Comparative histories of Midwestern states*, edited by James H. Madison. Bloomington: IN: Indiana University Press.

Baumgartner, Frank R., and Beth L. Leech. 1998. *Basic interests: The importance of groups in politics and in political science*. Princeton: Princeton University Press.

Birnbaum, Jeffrey H. 1993. *The lobbyists: How influence peddlers work their way in Washington*. New York: Times Books.

Coffman, Jack. 1993. Senate panel clamps down on special-interest money. *St. Paul Pioneer Press*, 1 April, A1.

———. 1993. IRs propose ban on PAC contributions to campaigns. *St. Paul Pioneer Press*, 22 January, B1.

Donnay, Patrick D., and Graham P. Ramsden. 1995. Public financing of legislative elections: Lessons from Minnesota. *Legislative Studies Quarterly* 20: 351–364.

Donnay, Patrick D., and Graham P. Ramsden. 1998. The history and performance of Minnesota's publicly funded elections. In *Perspectives on Minnesota government and politics*, edited by Steve Hoffman, et al. Minneapolis, MN: Burgess Publishing..

Drew, Elizabeth. 1999. *The corruption of American politics: What went wrong and why*. Secaucus, NJ: Birch Lane Press.

Elzzar, Daniel. 1984. *American federalism: A view from the states*. New York: Harpercollins.

Elazar, Daniel, J., Virginia Gray, and Wyman Spano. 1999. *Minnesota government and politics*. Lincoln, NE: University of Nebraska Press.

Gais, Thomas. 1998. *Improper influence: Campaign finance law, political interest groups, and the problem of equality*. Ann: Arbor: University of Michigan Press.

Loftus, Tom. 1994. *The art of legislative politics*. Washington, D.C.: Congressional Quarterly.

Lorenz, Sarah Ruth. 2001. Campaign finance: An ongoing debate. *Perspectives* 27 (2):14–17.

Magleby, David B., and Candice J. Nelson. 1990. *The money chase: Congressional campaign finance reform.* Washington, D.C.: Brookings.

Malbin, Michael J., and Thomas L. Gais. 1998. *The day after reform: Sobering campaign finance lessons from the American states.* Albany, NY: The Rockefeller Institute Press.

Paulson, Todd, and David Schultz. 1998. Bucking Buckley: Voter attitudes, tobacco money, and campaign contribution corruption in Minnesota politics. *Hamline Journal of Public Law and Policy* 19: 449–496.

Salmore, Stephen A., and Barbare G. Salmore. 1994. The transformation of state electoral politics. In *The state of the States,* edited by Carl E. Van Horn. Washington, D.C.: Congressional Quarterly.

Schultz, David. 1999. The price of admission: money and influence in Minnesota politics. Unpublished paper.

Smith, Dane. 1993. Bills take aim at power of PACs in state politics. *Star Tribune,* 7 March, B1.

Sorauf, Frank J. 1992. *Inside campaign finance: Myth and realities.* New Haven: Yale University Press.

Thompson, Joel A., and Gary F. Moncrief. 1998. *Campaign finance in state legislative elections.* Washington, D.C.: Congressional Quarterly Press.

Warren, Mark A. 2001. *Democracy and association.* Princeton: Princeton University Press.

CHAPTER 11

Term Limits and Campaign Funding in Michigan: More Money, More Candidates, More Wealth

Marjorie Sarbaugh-Thompson
Lyke Thompson
Lisa Marckini
John Strate
Richard C. Elling
Charles D. Elder

Introduction

Term limits advocates claimed that expelling long-term incumbents from office would sever the ties between special interests and elected officials. Thus, a term limits law was seen by some of its advocates and supporters—both in Michigan and nationally—as a way to limit the influence of special interest money in state politics (Niven, 2000; Anderson 1992). On the other hand, ed-

The authors gratefully acknowledge funding for this project from the following sources: Vice President for Research, Wayne State University; the State Policy Center, Wayne State University; the Hewlett Packard Corporation; College of Liberal Arts, Wayne State University. We also wish to thank our student assistants, Nirupma Banka, Lisa Marckini, Eric Rader, Jovan Trpovski, Tricia Ketterer, Simone Dietrich, Kelly LeRoux, and Pamela Walsh for their hard work on this project. Additionally, we are deeply indebted to Mark Grebner of Practical Political Consultants for generously providing 1990 campaign finance reports on microfiche and a microfiche reader.

itorials in national and local newspapers, as well as some advocates of campaign finance reform, such as Common Cause, warned that term limits were not a substitute for campaign finance reform (Niven, 2000; *Detroit Free Press* 1992a).

In the following discussion we explore the effects of term limits on campaign contributions. As we have argued elsewhere (Orr, et al. 2001), effects of term limits are likely to differ depending on the severity of the laws and the characteristics of the state and its political institutions, including its campaign finance laws. The combination of stringent term limits and a highly professionalized legislature mean that effects of term limits in Michigan are likely to be among the most profound, and campaign finance behavior is one of many areas in which these effects are expected. Gierzynski, describing a framework for comparative analysis of campaign finance behavior, identifies term limits as one of the legal factors that should be considered. As he argues "term limits may increase the importance of money in elections because of the reduced effect of incumbency: there will be more open-seat contests, for which money is more important…and less accumulation of the personal support that comes with incumbency" (Gierzynski1998).

Term Limits in Michigan

Term limits laws vary widely in their severity. Seven states impose lifetime limits on service, while twelve others restrict consecutive years of service. Michigan is one of the seven states with a lifetime limit. Michigan State Representatives may serve for six years, (three two-year terms), and State Senators may serve for eight years, (two four-year terms). Only two states limit combined service in both chambers to fewer years.[1] Therefore, Michigan's are among the most stringent limits on legislative service. In 1998, sixty-four of Michigan's State Representatives were prohibited from running for reelection.

In 1992 nearly 59% of Michigan's voters supported a term limits ballot initiative. The final legal challenge failed in March of 1998 when the Michigan Supreme Court ruled that the part of the law limiting the service of state officials was constitutional. The first cohort of representatives were to be termed out in November of that year. The lengthy court fight and the potential that

---

1. Nebraska limits service to fewer total years than does Michigan, but it has a unicameral legislature.

the law might not take effect muted the anticipatory effects of term limits seen in California (Faletta, et al. Forthcoming). The exodus from the Michigan State House precipitated by term limits was larger than that experienced by California when its first General Assembly members were termed out of office.

The nature of the legislatures in the nineteen states with term limits differ dramatically, and these differences are likely to produce unique effects. Michigan is one of two states with highly professionalized legislatures that have adopted term limits.[2] Michigan legislators are paid well, with Representatives receiving more than $70,000 per year. Both chambers meet annually, with no limits on session length, and both chambers employ numerous partisan and non-partisan staff, as well as providing each legislator with money to hire personal staff.

Michigan's legislature consists of a 110-member House of Representatives and a 38-member Senate. State representatives run for office every two years; State senators run for office every four years. All state senators in Michigan run for reelection simultaneously, and their election coincides with the state's gubernatorial election. These elections are held in even numbered, non-presidential election years. Throughout the 1990s, Republicans controlled the Michigan Senate. Partisan control of the State House of Representatives changed regularly throughout the 1990s. Both labor and business are active in the state and provide financial and political support to candidates for seats in the state legislature.

Both legislative chambers have numerous standing committees, in which much of the work of the legislature is done. Legislation must be supported by a majority of the members of a committee before being considered by the full chamber.

Compared to other state legislative leaders, Michigan's are among the most powerful. (Francis 1985; Hamm, et al. 1999). The Speaker of the House and the Majority Leader of the Senate may assign bills to committees as they see fit, even if the bill does not necessarily seem to fall under the jurisdiction of that committee. Therefore, the leaders can strongly influence a bill's chance to reach the chamber floor for a vote. Additionally, these leaders choose committee chairs and assign members to committees. Although the leaders generally respect committee requests made by minority party leaders and work with or defer to the appropriations committee chair on subcommittee chair selection, they are not formally required to do so. Most House committee

---

2. Levels of professionalization are based on Squire's (1992) index. California is the other term-limited state with a highly professionalized legislature. The limits adopted in California are the same stringent ones adopted in Michigan.

chairs and most caucus leaders were termed out of office at the end of the 1997–98 session. In the 1999–2000 session, eleven freshmen chaired standing committees in the House.

Campaign Finance Laws in Michigan

Michigan, like many states, limits the amount that citizens and groups may contribute to candidates running for elective office. Contribution limits were first adopted in 1974, but did not take effect until the 1976 election cycle. The 1974 campaign finance bill required that office holders disclose any fund raising done while in office, including any non-monetary support received. Reporting deadlines required that reports be filed both before and after both primary and general elections during election years and annually following non-election years. With the exception of gubernatorial races, there is no public funding for campaigns in Michigan.

After its passage, Common Cause described the 1974 Michigan campaign finance bill as "loophole-ridden." Loopholes included the following: committees spending less than $200 were exempted from disclosure requirements; sums less than $10 could remain anonymous; contributions to political parties could be made with an understanding that the party would contribute an equal amount to a specific candidate (thereby providing a mechanism for anonymous contributions); political party expenditures on behalf of a candidate were not included in campaign spending totals; and heavy spending in the last three weeks of a political campaign would not be reported until after the election (Tingwall 1974). Furthermore, the 1974 Michigan campaign finance law prohibited the Secretary of State's office from retaining campaign committee reports after six years, making it difficult to trace patterns of contributions across time.

In Michigan, independent PACs may contribute up to ten times the contribution limit for individual citizens. Currently those limits are $500 for individuals giving to a state representative candidate and $1,000 for individuals giving to a state senate candidate. These limits apply for the entire election cycle.

In *Austin v. Chamber of Commerce*, 494 U.S. 652 (1990), the U.S. Supreme Court ruled that corporate entities must establish PACs through which to channel campaign contributions instead of using member dues to make contributions. In response to this restriction on business organizations, the legislature has debated bills that would require that unions be prevented from using dues paid their members to fund union PAC contributions unless the member signed a statement giving the union permission to use his or her dues for political purposes. To date, these efforts have failed. It is not clear that

Austin v. Chamber of Commerce limits corporate- or other PAC-giving because it is so easy to form an independent political action committee (PAC) in Michigan.

Michigan's law permits any group of twenty-five individuals to establish a PAC as long as the group gives to at least three different individuals and registers with the Secretary of State six months before the election. Therefore, there are 945 independent PACs listed with the Secretary of State's office. Often the names chosen for these PACs do not reveal clearly, and sometimes seem chosen to obscure, the interests represented. Therefore, contributions are often difficult for voters and watchdog groups, as well as academic researchers, to interpret and classify.

Political parties in Michigan are permitted to contribute separately at the state, county and district levels. Each of these three levels may contribute up to ten times the contribution limits for individual citizens. Further, each caucus in each chamber of the legislature is permitted to contribute unlimited amounts to candidates running for office in that chamber. The only restriction is that caucus committees cannot contribute to candidates in primary elections if an opponent is running, and there may be only one caucus committee per party per chamber.[3] Although caucus committees may not contribute in contested primary elections, political parties may support one or more of the contestants. Given the ability of political parties and caucus PACs to funnel large sums of money to candidates in state house and senate races, these races can become extremely expensive. For example, in 2000 one candidate for the state house raised nearly $700,000 dollars, with more than $500,000 of this sum coming from the political party or caucus committees (Michigan Campaign Finance Network. 2001a).

Subsequent to the initial 1974 campaign finance bill, progress in regulating campaign contributions occurred incrementally through amendments. For

---

3. This is the result of an amendment to the campaign finance law, HB 5410, which created four caucus committees—one per party per chamber—to increase the ability to track contributions. According to Gongwer Reports (1992), Democrats amended the bill to limit contributions to $5,000 per chamber for each contributor. The Senate version removed these limits. This amendment, passed after term limits were adopted but before they were implemented, centralized control over caucus funds. Although it makes it easier to distinguish between caucus committees and independent PACs, which improves disclosure of the money given, it does not limit the amount of money, and it centralizes control of caucus money, limiting the ability of factions within the caucus from providing access to caucus funds for those candidates who may not be as supportive of or supported by caucus leaders.

example, in 1997 investors, developers and upper-level employees of casinos were prohibited from making campaign contributions. Common Cause of Michigan advocates restricting campaign contributions by all industries regulated by the state, but believes that that proposal lacks support among Michigan's legislators (Common Cause 1997a).

Legislative efforts to expand public funding for state legislative races floundered in the early 1990s in the face of state budget shortfalls and the then-dismal state of the state's economy (Gongwer Reports 1992). Citizen commitment to public funding seems to have declined, with fewer than 8% of taxpayers checking the box on their 1994 tax return that would earmark $3 (individual returns) or $6 (joint returns) of their tax for the State Campaign Fund. The check-off for public campaign funding does not raise the taxpayer's tax bill, but simply allocates tax money to the fund. In 1976, when the program began, 26% of taxpayers participated. Common Cause of Michigan believes that lack of public participation may jeopardize the existing public funding program for gubernatorial races (Common Cause 1997b). Thus, prospects for expanding public funding to include other statewide or state legislative elections seem slim, at best.

Methodology and Data

Term limits were adopted in 1992 in Michigan. Legislators were first termed out of the State House in 1998. In 2002 the first cohort of State Senators will be termed out of office. The research presented here is part of an on-going comprehensive investigation of term limits' effects on state government in Michigan. We began investigating the effects of term limits in 1998, shortly before the first cohort of representatives were to be termed out of office. As part of that investigation we have conducted face-to-face interviews with legislators before and after term limits and analyzed election results, as well as analyzing campaign contributions. Readers interested in an overview of our investigation of term limits are referred to Orr, et al. (2001).

In the following discussion we explore the effects of term limits on campaign contributions, especially those of special interests. We report two different sets of analyses: 1) a comparison of all campaign contributions made to all candidates for two comparable election cycles before and after term limits (1990 and 1998) for both the House and Senate and 2) annual contributions for two sets of members of the state house, one before and one after term limits. Annual contributions are given during the year following an election and thus are less likely to be made by a desire to help a candidate win election than to gain access to representatives who are already serving in the legislature. We compare contributions given in 1997 (reported in 1998) and given in 1999 (reported in 2000).

In our comparison of the 1990 and 1998 campaign, contributions for the House and Senate, we use a non-equivalent control group design (Campbell and Stanley 1963). Members were termed out of the House at the end of the 1997–98 session; no senators will be termed out of office until 2002. Thirty of the thirty-eight incumbents ran for reelection to the Senate in 1998, three more than the twenty-seven Senate incumbents who ran in 1990. There were seventeen open-seat races for the 1990 House; in 1998 there were sixty-four. Therefore, the House experienced the "treatment," massive turnover precipitated by term limits, while the Senate served as the control group. With incumbents still running in most State Senate races, we would not anticipate sizeable effects of term limits on State Senate campaign contributions.[4] Hence, if term limits do indeed impact patterns and dynamics of campaign contributions, they should be evident in the case of the Michigan House, but not in the State Senate.

This design helps act as a control of the effects of history that could otherwise confound the effects of term limits. For example, Gierzynski and Breaux find that "[t]he 1996 election was a watershed for 'soft money'...raised by national party committees...These numbers represent a substantial jump in the resources of the political parties, including state and local parties, and raise new questions about party involvement in the financing of elections" (Gierzynski and Breaux 1998). We would expect this influx of money to political parties to affect both the State House and the State Senate in similar ways. Divergent effects on the two chambers would lend support to term limits as a contributing factor.

The Secretary of State's Bureau of Elections began providing electronic files of campaign finance reports in 1994, and subsequently made those reports available on-line. Currently it is possible to download individual campaign finance reports from the Secretary of State Web site at www.sos.state.mi.us. The 1998 campaign finance data used in this investigation were downloaded from the Michigan Secretary of State's Web site. The 1990 campaign finance data were typed by term limits project members from the microfiche collection mentioned earlier. For these two election cycles, we have data from the House and the Senate for all five reports filed by candidates during the year before

---

4. There was a slight increase in competition for Senate seats as termed out House members challenged incumbents.

the election and the year of the election. These five reports are: the annual reports (which are filed on January 31 of the year of the election but cover contributions for the preceding twelve months); the pre-primary report; the post-primary report; the pre-general report; and the post-general report.

In choosing the years to compare, we wanted to avoid anticipatory effects of term limits that might have occurred after voters passed term limits in 1992. We were concerned that, after the term limits law passed, different kinds of candidates might have been attracted to run for the legislature and that these candidates might have appealed to different types of contributors. Therefore, we sought a baseline election that occurred prior to the adoption of term limits. Even though the Secretary of State's office no longer had campaign contribution data for elections held prior to the adoption of term limits, we fortunately found a privately held set of microfiche for most candidates for the 1990 election.[5]

In the second part of the investigation presented here, we compared the annual reports filed by House members serving in the 1997–98 sessions to those filed by House members serving in the 1999–2000 session to explore whether interest groups use campaign contributions to seek access to legislators who have already been elected. Because these contributions are given during the year after the representative won election, it is unlikely that the primary purpose of this giving is to help candidates win election. Instead, it is more likely that giving during non-election years is designed to gain access to representatives who serve on committees handling policies of interest to particular groups of contributors.

The annual reports are filed in the January after the calendar year in which the contributions are made. Therefore, contributions listed on the 1998 annual report were given to the last pre-term-limits representatives during the calendar year 1997, not an election year. Readers are reminded that the contributions made during 1997 were listed on the annual report before the Michigan Supreme Court upheld the term limits law's constitutionality in March 1998. Therefore, many, if not most, House members did not believe that they would be termed out of office. Similarly, contributions listed on the 2000 annual report were given to the first post-term-limits cohort of representatives in 1999, the year after they were elected. Using these data, we explore whether the amount of money given to representatives after they win

5. We gratefully acknowledge the contribution of Mark Grebner of Practical Political Consultants who provided microfiche campaign contribution reports and donated a microfiche reader. Additionally, we are grateful to the State Policy Center at Wayne State University, which provided funding for graduate students who entered and coded these data. This research would not have been possible without their generous assistance.

election changes after representatives are term limited. Further, we assess whether, after term limits, interest group contributions are more or less targeted toward representatives serving on several committees with jurisdiction over issues of interest to specific categories of groups (e.g., business PACs or labor PACs). If term limits sever the ties between special interests and elected officials, we should see a decline in these sorts of contributions, and committee service should play little or no role in interest groups' giving patterns.

In this part of our investigation, we employ a variant of the separate-sample pretest-post-test design (Campbell and Stanley 1963) in which forty-six House members served during both 1997–98 and 1999–2000 session and so were part of both the pre-test and post-test group. The other sixty-four members of the House were part of only the pre-test group (before term limits), and sixty-four others were part of only the post-test group (after term limits).

In this chapter, we have complete data only for the 2000 House annual reports. This is the result of changes in the availability of campaign finance data through the Michigan Secretary of State's office. Throughout the 1990s, these data were increasingly accessible to the general public, to watchdog groups, and to academic researchers. In 2000 the Michigan Secretary of State's office no longer entered data from handwritten campaign committee financial reports. Beginning in July of 2001, the Secretary of State's office began posting on their Web site only the reports filed electronically by the candidate. Electronic filing was voluntary. Therefore, watchdog groups and academic researchers were confronted by a return to the pre-1994 era, in which data that were not filed electronically were available only as PDF images of handwritten or, occasionally, typewritten sheets. To further complicate data gathering, many candidates filed only some of the required reports electronically, filing others on handwritten sheets. This change is the result of an amendment to the campaign finance bill that will require electronic filing of campaign finance reports for committees that raise more than $20,000, beginning on January 31, 2004. It is not clear at this time whether the Secretary of State's office will return to hand entry of data provided by committees not required to file electronically.[6] Even when the mandatory electronic filing requirement takes effect, many House candidates will not be required to file electronically. The median amount raised for State House races in 1998 was $15,300 (in unadjusted 1998 dollars). The $20,000 cut off will mean that data for approximately 58% the State House candidates

---

6. The National Institute on Money in State Politics (NIMSP) and the Michigan Campaign Finance Network have noticed this also (Personal correspondence with the lead author 2001).

would not have been filed electronically under the mandatory filing requirement. This would seem to reduce disclosure.

In the analyses that follow, we compare campaign contributions from three different years. To adjust for inflation, we used the July Consumer price index from 1990, 1998 and 2000 to discount 1998 and 2000 campaign contributions to their 1990 equivalents.[7] Unless otherwise noted, all monetary amounts discussed in the manuscript or presented in the tables are adjusted to their 1990 equivalents.

Interaction between Term Limits and Campaign Contributions

Limits on campaign contributions, such as those in Michigan, have been shown to reduce campaign spending, although their effect is somewhat limited. Hogan (2000) estimates that contribution limits reduce incumbent campaign spending by eighteen cents per eligible voter, but he found no statistically significant effect of contribution limits on spending in open seat races. Given that term limits increase the number of open seat elections, upon which contribution limits have little effect, we expected that overall House elections would have become more expensive after term limits. Further, given that open seat elections are generally won by the candidate who raises the most money (Gaddie & Bullock 2000), money may become more important for winning in post-term-limits elections.

Conversely, individual campaign contributions under term limits could decline if candidates become less willing to raise and spend large sums to gain a legislative seat that they can hold, at best, for only a few years (Mitchell 1991). Moreover, from an interest group perspective, there may be little value in using campaign contributions to cultivate an on-going relationship with a state legislators who can only serve for a few years, especially if the legislator's policy expertise and influence over other legislators is limited by transience (Porter 1974).

To explore these related questions, we compared both total and mean contributions for the House in 1990 and 1998 and compared the changes in the pattern in the 1990 and 1998 Senate. As is evident in Table 1, we have campaign finance reports for only about half of the candidates who ran for the State House in 1990. If candidates raise less than $1,000 per election, with the primary and general elections each counting as separate elections, they are not required to file campaign contribution reports and are granted a reporting waiver by the Secretary of State. Although many, possibly even most, of the

---

7. We divided the 1998 dollars by 1.23454 and divided the 2000 dollars by 1.325153 to convert them to their 1990 equivalents.

missing reports can be attributed to filing waivers, not all can be. Given the nature of our 1990 data, we suspected that some candidates' reports were lost. Underestimating the contributions in 1990 could inflate the effect of term limits. Therefore, we estimated the amount of money raised by candidates without reports. Details of the four estimates appear in Table 1.

In the 1998 House, 121 candidates, 21.3% of those running, were eligible for reporting waivers. Although they raised some money, we do not know how much exactly, only that they raised a small amount. We used the same method used for the 1990 data to estimate amount that 1998 candidates with reporting waivers may have raised.

Although the estimated contributions increase the total amounts raised and reduce the means for both chambers in both elections, the increases resulting from the estimates are, as we expected, more dramatic for both 1990 elections. Both the reported contributions and estimated contributions for each of the two chambers for the 1990 and 1998 elections appear in Table 1.

For the State House, both the estimated and the reported amounts provide the same pattern of change between 1990 and 1998, but the changes are smaller when we use the estimates. As expected, the number of candidates running for the state house increased dramatically from 1990 to 1998. Also as expected, the total contributions to all Michigan state house candidates increased dramatically with the advent of term limits, by $4.26 million, using reported amounts, or by $3.5 million, using estimated amounts. Also, as we expected, the mean contributions per state house candidate decreased from 1990 to 1998. Even with these sizeable increases in state house contributions, there were so many more candidates running that the average amount raise by an individual candidate declined by $13,200, using reported amounts, or by $11,404, using estimated amounts. Further, the maximum raised by an individual candidate declined from 1990 to 1998 by $78,000.[8]

In the State Senate there were slightly fewer candidates running in 1998 than in 1990. Therefore, we expected to see a slight decrease in the total amount contributed. Using the reported amounts, the total amount of money reported for State Senate races increased only slightly, by approximately $355,000. Using estimates to adjust for missing records and candidates with reporting waivers, we found the total amount raised decreased by nearly $1.9 million. Using reported amounts, the mean contributed to each candidate de-

8. Although complete data are not yet available for the 2000 campaign contributions, Michigan Campaign Finance Network provides data for the five most expensive races in the state in 2000. Two of the candidates in these races raised more than the maximum amount raised by a candidate in 1990. Therefore, this may vary across time with or without term limits.

Table 1
Changes in Campaign Contributions Between 1990 and 1998

	1990 Election	1998 Election	Change	% Change
House Candidates in Primary and General Elections				
Candidates Running	321	541	220	68.54%
Mean Reported Only	$36,446	$23,246	−$13,200	−36.22%
Standard Deviation	$39,402	$32,991		
Mean Reported and Estimated	$30,975	$19,571	−$11,404	−36.82%
Standard Deviation	$34,320	$30,157		
Median Reported Only	$28,537	$12,393	−$16,144	−56.57%
Median Reported and Estimated	$22,860	$7,617	−$15,243	−66.68%
Total Reported	$6,086,562	$10,344,808	$4,258,246	69.96%
Total Reported and Estimated*	$7,557,893	$11,057,884	$3,499,991	46.31%
Mean Number of Gifts	183	88	−95	−51.91%
Standard Deviation	160	111		
Total Number of Gifts	30603	39375	8772	28.66%
Maximum Number of Gifts	854	743	−111	−13.00%
Maximum Raised	$349,088	$270,259	−$78,829	−22.58%
Candidates Reporting	167	445		
Candidates Estimated	77	120		
Candidates Reported & Estimated	244	565		
Senate Candidates in Primary and General Elections				
Candidates Running	128	122	−6	−4.69
Mean Reported Only	$87,104	$76,038	−$11,066	−12.70%
Standard Deviation	$96,838	$93,261		
Mean Reported & Estimated	$74,599	$57,989	−$16,610	−22.27%
Standard Deviation	$84,780	$83,303		
Median Reported Only	$51,810	$45,593	−$6,217	−12.00%
Median Reported and Estimated	$36,847	$24,098	−$12,749	−34.60%
Total Reported	$6,184,394	$6,539,306	$354,912	5.74%
Total Reported and Estimated*	$8,951,820	$7,074,751	−$1,877,069	−20.97%
Mean Number of Gifts	390	258	−132	−33.85%
Standard Deviation	344	274		
Total Number of Gifts	27713	22147	−5566	−20.08%
Maximum Number of Gifts	1510	1166	−344	−22.78%
Maximum Raised	$369,361	$450,439	$81,078	21.95%
Candidates Reporting	71	86		
Candidates Estimated	49	36		
Candidates Reporting & Estimated	120	122		

* An explanation of the equations used to estimate missing values appears immediately before the references section at the end of this chapter.

creased by $11,066 from 1990 to 1998. Using estimated contributions leads to an even larger decrease of $16,610 in mean contributions raised for elections to State Senate seats.

The different pattern found in the senate and house races between these two elections suggests that term limits are associated with an increased number of candidates running for office and an increased total amount of money spent on the races. It is less clear the term limits are implicated in the decreasing amounts raised by individual candidates. The mean contributions fell for State Senate candidates as well as for State House candidates, but the decreases are larger for the State House candidates, suggesting some possible effect of term limits on amounts given by individuals.

Comparing the reported and estimated contributions suggests that the reported contributions tend to overstate the difference between the 1990 and 1998 elections. This is true for both the House and the Senate, because there appear to be some missing reports in the 1990 data for both chambers. We do not have an adequate way to estimate the contributions given by different types of donors and must rely on the reported amounts. Therefore, we focus on differences in the pattern of contributions between the House and the Senate in the following discussion.

Changes in the Proportion of Contributions Received from Different Types of Donors

Term limits advocates hoped to sever the ties between special interests and elected officials. To see whether different types of groups contributed differently to members of a term-limited legislature, we classified contributions into fifteen categories of donors: individual, corporate, peak trade associations, education associations and unions, public sector unions, private sector unions, government and non-unionized public employees, ideological groups, legal professionals including lobbyists, political candidate committees, caucus and caucus leaders, agriculture, medical professionals, political parties, and personal or family resources. Despite concerted efforts to determine the interests represented by each PAC in our data, we have some contributions that we could not classify. For the 1990 House such contributions amount to $146,843; for the 1990 Senate to $277,114; for the 1998 House, to $115,435; and, for the 1998 Senate, to $77,954.

Differences in the proportion of campaign contributions from four different types of contributors are summarized in Figure 1: individual contributions, personal resources, partisan PACs and other PACs. Partisan PACs include three categories of PACs: candidate committees, caucus and caucus leaders, and political parties. Other PACs include all ten other categories: all

Table 2
Proportion of Contributions from Types of Contributors

	House			Senate		
	1990	1998	Difference	1990	1998	Difference
Individuals	32.4%	29.1%	−3.3%	32.2%	37.8%	5.6%
Business PACs	26.1%	18.2%	−7.9%	25.5%	21.9%	−3.6%
Labor PACs	11.6%	7.4%	−4.2%	9.8%	5.3%	−4.5%
Caucus & Other Politicians	9.1%	14.9%	5.8%	9.6%	5.3%	−4.3%
Political Parties	2.7%	2.2%	−0.5%	7.1%	16.1%	9.0%
Personal or Family	5.4%	18.7%	13.3%	2.8%	3.9%	1.1%
Ideological Groups	2.2%	1.1%	−1.1%	1.8%	1.1%	0.7%
Lawyers & Lobbyists	2.1%	2.9%	0.8%	2.0%	2.4%	0.4%
Medical Professionals	4.0%	2.0%	−2.0%	2.8%	3.1%	0.3%
Agriculture PACs	0.4%	0.6%	0.2%	0.6%	0.3%	−0.3%
Government Sector	1.6%	1.6%	0.0%	0.9%	1.6%	0.7%

the business PACs and agriculture, all the labor PACs, the government sector, ideological groups, and medical and legal professionals.

We found these other PACs' contributions, as a proportion of all contributions, declined from 1990 to 1998 for the House, but given that this pattern is mirrored in Senate contributions, we are not convinced that this is a decline attributable to term limits. The proportion of contributions received by candidates from partisan sources increased in both the House and the Senate from 1990 to 1998. Nationally, there is a well-documented increase during the 1990s in the amount of soft money used by political parties for issue advocacy. This increase may have been accompanied by an increase in "hard money" from party organizations, either local, state or national, or from state legislative caucus committees based in each chamber. Thus, again, we hesitate to attribute this increase to term limits.

The share of candidates' contributions given by individual donors decreased for the House from 1990 to 1998, while it increased in the Senate. The movement in opposite directions across the two chambers suggests that term limits may be implicated in this change. An even more dramatic divergence between the House and Senate contribution patterns is revealed by investigating the share of contributions provided by the candidate's own and his or her family's resources.[9] The share of contributions coming from personal or family resources

9. In some earlier work, we treated the candidates and his or her family members as individual donors (see Marckini, et al. 1999; Thompson, et al. 2001).

Figure 1
Proportions of Contributions by Types of Donors

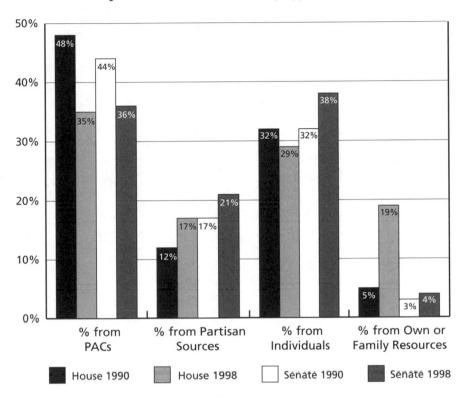

increased in both chambers from 1990 to 1998. The increase in the Senate was extremely small, one percent. In the House, the increase was large—14%.

Therefore, for an individual candidate, term limits appear to have had little impact on the extent to which candidates might depend on partisan PACs and other PACs to fund their campaigns. On the other hand, term limits seem to reduce the relative dependence of candidates on individual donors and increase their dependence on their personal wealth to fund their campaigns.

Combining our fifteen categories into the four major types of contributors may obscure some important changes within these categories, however. This proves true for both partisan sources of contributions and for all other PACs. As Table 3 illustrates, as a proportion of total contributions, four types of donors increased their relative shares in funding House races in 1998 compared to races in 1990. These four are: agriculture PACs; lawyers and lobbyists; personal wealth; and caucuses, chamber leaders, and other political ac-

Table 3
Amounts Contributed by Different Types of Contributors

	House			Senate		
	1990	**1998**	*difference*	**1990**	**1998**	*difference*
Individual	$1,973,278	$3,010,685	*$1,037,407*	$1,990,502	$2,468,028	*$477,526*
Corporate	$519,921	$608,840	*$88,919*	$612,212	$568,425	*–$43,787*
Peak Trade Groups	$1,067,363	$1,272,201	*$204,838*	$965,867	$866,386	*–$99,481*
Subtotal Business	**$1,587,284**	**$1,881,041**	***$293,757***	**$1,578,079**	**$1,434,811**	***–$143,268***
Education Ass'ns	$148,357	$254,812	*$106,455*	$134,170	$111,742	*–$22,428*
Public Sector Unions	$98,169	$87,843	*–$10,326*	$57,125	$44,315	*–$12,810*
Private Unions	$460,050	$418,500	*–$41,550*	$439,451	$192,142	*–$247,309*
Subtotal Labor	**$706,576**	**$761,155**	***$54,579***	**$630,746**	**$348,199**	***–$282,547***
Political Candidates	$18,059	$99,108	*$81,049*	$59,073	$39,555	*–$19,518*
Leaders & Caucus	$537,187	$1,450,135	*$912,948*	$541,109	$306,829	*–$234,280*
Political Parties	$162,735	$229,288	*$66,553*	$437,196	$1,049,718	*$612,522*
Subtotal Political	**$717,981**	**$1,778,531**	***$1,060,550***	**$1,037,378**	**$1,396,102**	***$358,724***
Personal or Family	$329,605	$1,935,383	*$1,605,778*	$174,954	$254,259	*$79,305*
Ideological Groups	$131,155	$110,208	*–$20,947*	$112,628	$74,102	*–$38,526*
Lawyers & Lobbyists	$128,605	$301,848	*$173,243*	$120,550	$154,181	*$33,631*
Medical Professionals	$240,470	$205,899	*–$34,571*	$169,771	$203,918	*$34,147*
Agriculture	$24,716	$63,137	*$38,421*	$35,923	$20,212	*–$15,711*
Government Sector	$100,049	$164,391	*$64,342*	$55,949	$107,539	*$51,590*
Total Reported	**$6,086,562**	**$10,344,808**	***$4,258,246***	**$6,184,394**	**$6,539,306**	***$354,912***

tors. Only the latter two increased their proportion by more than 1%. On the other hand, four types of contributors decreased their share of contributions to 1998 Senate races compared to races in 1990. These were business PACs; labor PACs; caucuses, chamber leaders and other political actors; and agriculture PACs. The last of these decreased their shares of contributions by less than 1%.

In Figure 2 we examine in greater detail the differences between the two chambers across the two elections for the four subgroups of PACs that changed their proportion of giving by at least 5%. We examine the following: business PACs, labor PACs , political parties, and other sources of partisan contributions (leadership PACs, caucus committees, and other elected officials' committees).

Although the share of contributions received from business PACs declines in both chambers from 1990 to 1998, the drop is much larger in the House. Indeed, as a share of overall contributions, the proportion from business PACs in 1998 House races decreased by more than twice their decline as a proportion for 1998 Senate races. This decrease suggests that term limits might have decreased the willingness of business PACs to contribute to candidates under

Figure 2
Proportion of Contributions by Specific Subgroups of Contributors

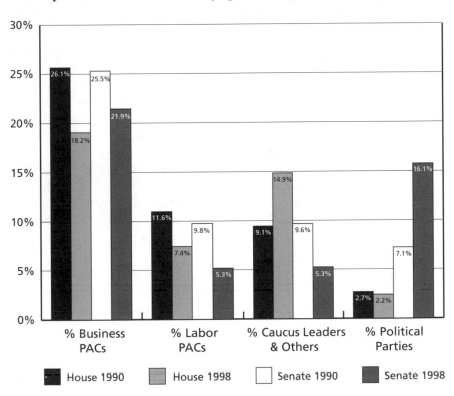

term limits. Yet, in absolute amounts, which we will discuss shortly, business increased its level of contributions—just not at a level equivalent to the dramatic increase in money spent on 1998 House races overall.

The proportion contributed by labor PACs also declined for both chambers from 1990 to 1998. For labor, however, the decline was roughly proportional for both chambers, suggesting that term limits had little or no effect on contributions from labor PACs.

The patterns of contributions from caucus committees and from leaders and other political actors' committees suggest that term limits may have an effect on these sources of contributions. The proportion of money received from these sources rose by more than half in the House from 1990 to 1998, while declining by nearly half in the Senate. On the other hand, the proportion of contributions from political parties more than doubled in the Senate from 1990 to 1998 while remaining virtually unchanged in the House. This suggests to us that term limits affect the decisional calculus of partisan sources of contributions dramatically and differentially.

If the proportion of funding received from a type of donor is associated with relative amount of influence exerted by that source of funding, then term limits advocates might be pleased to see that the relative amount given by business PACs declined more in the House than in the Senate, because this would suggest that term limits might attenuate the ties between business interests and elected officials. Although we are not confident that the amount of money given is proportionate to the amount of influence exerted, this seems to be an implicit assumption of campaign reformers and some term limits advocates.

Using this same assumption, we suspect that term limits advocates might be pleased that political parties share of contributions in the House declined from 1990 to 1998, while rising in the Senate. Thus, term limits advocates might claim that term limits reverses that national trend toward greater involvement of political parties in campaign funding. We would want to investigate this apparent change more closely and over a longer period of time, however.

On the other hand, term limits seem to increase the role played by caucus committees and other political actors. We believe that the dramatic increase in the proportion of campaign funding received from the caucuses, chamber leaders, and other political actors might not please term limits advocates. Further, we believe this increase is a more robust finding because it is confirmed by our previous findings based on interviews that caucus leaders are becoming much more influential and powerful in the post-term limits House (Trpovski, et al. 2001).

Amount of Money Contributed by Different Types of Donors

The total amount of money raised for House races for 1998 increased so dramatically that proportions can provide misleading impressions of the extent to which some donors increased their contributions in absolute terms. Some types of contributors may have given a lot more money during the 1998 election cycle than they did in 1990, but, as a proportion, their giving could have decreased. Therefore, we present in Table 3 a summary of the amount contributed by each of fifteen categories of contributors.

Despite the overall increase in the amount of money raised for 1998 House races, four individual categories of contributors decreased their giving: private sector unions, public sector unions, medical professionals, and ideological groups. The size of the decrease was relatively small, however—less than $50,000 in each case.

Although, as noted above, the share of the contributions to the 1998 House races coming from individual donors decreased, the absolute amount contributed by individuals increased over the amount contributed by individuals for 1990 House races by slightly more than one million dollars. Campaign funding from the candidates' personal resources increased both as a proportion and in absolute amount from the 1990 to the 1998 House races. This source of funding increased more than any other category, by slightly more than $1.6 million.[10]

In absolute terms, the amount contributed by partisan sources increased by more than one million dollars in House races from 1990 to 1998. Most of this increase is accounted for by the more than $1.4 million given by the chamber caucus committees and by chamber leaders' PACs. Contributions from political parties increased slightly, by approximately $66,500. Contributions from fellow candidates increased by approximately $81,000.

For the Senate we find several different patterns. Although three of the fifteen types of contributors, (individuals, personal resources, and political parties), increased the amounts they gave in 1998, these increases were much smaller—less than half the size they were in the 1998 House races. Both individual donors' and political parties' contributions to Senate candidates increased by less than $500,000, or less than half their increases in the House, and candidates' reliance on their personal resources increased by a mere $79,305 in the Senate compared to the $1.6 million increase in the House.

Further, contributions from ten types of contributors decreased in the Senate. Two types of contributors, private sector unions and leaders and caucus committees, decreased their giving by more than $200,000, and a third, peak trade groups, decreased giving by nearly $100,000. Seven other categories of donors decreased their giving for 1998 Senate races, compared to 1990 Senate races, but by smaller amounts. These were corporate PACs, education associations, public sector unions, political candidate committees, ideological groups, and agriculture. Therefore, it seems clear that the increase we find in House campaign contributions is not part of a general trend affecting both state legislative bodies.

In absolute numbers, the total amount reported by House candidates from individual donors increased by more than one million dollars from 1990 to 1998. Yet, because the total amount reported increased by four million dollars,

---

10. We classified individual donors as family members if they had the same last name as the candidate. This may have resulted in slippage, because female relatives may not share the candidate's last name and some candidates with more common last names might have received some contributions from people with the same last name who were not family members. Because these potential sources of error would pull our estimates in opposite directions, we assume that much, if not most, of this error will cancel itself out.

the proportion raised from individual donors declined. It is not clear that influence wielded is proportionate to money given, although this appears to be a working assumption of some term limits advocates and campaign finance watchdog groups. If this assumption has some basis in reality, then, despite concerted efforts (indicated by giving more money) to preserve their influence over their elected representatives, the relative influence (amount given by individuals as a proportion of all giving) may have declined. Therefore, relatively speaking, the ability of citizens to exert more influence than PACs and political groups may have declined instead of increased in a term-limited legislature.

As Table 3 indicates, candidates running under term limits in the 1998 House relied heavily on their personal resources to fund their campaigns—much more heavily than did Senate candidates in 1998 or either House or Senate candidates in 1990. This represents a major infusion of money—an increase of $1.6 million—suggesting that open seats in a term-limited legislature not only attract more candidates but more candidates capable of funding a portion of their own campaigns.

In absolute terms, contributions from all three types of political contributors rose in the House from 1990 to 1998. In the Senate only one type of political contributor gave more to candidates in the 1998 Senate races—political parties. The other two types of political contributors—other candidates and leaders' PACs or caucus PACs—gave less to Senate candidates in 1998 than they did in 1990. As noted earlier, Gordon and Unmack argue that under term limits in California "(t)he uncertainty about members' voting patterns and committee assignments created by the high levels of turnover in the Assembly leave PACs with fewer cues about how a member will vote. Party identification, however, remains a fairly reliable indicator of political ideology, and is thus one of the few 'constants' left for PACs to use when making their allocation decision" (1999). This decisional calculus could indeed account for the increase we found in giving by caucus committees in the 1998 House. On the other hand, the dramatic increase in giving through political parties in the Senate cannot be explained by uncertainty. In the Senate, more incumbents (thirty) ran for reelection in 1998 than did in 1990 (twenty-seven). Further, many of the non-incumbents were termed-out House members, whose ideology should have been well known. Therefore, there should have been more, not less, certainty about the ideology of Senate candidates even in open seat races, providing business PACs, labor PACs and other types of PACs with little incentive to channel their donations through political parties.

Effects of Open and Competitive Seats on Campaign Contributions

Open seat elections became much more common under term limits. Open seats in competitive districts provide opportunities to gain partisan control, and under term limits incumbents will regularly vacate these seats. Therefore, it is important to analyze the patterns of contributions for competitive, open seat elections in order to understand effects term limits are likely to have on campaign contributions.[11] Table 4 compares the mean contributions from all types of contributors for competitive and non-competitive seats in open and closed seat races.[12] We found that candidates running in competitive, open seat elections received more money than did other candidates in both for both elections chambers. There were no statistically significant differences in the mean amount of money raised attributable solely to either the effect of an incumbent running or the effect of the competitiveness of the district for any of these four elections. The only statistically significant difference we found was an interaction effect for open, competitive seats for the 1990 House races and the 1998 Senate races. Although in all four elections candidates in open, competitive seat races received higher mean contributions than candidates in the other three kinds of races, this effect was not statistically significant in the 1998 House races and the 1990 Senate races. In general, then, we see little or no effect of term limits on the distribution of total contributions for open seat races or for competitive races.

We do, however, find differences in contributions from specific types of donors that suggest an effect of term limits. As the results presented in Table 5 indicate, the effect of open seat elections on PAC contributions provides mixed support for Gordon and Unmack's argument that PACs are reluctant to contribute when uncertainty about the candidate's ideology is high (1999). In 1998, with sixty-four open seat races and many new faces, individual candidates in open seat races received much less financial help from PACs than

---

11. To identify competitive seats, we relied on a measure of base partisan voting created by Bill Ballinger of *Inside Michigan Politics*. He calculates the average base partisan vote using the vote for State Board of Education candidates. For the 1990 elections we used his measure from the five elections from 1982–1990, and, for the 1998 election, we used his measure from the five elections from 1992 to 2000. Districts with based partisan voting greater than 45% but less than 55% were classified as competitive.

12. Because we analyze data from all candidates reporting contributions instead of a sample, we occasionally discuss findings that are substantively significant, even if they lack statistical significance. Additionally, because we are not sampling, the small number of cases in some of the types of elections present fewer problems than they would if we relied on only a sample of cases.

Table 4
Effect of Competitive and Open Seat Elections on All Contributions

	Open Seat		Incumbent Running		Open Seat		Competitive		Interaction	
	Competitive	Non-competitive	Competitive	Non-competitive	F	sig.	F	sig.	F	sig.
1990 House Mean	$63,072	$28,807	$34,494	$34,620	0.44	0.63	0.99	0.50	5.94	0.02
standard deviation	$53,245	$26,576	$28,115	$41,496						
number of candidates	17	30	34	86						
1998 House Mean	$31,521	$17,807	$28,348	$24,215	0.11	0.79	3.47	0.31	1.20	0.28
standard deviation	$50,460	$20,720	$29,368	$19,872						
number of candidates	129	225	22	68						
1990 Senate Mean	$130,901	$60,410	$109,346	$71,101	0.11	0.79	11.37	0.18	0.33	0.57
standard deviation	$125,380	$59,518	$107,617	$88,507						
number of candidates	7	8	21	35						
1998 Senate Mean	$185,195	$74,215	$84,120	$73,047	1.05	0.49	1.49	0.44	2.74	0.10
standard deviation	$143,203	$70,362	$122,403	$85,177						
number of candidates	4	13	13	51						

Table 5
Effect of Competitive and Open Seat Elections on PAC Contributions

	Open Seat		Incumbent Running		Open Seat		Competitive		Interaction	
	Competitive	Non-competitive	Competitive	Non-competitive	F	sig.	F	sig.	F	sig.
1990 House Mean	$25,433	$6,843	$19,084	$18,981	0.10	0.81	1.02	0.50	7.95	*0.01*
standard deviation	$28,222	$7,911	$17,935	$17,975						
number of candidates	17	30	34	86						
1998 House Mean	$8,148	$5,006	$16,219	$14,261	214.61	**0.04**	18.60	0.15	0.16	0.69
standard deviation	$11,874	$6,897	$23,643	$14,119						
number of candidates	129	225	22	68						
1990 Senate Mean	$49,350	$17,798	$44,134	$36,851	0.33	0.67	2.56	0.36	0.78	0.38
standard deviation	$62,780	$26,972	$45,109	$47,844						
number of candidates	7	8	21	35						
1998 Senate Mean	$57,487	$25,650	$25,930	$28,122	0.73	0.55	0.76	0.54	2.96	**0.09**
standard deviation	$24,034	$25,619	$32,854	$31,177						
number of candidates	4	13	13	51						

did incumbents who ran—regardless of whether the district was competitive or non-competitive. This difference could reflect reluctance to give under high uncertainty; it could also reflect the large number of candidates running in these races. The pattern stands in stark contrast to the pattern in the other three elections. In all three other elections, candidates running in open, competitive seat races received more money than candidates running in any of the three other types of elections. This effect on PAC giving appears to be attributable to term limits.

We found a statistically significant interaction effect for open, competitive seat elections in two of the four elections: the 1990 House and the 1998 Senate races. The mean amounts given by PACs (excluding political PACs) to candidates in races for the open, competitive seats in the 1990 House and 1998 Senate seem to contradict the argument that uncertainty constrains giving. Term limits provides a plausible, although partial, explanation for this apparent anomaly. In 1998 many candidates for the State Senate were termed-out members of the State House.

Therefore, their ideology, voting record, and personal credibility were well known. Uncertainty does not, however, explain the high levels of PAC contributions to candidates in open seat, competitive races for the 1990 House. In this same year, PACs contributed at very low levels to candidates in open seat, non-competitive elections. Thus, their level of giving to candidates in open seat, competitive races may suggest that a desire for partisan control of the chamber that, at least prior to term limits, could overcome the constraint of uncertainty about the candidates. Alternatively, with fewer candidates running in open, competitive races, (seventeen in 1990 compared to 129 in 1998), perhaps candidates' ideologies could be examined by contributors thoroughly, thereby reducing uncertainty.

With larger numbers of open seat elections, term limits increase the chance that partisan control of the chamber will change, except in a few one-party dominated states. In Michigan, even without term limits, partisan control of the House changed every two years during the 1990s, featuring the infamous "stereo speakers" in 1992, when control was shared equally by fifty-five Republicans and fifty-five Democrats. This leads us to expect that party contributions, especially from the caucus, may increase dramatically after term limits, and that these contributions will be targeted toward open seats in competitive districts.

Evidence gathered in our interviews with term-limited representatives suggests that caucus leaders may use their ability to fund candidates in these races to insure that representatives cast votes that support the caucus positions, even when representatives disagree with that position (Trpovski, et al. 2001). If this, indeed, persists as a long-term trend, it is likely to provide further motivation for PACs to contribute to the caucus and political party instead of to the candidates directly.

As Table 6 illustrates, partisan sources contribute heavily to candidates in open, competitive seat races. Additionally, in the Senate, but not in the House, they contribute heavily to competitive races even when an incumbent is running. This is consistent with the importance that these groups place on gaining and retaining partisan control of the chamber. In the House, this pattern of giving appears to be affected only slightly by term limits. The mean amount given to individual candidates in open, competitive seat races was approximately $10,000 less than that given in comparable races for the 1990 House. This suggests that even donors with deep pockets, such as political parties and chamber caucuses, cannot give as heavily to each individual candidate when there are so many candidates. Also, the amount of money given by partisan sources to candidates in open seat, competitive races in the Senate more than tripled from 1990 to 1998. This suggests that termed out representatives running against each other in these elections were formidable opponents through whom each party hoped to increase or retain its share of Senate seats. If this is a harbinger of things to come, races for the State Senate under term limits are likely to attract large amounts of money.

Changes in Post-election Contributions to Sitting Representatives

Various studies have found that political action committees tend to concentrate their contributions on incumbents of either party, especially those holding leadership positions (Eismeier and Pollock 1986; Gordon and Unmack 1999; Thompson and Cassie 1992; Thompson, Cassie, and Jewell 1994). It is generally difficult to tell whether PACs give to candidates because they want to see ideologically sympathetic candidates elected and reelected or whether they give to candidates because they want to influence elected officials to vote in ways that they might not if left to make up their own minds. To try to disentangle these effects, we created a data set in which we used only contributions listed on each elected representative's annual report (contributions made in the calendar year *after* the candidate won election). We did this for each member of the State House for the 1997–98 session, the last before representatives were termed out of office, and each representative in the 1999–2000 session, the first session in which being a long-term incumbent meant serving a third term.

Virtually all representatives serving in these sessions received contributions in the year following their election, including the flock of lame ducks. Campaign contributions given to them could be transferred to a candidate's committee so that he or she could run for the State Senate or for another state-

Table 6
Effect of Competitive and Open Seat Elections on Political Contributions

	Open Seat		Incumbent Running		Open Seat		Competitive		Interaction	
	Competitive	Non-competitive	Competitive	Non-competitive	F	sig.	F	sig.	F	sig.
1990 House Mean	**$21,090**	**$4,935**	**$2,417**	**$1,503**	2.10	0.38	1.25	0.46	16.32	0.00
standard deviation	$21,494	$15,323	$5,821	$4,970						
number of candidates	17	30	34	86						
1998 House Mean	**$11,594**	**$700**	**$1,873**	**$1,239**	0.801	0.535	1.263463		4.226	0.04
standard deviation	$34,140	$2,319	$2,361	$3,700						
number of candidates	129	225	22	68						
1990 Senate Mean	**$26,199**	**$1,979**	**$23,802**	**$9,666**	0.28	0.69	14.47	0.16	0.22	0.64
standard deviation	$28,820	$3,500	$44,610	$36,757						
number of candidates	7	8	21	35						
1998 Senate Mean	**$92,212**	**$8,432**	**$28,569**	**$10,708**	0.867	0.523	2.378	0.366	3.857	0.05
standard deviation	$101,215	$24,531	$84,018	$40,550						
number of candidates	4	13	13	51						

wide office, could be given to his or her political party, or could be returned to contributors. But the sixty-four lame ducks in the 1997–98 session and the twenty-one lame ducks in the 1999–2000 session could not use this money to seek reelection in the House. The others, although eligible to run for reelection to the State House, were more than a year away from a political campaign. Therefore, we consider it likely that giving during the annual reporting period is motivated by the prospect that the legislator could provide some sort of service while in office.

As Table 7 indicates, after term limits we found a statistically significant increase in the total amount of money contributed during the year after the election. The mean amount given to representatives during their post-election year rose to $17,540 per representative after term limits, compared to $8,429 before term limits. This was also true for ten of the fifteen categories of contributors. After term limits, only one type of contributor decreased the amount given in the year after the election. The mean amount contributed by public sector unions to each candidate decreased by $66 per representative. This amount was just barely statistically significant. Of the four types of contributors whose post-election year contributions did not differ statistically in a significant way before and after term limits, two—political parties and personal or family resources—would be expected to care more about helping a candidate win election than about exerting influence after the election. Therefore, the lack of statistically significant differences in these two sources of contributions lends further support to the hypothesis that money given to representatives already serving is unlikely to be designed to help elect like-minded representatives.

These results suggest that term limits have not severed the ties between special interests and elected officials. Indeed, if contributions are an indication of these ties, the ties to nine different types of special interests appear stronger than they were before term limits were adopted. These special interests include: corporations, peak trade associations, private sector unions, other elected officials, the caucus and its leaders, ideological groups, lawyers and lobbyists, medical professionals, and the government sector.

Targeting of Post-election Year Contributions

Committee assignments of incumbents are seen as an important factor in interest groups' decisions to make contributions to legislative candidates (Dow, Endrsby, and Menifield 1998; Grier and Munger 1986, 1991, 1993; Gopoian 1984; Endersby and Munger 1992). Gordon and Unmack find this to be especially true for committees that have the authority to regulate or otherwise

Table 7
Mean Post-Election Contributions Before & After Term Limits by Categories of Contributors

	1997–1998 House Session	1999–2000 House Session	F	sig.
Individual	$2,577	$4,651	7.644	0.006
standard deviation	*$5,331*	*$5,786*		
Corporate	$1,520	$2,574	16233	0.000
standard deviation	*$1,763*	*$2,100*		
Peak Trade Assn.	$2,059	$3,766	21.285	0.000
standard deviation	*$2,158*	*$3,226*		
School Associations	$54	$74	0.377	0.540
standard deviation	*$214*	*$254*		
Public Sector Unions	$238	$172	2.809	0.095
standard deviation	*$334*	*$244*		
Private Sector Unions	$237	$433	4.709	0.031
standard deviation	*$510*	*$800*		
Political PACs	$26	$1,465	15.159	0.000
standard deviation	*$90*	*$3,874*		
Leader & Caucus	$104	$1,320	11.097	0.001
standard deviation	*$523*	*$3,791*		
Political Parties	$25	$23	0.02	0.887
standard deviation	*$123*	*$81*		
Personal or Family	$187	$345	0.695	0.406
standard deviation	*$587*	*$1,898*		
Ideological Groups	$66	$145	10.198	0.002
standard deviation	*$165*	*$199*		
Lawyers	$384	$1,036	54.625	0.000
standard deviation	*$414*	*$827*		
Medical	$456	$665	5.139	0.024
standard deviation	*$672*	*$697*		
Agriculture	$7	$10	0.172	0.679
standard deviation	*$47*	*$36*		
Government Sector	$320	$670	17.205	0.000
standard deviation	*$396*	*$793*		
Total Mean Post-election $	$8,429	$17,540	24.59	0.000
standard deviation	*$9,374*	*$17,031*		
Number of Representatives	**110**	**110**		

impact the activities of powerful interests in a state. They call these "juice committees" and found that legislators serving on these committees received large contributions from interest groups that might be affected by the work of these committees. In their study of the California Assembly, they found that transportation, finance and insurance, and agriculture were "juice committees" (1999).

In Michigan, both labor and business are both sizeable donors, although business contributions are more than double those of labor's. Therefore, we identified committees that would deal with issues that would affect both these groups. We followed Gordon and Unmack's choices for many of the committees, expanding the list based on our interviews with representatives to include some that we knew dealt with issues that were of high interest for businesses. Although Gordon and Unmack classify agriculture as a "juice" committee, we excluded it from our list of business "juice" committees. There are two reasons for this. First, we coded agriculture PACs separately from business PACs in our data. Secondly, as a group, these PACs are among the smallest donors in Michigan. The committees we classified as "juice" committees[13] for business were: transportation, energy and technology (1999–2000) or public utilities (1997–1998), insurance, tax policy, great lakes and tourism (1999–2000) or marine affairs and port development (1997–1998), and the corresponding appropriations subcommittees that dealt with these areas. For labor, we classified education, insurance, and training and safety (1999–2000) or labor and occupational safety (1997–1998) as "juice" committees.

These two large, heterogeneous groups of PACs—labor and business—may be able to spread money fairly broadly and may incorporate some groups with conflicting interests. Therefore, we chose two smaller, more homogeneous groups of donors: agriculture and medical professionals. We investigated giving to the Agriculture and Natural Resources committee for the agriculture PACs and to the health policy committees and insurance committees and to the corresponding appropriations subcommittees for the Medical Professionals PACs. This gave us an opportunity to investigate targeting by fairly homogeneous groups of PACs with limited resources.

Further, we were interested in whether giving by the government sector itself (counties, townships, et cetera) was targeted and whether this giving was affected by term limits. We hypothesized that the appropriations committee and committees making decisions about public projects, such as roads and harbors, would handle issues of interest to governmental units.

Most representatives serve on several different committees, often four or more. Therefore, we felt that if we considered each committee separately, we would include among the non-members representatives who served on an-

---

13. Several committees were combined or eliminated when the Republicans assumed control of the House in 1999–2000. We linked committees from the two sessions based on the issues considered by each committee. For example, in 1999–2000 the House Committee on Energy and Technology deregulated telephone service and power companies. These issues were dealt with by the Public Utilities Committee in the 1997–1998 House.

other committee that the interest group might be targeting. To adjust for this problem, we combined members of all of the business "juice" committees into one category. We did the same thing for the representatives who served on any of the labor juice committees. Also we classified all the members of the health policy and insurance committees into a group likely to be targeted by medical professionals—as medical "juice" committees. We combined members of the appropriations committee and the transportation and great lakes or port development committees into a category of government "juice" committees. This still left us with some overlap, however. For example, we discovered that membership in the business "juice" committee-member group had a 0.26 correlation with membership in the labor "juice" committee-member group. Although there was some overlap, we felt that it was small enough that we should be able to discern tendencies of interest groups to target their contributions toward representatives most able to influence policies of concern to the group.

Additionally, we hypothesized that the political party of the representative would influence giving by special interests. For example, we suspected that Business PACs might be more likely to contribute to Republican committee members, while Labor PACs might be more likely to contribute to committee members who were Democrats. Therefore, we felt it would be important to control for the effect of party on giving.

Using analysis of variance we found considerable evidence that interest groups do direct their non-election year giving toward representatives serving on committees handling issues of concern to those interest groups. Further, we found that interest groups tended to target their contributions toward committee members even more after term limits than they did before. Thus, not only were the amounts being given to representatives after the election higher in the post-term limits house, as discussed previously, but the disparity between members of the interest groups' "juice" committees and other representatives was wider in most cases after term limits than it was before.

As Table 8 indicates, members of business "juice" committees received more from business PACs than did non-members during both sessions. This difference was statistically and substantively significant, with "juice" committee members receiving roughly twice the amount that non-members did. Further, we found that the amount given to members and non-members of these committees increased in 1999 to about 1.5 times the amount given in 1997. In 1997 representatives received an average of $3,579 from business PACs in the year after their election. In 1999 this rose to an average of $6,340 per representative. Additionally, partisan control of the chamber was an important factor in business PAC giving after the election. For both sessions, "juice" committee members of the party in control of the chamber, and, hence, in control of the com-

Table 8
Contributions by Different Sectors to Juice and Non-Juice Committees,
by Session and by Party, Michigan Legislature

	Session 1997–1998				Session 1999–2000			
	Republican		Democrat		Republican		Democrat	
	Non-juice	Juice	Non-juice	Juice	Non-juice	Juice	Non-juice	Juice
Business PACs								
mean	$1,864	$3,734	$2,728	$5,223	$5,863	$10,129	$2,849	$4,327
s.d.	$1,726.	$3,907	$1,669	$4,596	$3,122	$5,996	$2,144	$2,404
n	23	31	23	33	19	39	23	29
Labor PACs								
mean	$127	$217	$1,121	$743	$438	$358	$928	$1,076
s.d.	$206	$338	$1,277	$733	$413	$328	$1,311	$1,465
n	26	28	19	37	26	32	28	24
Govt. Sector PACs								
mean	$145	$344	$346	$431	$574	$1,183	$326	$500
s.d.	$233	$441	$306	$480	$459	$1,203	$360	$305
n	28	26	23	33	26	32	29	23
Medical Prof. PACs								
mean	$162	$772	$281	$1,179	$640	$1,221	$346	$637
s.d.	$227	$892	$209	$1,059	$432	$1,070	$472	$528
n	37	17	39	17	36	22	34	18

Table 9
Tests of Between-Subjects Effects for Contributions
from Different Types of Donors

	Business PACs		Labor PACs		Govt. Sector PACs		Medical Prof. PACs	
Source of Effects	F	Sig.	F	Sig.	F	Sig.	F	Sig.
Corrected Model	15.37	0.000	5.20	0.000	8.80	0.000	10.91	0.000
Intercept	304.92	0.000	113.16	0.000	148.34	0.000	230.46	0.000
Session	20.93	0.000	1.58	0.211	17.38	0.000	1.70	0.19
Party	9.45	0.002	33.56	0.000	11.40	0.001	1.05	0.307
Juice Committee	23.12	0.000	0.22	0.639	4.143	0.043	46.57	0.000
Session*Party	28.21	0.000	0.44	0.507	14.88	0.000	16.57	0.000
Session*Committee	0.43	0.51	0.57	0.452	2.49	0.116	3.39	0.067
Party*Committee	1.06	0.31	0.26	0.610	3.04	0.083	0.00	0.99
Session*Party* Committee	2.63	0.11	2.19	0.140	1.03	0.311	2.81	0.095

* bold type indicates statistical significance at the p = 0.10 level or less

mittees, received more money from business PACs. This same pattern affected non-members, too. Thus, representatives who were not on the "juice" committees and not members of the party in control of the chamber received the lowest average amounts of money from business PACs in both 1997 and 1999.

Labor PACs display an entirely different pattern. As shown in Table 9, we found that Labor PACs did not contribute differentially to members and non-members of labor "juice" committees. Instead, Labor PACs contributed to Democrats, regardless of their committee assignments and regardless of the partisan control of the chamber. Although Labor PACs gave more money to representatives in 1999, the average increased from $529 per representative to $679, a mere $150 difference.

From 1997 to 1999, medical professionals increased their giving by a small amount ($219 per representative) that is not quite statistically significantly different (p = 0.15). These results are presented in Table 10. Most of the increase in giving resulted from increased giving to representatives who were not members of committees likely to deal with issues of interest to medical professionals. Even with the narrowing of this differential, medical professionals gave more to members of these committees In 1997, representatives on their "juice" committees received an average of $975 during the year after their election. In 1999 this average declined slightly to $958. Medical professionals gave a mere $223 per representative in 1997 to those not serving on these committees. This average rose to $497 for non-member representatives in 1999. Thus, although medical professionals' giving is still statistically significantly targeted toward members serving on committees handling issues of interest to them, this effect may have diminished somewhat in 1999. Term limits may have reduced this differential. Alternately, it is possible that in 1999 there was an issue before a committee that we did not include in our category of medical issues "juice" committees, an issue that attracted giving from medical professionals. A Representative's political party did not statistically significantly affect giving by medical professionals, so we excluded it from our analyses.

Finally, we found that public sector entities, such as townships or county road commissions, gave in ways that resembled giving by business PACs, but the amounts given were much smaller. This type of contributor gave more to members of committees handling issues affecting them and more to members of the party in control of the chamber, and the amounts given increased from 1997 to 1999. In 1997, Democrats held a majority of the seats in the House, and if they served on committees handling issues of interest to public sector entities, they received an average of $431 from these contributors. Republicans on these same committees received $344, on average. Democrats and Republicans not on these committees received $346 and $145 on average, respectively. In 1999, Republicans controlled the House. In the year after their election, Republicans on committees handling issues of interest to these donors received an average of $1,183, and Democrats on these committees received an average of $500. Republicans and Democrats not on these committees received an average of $574 and $326, respectively. Again we find evidence that interest groups contribute to elected officials who can provide service, and term limits has not eliminated this tendency.

Conclusions

The term limits law in Michigan appears to have affected campaign contributions, but not necessarily in ways that its architects envisioned. Races for seats in the term-limited House are more expensive. If more expensive House races mean that voters are increasingly well informed about candidates and that more voters feel that they have a choice on election day, then increased cost of the elections may be worthwhile. There is some evidence that competition in Michigan has increased since 1990, but the evidence is mixed and the role played by term limits is not clear (Faletta, et al. Forthcoming). Compared to 1990 there were more contested primary elections in 1998, and voter turnout was higher for both primaries and the general election in 1998 than it was in 1990. Further, there were fewer elections won by a landslide margin of victory (20%) in 1998 than there were in 1990. This would seem to suggest that, by increasing the number of open seats and the amount of money spent to fund races, term limits may have contributed to greater competition and voter participation. On the other hand, in 1994 voter turnout was nearly the same as in 1998, and fewer elections were won by landslide margins of victory than in either 1998 or 1990. Therefore, it is difficult at this point to say whether the influx of money and candidates wrought by term limits has increased the competitiveness of elections or the level of participation by voters.

Citizens, including some who supported term limits, might be alarmed to learn of other trends we found. In our previous work we found little evidence that term limits produces a new breed of citizen legislators (Rader, et al. Forthcoming). For example, the greater reliance on the candidates' family resources means that the "citizen" legislators promised by term limits proponents may be wealthier citizens instead of a broad cross-section of the state's citizens. Thus, instead of increasing the "representativeness" of elected representatives, term limits may lead to an increasing upper-class bias among elected officials.

Individual donors gave more money overall to candidates running for the House in 1998, but, as a proportion, their share of the money raised declined. It is not clear what this means in terms of responsiveness of elected officials to their constituents. If the amount of money given is associated with the influence of the group, as is sometimes assumed, then citizens of Michigan may find themselves giving more money for less influence. In our previous work, we found relatively little impact of term limits on responsiveness of legislators to their constituents (Wilson, et al. 2001).

The dramatic increase in the number of candidates is associated with less giving from business PACs to candidates running in open seat elections. This might seem to be a positive effect of term limits. It may be explained by uncertainty about candidates' ideologies, as other scholars have found. The increased targeting of post-election business PAC contributions toward members of "juice" committees is consistent with this explanation. However, the targeting of post-election contributions, as well as the overall increase in these contributions made by business PACs, challenges the positive assessment of term limits' effect on business PAC contributions. It suggests that, after term limits, business PACs may be spending less to help pro-business candidates win election and more to influence key representatives after they are elected.

The advent of term limits is associated with a dramatic increase in giving by chamber caucuses and party leaders. The increasing role of political parties and caucus PACs in funding elections may appeal to some political scientists who advocate a return to the era of strong parties, but some citizens are attracted to elected officials who are more independent. At the very least, citizen legislators were supposed to reflect the views of their constituents more closely. It seems likely that voting the caucus position could conflict with responsiveness to constituents' wishes. Further, in Michigan, with a closely balanced partisan split among the electorate, an increase in partisanship may limit bipartisan compromises that historically balanced strong competing interests in state politics. This finding is consistent with evidence from our interviews that caucus leaders are becoming more powerful and that bipartisanship has declined (Trpovski, et al. 2001).

Finally, we find no evidence that the ties between special interests and legislators have been severed with the advent of a term-limited House. In fact, we find substantial evidence that they are alive and well, and perhaps even stronger than they were without term limits. Under term limits, eleven of the fifteen categories of PACs we analyzed increased their giving to elected officials in the year after the candidate's election. The mean amount received by candidates in the year after their election more than doubled between 1997–1998 and 1999–2000. Further, we find some slight, although mixed, evidence that the targeting of contributions by business PACs and government entities increased between the 1997–1998 and the 1999–2000 sessions. We find evidence that only medical professionals' PACs have spread their giving slightly more broadly, but that they still target their contributions toward candidates who can help them on important issues. We intend to extend this part of our investigation in our ongoing research on term limits.

Term limits may offer other advantages for a state's political institutions and political climate, but in Michigan term limits are no substitute for campaign finance reform. Indeed, we find that they may even make it more important to address problems of funding campaigns.

Note on Estimated Data in Table 1

The problem we faced was that there was some missing data in each year for each chamber. Some of these were missing because candidates filed for waivers that attested that they had not spent more than $2,000 across the primary and general election. Some reports were missing because they may have been lost from the microfiche files we were provided. We did, however, know a number of characteristics of the candidates for whom contribution data were missing. These included their vote totals, their party, whether they were running for an open seat or not, and whether they were running for a competitive seat or not. So we used regression to predict the total contributions for each candidate, using these variables as predictors for all the cases that did have reported contributions. This was done four times—for each session and each chamber. Based upon these equations, we also predicted contributions for the candidates for whom we did not have reports. Adding these together, we had an estimated total contribution for each house. The equations varied by chamber and by election. Given that equations used logs, we had to take the antilogs of the predictions to get our final results.

For the 1990 House the equation was:

Logged Total Contributions=8.079+(0.000092*total vote)+(0.962*Democratic Party dummy).

The R2 was 0.326. All variables in this and the other final equations were significant at least at the 0.05 level.

For the 1990 Senate the equation was:

Logged Total Contributions=9.591+(0.00003782*total vote)+(−0.615*Democratic Party dummy)+(0.706*competitive race dummy). The R2 was 0.459.

For the 1998 House the equation was:

Logged Total Contributions=8.059+(0.0001005*total vote)+(−0.278*Democratic Party dummy)+(0.249*competitive race dummy)+(0.469*open seat dummy). The R2 was 0.379.

For the 1998 Senate the equation was:

Logged Total Contributions=9.493+(0.00003643*total vote)+(−1.019*Democratic Party dummy). The R2 was 0.351.

References

Anderson, Patrick L. Papers. 1992. State Archives of Michigan. Department of State. Bureau of History. Lansing, MI.

Campbell, Donald T., and Julian C. Stanley. 1963. *Experimental and quasi-experimental designs for research*. Boston: Houghton Mifflin.

Common Cause.1997a. Casino contributions prohibited. Retrieved [November 20, 2001]: http://commoncause.org/states/michigan/release1.htm.

———. 1997b. Editorial memorandum: Michigan's gubernatorial public funding in jeopardy; former governors, common cause and league of women voters urge taxpayers to use check-off. Retrieved [November 19, 2001]: http://commoncause.org/states/michigan/release1.htm.

Detroit Free Press. 1992a. Term limits: They may be legal, but they would be a mistake. *Detroit Free Press*, 17 March, 12A.

———. 1992b. Term limits: Proposal B would weaken your vote and the state. *Detroit Free Press*, 14 October, 8A

Dow, Jay K., James Enderby, and Charles E. Menifield. 1998. The industrial structure of the California assembly: Committee assignments, economic interests, and campaign contributions. *Public Choice 94*; 67–83.

Eismeier, Theodore J., and Philip H. Pollock III. 1986. Strategy and choice in congressional elections: The role of political action committees. *American Journal of Political Science 30*:197–21.

Endersby, James W., and Michael C. Munger. 1992. The impact of legislator attributes on union PAC campaign contributions. *Journal of Labor Research* 13: 79–97.

Faletta, J.P., Charles D. Elder, Marjorie Sarbaugh-Thompson, Mary Herring, Eric Rader, and Shannon Orr, with Stanley Caress. Forthcoming. Term limits effects on the electoral environment and composition of the California state Assembly and Michigan state House of Representatives. *The American Review of Political Science.*

Francis, W. L. 1985. Leadership, party caucuses, and committees in U. S. state legislatures. *Legislative Studies Quarterly* 102: 243–257.

Gaddie, R.K., and C. S. Bullock, III. 2000. *Elections to open seats in the U. S. House.* Lanham, MD: Rowman and Littlefield Publishers, Inc.

Gierzynski, Anthony. 1998. A framework for the study of campaign finance. In *Campaign finance in state legislative elections*, edited by Joel Thompson and Gary Moncrief. Washington, DC: Congressional Quarterly Press.

———, and David A. Breaux. 1998. The financing role of parties. In *Campaign finance in state legislative elections*, edited by Joel Thompson and Gary Moncrief. Washington, DC: Congressional Quarterly Press.

Gopoian, J. David. 1984. What makes PACs tick? An analysis of the allocation patterns of economic interest groups. *American Journal of Political Science* 30:197–213.

Gongwer Reports. 1992. Gongwer News Service, Inc. Lansing, MI. May 4, p. 2.

Gordon, Stacy B., and Cynthia L. Unmack. 1999. The effect of term limits on PAC allocation patterns: The more things change....Paper prepared for delivery at the Midwest Political Science Association, 57th Annual Meeting, 14–17 April, Chicago, Illinois.

Grier, Kevin B., and Michael C. Munger. 1986. The impact of legislator attributes on interest group campaign contributions. *Journal of Labor Research* 7: 349–361.

———. 1991. Committee assignments, constituent preferences, and campaign contributions. *Economic Inquiry* 29:24–43.

———. 1993. Comparing interest group PAC contributions to House and Senate incumbents, 1980–1986. *Journal of Politics* 55: 615–643.

Hamm, K.E., R.D. Hedlund, and N. Martorano. 1999. The evolution of committee structure, powers and procedures in twentieth century state legislatures. Paper presented at the Annual Meeting of the American Political Science Association, Atlanta, GA., 1–5 September.

Headlee, Richard. 1992. Proposal B—yes: Term limits will end gridlock, sleaze. *Detroit Free Press*, 12 October, 7A.

Hogan, Robert E. 2000. The costs of representation in state legislatures: Explaining variations in campaign spending. *Social Science Quarterly* 81 (4): 941–956.

Marckini, Lisa, John Strate, and Eric Rader. 1999. Term limits and campaign contributions in the Michigan house of representatives. Paper presented at the annual meeting of the American Political Science Association, Atlanta, GA., 1–5 September.

Michigan Campaign Finance Network. 2001a. Campaign finance talk. Michigan Campaign Finance Network: Lansing. MI.

———. 2001b. *More money, less disclosure.* Michigan Campaign Finance Network: Lansing, MI.

Mitchell, Cleta. 1991. Term limits? Yes! *Extensions.* Norman, OK: Carl Albert Research Center.

Niven, David. 2000. Revolutionary headlines: Media coverage of legislative term limits. Paper presented at the Coping with Term Limits Conference, 12–13 April, Columbus, OH.

Orr, Shannon, Eric Rader, Jean-Philippe Faletta, Marjorie Sarbaugh-Thompson, Charles Elder, Lyke Thompson, John Strate, and Richard Elling, 2001. A naturally occurring quasi-experiment in the states: research on term limits in Michigan. *State Politics and Policy Quarterly* 1: 433–445.

Porter, H. Owen, 1974. Legislative experts and outsiders: The two-step flow of communication. *Journal of Politics* 36: 703–730.

Rader, Eric, Charles D. Elder, and Richard Elling. Forthcoming. Motivations and behaviors of the "new breed" of term limited legislators. *The American Review of Political Science.*

Squire, Peverill. 1992. Legislative professionalization and membership diversity in state legislatures. *Legislative Studies Quarterly* 17: 69–79.

Thompson, Joel A., and William E. Cassie. 1992. Party and PAC contributions to North Carolina state legislative candidates. *Legislative Studies Quarterly* 17: 409–416.

———, and Malcolm Jewell.1994. A sacred cow or just a lot of bull? Party and pac money in state legislative elections. *Political Research Quarterly* 47: 223–237.

Thompson, L., Richard Elling, John Strate, Eric Rader, and Lisa Marckini. 2001. Term limits and campaign contributions in the Michigan legislature. Paper prepared for delivery at the Annual Meeting of the Midwest Political Science Association, Chicago, 19–22 April.

Tingwall, John. 1974. "Common Cause Hits Campaign Reform Bill." *Michigan State News*, 26 September.

Trpovski, Jovan, Marjorie Sarbaugh-Thompson, and John Strate. 2001. Conflict and control in committees in a term limited legislature. Paper delivered at the 2001 Annual Meetings of the American Political Science Association, San Francisco, CA, 30 August–2 September.

Wilson, Chris, Charles D. Elder, Lyke Thompson, and Richard Elling. 2001. Term limited legislators' responsiveness to constituents: The case of the Michigan House of Representatives. Paper delivered at the 2001 Annual Meetings of the American Political Science Association, San Francisco, CA, 30 August–2 September.

CHAPTER 12

FOOL'S GOLD: PARTY POLITICS AND CAMPAIGN FINANCING IN CALIFORNIA

Craig B. Holman

California's political campaigns for state office have long been the most costly in the nation. The state is geographically spread out, the population vast and the media markets expensive. It is no wonder that California state campaigns are expensive affairs.

However, these factors cannot account for the degree of rising campaign costs in the state. Each election cycle witnesses new records in campaign spending, far above the rate of inflation. Candidates, committees, and party organizations have become nothing short of obsessed with the money chase, convinced that political fortune lies in their pocketbooks. The campaign industry of consultants, pollsters, and media buyers know how to spend that money and have reaped record profits. And, home to much of the nation's wealth, some financial contributors seem willing to satisfy the fund-raising frenzy.

But not the voters. Californians have grown increasingly cynical with state government and downright angry with the flow of money into politics. Turning to ballot initiatives to get what the legislature has refused—to provide caps on money in politics—voters have approved three campaign finance reform measures in just a decade prior to 1998, only to have each one challenged by the parties and others, and thrown out by the federal courts.

Finally, in November 2000, Californians approved another campaign finance measure that few seem interested in challenging in court. In fact, some of the same persons who had been suing against reform over the last decade wrote and financed the campaign for the new measure. Proposition 34, the campaign finance reform measure approved by voters in the 2000 general election, gives California its first-ever contribution limits to candidates, but places virtually no cap on campaign fund raising and spending by the parties.

This chapter charts the rising patterns of campaign contributions and expenditures in California state elections and offers an assessment of the impact of Proposition 34 on campaign financing. In assessing campaign finance activity in California, this chapter first examines the trials and tribulations of the campaign finance reform movement through the state's history. The historical analysis is followed by a description of the current regulatory regime. Campaign financial activity in state elections is then documented from the 1980s to the 2000 election cycle, and the likely impact of California's new regulatory regime on this financial activity is evaluated.

History of Campaign Finance Reform in California

With Congress unwilling or unable to fix the federal campaign finance law, the campaign finance reform movement has largely turned to the states as laboratories of reform to promulgate and test new campaign finance programs. A wide array of reform experiments have emerged at the state level in recent decades, most of which have been challenged by opponents of reform in the courts under the constraints of the *Buckley* decision. Some lower federal courts have expanded the constraints against reform far beyond what was expressed by the U.S. Supreme Court, causing additional problems for meaningful campaign finance laws at the state level.

Such lower court rulings have weighed especially heavily on California. Ironically, for a state that has repeatedly developed and approved some of the nation's most innovative campaign finance laws, California, until recently, was one of only seven states that had no limits at all on money in politics.[1] But this was not for want of trying to regulate money in politics.

100 Years of Trying

After more than 100 years, California's efforts to remedy the problems of excessive money in politics have all been in vain. The problems that demanded the first attempts at reform remain common in today's politics, only worse. For example, the state's very first campaign finance law—the Piece Clubs Act

---

1. The seven states that had no limits on corporate, union, PAC or individual contributions and expenditures in campaigns as late as 1998 were: California, Colorado, Idaho, Illinois, New Mexico, Utah, and Virginia.

of 1878—was approved by the California legislature in response to allegations of extortion of public officials by special interest groups in the City of San Francisco in exchange for endorsements. Today, newspaper stories as well as FBI sting operations have documented public officials extorting money from special interest groups in exchange for legislation. In 1893 the legislature banned transfers of funds and limited expenditures. Today, the legislature again acted to limit contributions and expenditures by gaining voter approval of Proposition 34. But even with this act in place, campaign fund raising continues to break all previous records, assisted in part by a governor who has been raising a million dollars a month since assuming office. California's track-record over the last century can much more accurately be called *deform* than *reform*.

Concern over the corrupting influence of money in politics in California began with its founding in 1849. Unlike the U.S. Constitution, the California Constitution specifically prohibits bribery in elections. Less than thirty years later, the legislature approved the first campaign finance law, the Piece Clubs Act noted above, which applied only to San Francisco. Between 1890 and 1893 the movement to regulate the flow of money in California politics gained unusual momentum with innovative programs.

The Purity of Elections Act of 1893, modeled on the British Corrupt and Illegal Practices Act, included several innovative campaign finance restrictions which had no precedents in the United States. The Purity of Elections Act established expenditure ceilings for state candidates based on a percentage of the salary for the office sought. A candidate for a two-year legislative term, for example, could not spend more than 10% of the salary for that office on the campaign. A candidate for a four-year term could not spend more than 20% of the salary for the office sought. Inter-candidate transfers were prohibited. Campaign money had to be spent for campaign purposes. Independent expenditures were prohibited. Candidates had to appoint a campaign committee as a depository of all campaign funds, and the committee had to file sworn statements of all contributors to the campaign (although not the amounts contributed). Failure to comply with the law could result in forfeiture of office.

California's Purity of Elections Law was one of the nation's most thorough and stringent campaign finance laws on the books. Three years after passage, however, the courts began to weaken the law. Predating the U.S. Supreme Court's *Newberry* decision, the California Supreme Court ruled that parties are "a law unto themselves" and thus nothing in the Act could apply to primary elections, but could only apply to general elections [*People v. Cavanaugh*, 112 Cal. 674 (1896)]. The legislature swiftly responded by approving the Purity of Primary Elections Act of 1897, noting that party committees had become the primary instruments of corruption in American politics and were most in need of the regulatory framework that applied to other elections and committees. The state court reacted in turn and declared the new law unconstitutional, because the title of the Act was misleading and because a special oath required of voters was unlawful [*Spier v. Baker*, 120 Cal. 370 (1898)].

In 1901, the California Supreme Court leveled the final blow against the Purity in Elections Act with two subsequent rulings. Both rulings affected Mayor-Elect George Clark of San Francisco. Clark had declined to file a sworn statement listing his contributors and filed some erroneous statements of expenditures. In the first case, the court ruled that an affidavit requirement created an unconstitutional oath of office [*Bradley v. Clark*, 133 Cal. 196 (1901)]. In the second case, the court ruled that a discrepancy of $22 in Clark's expenditure filings was too trivial to punish [*Land v. Clark*, 132 Cal. 673 (1901)].

Although these rulings seemed to be based on rather minor circumstances, the ramifications were far from trivial. Elections officials perceived the court as hostile to the campaign finance reform law and thus decided to cease enforcing its requirements. Ironically, the lawyer responsible for undoing the Act in favor of the parties was Hiram Johnson, a lawyer who later would usher in the Progressive reform movement in California when he was elected governor in 1910.

Hiram Johnson's election in 1910 brought with it a series of political reforms unrelated to campaign finance, but which had a dramatic effect on corrupt party politics in the state. The initiative, referendum, and recall reforms, called "freak legislation" by the *New York Times*, were ratified by the Progressive-dominated legislature the following year, and citizens were granted the power to ratify legislation directly, with or without the support of the parties or legislature. Two years later, the Progressive-dominated legislature also passed the Direct Primary Act of 1913, which established a primary system and some reporting requirements for candidates (although not committees).

Nevertheless, campaign finance reporting remained very spotty. And, even though spending limits were still on the books from the 1893 Purity of Elections Act, none of these requirements were enforced. In fact, no action had been taken for a campaign violation in fifty years, so the spending limits were eliminated by the legislature in 1949. In 1953, an Assembly committee reported that the disclosure requirement still on the statute books was "so defective that it is worthless as an instrument for achieving fair and honest elections in the state"(Comment 1953).

Lobbyist Artie Samish and the Art of Influence

In the 1930s, lobbying the California legislature reached new heights with tactics fine-tuned by one lobbyist in particular: Artie Samish. Samish learned that legislators could be more easily influenced by campaign contributions than by logic and persuasion. Rather than giving oratorical presentations before legislative committees, Samish organized a solid base of campaign contributors and began bankrolling legislative campaigns, much in the same style that had been perfected by the parties earlier. The clients Samish came to represent, and solicited funds from, included the liquor industry, tobacco industry, railroads, banks, and gambling, to name a few. As legislators grateful for Samish's assistance rose to committee leadership positions, Samish's power became so great that he could claim without much exaggeration to be the "secret boss" of California politics. Samish once boasted: "I'm the governor of the legislature. To hell with the governor of the state" (Farrelly and Hinderaker 1951). Then-Governor Earl Warren agreed: "[O]n matters that affect his clients, Artie unquestionably has more power than the governor" (Velie 1949).

Samish's downfall was his own doing. He loved boasting of his money and his power over the legislature. In one fateful interview, Samish posed with a dummy sitting on his lap named "Mr. Legislature." Embarrassed by the truth being made public, the legislature responded by removing Samish from the roster of lobbyists and banned him from appearing before the legislature ever again.[2] Two years later, Samish was convicted of tax evasion and sentenced to federal prison.

Following the departure of Samish, Governor Warren called a special session of the legislature and induced it to pass the 1949 Collier Act. The law required lobbyists to register and report their expenditures, although lobbyists filed with a legislative committee rather than an independent watchdog agency. Disclosure by candidates continued to be lax under the old 1893 legislation. This was the last of campaign finance reform legislation in California, until the 1974 gubernatorial candidacy of Jerry Brown.

Beginning in the mid-1970s, citizens of California realized that meaningful campaign finance reform no longer could be achieved through the legislature. The early reform zealotry of the 1890s legislature had long since vanished, and legislators since the 1930s had grown dependent on campaign money and enjoyed the incumbency advantage of securing large campaign war chests.

2. Sen. Con. Res. 11, Cal. Stats. Extra Sess. 1949, ch. 33, p. 248.

In 1973, Jerry Brown decided to run for governor but felt he needed a campaign edge. Brown decided to sponsor a comprehensive campaign finance reform initiative for the 1974 primary election ballot. When it became apparent to the legislature that Brown's initiative, the Political Reform Act of 1974, was likely to qualify for the ballot, the legislature decided to pass its own disclosure bill to undercut popular support for comprehensive reform. It passed the Waxman-Dymally Campaign Disclosure Act, requiring disclosure of campaign finances, and the Moscone Governmental Conflicts of Interest Act, requiring recusal of public officials from decisions bearing potential conflicts of interest. Both measures were largely taken from provisions of the initiative. Despite the last-minute passage of the legislative measures, the Political Reform Act appeared on the June ballot as Proposition 9 and easily won approval with 70% of the popular vote. Jerry Brown was elected governor later that year.

Proposition 9 was primarily a comprehensive disclosure measure. It also permitted local jurisdictions to develop their own campaign finance programs independent of the state. Many of its proponents believed thorough disclosure would shock the public and lead to other measures by the legislature to reduce the role of money in politics. Others believed that disclosure would serve as a "disinfectant" against corruption and shame politicians into self-regulating their contributions and expenditures. But, similar to the experience with the Publicity Acts at the federal level, none of this happened. It simply reaffirmed the public's suspicions that special interest groups make large contributions to office holders in an effort to gain access or favor, that large contributions are made to incumbent office holders of any and all parties and political persuasions, and that incumbents enjoy a huge campaign cash advantage over challengers.

The California legislature did not seriously visit the harder questions of contribution and spending limits for almost a decade after the adoption of the Political Reform Act. In 1982, Assembly Speaker Willie Brown introduced a comprehensive reform program which included public financing of legislative races. In his early years as Speaker of the Assembly, Brown had made campaign finance reform one of his major causes. The Assembly passed the far reaching measure (AB 3187), but it was quickly killed after receiving only one vote in its first Senate committee hearing. There were a few other campaign reform bills bandied about in the halls of the legislature in subsequent years, but all of these bills perished in committees.

In 1983, Republican Ross Johnson introduced AB 1751, which called for limits on contributions and expenditures and provided some public financing as a means to encourage candidates to abide by the spending limits. The measure was swiftly defeated by the Senate. But Johnson did not give up so easily. He solicited money from supporters, chipped in $58,000 of his own money, and issued a loan from his own campaign funds to mount an initiative drive. In May 1984, Johnson startled the political establishment when he qualified his measure as an initiative for the ballot, designated Proposition 40.[3]

Proposition 40 would have limited contributions from individuals, political action committees and parties to $1,000 each per fiscal year for state candidates. Corporations and unions would have been prohibited from making direct contributions to candidates. Contributions to independent expenditure committees would have been restricted to $250 per year. Candidates would have been permitted to collect funds for only one campaign at a time and could not carry over campaign funds for future elections, even those funds collected prior to ratification of the initiative. The measure also would have established a $1 million public fund to provide matching public financing to opponents of candidates using personal wealth in their campaigns.

Later that summer, the Fair Political Practices Commission (FPPC)—the governmental agency established by the Political Reform Act to monitor and disclose campaign finances—issued a 400-page report which was mostly unfavorable toward the initiative. The report predicted that the measure would have reduced campaign spending by 64% but would favor incumbents and harm challengers. Much of California's reform community, including Common Cause, agreed with the conclusions of the FPPC and opposed Proposition 40. Common Cause also believed that the amount of public financing was far too little to provide much of an impact. For example, a single Assembly candidate who spent a small fortune of his own personal wealth to win office in 1982, Tom Hayden, would have broken the bank. Common Cause was also hoping to run a much more comprehensive public financing program in the next few years and thought that passage of Proposition 40 would slow momentum for additional reforms.

By the time the election rolled around, Proposition 40 had almost no backing except for the author himself. Common Cause joined the Chamber of Commerce and the political parties in opposing the measure. Johnson was unable to encourage even other members of the legislature to support the measure. Most of the state's newspapers editorialized against Proposition 40. It was soundly defeated at the polls, with only 34% of voters favoring the initiative.

Contemporary Reform Efforts

Four years later, Common Cause and the League of Women Voters did indeed qualify a comprehensive public financing initiative for the June 1988 bal-

---

3. Ross Johnson, who is now in the California Senate, no longer supports the idea of public financing of campaigns.

lot. Known as Proposition 68, the measure would have limited contributions to $1,000 per election for individuals, and $2,500 for PACs and parties. It would have established voluntary spending ceilings and provided extensive partial public financing of legislative campaigns, matching small private contributions of $250 or less.

But Proposition 68 was not alone on the ballot. Ross Johnson, along with Senators Joseph Montoya and Quentin Kopp,[4] sponsored another competing initiative, Proposition 73, which qualified for the same ballot. Proposition 73 contained many of the same elements of Johnson's earlier measure, except that Proposition 73 specifically prohibited any public financing of campaigns.

Californians were so eager for comprehensive campaign finance reform that voters approved both measures. Proposition 68 garnered 52.8% approval in the election, while Proposition 73 received 58.0% of the vote. Since the contradictory measures were approved at the same election, the California Supreme Court ruled that Proposition 73 took precedence because it received more votes [*Taxpayers to Limit Campaign Spending v. FPPC*, 51 Cal. 3d 744 (1990)]. However, a federal district court, and later a federal appellate court, invalidated almost all of Proposition 73 because its contribution limits were based on a fiscal year rather than a calendar year or an election [*SEIU v. FPPC*, 747 F.Supp. 580 (1990); and *SEIU v. FPPC*, 955 F.2d 1312 (1990); denied, 505 U.S. 1230]. An effort by Johnson to encourage the California Supreme Court to "judicially reform" Proposition 73 by changing the per-fiscal-year provision to a per-calendar-year provision was rejected by the court [*Kopp v. FPPC*, 11 Cal. 4th 607 (1995)]. All that was left of Proposition 73 under Judge Lawrence Karlton was the provision prohibiting any public financing of campaigns (California Government Code Section 85300) and the contribution limits only for special elections which are unaffected by the fiscal year fund-raising period. Proponents of Proposition 68 appealed to the state Supreme Court to re-validate the stronger measure, since Proposition 73 was dismissed almost in total, but the court refused to do so by a vote of 4-to-3 [*Gerken v. FPPC*, 6 Cal. 4th 707 (1993)].

A later court ruling determined that the prohibition against public financing of campaigns applies to all state and county campaigns and general law city campaigns. However, a charter city possesses the authority by virtue of its charter to provide public financing of city campaigns [*Bradley v. Johnson*, 4 Cal. 4th 389 (1992)]. The cities of Long Beach, Los Angeles, Oakland, and San Francisco provide partial public financing of local elections.

---

4. Several years later, Senator Montoya was convicted of corruption charges and served time in federal prison.

Subsequent citizens' initiatives have attempted over and over again to modify the state's campaign finance system. Four statewide initiatives were presented to voters: Proposition 131 in 1990, Propositions 208 and 212 on the same ballot in 1996, and Proposition 25 on the March 2000 ballot.[5] Of these, only Proposition 208 was ratified by voters, overwhelmingly supported by 61.3% of them.

Proposition 208 and the Legislature's "Secret Deal"

Proposition 208, approved by voters in 1996, proposed contribution limits ranging from $250 up to $1,000 per election for state candidates and lower contribution limits for local candidates. Proposition 208 went into effect in 1997 and effectively shut down all campaign solicitations in the state due to its fund-raising period in which candidates were prohibited from raising funds until one year before the election for statewide campaigns and six months prior to all other campaigns. The California Pro-life Council, the Democratic and Republican parties, the state labor unions, and state mailer firms all filed suits against Proposition 208. Although these disparate groups were based all over the state, from San Diego to San Francisco, they all filed in Judge Lawrence Karlton's Sacramento court, the same court with history of invalidating campaign finance laws. On January 6, 1998, Judge Karlton suspended the law with a "preliminary injunction" following a three-week trial [*California Prolife Council v. Scully*, 989 F. Supp. 1282 (1998)]. The Ninth Circuit Court of Appeals ordered that Karlton conduct another trial and issue a final

---

5. Proposition 131 was a far-reaching hodgepodge initiative that included everything from term limits to ethics laws and campaign finance reform. It was sponsored by Attorney General John Van De Kamp, who was trying to use the issue to further his gubernatorial bid. The 14,000-word tome proved too much for voters to understand and thus was rejected at the polls (along with Van De Kamp's bid for governor). Proposition 212, on the same ballot as Proposition 208, would have imposed strict $100 contribution limits, but was also rejected by voters largely because the measure contained a drafting error which would have accidentally deleted the state's ethics laws.

Sponsored by millionaire Ron Unz, Proposition 25 proposed extremely high contribution limits of $3,000 for legislative candidates, $5,000 for statewide candidates, and aggregate contribution limits of how much any one person can give to all state candidates to $50,000 per election. Bowing to pressure from Republican party leaders, Unz also drafted a soft money loophole into the measure to allow unlimited contributions to party committees used for non-candidate media advertising and party-building activities. The reform community split on this measure, with Common Cause supporting it as "better than nothing," and the League of Women Voters opposing its high contribution limits and soft money loophole. Proposition 25 was rejected by voters in every county of the state.

ruling on a timely basis [*California Prolife Council v. Scully*, 164 F.3d 1189 (1999)].

Few expected Karlton to uphold the law. Proponents of Proposition 208 desired a quick final ruling from Karlton so that they could appeal to the Ninth Circuit. When, after three years, it appeared that a ruling was finally forthcoming, opponents of the measure pursued an additional tack.

An unofficial survey of the lawyers suing against Proposition 208 by a Republican legislative consultant found that the lawyers believed the Ninth Circuit Court of Appeals might eventually reinstate the law.[6] Consequently, one of the lawyers for the Democratic party drafted an alternative measure that would specifically revoke Proposition 208. Since the measure would have to be approved by voters in order to supersede Proposition 208, it contained a set of more lenient campaign finance limitations and was offered as a reform measure.

The twenty-eight-page alternative measure was substituted for a bill (SB 1223) that had already been ratified by both houses of the legislature and was in conference committee. It was first released to the public at 1:55 on the morning of the conference committee hearing and was ratified by the committee eight hours later in a fifteen-minute session with no opportunity for public comment.[7] On July 7, 2000, the Governor signed the bill with reservations stating, in part: "This bill was devised largely in secret, without input from the public or knowledgeable sources" (Matthews 2000). The bill was then placed on the next statewide ballot for voter approval as Proposition 34.

Since the measure was a legislative measure, the presiding officer of the senate—the author of SB 1223—was empowered to select who would write the arguments for and against the measure for publication in the state ballot pamphlet. Although universally opposed by the campaign finance reform community,[8] the presiding officer chose another legislator to represent the oppo-

---

6. The Assembly Republican caucus bill analysis of SB 1223 began on the first page, noting that previous votes on the measure were irrelevant because "this is a totally new bill," followed with: "NOTE: This consultant has polled all three appellate attorneys (Democrat and Republican) handling the Prop. 208 case, and they are unanimous in their opinion that Proposition 208 will eventually be put back in place by the courts." Jack Wells, Policy Consultant, Assembly Republican Bill Analysis, "SB 1223," Elections, Reapportionment and Constitutional Amendments Committee (5 July 2000). On file with the author.

7. Although the chair of the committee and sponsor of the bill, Sen. John Burton, insisted that members of the public could have disrupted the committee vote, if the public really felt concerned about the issue.

8. The "reform community" as defined here was represented by California Common Cause, the League of Women Voters, AARP, CalPIRG, Americans for Democratic Action, Californians for Political Reform and others.

sition in the ballot pamphlet.[9] Consequently, the official opposition argument published in the ballot pamphlet urged voters to vote against Proposition 34 because it is "…a scheme to limit the amount of money that can be spent by candidates for State office"—a seemingly specious argument that prompted an unsuccessful lawsuit by the reform community to replace the official opposition.[10] The attorney general's summary of the measure in the ballot pamphlet neglected to mention that it would repeal Proposition 208. On November 7, 2000, voters approved the measure, casting Proposition 34 as the state's current campaign finance regulatory regime.

Proposition 34's Regulatory Regime

Proposition 34 establishes California's regulatory regime for campaign financing as of 2001. In a concession to Governor Gray Davis, the contribution limits affecting gubernatorial races do not kick in until after the 2002 gubernatorial election. The key elements of this new regime include:

- Repealing the contribution limits and spending ceilings of Proposition 208.
- Creating higher contribution limits in its place for individuals, ranging from $3,000 per election to legislative candidates to $20,000 per election to gubernatorial candidates.
- Restricting contribution limits to and from party committees to apply only to funds used for direct contributions to candidates. Funds used for party expenditures in support or opposition to candidates or any other party activity are not limited.
- Setting higher voluntary spending ceilings, with the primary incentive to agree to the ceilings being a notation of participating candidates in the state ballot pamphlet.
- Disclosing the sources of issue ads costing $50,000 or more that clearly identify a candidate for state office within forty-five days of an election but that avoid using the "magic words" of "express advocacy."

In addition to lifting the strict contribution limits and spending ceilings of Proposition 208, the primary objective of Proposition 34 is to cast political

---

9. According to California law, the presiding officer of the senate must select a legislator who voted "no" on the bill to write the official opposition argument for the ballot pamphlet [California Elections Code Section 9042]. The official opposition argument was drafted by Senator Bill Morrow and Assembly Member Brett Granlund.

10. *Greenlee v. Jones.* 2000. Sacramento Superior Court. Unpublished. 1 August.

parties as central players in the campaign finance game. Unlike other entities, political parties may make unlimited contributions to candidates and receive substantial funds from any entity for that purpose. Parties may also receive unlimited contributions from any entity to use for party expenditures for or against candidates or for party-building activities.

At the same time, Proposition 34 sets contribution limits from other persons to candidates at comfortably high levels, accommodating most contributors. The contribution limits established under Proposition 34 are among the highest in the nation. Even the lowest contribution limit of $3,000 per election for legislative candidates is three times the limit imposed upon federal candidates by the Federal Election Campaign Act (FECA).

As shown in Figure One, Proposition 34's regulatory regime is considerably looser than that of Proposition 208, but nevertheless brings California out of the category of the few states with no limits on campaign finance. Transfers between candidates are limited to $3,000 per election, and a system of voluntary spending ceilings is offered. The spending ceiling program, however, lacks an effective incentive to encourage candidates to abide by the ceilings. No public funds are offered for participation in the program. The primary incentive is a notice in the state ballot pamphlet in which candidates agree to limit their expenditures.

Proposition 34 also imposes some interesting disclosure requirements. One such provision addresses the newly-emerging problem associated with issue advocacy. In its 1976 landmark decision, *Buckley v. Valeo,* 424 U.S. 1 (1976), the U.S. Supreme Court attempted to devise a test to distinguish issue advocacy (political speech that is not designed to influence candidate elections) from express advocacy (political speech designed to promote the election or defeat of candidates), the latter of which is subject to campaign finance laws and regulations. Without any substantive evidence, the court explained in footnote 52 that campaign ads could be distinguished from issue ads by the use of such words as "vote for," "elect," or "vote against." In what has since become known as the "magic words" test, most federal and state campaign finance laws are interpreted by the courts and elections agencies to apply this standard in determining which ads are subject to regulation and which are not.

The practical result of the magic words test has been to exempt most advertisements sponsored by independent groups in federal and state elections from campaign finance laws. A comprehensive study of the content of political television commercials in the 2000 federal elections found that few campaign advertisements employ the magic words (Holman and McLoughlin 2002). Campaign ads simply are more persuasive by not blatantly proclaiming, "Vote for me!" The federal study found that almost 90% of all candidate ads did not use any of the magic words of express advocacy.

Figure One
Key Changes Made by Proposition 34

	Political Reform Act of 1974	Proposition 208	Proposition 34
Contribution Limits per Election by Individuals			
Legislative	No Limits	$250*	$3,000
Statewide	No Limits	$500	$5,000
Governor	No Limits	$500	$20,000
Contribution Limits per Election FROM Political Parties			
Legislative	No Limits	25% of Spending Ceiling	No Limits
Statewide	No Limits	25% of Spending Ceiling	No Limits
Governor	No Limits	25% of Spending Ceiling	No Limits
Contribution Limits per Year TO Political Parties			
Per Person	No Limits	$500	$25,000 for purpose of candidate contributions; no limits otherwise
Contribution Limits per Year to PACs			
Per Person	No Limits	$500	$5,000 for purpose of candidate contributions; no limits otherwise
Limits on Transfers per Election Between Candidates/Legislative Caucuses			
Per Candidate	No Limits	Prohibited	$3,000
Voluntary Spending Ceilings			
Assembly			
Primary	No Limits	$100,000	$400,000
General	No Limits	$200,000	$700,000
Senate			
Primary	No Limits	$200,000	$600,000
General	No Limits	$400,000	$900,000
Governor			
Primary	No Limits	$4,000,000	$6,000,000
General	No Limits	$8,000,000	$10,000,000

More troublesome is the application of the magic words test to party-sponsored and group-sponsored ads. While all candidate-sponsored ads are assumed to be campaign ads and thus are subject to regulation whether or not the magic words are used, such is not the case with non-candidate-sponsored ads. Most federal and state jurisdictions will exempt party- and group-sponsored ads from campaign finance laws if they do not use the magic words. Consequently, as found in the study of the 2000 federal elections, about 98% of party and group television ads in 2000 fell outside the laws (Holman and McLoughlin 2002).

Proposition 34 in California state elections, like the McCain-Feingold bill in federal elections, changes the standard for defining express advocacy for purposes of disclosure. Instead of the magic words test, it applies a forty-five-day bright-line test in which any advertisement costing $50,000 or more that mentions a candidate within forty-five days of an election is classified as electioneering in nature and the sponsors must disclose their funding sources. This particular provision of Proposition 34 requires that the disclosure be done via the Internet onto the Secretary of State's Web site within forty-eight hours of paying for the ad.[11]

Another innovative disclosure provision of Proposition 34 involves paid spokespersons. This provision arose from a 1998 campaign against a ballot measure. A grass-roots consumer organization attempted to take on California's utility industry by qualifying an initiative to the ballot (Proposition 9) that called for a 20% cut in electricity rates and an end to surcharges levied on ratepayers to pay for costly nuclear power plants. The utility companies rallied to oppose the measure, amassing a $40 million campaign war chest—twenty times more than the campaign budget gathered by proponents of the measure. In the course of the campaign, the public was surprised to see that the utilities' leading spokesperson in television commercials against Proposition 9 was David Horowitz, a well-known consumer activist in charge of a rabble-rousing consumer group called "Fight Back!" It was learned only after the filing of campaign finance reports that Horowitz' group was paid $106,000 by the utility industry to become their on-air spokesperson against Proposition 9 (Shuit 1998). The measure went down in defeat and became the third most expensive initiative campaign in California's history, with nearly all of the expenditures from the "no" side.

Proposition 34 now requires that any person who appears in an advertisement for or against a ballot measure who is paid $5,000 or more for the appearance shall immediately disclose that payment. A notice must be included in the ad itself, stating that the spokesperson is being paid for the endorsement.[12]

While several provisions of California's new campaign finance regulatory regime have enhanced disclosure requirements, this is not the case when it comes to party activities. Like many other states, Proposition 34 exempts internal membership communications from the campaign finance law. Unions, for example, may send out a union newsletter to their members endorsing particular candidates or ballot measures without being subject to contribution limits or disclosure requirements. Unlike other states, however, Proposition 34 applies this exemption to party communications—in essence allowing parties to disseminate campaign advertisements to anyone in the state who declared a

11. California Government Code Section 85310.
12. California Government Code Section 84511.

similar party affiliation without being subject to campaign finance laws. In the case of California, nearly 80% of the state's registered voters have declared party allegiances (Barone and Ujifusa 1995). Although the parties have to target the dissemination of their "member communications" through direct mailings and the like, this is a huge free ride for party electioneering activity.

The member communications exemption has become a focal point of conflict between state elections administrators and local officials. In California, local jurisdictions may establish their own campaign finance regimes so long as the local regimes are stronger but not weaker than that required by the state.[13] In fact, some seventy localities throughout the state impose their own campaign finance regimes over local elections.[14] Los Angeles is one such jurisdiction. The Los Angeles campaign finance ordinance requires organizations that finance member communications to disclose their sources of funding. Member communications by labor unions have long been a significant campaign activity in city elections.

With the member communications exemption suddenly applied to the parties, the Democratic party declined to abide by Los Angeles' disclosure requirement, claiming that state law superseded the local ordinance. The party spent nearly $700,000 on member communications in Los Angeles' 2000 municipal elections and, buttressed by a favorable ruling from the state elections agency that state law prevails in this instance, successfully evaded the city's disclosure requirement (Ford 2001).

Campaign Financial Activity in California

In order to develop a clearer picture of money in California politics, it is useful to describe recent trends in party competition and the state's electoral process. The California Legislature is divided into the Assembly, consisting of

13. In California, both the state constitution and the statutory Political Reform Act permit some degree of local autonomy, which has been upheld by the courts. Local jurisdictions which desire to codify their own rules of conduct organize their jurisdiction as a charter county or charter city (as opposed to a general law county or general law city). Charter jurisdictions then draft their own charter (equivalent to a local constitution) which modifies certain laws to local needs. General law communities must abide by state laws and cannot modify these laws. Such "modification" of state laws usually means enhancing or strengthening state requirements, or imposing new requirements where none exist at the state level. Modifications generally do not permit localities to weaken or dismantle state mandates.

14. JoAnn Fuller, Memorandum on Local Campaign Finance Ordinances (2000). On file at California Common Cause, Sacramento.

eighty officeholders representing districts of about 420,000 residents, and the Senate, consisting of forty officeholders representing districts double the size of Assembly districts. Following the 2000 elections, Democrats enhanced their partisan advantage in both chambers. In the Assembly, Democrats held fifty seats to the Republicans' thirty seats. In the Senate, Democrats held twenty-five seats compared to the Republicans' fifteen seats.

Since the 2000 elections, California holds partisan primary and general elections to select most of its state officeholders. (Most local elections are non-partisan.) From 1960 through 1996, state elections had operated under the "closed primary" system, in which only party members could participate in the election of their own party's candidates. In the general election, voters from all parties, as well as those with no party affiliation, could cast ballots for any candidate.

In 1996, voters in California approved Proposition 198, establishing a "blanket primary" system, in which any voter could cast ballots for candidates of any party, even dividing their votes among candidates of different parties in the same primary election.[15] But the U.S. Supreme Court invalidated the blanket primary mid-way between the 2000 elections, and the legislature adopted a modified closed primary system in which voters may register as "decline to state," and the parties may voluntarily allow such voters to cast ballots in their primaries. Both major parties have indicated they will allow such voters to participate in the next statewide primary.[16]

Electoral competition in California's state election has increased significantly in recent years—mostly attributable to the state's term limits initiative ratified by voters in 1990 (Proposition 140). Legislative service in the Assembly is limited to six years (three terms) and in the Senate to eight years (two terms). This limitation has produced more candidates and closer elections. Compared to the 1980s, when Assembly incumbents clung to their office-

---

15. The "blanket primary" systems stands in contrast to both the "closed primary" system and the "open primary" system. In the closed system, voters must declare affiliation to a party sometime before Election day and choose from only candidates of the same party. In the open primary, voters may declare their party allegiance at the voting booth, and then choose from only those candidates of the same party. In a blanket system, voters may choose from among any candidates of any party. The blanket primary has since been invalidated by the U.S. Supreme Court. In a 7-to-2 decision the Court ruled that "California's blanket primary violates a political party's First Amendment right of association." *California Democratic Party v. Jones*, 530 U.S. 567 (2000).

16. As of February 2000, 13.9% of California voters registered as "decline to state." E. Dotson Wilson and Brian Ebbert. "California's Legislature." (Oct. 2000) Report published on-line: www.ca.gov

holder status for an average of 4.5 terms, term limits have drastically cut incumbency longevity (Clucas 1995). As a result, California's legislative campaigns over the last two decades have seen more major party candidates in primary elections, a slimmer average margin of victory in elections, and a
decrease in the number of unopposed candidates (Daniel and Lott 1996).

But, as discussed below, these term limits have increased the prevalence of
"non-incumbent officeholders," as officeholders shuffle from office to office.
This has helped place political parties in an increasingly important role of
preserving the longevity of existing officeholders as they change offices. They
also provide opposing challengers as well as new candidates in open seat
races, if the open seat candidates happen to be running against non-incumbent officeholders.

Money has become ever more important in California politics since the state's
first attempts to place a lid on money in politics. Although California's Political
Reform Act of 1974, and as subsequently amended, consisted of one of the nation's premier disclosure laws, contributions and expenditures have continued to
rise each election cycle. Incumbents remain the primary beneficiaries of special
interest contributions and almost always out-raise their opponents by hefty sums.
Even overt political corruption in state politics has not waned. Over the last two
decades, twenty-two California state officeholders, legislative staff, or lobbyists
have been convicted of bribery charges—averaging almost one per year.[17]

One of the more recent corruption scandals involved elected Insurance
Commissioner Charles Quackenbush. The Insurance Commissioner sought
settlements with insurance companies that were slow or negligent in paying

---

17. Of the corruption convictions in California state politics, one FBI agent, James
Wedick, conducted the investigations that led to fourteen of the convictions in one nine-
year probe, known as "Shrimpgate." With undercover FBI agents offering money for legislative support of a phony bill to facilitate a fictitious shrimp processing company, the
agents found plenty of takers. When a reporter suggested to one Assembly member that
quid pro quo arrangements may continue through unlimited campaign contributions, the
legislator tersely responded: "Prove it!" Another Assembly member, who had avoided any
implication in the FBI sting probe, had routinely eschewed social contact with lobbyists,
calling the practice "morally corrosive." As a result, he was also among the five worst campaign fund raisers among Assembly Democrats. An additional reward for his attention to
appearances: after a decade in the Assembly, he received no committee chairmanships. "The
Legacy of the Capitol Sting." California Journal (1 August 1994).

A second just-completed investigation by Wedick led to the conviction of sixteen more
public officials and lobbyists in California, mostly at the local level, and has earned Wedick
honors among the Federal Bureau of Investigation. Jerry Bier, "Feds Close Inquiry Into
Corruption," Fresno Bee (2 July 2001).

off insurance claims resulting from the 1994 Northridge earthquake. The settlements frequently were in the form of company contributions to Quackenbush-controlled nonprofit committees in amounts much smaller than official fines. These funds sometimes were used by Quackenbush to purchase television advertisements featuring the rising-star politician in "public service" television spots; others went to activities that personally benefitted the politician's family. Quackenbush resigned in June of 2000 under pressure of pending investigative proceedings by the legislature and moved to Hawaii (Ellis and Ingram 2001).

The prevalence of scandals and corruption in California politics stems largely from the growing value elected officials place on money in politics. With virtually no checks on the flow of money into campaign coffers and officeholder accounts, the amount of funds spent on elections has steadily and dramatically increased in California politics well beyond the rate of inflation. Incumbents are privy to ever-larger campaign war chests; officeholders solicit campaign funds year-round, whether or not they are engaged in an election; and challengers feel compelled to join in the fund-raising frenzy in order to compete. All of this has amounted to a campaign finance system out of control.

The Data Collection

Despite priding itself as a state with a thorough campaign finance disclosure system, compiling California's campaign data in any meaningful and comparative way is a Herculean task. Without a doubt, state law does require all viable candidates, parties and political committees to file regular reports of campaign contributions, expenditures, loans and debts. The records are maintained in paper and microfiche format in Sacramento and Los Angeles to facilitate access. Beginning in 2000, the state introduced an electronic filing system, placing many of these records on-line for anyone to peruse. But major problems in public access to these data persist.

The sheer number of filings in California makes aggregation and analysis of the data a major research project, requiring a long-term commitment of resources and personnel. This is beyond the scope of most watchdog groups or even the press. Instead of conducting comprehensive analyses of the data, watchdog groups like Common Cause will often streamline their efforts and study, say, the top ten recipients of campaign money.

Because of the quantity of filings, it even takes the Secretary of State's office—one of whose roles is to provide public access to campaign finance data—years to compile and publish reports of aggregate campaign finance activity. Understandably, these reports tend not to be comprehensive. Instead, they usually provide a snapshot of total campaign fund-raising and spending activity.

California's electronic filing program, once heralded as the "Cadillac of electronic reporting," has come out of the starting gate looking a lot more like a Volkswagen Beetle.[18] Technical problems delayed implementation of electronic filing in 1998. About a third of the candidates who were supposed to file electronically at that time did not bother to do so because of software complications. In 2000, the second election cycle with electronic reporting, only candidates and committees raising or spending $100,000 or more in the primary election or $50,000 or more in the general election were required to file electronically in order to ease the transition into the program. Many candidates and committees that reached this threshold declined to participate in the electronic program, probably more out of ignorance than a deliberate attempt to flout the law. But the result has been a data set for the 2000 elections that understates actual contributions and expenditures in some candidate races. Minor party candidates are not included in the data set, and major party candidates who ignored the electronic reporting requirements or who raised or spent less than $50,000 are also not included.

Nevertheless, data collected by the professional researchers at the National Institute on Money in State Politics in Helena, Montana, combined with the electronic filings reported to the Secretary of State and coded by the author, provide a fair picture of fund-raising and spending patterns in California's 2000 elections. This data is then supplemented with independent research conducted by the Secretary of State's office and other organizations.

The Upward Spiral of Campaign Fund Raising and Expenditures

Prior to the new campaign finance regime of Proposition 34, California was one of a handful of states with no limits on campaign fund raising and expenditures—except for a few brief periods in which voter-approved initiatives awaited court challenge, such as the 1997 Proposition 208 that closed down off-year fund raising before an injunction was issued. And the numbers reflect this lack of limits.

---

18. For greater discussion of the trials and tribulations of establishing electronic reporting systems, and a state-by-state comparative analysis of such systems, see Paul Ryan and Robert Stern, "A Survey of State Electronic Reporting Systems," paper presented before the annual meeting of the Council of Governmental Ethics (2001); and Craig Holman and Robert Stern, "Access Delayed Is Access Denied," *Public Integrity* (Winter 2001).

Figure Two
Aggregate Spending in Legislative Races, 1975–2000

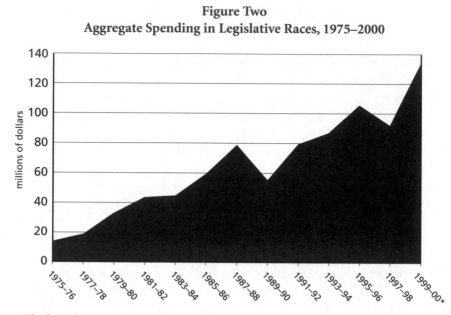

* The figure for 1999–2000 is fundraising by legislative candidates with $100,000 or more in receipts.

As shown in Figure Two, aggregate spending by state legislative candidates in primary and general elections combined, from the 1976 election cycle through the 2000 election cycle, resembles that of going from the Great Plains to the Rocky Mountains. Aggregate spending in legislative races has risen from less than $20 million in the mid-1970s to about $130 million in 2000. Throughout this period, there have been only two notable aberrations in the patterns of escalating expenditures: the 1989–1990 election cycle, following passage of Proposition 73's contribution limits, and the 1997–1998 election cycle, following passage of Proposition 208. Except for these two periods of brief regimes of campaign finance limitations, the rise in campaign financial activity in legislative elections has been certain and dramatic, even without any consideration of changes in the number of candidates running for office.

The same trend is evident in California's gubernatorial elections. Comparing aggregate general election spending by major party candidates for governor from 1976 through 1998 (the last gubernatorial election) shows a consistent and sharp growth in spending for each election cycle. Spending in the 1998 gubernatorial election increased more than nine-fold over spending in 1976. As shown in Figure Three, even in just the last two election cycles, overall spending by the gubernatorial candidates increased by 62% between 1994 and 1998.

Figure Three
Spending in California's Gubernatorial Races,
1976 through 1998 Elections

Year	General Election
1976	$5,709,806.00
1982	$11,776,022.00
1986	$15,702,647.00
1990	$29,256,520.00
1994	$31,806,877.00
1998	$52,487,133.00

Source: California Secretary of State, Campaign Receipts, Expenditures, Cash-on-Hand and Debts, 1998 Primary and General Election. Available on the Secretary of State's Web site: www.ss.ca.gov

Not surprisingly, these levels of campaign spending for state office routinely place California among the costliest in the nation. Aggregate expenditures for legislative races in California usually are the highest in the nation, and aggregate expenditures for gubernatorial and other constitutional offices always place California among the most expensive states.

In fact, the levels of campaign spending in California state elections compared to nearly all other states is utterly staggering—both in terms of aggregate levels, average expenditures, and individual races. For example, state legislative candidates in Idaho collected and spent a total of $1.8 million in 1994. Idaho's gubernatorial candidates raised and spent $3.5 million (Thompson and Moncrief 1998). Compare those levels of spending to California's $86 million spent on legislative races and $32 million spent on gubernatorial races in the same year. A selection of states, ranging from full-time legislatures in California, Illinois, and Wisconsin, to part-time citizen legislatures in Montana and Maine, shows the extent of the disparity between California and other states in terms of average and median spending as well. Average and median spending for contested House races in California's 1994 elections were three times greater than the next most expensive state, Illinois, and about eighty times greater than campaign expenditures in states like Wyoming and Maine (Thompson and Moncrief 1998).

Some cross-state comparisons of campaign financial activity in the 2000 election cycle is made possible by the research of the National Institute on Money in State Politics, a research institution that collects and analyzes state financial databases. As shown in Figure Four, even using the under-stated electronic filing database for California, fund raising by California legislative candidates has far exceeded legislative fund raising in all other states for which data is available, including states like Florida and Texas that are known to have

Figure Four
Campaign Fund Raising by Legislative Candidates by State, (Primary and General Elections Combined), 2000 Election Cycle

State	Aggregate Fundraising	Mean in Senate Races	Mean in House Races
California	$135.1 million	$598,617	$387,445
Illinois	$47.0 million	$260,844	$159,525
Texas	$43.2 million	$167,647	$113,339
Florida	$41.6 million	$238,283	$87,993
Tennessee	$13.2 million	$170,000	$47,742
South Carolina	$12.0 million	$72,889	$24,434
Indiana	$11.0 million	$33,153	$47,679
Missouri	$10.3 million	$90,476	$18,286
Iowa	$9.0 million	$69,583	$31,250
Kentucky	$8.8 million	$107,602	$22,870
Wisconsin	$7.2 million	$84,331	$21,561
Kansas	$6.5 million	$38,631	$12,097
South Dakota	$1.9 million	$10,801	$7,993

Source: Estimates for states other than California provided by National Institute on Money in State Politics

exorbitantly costly state elections. The fund-raising frenzy by legislative candidates in California exceeds that of other states in average contributions as well as aggregate solicitations.

The Growing Phenomenon of Non-Incumbent Officeholders

Consistent with fund-raising patterns in all other states, incumbents enjoy a substantial advantage over challengers as well as open seat candidates. This comes as no surprise. Many factors contribute to the incumbent's fund-raising advantage, ranging from the cynical explanation of special interests attempting to buy access and influence over sitting legislators to the more optimistic explanation that incumbents have greater name recognition. Obviously, these various factors play a greater or lesser role, depending on the particular officeholder and situation.

What is somewhat surprising is the prevalence of non-incumbent officeholders in the campaign fund-raising game. There are two general categories of non-incumbent officeholders in California politics. The first category is officeholders forced out of their offices by term limits (or occasionally their districts by redistricting) and running as a non-incumbent for another office (or in a different district). This type of non-incumbent officeholder running for reelection has become a prominent feature in California politics, as many of-

Figure Five
Distribution of Campaign Fundraising by Incumbency,
2000 Election Cycle

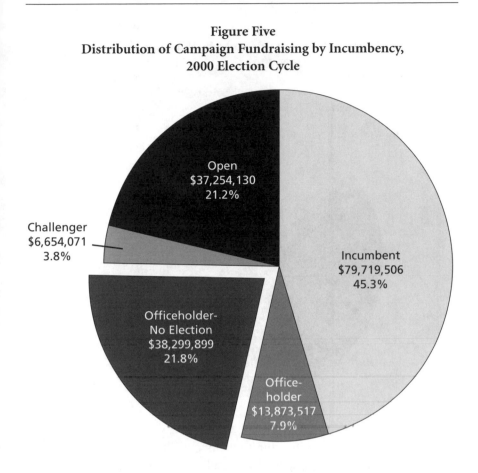

ficeholders are termed out of office each election cycle. The second category of non-incumbent officeholder soliciting campaign funds is an officeholder who is not running for election but is fund-raising anyway. Usually, this type of fund raiser is an officeholder who raises funds year-round, every year, whether or not the officeholder is in an election contest. This could be an officeholder who raises funds in an off-year and is not an official candidate, or he or she could be an officeholder who plans on leaving office but chooses to amass campaign funds for distribution to other candidates or committees.

The degree of fund raising by non-incumbent officeholders in California's 2000 election cycle was remarkable. Combining all candidates and officeholders who raised funds in the 2000 election cycle and who were required to electronically file their campaign activity, including those officeholders who were not even running for election, state candidates in California amassed a conservatively-estimated $189 million. As shown in Figure Five, non-incum-

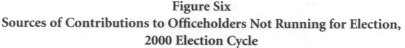

Figure Six
Sources of Contributions to Officeholders Not Running for Election,
2000 Election Cycle

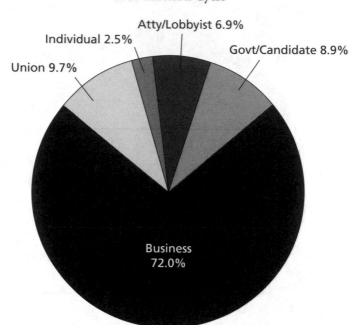

bent officeholders rank second behind incumbents in their success at soliciting campaign funds, accounting for 30% of all campaign money raised. Open
seat candidates rank third, and challengers a meager last, gathering only about
4% of all campaign funds.

Average funds raised by these candidates and officeholders also reflected
the inherent advantage enjoyed by holding a position in office, whether or not
the candidate was running as an incumbent. The high average amount raised
by officeholders who were not running for election lends considerable cre-
dence to the view that much fund-raising activity is intended to buy access or
influence with policy-makers. The very large sums of money given to officeholders who are not campaigning for office suggests that the contributions are
not election-related. The sources of these contributions also raise serious questions about the purpose of this money. As shown in Figure Six, business interests, unions, and attorneys and lobbyists, most of whom have issues pending before the legislative or executive branches of government, account for
nearly 89% of all contributions to officeholders not running for election. Most

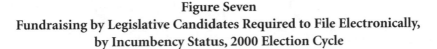

Figure Seven
Fundraising by Legislative Candidates Required to File Electronically,
by Incumbency Status, 2000 Election Cycle

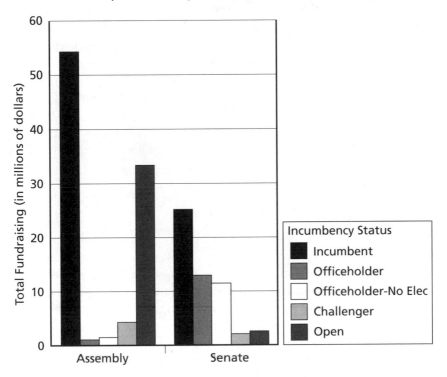

of the remainder comes from transfers from other candidates. Individuals provide only 2.5% of funds to officeholders not involved in an election.

Much of the non-incumbent officeholder fund raising went to constitutional officers, many of whom plan to run for reelection or some other office sometime in the future. As will be discussed below, Governor Gray Davis accounts for a major portion of the fund-raising activity by a non-candidate. It is thus useful to break down the numbers for legislative candidates versus constitutional officers.

As shown in Figure Seven, an interesting picture of fund-raising advantage by incumbency emerges when looking at patterns of fund raising by the Assembly and the Senate. Term limits have clearly had a significant impact on fund raising. In the lower house of the legislature, campaign money flows overwhelmingly to incumbents and open seat candidates. Challengers and, less so, non-incumbent officeholders are on the short end of the stick of campaign fund raising in the Assembly.

In the upper house of the legislature, however, incumbents must share the wealth with officeholders running for a new office and with officeholders not presently running for any office. The officeholders that are running for new office in the Senate tend to be termed-out Assembly members seeking to stay in the legislature. These officeholders dominate the open seat contests, driving most other open seat candidates out of contention. The officeholders not presently running for election largely tend to be soon-to-be termed-out senators seeking election opportunities in constitutional offices. A few of these officeholders, however, are amassing sizable campaign war chests and do not appear to be planning for any future election campaigns. Since these funds cannot be used for personal purposes in California, it is presumed that the retiring officeholders will transfer the funds to other candidates or committees.

The "$1 Million-a-Month" Governor and Sizes of Contributions to State Candidates

Following the most expensive gubernatorial election in history, in which Gray Davis was elected governor of California in 1998 in a $118 million campaign, Davis resumed fund raising weeks within settling into the Governor's Mansion for his next campaign (Morain 1999). In an era of no contribution limits, and no time period in which these contributions may be gathered, the new governor made an art of what is called the "eternal campaign." The next gubernatorial election was to be held four years later in 2002, but the fund-raising race already started—albeit only the Governor was in the running in the off-years.

With no election in sight for years and no opponents, Governor Gray Davis hit the fund-raising stump in earnest. Throughout each off-year, the Governor raised, on average, about $1 million-a-month—as discussed below, nearly all of it coming in very large sums from wealthy individuals and special interest groups. In fact, the Governor had not even disputed that he insists on a $100,000 minimum take before he will personally appear at a fund-raising event.[20]

---

20. California Governor Gray Davis' prolific fund raising has generated considerable controversy as well as advantages. On several occasions, journalistic accounts have correlated contributions and specific policy actions taken by the Davis Administration. In December 2001, a federal appeals court ruled that U.S. District Judge Lawrence Karlton erred in sealing allegations by former California Coastal Commissioner Marc Nathanson that he and Davis had conspired to fix cases pending before the commission in the 1980s in return for campaign contributions to Davis, then an Assembly member. Nathanson, convicted of corruption in a recent FBI sting operation, offered to cooperate with prosecutors in ex-

Figure Eight
Mean and Median of the Size of Contributions, by Level of Office,
2000 Election Cycle

	Count	Col %	Mean	Median	Std Deviation	Sum
Missing Data	7,858	5.6%	$1,598	$194	$6,352	$12,558,165
Assembly	77,356	55.2%	$1,218	$500	$3,752	$94,203,715
Statewide	12,676	9.0%	$1,221	$500	$3,828	$15,474,572
Governor	1,889	1.3%	$6,648	$2,500	$11,068	$12,558,361
Senate	40,362	28.8%	$1,333	$500	$4,184	$53,821,388
Table Total	140,141	100.0%	$1,346	$459	$4,294	$188,616,201

An analysis of sizes of contributions is revealing of the significance of the Governor's and legislative candidates' fund-raising activities. As shown in Figure Eight, the average and median sizes of contributions to legislative candidates and constitutional officers were roughly comparable between level of office, with the exception of the gubernatorial office. The largest absolute number of contributions in 2000 had been made to Assembly candidates, followed by Senate, statewide, and gubernatorial candidates, respectively. The largest size of contributions, in terms of both average and median size, were made to the gubernatorial "candidate"—solely, Gray Davis.

The average size of contributions for legislative and statewide candidates was rather even— between $1,200 and $1,300; the median contribution hovered at $500 for each of these offices. The average contribution made to Governor Gray Davis, however, reached $6,648, with a median five times that of other offices at $2,500. The standard deviation of the Governor's contributions indicate a wide disparity between sizes of contributions, with many six-digit contributions being made to the Governor.[21]

Nevertheless, candidates for all levels of office have relied upon a small pool of contributors for the bulk of their campaign funds. Breaking down total

---

change for a lighter sentence. Judge Karlton agreed to release documents about the corruption scandal only if the name of the "high political figure" involved was blacked out. But a California newspaper reported that the official was Davis, and the federal court later inadvertently released a document with the name still visible. Judge Karlton ordered the newspaper not to publish the name. The Ninth Circuit Court of Appeals overruled Karlton, stating that the "press must be free to monitor the courts." Dan Walters, "Could Sealed Documents Be A Smoking Gun on Davis' Funds?" Scripps Howard News Service (4 December 2001).

21. Contributions of $100,000 or more to Governor Gray Davis in 2000 came from: PaineWebber, Inc.; the Democratic party; Chevron Corp.; the California Dental PAC; Temescal Canyon Properties; and Metabolife International, Inc.

funds raised for each level of office by the median size of contribution by percentile shows that 3% or fewer of contributors provide about a quarter or more of campaign dollars for state candidates.

For example, the median contribution at the 99th percentile of total funds raised by all Assembly candidates was $15,148. Only 1% of contributions came in that median amount or greater to Assembly candidates in 2000. Yet those contributions accounted for 25% of all funds raised by Assembly candidates (see Figure Nine). The median contribution of the 99th percentile of funds raised by Senate candidates was $20,000. Again, only 1% of contributions came in that median amount or greater to Senate candidates, but they accounted for 29% of total funds raised by Senate candidates (see Figure Ten). The median contribution of the 99th percentile of funds raised by the Governor was $50,000. About 3% of contributions to the Governor came in that median amount or greater, but they accounted for 23% of all funds raised by the Governor (see Figure Eleven).

Conversely, the vast majority of contributions to state candidates in California came in fairly small amounts. About 70% of the total number of contributions to Assembly candidates came in amounts of the overall median for that office of $500 or less. Roughly 65% of the total number of contributions to Senate candidates came in amounts of the overall median of $500 or less (93% of contributions to Senate candidates came in amounts of $1,000 or less). Half of the number of contributions made to the Governor came in amounts of the overall median for that office of $2,500 or less.

Party Financial Activity in California

California has a long tradition of weak political parties. State party committees in California at the beginning of the twentieth century had been closely associated with the wave of political corruption in state government that gave birth to the Progressive era. With the election of Progressive gubernatorial candidate Hiram Johnson in 1910, California took a decisive turn toward non-partisanship and limiting the role of parties in politics.

California's Democratic and Republican parties have since evolved largely as fund-raising conduits for officeholders and their favored candidates. Primarily under the tutelage of gubernatorial or legislative leadership, California state party organizations tend to function more as legislative or leadership caucuses supporting and attempting to strengthen partisanship among officeholders. Thus, the financial relationship between party committees and officeholders is a key to measuring the impact of state parties in California politics.

Figures Nine, Ten and Eleven
ASSEMBLY: Percentage of Total Funds Raised vs. Percentage of Contributors

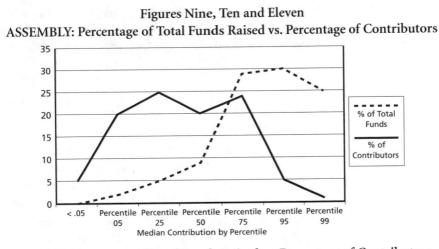

SENATE: Percentage of Total Funds Raised vs. Percentage of Contributors

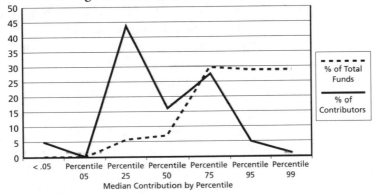

GOVERNOR: Percentage of Total Funds Raised vs. Percentage of Contributors

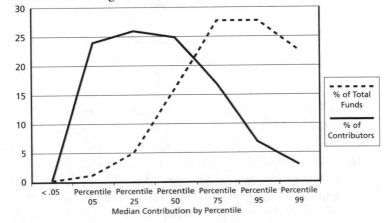

This financial relationship has three elements: sources of party funds; party contributions to candidates; and party expenditures. Each will be briefly examined in turn using electronically-filed campaign finance data for the calendar year 2000.

Sources of Party Funds

In terms of both partisan affiliation among voters, offices controlled, and financial resources, the Democratic party in California enjoys a significant advantage over the Republican party. The Governor and both houses of the legislature are currently controlled by Democrats, although it is not uncommon for voters to alter partisan control over the executive office.

The Democratic party is in a far healthier position than the Republicans financially. Party filings for the calendar year 2000 show Democratic receipts of more than $21 million and Republican receipts of about $16 million. Both parties, of course, carried over funds from previous years and also relied extensively on national party spending and soft money transfers, much of which is not reflected in these totals. Direct contributions to the state committee from national party committees, however, are captured in the total.

As shown in Figure Twelve, the primary source of Democratic financial strength is transfers from legislative leadership PACs and candidate committees. Nearly half of Democratic party receipts comes in the form of transfers from legislative officeholders and other candidate-controlled committees. Almost as much is donated from national (and to some extent, local) party committees. Even the New York state Democratic party contributed a substantial sum to its California counterpart. Unions provide a slightly larger share of the Democratic party receipts than business interests (6.4% to 4.4%), while contributions from individuals are small in proportion to the overall budget (2.3%).

Contributors to the state Republican party comprise quite a different animal. While national party contributions also are substantial for Republicans, providing the single largest bulk of state party receipts (44.3%), the California Republican party relies extensively on individual contributions (31.1%). Like its national counterpart, the Republicans have nurtured a hefty contributor base of individuals through direct mail and other solicitations. Unions account for barely a fraction of 1% of Republican receipts, while business interests comprise the third largest source of state party income (15.6%). Republican legislative caucuses and other candidate-controlled committees are a much less significant source for Republicans than for Democrats, which is probably reflective of their minority status in California government.

Figure Twelve
Sources of Receipts of California's Major Parties, Calendar Year 2000

	Count	Sum	Col Sum%	Mean
Democratic party				
Individual	39	$477,039	2.3%	$12,232
Union	85	$1,357,672	6.4%	$15,973
Business	123	$927,307	4.4%	$7,539
Leg. Caucus/Candidate	52	$8,994,555	42.7%	$172,972
Ideological group	10	$501,589	2.4%	$50,159
Party	72	$8,830,486	41.9%	$122,646
Table Total .00	381	$21,088,648	100.0%	$55,351
Republican party				
Individual	265	$4,924,853	31.1%	$18,584
Union	1	$10,000	.1%	$10,000
Business	788	$2,471,567	15.6%	$3,137
Leg. Caucus/Candidate	84	$1,277,612	8.1%	$15,210
Ideological group	13	$146,317	.9%	$11,255
Party	49	$7,012,146	44.3%	$143,105
Table Total .00	1200	$15,842,494	100.0%	$13,202
Table Total .00				
Individual	304	$5,401,892	14.6%	$17,769
Union	86	$1,367,672	3.7%	$15,903
Business	911	$3,398,874	9.2%	$3,731
Leg. Caucus/Candidate	136	$10,272,167	27.8%	$75,531
Ideological group	23	$647,906	1.8%	$28,170
Party	121	$15,842,632	42.9%	$130,931
Table Total .00	1581	$36,931,142	100.0%	$23,359

Another interesting comparison between the parties is the number and average size of contributions. Though the Democrats have taken in more total funds than the Republicans, the Republican party has received three times more contributions in terms of absolute numbers (1,200 contributions to the Republican party, compared to 381 contributions to the Democratic party). The average size of contributions to the Democratic party ($55,351) is thus much larger than the average size of contributions to the Republican party ($13,202). Ironically, the Republican party depends on a larger number of smaller contributions for its livelihood than the Democrats.

For the most part, fund raising by the parties in 2000 followed comparable time lines. As shown in Figure Thirteen, the peak of party fund raising occurred within thirty days of the general election. The Democratic and Re-

Figure Thirteen
Party Fundraising Activity During Calendar Year 2000

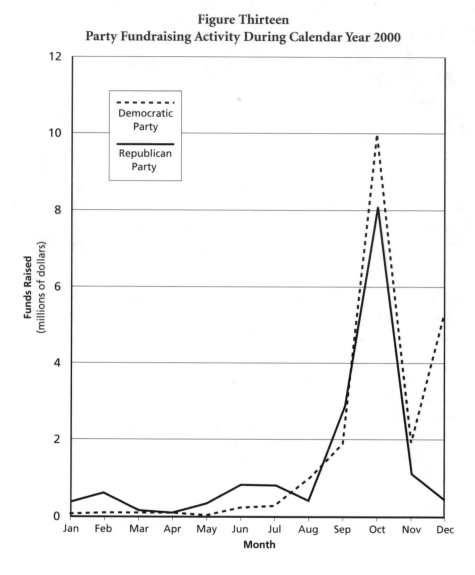

publican parties, however, part ways as the new year begins. Following Democratic electoral victories at the state level, the Democratic party experienced a sharp rise in fund raising that carried well into the year 2001. As shown in Figure Fourteen, the share of Republican party fund raising in 2001 has fallen off, while the Democratic organization appears to be building steam.

Figure Fourteen
Party Fundraising Activity During First Reporting Period, 2001

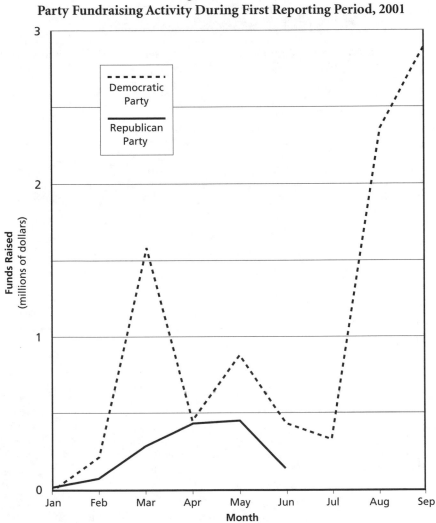

Party Contributions to State Candidates

Since only legislative candidates were up for election in 2000, nearly all of the parties' contributions to other committees targeted legislative candidates. As shown in Figure Fifteen, the state Democratic party shelled out more than $9 million in contributions to other committees, while the Republicans chose to contribute only about $2 million. The greatest share of Democratic party contributions was given to Assembly candidates, while the Republicans con-

Figure Fifteen
State Party Contributions to Other Committees,
by Level of Office, Calendar Year 2000

Democratic party	Count	Sum	Col Sum %
Assembly	1452	$4,986,175	53.6%
Senate	354	$2,868,590	30.8%
Const	2	$562	.0%
Governor	12	$195,000	2.1%
Local	6	$2,658	.0%
Party	5	$429,500	4.6%
Measure	104	$821,662	8.8%
Table Total .00	1935	$9,304,146	100.0%

Republican party	Count	Sum	Col Sum %
Assembly	44	$585,210	30.5%
Senate	72	$1,115,650	58.1%
Const	1	$5,000	.3%
Governor		.	.
Local		.	.
Party	3	$38,500	2.0%
Measure	4	$176,268	9.2%
Table Total .00	133	$2,055,461	100.0%

Table Total		.00	
	Count	Sum	Col Sum%
Assembly	1496	$5,571,384	49.6%
Senate	426	$3,984,240	35.5%
Const	3	$5,562	.0%
Governor	12	$195,000	1.7%
Local	6	$2,658	.0%
Party	8	$468,000	4.2%
Measure	108	$997,930	8.9%
Table Total .00	2068	$11,359,607	100.0%

tributed more to Senate candidates. Both parties gave a significant amount to ballot measure committees. The 2000 primary and general election ballots consisted of a variety of issues that concerned the parties, including campaign finance reform (opposed by the Republican and Democratic parties), consumer lawsuits (favored by trial lawyers and the Democratic party), and education reform (an issue with which Democrats wanted to be identified).

Advocates of strong parties sometimes argue that state parties can play an important balancing function between entrenched incumbents and challengers by providing challengers with an important source of funds. There is not much evidence of this balancing function in California party politics.

Figure Sixteen
Distribution of Party Contributions by Incumbency Status, All Offices,
Calendar Year 2000

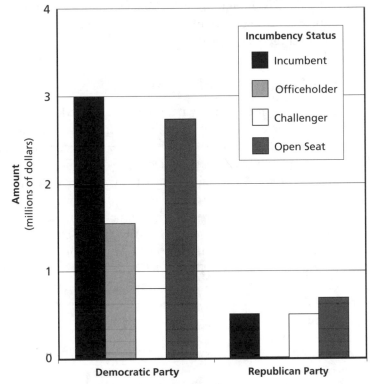

Challengers were not the primary beneficiaries of party contributions, especially among Democrats. As shown in Figure Sixteen, while the Republican party was more even-handed in its distribution of campaign contributions among incumbents, challengers and open seat candidates, the Democratic party threw most of its money behind incumbents and officeholders, and also supported open seat candidates. Challengers came up short on the list of Democratic gift recipients.

In Assembly races, challengers received only 14.5% of their contributions from the major parties. In Senate races, that figure fell to 12.3%. Incumbents received 36.3% of all party contributions in Assembly races, and 36.8% in Senate races. While few non-incumbent officeholders ran for election in Assembly contests, accounting for the lack of party contributions to officeholders in Assembly races, they received more than a third of all party contributions in Senate races.

Particularly for the state Democratic party, the pattern of distribution of campaign funds almost seemed like a revolving door. Officeholders provided a large chunk of party receipts, and the party turned around and gave much of it back to officeholders. Even more surprising was the extent of party support for incumbents, the candidates most assured of election victory and least in need of additional campaign cash.

Party Expenditures in State Elections

The comingling of financial activity between state and federal party committees obfuscates some of the party spending activity, making it difficult to offer a precise measurement of where and when the parties spent their funds.[22] Nevertheless, sufficient information is provided in the disclosure reports to give a reasonable representation of party spending activity at the state level.

Consistent with reports on party receipts, the California Democratic party enjoyed a distinct advantage over the Republican party in terms of total expenditures. As shown in Figures Seventeen and Eighteen, Democrats spent slightly more than $31 million in the calendar year 2000 on state elections, and the Republicans spent about $17 million. Some expenses appear grossly under-reported, such as those for staff salaries and administration for the Republican party.[23] But these are expenses that could have been absorbed by the previous year's budget and by unreported "soft money" expenses of the state or federal party committees.[24]

---

22. Data for contribution totals in the party expenditure reports do not exactly match the totals in the separate filings of party contribution reports. "Contributions" in the party expenditure reports were not as clearly identified as they were in the party contribution reports.

23. Data for contribution totals in the party expenditure reports do not exactly match the totals in the separate filings of party contribution reports. "Contributions" in the party expenditure reports were not as clearly identified as they were in the party contribution reports.

24. The concept of "soft money" arises by contrast with the concept of "hard money," the latter of which refers to funds raised under the restrictions of campaign finance law. The federal restrictions, for example, include bans on contributions from certain sources—corporate and union treasuries, and foreign nationals—and monetary limits on the amounts of contributions from all others. Political parties and groups that raise money for advertising that expressly advocates the election or defeat of a clearly identified federal candidate using the magic words must comply with those restrictions. But political parties and groups that seek to influence federal elections generally treat any advertisement that lacks magic words as if it were issue advocacy, which is exempt from certain aspects of campaign finance regulation depending on the sponsor. Other activities not directly related to cam-

Figure Seventeen
Democratic Party Expenditures by Type of Activity, Calendar Year 2000

	Count	Sum	Col Sum %
Contribution	1,514	$8,445,606	27.1%
Voter mobilization	487	$610,427	2.0%
Media-issue advocacy	985	$15,418,202	49.5%
Salaries/consultants	1,639	$2,222,272	7.1%
Administration	1,057	$4,316,796	13.9%
Fundraising	19	$109,757	.4%
Table Total .00	5,705	$31,127,156	100.0%

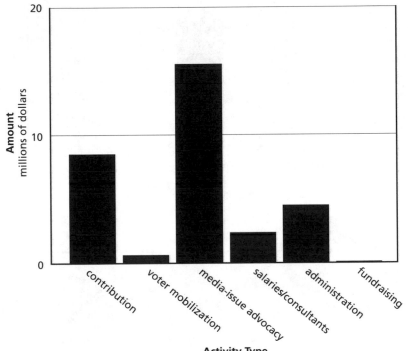

The most significant finding in these data is the area where the parties are *not* spending much of their money: voter mobilization. "Voter mobilization"

paigns are sometimes also treated as exempt from campaign finance laws. Funds used to pay for these types of ads can come from sources and in amounts outside federal campaign finance law. These funds are known as "soft money." Most state laws also provide a distinction between hard money, subject to campaign finance regulations, and soft money, not subject to state campaign finance and disclosure laws.

Figure Eighteen
Republican Party Expenditures by Type of Activity, Calendar Year 2000

	Count	Sum	Col Sum%
Contribution	98	$2,013,409	11.8%
Voter mobilization	578	$588,453	3.4%
Media-issue advocacy	113	$14,462,826	84.5%
Salaries/consultants	4	$26,953	.2%
Administration	17	$24,129	.1%
Table Total .00	810	$17,115,769	100.0%

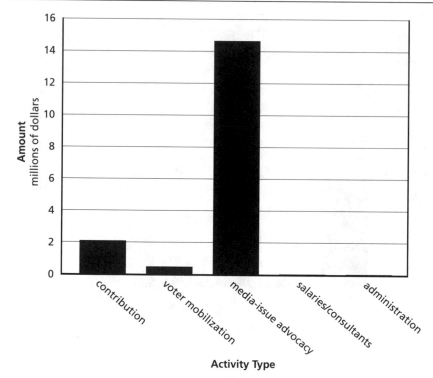

is defined as any activity intended to get out the vote (GOTV) or increase voter registration. These activities include GOTV phone banks, absentee ballot drives, voter registration, food for volunteers, and even costs associated with setting up and running a party Web site. Of course, many of these activities are paid for by candidate committees and local party organizations, sometimes even using funds that came in the form of state party contributions. But direct party expenditures on voter mobilization activities are relatively scarce for both the state Democratic and Republican parties.

This lack of attention by the parties on registering and getting voters out to the polls is not unique to the state organizations. It has been documented in other studies for national party committees as well.[25]

Instead of spending funds on mobilizing voters, the parties direct most of their expenditures to media advertising, direct mail and other types of electioneering issue advocacy. Media/issue advocacy expenditures frequently are financed by the state parties, using soft money funds transferred from federal party committees.

Conclusion: Assessing the Impact of California's New Campaign Finance Regime

In evaluating the potential impact of the new campaign finance regime imposed by Proposition 34 on state politics, the patterns of candidate and party fund raising and expenditures in the 2000 elections can be indicative.

First of all, California's new campaign finance regime does not appear likely to reduce aggregate fund raising and expenditures in state elections.

Proposition 34 was never really offered as a mechanism to cut overall money in politics. In fact, it sprang from a concern among officeholders and party leadership that a pending reform measure—Proposition 208—would dramatically curtail the flow of campaign money and was designed to thwart such an objective. California can expect to see more record-breaking campaign fund raising and expenditures in future election cycles.

Instead, Proposition 34 is likely to re-route some of the flow of campaigns funds. Candidates may still receive sizable contributions but within upper-range limits. These contribution limits are sufficiently high not to impact most contributors, but some contributors who wish to make very large contributions to candidates will have to find alternative avenues. As demonstrated earlier, these few contributors can account for a significant portion of a candidate's campaign budget. The corporations and labor unions that previously had made six-digit contributions to the Governor, for example, will eventually be limited to no more than $20,000 per election in direct contributions to the Governor.

---

25. See, for example, Ray La Raja and Elizabeth Jarvis-Shean, "Assessing the Impact of a Ban on Soft Money: Party Soft Money Spending in the 2000 Elections," Policy Brief, Institute of Governmental Studies and Citizens' Research Foundation (6 July, 2001); and Craig Holman and Luke McLoughlin, BUYING TIME 2000 (2002).

Proposition 34 codifies the parties as that alternative avenue for very large contributions. In addition to the maximum contribution an entity may give to a candidate, that entity may then make a $5,000 contribution to any PAC and a $25,000 contribution to a party committee, which can then be used by the PAC or party for contributions to the same candidate. That same entity may also make unlimited contributions to any PAC and party which can be used for expenditures by the committees in support of the same candidate. Given the close relationship of the parties with the candidates, the parties will emerge as the primary beneficiaries of any re-routing of campaign contributions. As one Capitol staffer said at the time Proposition 34 was placed on the ballot by the legislature: "We just made the state party chairman the second most powerful politician in California" (Walters 2000).

California's new campaign finance regime is likely to maintain the strong electoral advantages of incumbents and officeholders over potential challengers. As discussed above, the political parties tend to use their financial resources to support incumbents and non-incumbent officeholders running in open seats; challengers are not major recipients of party aid.

Party support of incumbents and non-incumbent officeholders should also be expected to help preserve the longevity of sitting officeholders in the halls of state government. As shown in Figure Nineteen, incumbents and non-incumbent officeholders have overwhelmed their opponents at the ballot box in the 2000 elections. With financial resources continuing to flow to these officeholders, either directly through contributions or through party support, the ability of new faces to gain a seat in government will remain a formidable task. Even in open seat races, non-incumbent officeholders will be able to count on strong party support against their opponents.

Meanwhile, officeholders who raise funds in a non-election year or who otherwise are not running for elective office will not find their fund-raising ability impeded by California's new campaign finance regime. Campaign war chests will continue to be amassed by officeholders in an effort to deter electoral competition or to prepare to seek higher office. Funds for these officeholders will continue to be solicited and received from the businesses, unions, and lobbyists with issues pending before the legislative or executive body.

Most importantly, the new campaign finance regime cannot reasonably be expected to curtail the extent of corruption that has come to define California politics. Campaign spending will continue at record-breaking levels, making candidates desperate for ever-larger sums of campaign cash, and the sources of large campaign contributions will remain influential players in the halls of government.

The California "Gold Rush" never really ended. It merely moved out of the foothills and into Sacramento.

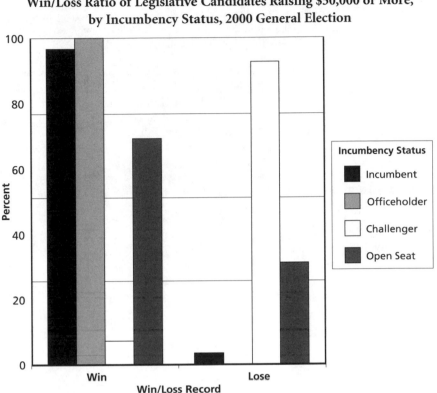

Figure Nineteen
Win/Loss Ratio of Legislative Candidates Raising $50,000 or More,
by Incumbency Status, 2000 General Election

References

Barone, Michael, and Grant Ujifusa. 1995. *The almanac of American politics, 1996.* Washington D.C.: National Journal.

Bradley v. Johnson, 4 Cal. 4th 389 (1992).

Buckley v. Valeo, 424 U.S. 1 (1976).

California Prolife Council v. Scully, 989 F. Supp. 1282 (1998).

California Prolife Council v. Scully, 164 F.3d 1189 (1999).

Clucas, Richard. 1995. *The speaker's electoral connection: Willie brown and the California assembly.* Berkeley: Institute of Governmental Studies Press.

Comment. 1953. Campaign contributions and expenditures in California. *California Law Review* 41: 305.

Daniel, Kermit, and John Lott. 1996. Term limits and electoral competitiveness: California state legislative rules. Unpublished paper. Cornell University Law Review.

Farrelly, David, and Ivan Hinderaker. 1951. *Politics in California: A book of readings.* New York: Ronald Press Company.

Ford, Chris. 2001. Political parties challenge local campaign rules. *Los Angeles Daily Journal*, 8 June, A1.

Gerken v. FPPC, 6 Cal. 4th 707 (1993).

Holman, Craig, and Luke McLoughlin. 2002. *Buying time 2000: Television advertising in the 2000 federal elections*. New York: Brennan Center for Justice.

Kopp v. FPPC, 11 Cal. 4th 607 (1995).

La Raja, Ray, and Elizabeth Jarvis-Shean. 2001. Assessing the impact of a ban on soft money: Party soft money spending in the 2000 elections. Policy Brief. Institute of Governmental Studies and Citizens' Research Foundation: 6 July.

Matthews, Jonathan. 2000. Proposition 34 seeks lighter campaign finance reform. Scripps-Howard News Service, 24 October, 1.

Morain, Dan. 1999. Governor race set spending record. *Los Angeles Times*, 4 February, A1.

SEIU v. FPPC, 747 F.Supp. 580 (1990).

SEIU v. FPPC, 955 F.2d 1312 (1990).

Shuit, Douglas. 1998. Utilities, others fight rate-cutting measure. *Los Angeles Times*, 18 October, A3.

Velie, Lester. 1949. Boss of California. *Reader's Digest* (November): 103–104.

Walters, Dan. 2000. Parties given a power pill. Scripps-Howard News Service, 6 July, 1.

———. 2001. Could sealed documents be a smoking gun on Davis' funds? Scripps-Howard News Service, 4 December, 1.

CHAPTER 13

STARTING AT HOME: CAMPAIGN FINANCE REFORM AT THE LOCAL LEVEL

Carl Castillo

Beneath the checkered quilt of state level experimentation lie the lesser-known attempts of city and county governments to protect the integrity of their local elections. Citizens at this level have long witnessed the dominating influence of private money in their elections. Voter cynicism flourishes in Philadelphia, where contributions as large as $100,000 are all too commonly given to candidates from individuals who then reap lucrative city contracts. In smaller localities, such as Alachua County, Florida, or Hayward, California, residents have seen their grassroots campaign traditions increasingly threatened by high-priced media-dominated elections supported by large contributors seeking to promote policy favoring their special interests. Recognizing a limited ability to change the system at the state and federal level, many of these citizens have decided to take charge of their elections at the level where they have the most control. In so doing, they give voice to an opinion that can be heard reverberating across the country: "Change begins at the local level."

The National Civic League's New Politics Program (NPP) has been tracking these changes since 1997. In 1998, NPP released a publication entitled "Local Campaign Finance Reform: Case Studies, Innovations, and Model Legislation" (Bainter and Lhevine 1998). In that report, seventy-five cities and counties were identified that had legislation limiting contributions to, or expenditures by, candidates for local office. Almost two-thirds of those reforms had been enacted since 1990. NPP has recently completed a national survey in preparation for a second edition of this report. The results indicate that, by the end of 2001, approximately 135 cities and counties now have these types of laws in place. There is no doubt: the winds of change are sweeping across America's communities.

The goals of local reformers are similar to those of their state counterparts. On the one hand, they aim to expose and reduce large private contributions given to candidates for public office. Such contributions are perceived as providing the contributor with increased access to, and influence over, candidates voted into office. On the other hand, these reformers attempt to control expenditures made by, or on behalf of, candidates during their campaigns for public office. Left uncontrolled, candidates that are either well financed, or supported by well-financed interests, are considered to have a decisive advantage in modern campaigns that are increasingly reliant on consultants, pollsters, and expensive media advertisements.

In attempting to reach these goals, reformers have experimented with a variety of distinct approaches. The resulting diversity is a true reflection of the unique conditions found in each community and, in particular, the options that are available. In evaluating options, reformers begin with reviewing the amount of autonomy that state law may have bestowed upon the local government in question. In states that offer what is known as municipal home rule authority, obtaining such authority is often the first hurdle. While the extent of the power that comes with "home rule" status varies from state to state, the effect is in essence the same; it allows for a transfer of power to make local laws from the state legislature to the applicable municipality. However, regardless of whether a municipality has home rule authority or not, state legislation may mandate a specific type of approach to regulating campaigns at the local level, prohibit local alternatives, or grant local governments authority to make such laws. In states where state law clearly restricts local alternatives, a certain amount of creativity may be necessary. In New York, for example, state law imposes mandatory contribution limitations for local elections ($30,700 per campaign for the New York City mayoral race in 2001), and restricts local governments from creating mandatory contribution limitations below this level. Without the authority to alter these high mandatory limitations, New York City instead chose to create contribution limits that were lower ($4,500 per campaign for the mayoral race) but voluntary, along with voluntary spending limits, both tied to an incentive program that provides public dollars that match private contributions for candidates that choose to participate in the program.[1] Given the differences, often subtle, that

---

1. New York City, N.Y. Charter, Chapter 46 (as last amended by Local Law No. 48 of 1998).

exist in state laws across the country, local reformers are always advised to seek counsel to determine the options that are legally permitted.

Population size is another factor that may restrict the options available to the local reformer. Small towns can be successful using voluntary contribution and spending limits with very modest incentives for compliance. In Alta, Utah, a town with just over 400 residents, the only incentive for the mayoral candidates to comply with the $200 contribution limit and the $1,000 spending limit is the looming pressure of a public announcement by the town clerk listing off the candidates that have agreed to the limits and those that have not.[2] Large cities, however, usually have the need for, and the ability to create, a more comprehensive regulatory system. For example, in 1990, Los Angeles, California, established a five-member ethics commission that is currently staffed by twenty-five full-time employees. In addition to regulating the city's ethics and lobbying rules, the Ethics Commission administers a campaign finance program that regulates everything from fund-raising time restrictions and contribution limits to voluntary spending limits, matching public dollars, and regulation of independent expenditures.[3]

Public awareness of an existing or potential problem with money in politics is another factor limiting the options available to the local reformer. In places like Miami-Dade County, Florida, where between 1993 and 1998, a whopping 263 public officials had criminal charges lodged against them, 171 of them that were convicted (*Minneapolis Star Tribune* 1998), the normally fiscally conservative county was able to find support for passage of a program to publicly finance campaigns. In other places, where corruption is rare and campaigns are still conducted in a grassroots manner, reformers often find small, incremental reforms aimed mostly at educating contributors and candidates to be the most effective way to lay the groundwork for future efforts.

Although the differences in local communities are reflected in a myriad of different ordinances and charter amendments, there are certainly patterns, or models, that have emerged over the last twenty-five years. In order to discuss the different approaches, it is easier to view them as fitting into one of two general categories: those that aim to expose or reduce large contributions to candidates; and, those that aim to control expenditures made by, or on behalf of, candidates during their campaigns for public office. This separation is perhaps less than perfect and may be somewhat artificial. Approaches under one category commonly have the effect of indirectly meeting part of the goal of the other category. Nonetheless, categorization is used in order to allow the

---

2. Alta, Utah, Ordinance No. 1997-0-1 (1997).
3. Los Angeles, Cal., Code § 49.7.1 et seq.

reader to focus on what is considered the most direct influence of the approaches contained therein.

Rather than provide detailed case studies of how a system works in any particular local government, the remainder of this article outlines a variety of different approaches to campaign finance reform currently employed by local governments. Some examples are also combined with brief descriptions of the results associated with these approaches. The hope is that this brief survey will remind state reformers to always consider the experience with, and support for, campaign finance reform in cities and counties across the country.

Local Efforts to Expose or Reduce the Influence of Large Contributions

Disclosure

Most local governments have had a long tradition of requiring disclosure of campaign contributions and expenditures. Disclosure allows voters to draw their own conclusions about whether they approve of how a candidate has chosen to finance his or her campaign. Obtaining this information, however, usually requires the self-initiated citizen to visit the city clerk's office, where the records may be maintained at varying levels of organization. The most common complaint with this system is that the average voter has neither the time nor understanding to undertake the research effort. Moreover, even when an investigative reporter makes a diligent effort to review the financial records, a meaningful understanding of the money trail is often difficult, if not impossible, to create. With the advent of the Internet, however, many local governments have begun to post such information on their Web sites to increase public access. The City of Seattle, Washington, may provide the best example of this approach. Beyond the basic information that one would expect to find, Seattle's highly interactive Web page (available at http://www.ci.seattle.wa.us/ethics/) allows one to research a surprising array of information, including contributions by neighborhood, contributions and expenditures by type, employers of contributors, historical comparisons, and candidate compliance rates (Seattle Ethics and Elections Commission 2001).

Contribution Limits

Moving beyond basic disclosure, the most common approach used at the local level is a limitation on the amount of money that can be given to a candidate for local office (Bainter and Lhevine, 1998). As mentioned above, such limitations can be voluntary, as they are in Alta, Utah, or in New York City. More often, however, these limitations are mandatory, as in the case of Fort Collins, Colorado, which prohibits individuals from contributing more than $100 to any candidate for mayor, or more than $75 for any candidate for city council. Many local governments also choose to make separate limitations, or outright bans, on particular sources of contributions, such as corporations, unions, political action committees, or political parties. Some, such as Belmont, California, have enacted so called "pay-to-play" ordinances that attempt to prevent the decision to award city contracts from being influenced by large contributions made by current or perspective contractors. The law in Belmont states:

> No person who contracts with the city, either for the rendition of personal services or for the furnishing of any material, supplies or equipment to the city, or for selling any land or building to the city, directly or indirectly, shall make any contributions to a candidate or committee at any time between the commencement of negotiations for and during the completion of the performance under, or the termination of negotiations for, such contract or the furnishing of material, supplies, equipment, land or building, whichever occurs later. (Belmont, CA., Code §8.5-8)

Taking a different approach to reaching the same goal, Hamilton, New Jersey, recently passed a "pay-to-play" ordinance that relies on the township's right to establish rules and procedures for contracting. Under the ordinance, "professional business entities," as defined, are limited to $300 in the amount that they can contribute to candidates for mayor or city council "between the time of first communications between the business entity and the Township regarding a specific professional services agreement and the later of the termination of negotiations or the completion of the contract or agreement." The township is also prohibited from entering into a contract with such specified professional business entities if they have in fact made contributions in excess of the limits to a "candidate or holder of public office having ultimate responsibility for the award of a contract...within one calendar year immediately preceding the date of the contract or agreement."[4]

---

4. Hamilton, N.J., Ordinance No. 01-038 (2001).

Time Limits

Other local governments have chosen to focus on the timing of the contributions rather than the amount. Little Rock, Arkansas, for example, was concerned with the actual intent and influence of campaign contributions made to political office-holders soon after an election and years in advance of the beginning of the next election. Accordingly, in 1997, the city passed a law that required contributions to regular election campaigns to be limited "to the period beginning immediately before the election [June 1] and ending December 1 immediately after the election."[5] One indirect consequence of this approach is that it tends to decrease the fund-raising advantage of incumbents, thereby reducing the inherent disadvantage that challengers often face in their campaigns (Castillo, et al. 2001).

Conflict of Interest Approaches

Some local governments have chosen to avoid regulating contributions altogether. Instead, they have focused on the conflict of interest that can exist when a contributor gives a large amount of money to a candidate who later, as an officeholder, votes or debates on an issue that directly impacts that contributor. Westminster, Colorado, for example, amended its charter in 1996 to extend the application of its conflict-of-interest law to cover contributions to the campaigns of city council members.[6] Under the law, any candidate who accepts more than $100 is said to have a conflict of interest in any official action that involves providing a benefit to that contributor, unless the benefit is "merely incidental to an issue or question involving the common public good." As a result, the official is required to abstain from debating or voting on the issue. A review of the elections since the charter amendment has shown that, while the number of contributions have continued to increase, contributions over $100 have decreased (Bainter and Lhevine 1998; Castillo, et al. 2001).

---

5. Little Rock, Ark., Ordinance 17.408 § 2
6. Westminster, Colo., Charter § 5.12.1

Local Efforts to Control Expenditures Made By, or on Behalf of, Candidates for Public Office

Mandatory Spending Limitations

As is the case at all levels of government, the U.S. Supreme Court decision in *Buckley v. Valeo* (424 U.S. 1 [1976]) has, for the most part, prevented local governments from mandating campaign expenditure limitations. Nonetheless, there have been exceptions. Cincinnati, Ohio, had mandatory spending limitations in place for three years until the U.S. 6th Circuit Court of Appeals held them unconstitutional in 1998 (*Kruse v. City of Cincinnati*, 142 F.3d 907 6th Cir. [1998]). Albuquerque, New Mexico, continues to have mandatory campaign spending limits on the books after twenty-seven years.[7] A recent decision challenging the Albuquerque law revealed some interesting facts. In a decision denying a request for an injunction (*Homans v. City of Albuquerque*, CIV 01-917MV/RLP D.N.M. [2001]) Judge Vazquez of the U.S. District Court for the District of New Mexico interpreted the U.S. Supreme Court decision in *Buckley* as establishing not an outright ban on expenditure limitations, but a requirement that a compelling governmental interest exist for such restrictions to be maintained. In finding that a compelling interest existed in "preserving the public faith in democracy," the judge reviewed the impact of Albuquerque's long electoral history with expenditure limitations. Among the facts she noted were the following: a zero percent success rate for mayors seeking reelection; an approximately 40% voter turnout that contrasted with the 25 to 35% turnout found in other major cities; and a distinct inverse correlation between voter turnout and the amount spent by candidates on campaigning. The Tenth Circuit subsequently ordered the city to halt its enforcement of the law while the lawsuit continued. (*Homans v. City of Albuquerque*, No. 01-2271 10th Cir. [2001]).

Voluntary Spending Limitations

Most local governments have chosen to craft expenditure limitations to minimize the chance of judicial scrutiny. This has meant the establishment of voluntary spending limitations, with incentives offered for candidate compliance ranging from public shaming to public financing. As mentioned above,

---

7. Albuquerque, N.M., Charter, Article 13, §4

some governments such as Alta, Utah; Richland, Washington; or Concord, California, use the force of public pressure to encourage candidates to adhere to expenditure limits. Through various means, including city Web sites, newspapers, voter information guides, and even ballot notations, these governments have formalized a process of making public the names of candidates that have chosen to adhere to voluntary spending limits and those who have not. Some cities, such as Chapel Hill, North Carolina, and Boulder, Colorado, used this same approach in the late 1990s, differing only in that the publication was conducted as part of an un-codified concerted campaign between citizens and the media to work with candidates rather than through the government. Both Chapel Hill and Boulder used these informal approaches successfully to later garner support for more extensive campaign finance laws that were eventually enacted. Beyond publication, some cities such as Gilroy, or Beverly Hills, California, have chosen to establish variable contribution limits as an incentive for compliance with expenditure limitations. Under this scenario, candidates that agree to adhere to set expenditure limitations have their contribution limits increased, sometimes by as much as double or triple of what they would otherwise have been. The cities that have been most effective with these types of voluntary spending limits tend to use all or a combination of the above incentives. San Jose, for example, passed a law in 1997 that allows candidates that agree to comply with spending limits (varying in each election, based on population) to receive individual contributions of as much as $250 for city council races or $500 for mayoral races.[8] This is in contrast to the $100 and $200 limits the candidates would face without such an agreement. Furthermore, candidates agreeing to participate in the program receive a designation on the ballot, ballot pamphlet, and sample ballot. Finally, candidates have their spending limits tripled if their opponents have not agreed to the spending limits and have spent 75% of the set expenditure limits. In the elections since this law was passed, all candidates have complied with the expenditure limitations, and the city has seen a significant decline in the amount spent by the highest spending candidates.

Public Financing of Campaigns

Public financing of campaigns is another method to encourage candidate compliance with expenditure limitations. Nevertheless, this approach deserves special attention because it is often seen as the most effective incentive and be-

---

8. San Jose, Cal., Ordinance No. 25257 (1997).

cause it can also have the additional effect of creating financially viable candidates that did not exist before. Nevertheless, it remains a very controversial approach among the public at-large because it means money out of the public purse and occasionally new taxes. As of 2001, at least thirteen cities and counties had laws providing for publicly financed elections. Tucson Arizona, New York City, and Los Angeles have had public financing in place for over a decade and, consequently, have had the longest history from which to learn from. Cary, North Carolina; Miami-Dade County, Florida; and Cincinnati, Ohio, have all enacted a form of public financing for elections within the last year. All thirteen of these governments have chosen to implement a system of partial-public financing rather than the full-public financing that is now seen in some states. Miami-Dade County, however, stands out for having passed a partial-grant system rather than the matching funds system available in most of the other localities. The main difference with this system is that, once candidates qualifiy for public funding, they receive the entire amount of public funding allowed, without having to match it with receipt of private contributions.

Tucson, Arizona, the city with the longest history of using a public financing system, has shown indications of success. In 1985 Tucson amended its charter to establish a partial public financing system for campaigns for local office.[9] Under the system, a city council candidate qualifies by collecting 200 contributions of $10 or more from local citizens; 300 contributions of the same size are required for candidates for mayor. After qualifying, the candidate signs a legal document agreeing to limit spending to no more than the designated formula (29 cents per registered voter in council races and 58 cents in mayoral races, with an annual adjustment for inflation and population changes). The candidate also agrees to spend no more than 3% of his or her own money on their campaign. In return, the city periodically audits the campaign to assure compliance and matches every dollar raised privately by the candidate with a public dollar. At the end of the campaign, unspent public dollars are returned to the city. In early 2001, Professor Thomas Volgy, former mayor of Tucson, conducted a review of the program (Volgy 2001). In his review, Professor Volgy described six key measures of the program's success. First, he found a decrease in candidate spending. The combined cost of the winning and losing mayoral campaigns in the last four election cycles were described as substantially below what they were in the early 1980s. In constant non-inflationary dollars, the contenders in the 1999 mayoral race spent 26%

---

9. Tucson, Ariz., Charter, Chapter XVI, Sub-chapter A.

less than their counterparts in 1983—sixteen years earlier and before campaign finance reform.

Second, since 1985 every candidate that has chosen not to adhere to the limits lost his or her election, including a popular incumbent. Third, bucking the national trend, candidates who spent less still won. Fourth, the incumbency factor has been diminished. Before campaign finance reform in Tucson, one person occupied the mayor's office for sixteen years. Since then, four new elections have brought three new mayors to office. Fifth, there has been a change in campaign culture. Television advertising has been minimized, while radio advertising, coffees, rallies, and a variety of grassroots-style of voter contact efforts have increased. Finally, according to Professor Volgy, the candidates and the public have accepted the law.

One reason for the program's popularity may be that, since the law's passage, there has not been any need to increase taxes. The November 2001 city council elections, however, have begun to reveal some limitations in the program. According to the *Arizona Daily Star*, that election saw more than $100,000 of independent expenditures made on behalf of two Republican council candidates that went on to win their races, despite the fact that voter registration indicated party affiliation was tilted three to two against them. Professor Volgy, who sits on a blue-ribbon commission examining city charter changes, claims that the answer to the problem associated with independent expenditures is to provide candidates with 50 cents for every dollar raised by independent campaign committees opposing them. As explained further below, independent expenditures may well be the newest and most complicated challenge facing the success of public financing programs at the local level.

Independent Expenditure Limits

Whenever some entity other than the candidate or candidate's committee spends money that directly influences an election, it could be characterized as an independent expenditure. However, most governments use the term "independent expenditure" specifically to apply only to those expenditures that expressly support or oppose a candidate and that are made independently and without the coordination of any candidate. Using this latter definition, political party registration drives, issue advertisements, and other expenditures, no matter how closely tied to the outcome of an election, are not included in the expenditure total. As mentioned above, independent expenditures are revealing themselves as an increasing challenge to local level reforms.

Los Angeles, California, may provide the best example of the difficulty of attempting to regulate independent expenditures. The most recent 2001 elections witnessed an explosion of independent expenditures (Center for Governmental Studies 2001). Under Los Angeles' comprehensive campaign finance system, independent expenditures are regulated in three ways. First, there is a $500 limit per person per calendar year in the amount that may be contributed to any committee that makes independent expenditures to support or oppose a city candidate or candidates. Second, reporting is required by persons making independent expenditures totaling $1,000 or more. Third, candidates receiving public financing are released from their spending limitations once independent expenditures made in support of, or in opposition to, any candidate in a particular race, either alone or in the aggregate, exceed $50,000 for the council race or $200,000 for the mayoral race. As a result of the increasing independent expenditures, spending limits have been suspended with increasing frequency. In the 2001 elections, the limits were lifted in five races, including the race for mayor, leading to expenditures far exceeding the expenditure limitations (Center for Governmental Studies 2001). As a result of these independent expenditures, the expenditure limitations in Los Angeles are beginning to be seen as nothing more than illusory. In order to combat this problem, Los Angeles has no choice but to consider new approaches to regulating independent expenditures.

Conclusion

Local efforts at campaign finance reform should be recognized and encouraged if for no other reason than because they are necessary. The problems caused by private money in politics is every bit as real and as damaging to representative democracy in cities and counties as it is at the state and federal level. The commitment to encouraging such reforms should not be any less vigorous because of the difficulty in determining which approach is best in any given situation. As is the case at the state level, an understanding of the successes and failures directly associated with any approach is a difficult task. The problem is exacerbated at the local level, especially in smaller cities, because of a lack of funding and, therefore, lack of attention given to reviewing and analyzing election data. Moreover, campaign finance reform at the local level is, by and large, still in its infancy, and there have been relatively few elections to study. A truly objective evaluation of any one program might require drawing a statistically relevant relationship between the law and its impact on such measures as the following: number of contributors; total contributions raised; total expenditures made; number and diversity of candidates; incumbency rates; and even voter turnout. The existence of an endless number of independent variables, such as term limits, unusually popular incumbents, and changes in the economy, however, requires that the true impact of a program be evaluated in the aggregate by reviewing a group of similar approaches in different places over different periods of times. From this perspective, it is fortunate that the last decade has brought with it a significant increase in the number of local governments that have chosen to employ some form of campaign finance reform.

With each new charter amended and ordinance passed, local governments incrementally move towards incorporating past successes, avoiding ineffective approaches, and occasionally adding something completely new. In so doing, these laboratories of experimentation continually work together to improve democracy. In fact, democracy is strengthened not only by the impact of these measures but also by the process by which they come into being. Each time that a city or county makes a change to its system of financing campaigns, the change is usually preceded by a large groundswell of citizen involvement. In fact, there may be few policy changes more unlikely to expect elected representatives to self-initiate than those associated with how their campaigns are financed. Getting the issue on the agenda usually requires a significant amount of citizen engagement and activism—an outcome that can be considered positive in its own right. The experience is often particularly empowering at the local level, where a strong grassroots campaign is most likely to translate directly into success. One way or another, the movement for local reform is an important step in preserving and restoring democracy.

References

Bainter, R., and P. Lhevine. 1998. *Local campaign finance reform: Case studies, innovations and model legislation.* Denver, CO: National Civic League.

Castillo, C., M. Krumme, M. McGrath, and M. Nord. 2001. *Addendum to local campaign finance reform: Additional case studies.* Denver, CO: National Civic League

Center for Governmental Studies. 2001. *Campaign financing in the city of Los Angeles. Eleven years of reform: Many successes—more to be done.* Los Angeles: Center for Governmental Studies.

Minneapolis Star Tribune. 1998. Miami's vice; ethics patrol hits Miami // A rash of scandals in high places has led to a new push for good behavior. *Minneapolis Star Tribune,* 29 July.

Seattle Ethics and Elections Commission. Elections. Date retrieved: November 27, 2001: http://www.ci.seattle.wa.us/ethics/elpub/el_home.htm

Volgy, T. J. 2001. *Politics in the trenches.* Tucson, Arizona: University of Arizona Press .

ABOUT THE AUTHORS

Carl Castillo is the Director of the New Politics Program of the National Civic League. The mission of the New Politics Program is to recognize and promote innovative political reform at the state and local level. For more information on the program and their projects, visit http://www.ncl.org/npp or call the National Civic League at (303) 571-4343.

Christopher A. Cooper, a native of South Carolina, is a Doctoral candidate in political science at the University of Tennessee, Knoxville. His research focuses on political communication, state politics, Congress and political socialization. His work on socialization is forthcoming in *Social Science Quarterly*. He is currently working on a large project examining the role of the media in the State Legislature.

Jerold J. Duquette is an Assistant Professor of Political Science at Central Connecticut State University. A Massachusetts native and current resident, Professor Duquette's research interests include Massachusetts politics as well as national politics. In 2000, his first book, *Regulating the National Pastime*, was published by Greenwood/Praeger. Professor Duquette earned a Ph.D. and M.A. in political science from the University of Massachusetts at Amherst, an M.P.A. from The George Washington University, and a B.A. in politics from The Catholic University of America. He has served as a Congressional staffer on Capitol Hill, as well as a policy analyst at the U.S. Environmental Protection Agency. Professor Duquette is frequently asked to provide commentary and analysis on state and local politics for Western Massachusetts media outlets.

Charles Elder is a professor of political science at Wayne State University. He teaches courses in public policy, American politics, and methodology, and has received two university-wide awards for his teaching. He is a former deputy dean of the College of Liberal Arts and former chair of the Department of Political Science. Professor Elder's publications include three books and numerous articles and book chapters. He was awarded the Aaron Wildavsky Enduring Contribution Award in 1998 by the Public Policy Section of the American Political Science Association for his co-authored book on *Par-*

ticipation in American Politics: The Dynamics of Agenda-Building. He is currently a member of the departmental research team studying the impact of term limits on the Michigan State Legislature, and he is also engaged in research, updating and extending his earlier co-authored work on "Life Span Civic Development and Voting Participation," which was published in the *American Political Science Review.*

Richard Elling is a professor and chair in the Department of Political science at Wayne State University. He teaches courses in public administration, American federalism, and intergovernmental relations. Recent publications include a chapter on state administration in the seventh edition of *Politics in the American States: A Comparative Analysis* (Congressional Quarterly Press, 1999). Two co-authored articles published in 2000 are "Let Them Eat Marblecake: The Preferences of Michigan Citizens for Devolution and Intergovernmental Service Provision" (*Publius*), and "Mapping Patterns of Support for Privatization in the Mass Public: The Case of Michigan" (*Public Administration Review*). Current research includes the Michigan legislative term limits project, in collaboration with several other members of the Department of Political Science. He was a recipient of a Probus Club Award in 1993. In 1994 he received a Wayne State University Board of Governors Faculty Recognition Award for his book *Public Management in the States* (Praeger, 1992).

Rich Engstrom teaches political science at the University of Wyoming. His research interests include the role of interest groups in elections, government budgeting, and questions surrounding the process of representation. His Master's thesis (Louisiana State University, 1994) was on the effectiveness of independent expenditures in Congressional elections. He received his PhD in political science from Rice University in May of 2001.

Dr. Robert K. Goidel is an Associate Professor of Political Science at Indiana State University. He is the co-author of a book and several journal articles examining various aspects of campaign finance in legislative and gubernatorial elections.

Jan C. Hardt is associate professor of political science at the University of Central Oklahoma. She has published several book chapters, most recently in *Oklahoma Government and Politics.* She also serves as co-editor of *Oklahoma Politics,* a journal published by the Oklahoma Political Science Association. She received her Ph.D. in political science from the University of Maryland, College Park, in 1993.

Dr. Craig Holman is currently Senior Policy Analyst with the Brennan Center for Justice at New York University. Previously, he served as Project Director, National Resource Center (NRC), a private research institution associated with the Center for Governmental Studies in Los Angeles. Holman was also

Executive Director of the Californians for Political Reform (CPR) Foundation, a nonprofit public interest organization committed to the defense and implementation of campaign finance laws in California. He has authored and co-authored several studies on campaign finance reform and the initiative process, including three books, entitled *The Price of Justice: A Case Study in Judicial Campaign Financing* (1995); *To Govern Ourselves: Ballot Initiatives in the Los Angeles Area* (1992), and *Democracy by Initiative* (1992). Some of his other publications include: "Access Delayed Is Access Denied: Electronic Reporting of Campaign Finance Records," *Journal of Public Integrity* (2001); "Judicial Review of Ballot Initiatives," *Loyola Law Review* (Summer 1998); *Campaign Money on the Information Highway: Electronic Filing and Disclosure of Campaign Finance Reports* (1997).

Edward M. Mansfield is a partner with the Des Moines law firm of Belin, Lamson, McCormick, Zumbach, and Flynn in Des Moines, Iowa. Mr. Mansfield received his B.A. in government from Harvard in 1978 and his J.D. from Yale in 1982. Following his graduation from Yale, Mr. Mansfield clerked for the Honorable Patrick E. Higginbotham of the U. S. Court of Appeals from the Fifth Circuit, and then worked for the Phoenix, Arizona law firm of Lewis and Roca, before moving to Iowa in 1996. Mr. Mansfield is a frequent speaker and has recently published articles in the Kentucky Law Journal, the Drake Law Review, and the American Bar Association's Litigation Magazine. Mr. Mansfield has taught election law at Drake Law School since 1997.

Dr. James L. McDowell is a Professor of Political Science at Indiana State University. He has contributed chapters to three books on Indiana politics and published several articles on various aspects of the state legislative process. Additionally, he has presented papers at various academic conferences on state campaign finance practices.

Lisa Marckini is a doctoral candidate in political science at Wayne State University. Her areas of concentration include policy studies, American institutions, and political theory. Her dissertation focuses on the distinctive voting patterns associated with the representation of city, suburban, and non-metropolitan districts in the U.S. Congress and how these patterns have changed since the 1960s. Her work in this area has appeared in *Social Science Quarterly* and in the *Urban Affairs Review*. She is currently employed as project manager for Public Policy Associates, a research and evaluation firm based in Lansing, Michigan. Previously she worked as a graduate research assistant on a multi-year research project investigating term limits in Michigan.

Anthony J. Nownes earned his Ph.D. at the University of Kansas. He has taught at the University of Utah and, since 1993, at the University of Tennessee, Knoxville. As associate professor of political science, he offers courses on organized interests, political parties, mass media, and popular culture. Professor Nownes has done extensive research on organized interests in American politics, and his articles have appeared in *American Politics Quarterly, Journal of Politics, Political Research Quarterly*, and *Social Science Quarterly*. His book, *Pressure and Power: Organized Interests in American Politics*, was recently published by Houghton Mifflin.

Darryl Paulson is a professor of Government at the University of South Florida's St. Petersburg campus. Professor Paulson earned his doctorate from Florida State University and specializes in political parties and elections, Florida politics, Congress and urban government. He is the recipient of a National Teaching Fellowship from the Department of Education and of three undergraduate teaching awards from USF. In addition to his classroom activities, Professor Paulson has served as an expert witness in numerous court cases, including two appearances in Federal District Court on the reapportionment of the Florida Legislature. Paulson was invited by the United States Commission on Civil Rights to participate in the recent hearings on *Allegations of Election Day Irregularities in Florida*. He has served as a campaign consultant and as a political analyst for many media outlets. Professor Paulson has been interviewed over 2000 times by the print and broadcast media, including *The New York Times, USA Today, The London Financial Times*, National Public Radio, Inside Politics on CNN, CNN Headline News, and C-Span. He currently serves as political analyst for WTVT-TV, Channel 13, the local FOX affiliate in the Tampa Bay area. In 1994 Professor Paulson was named a Salvatori Fellow at the Heritage Foundation in Washington D.C.

John David Rausch, Jr., is an Assistant Professor of Political Science at West Texas A&M University. He earned a PhD in Political Science from the University of Oklahoma, where he was a graduate fellow in the Carl Albert Congressional Research and Studies Center. An American Political Science Association Congressional Fellow in 1992–93, Dave worked on campaign finance issues and other congressional reform proposals in the office of former Representative Bob Inglis (R-SC). He has published numerous journal articles and book chapters on direct democracy, legislative term limitations, religion and political participation, and gubernatorial campaigns.

Kent Redfield is a professor of Political Studies at the University of Illinois, Springfield (UIS), and the Associate Director of the Illinois Legislative Studies Center at UIS. He received his undergraduate degree in political science from the University of Utah and his M.A. and Ph.D. in political science from the University of Washington. Prior to joining the faculty at the University of

Illinois, Springfield, in 1979, Dr. Redfield worked for four years as a member of the research/appropriations staff for the Speaker of the Illinois General Assembly. He is a co-author of *Lawmaking in Illinois* and a contributor to the *Almanac of Illinois Politics*, which is now in its sixth edition. Dr. Redfield has been engaged in research on the financing of political campaigns in Illinois since 1991. The results of that research have been presented in numerous research reports, a series of articles in *Illinois Issues*, a 1994 book on financing legislative elections in Illinois entitled *Cash Clout*, and a recently published book on the role of money in Illinois politics entitled *Money Counts*. In the fall of 1997 Dr. Redfield received a grant from the Joyce Foundation to fund the Sunshine Project. The purpose of the project is increase public awareness and knowledge of the role of money in Illinois politics. Funding for the project has been renewed through 2002.

Marjorie Sarbaugh-Thompson is an associate professor of political science at Wayne State University. She teaches classes in policy analysis, organization theory, and public policy. Her research focuses primarily on change in public sector organizations. Her work has appeared in several scholarly journals including *Administration and Society, Social Science Quarterly, Organization Sciences, the American Review of Public Administration*, and *State Politics and Policy Quarterly*. She is the principal investigator for a multi-year study of the effects of term limits in Michigan. Her other research interests include citizen participation in decision making in Community Development Block Grants and the responsiveness of local public officials to morality issues.

David Schultz is director of the Doctoral Program in Public Administration and professor in the Graduate School of Public Administration and Management at Hamline University, where he teaches classes including professional ethics, legislative process, research methods, housing and economic policy, and public policy. David is also an adjunct professor of law at the University of Minnesota where he teaches a class on election law. Professor Schultz has taught political science, law, and American politics since 1989, and he is the author of twelve books and over thirty articles on topics ranging from civil service reform, campaign finance reform, land use, constitutional law, to the media and politics. His most recent publications include *The Encyclopedia of American Law* (Facts, On File, Inc. 2002); *Leveraging the Law: Using the Courts to Achieve Social Change* (Peter Lang, 1998) and *Inventors of Ideas: An Introduction to Western Political Philosophy* (St. Martin's Press, 1998). Professor Schultz has testified before the Minnesota and New Mexico legislatures on campaign finance reform and is a nationally recognized expert on this topic, with hundreds of media appearances in local, national, and international newspapers, magazines, television, and radio.

Charles Smithson, General Counsel to the Iowa Ethics and Campaign Disclosure Board, the state's regulatory agency for political campaigns. Charles Smithson has been Legal Counsel and Legislative Liaison for the Iowa Ethics and Campaign Disclosure Board since June of 1998. Prior to joining the Board, he served as Legal Counsel for the Kansas Commission on Governmental Standards and Conduct for three years. During his tenure with the Commission he was voted one of the 100 most influential political figures in the state of Kansas. Mr. Smithson is a frequent lecturer on campaign finance and other governmental ethics issues. He received his Bachelor of Arts degree from Westmar College with a triple major in history/political science/sociology in 1990, and received his Juris Doctor from Washburn University School of Law in 1994. Mr. Smithson is licensed to practice law in the federal and state courts of Iowa and Kansas and the U.S. Court of Appeals for the 8th and 10th Circuits.

John Strate is an associate professor of political science and director of the Master's in Public Administration Program at Wayne State University. He teaches graduate courses in elementary statistics, advanced statistics, and policy analysis, as well as undergraduate courses in introductory political science, American government, biopolitics, and policy analysis. Areas of research interest include physician assisted suicide, legislative term limits, empowerment zones, and good Samaritan laws. Recent publications include articles in *Social Pathology*, *Ohio Northern University Law Review*, *Politics and the Life Sciences*, *Criminal Law Bulletin*, and *Journal of Politics*.

Lyke Thompson is a professor at Wayne State University in the Department of Political Science and in the College of Urban, Labor, and Metropolitan Affairs. He teaches classes in policy analysis and evaluation, urban administration, Michigan politics, and Detroit politics. His research specializes on program evaluation and policy analysis, with recent concentration on community development, state policy on disabilities, and the impact of term limits. He has published in the areas of urban labor markets, citizen attitudes about service delivery, welfare reform, service collaboration, and evaluation theory and design. Recent publications include: "A Naturally Occurring Quasi-Experiment in the States: Research on Term Limits in Michigan," "Mapping Patterns of Support for Privatization in the Mass Public: The Case of Michigan," "Let Them Eat Marblecake: The Preferences of Michigan Citizens for Devolution and Intergovernmental Service Provision," "Dimensions of Collaboration and Family Impacts, an edited book *The Politics of Welfare Reform* (with Don Norris) and "Emergent Design" in *Evaluation and Program Planning*. Current research projects include an evaluation of family service coordination, research on decision making on community development projects, and an evaluation of term limits in Michigan.